Instructional Strategies
for physical education

Instructional Strategies
for physical education

Joyce M. Harrison
Brigham Young University

wcb
Wm. C. Brown Company Publishers
Dubuque, Iowa

Book team

Edward G. Jaffe Editor
Judith A. Clayton Associate Developmental Editor
James M. McNeil Designer
Patricia L. A. Hendricks Production Editor
Mary M. Heller Visual Research Editor
Mavis M. Oeth Permissions Editor

Consulting Editor
  Aileene Lockhart
  Texas Woman's University

Photo Credits

John Avery: 116, 157, 242, 294, 489; James L. Ballard: 71, 232, 408, 480; Bob Coyle: 26, 458; Robert Eckert/EKM Nepenthe: 93; Rohn Engh: 133; Courtesy of Evanston Recreation Department: 468; Stan Greenwood: 53; Jean-Claude Lejeune: 35, 340, 442; Allen Ruid: 180, 194, 392; James L. Shaffer: 8, 47, 114, 326, 367, 369, 509; United Press International: 251

contents

unit 3

Planning the instructional program 167

preface

The purpose of this book is to help teachers and prospective teachers acquire the skills necessary to design and implement effective instructional programs in physical education. Effective programs require both effective instruction and a balanced curriculum. Either one without the other results in failure to educate students physically. Therefore, it is essential that prospective teachers be instructed in both aspects of the physical education program included in this book—curriculum and instruction.

In the past, curriculum theory and design have been delayed until graduate school. However, since many beginning teachers are involved in curriculum development, an attempt has been made in the text to integrate the process of curriculum design with that of designing instructional strategies. The curriculum chapters relate specifically to the entry-level teacher and can be taught most effectively by forming curriculum committees of three to five students and actually designing a curriculum.

Unit 1 provides an introduction to the teaching world. Unit 2 presents the theory essential to an understanding of the learning process. This is followed in unit 3 by a presentation of the skills essential to the instructional process. This serves as a basis for both curriculum and instruction. Effective classroom management is presented in unit 4. Unit 5 takes the prospective teacher through the process of curriculum design and the evaluation of the instructional program.

The book follows the progression usually followed in teaching undergraduate physical education majors. That is, it assumes that lesson and unit planning and basic instructional skills are prerequisite to an understanding of the curriculum. It is suggested that students apply the principles taught by actually writing lessons and units and designing a curriculum as suggested in the various units of the text. In this way the entire process will be more meaningful to the learner.

The book is divided in such a way that portions of it can be used in several classes. For example, unit 1 can be used in an introductory class, units 2, 3, and 4 in a class on methods of teaching physical education, and units 1 and 5 to teach a separate unit on the curriculum. The entire text can also be used in one traditional methods course.

This text is different in its approach in that it ties together all three of the learning domains—cognitive, psychomotor, and affective—as a basis for the design and implementation of instructional strategies. In addition to the background theory, a large number of practical applications and examples are provided. The recent emphasis by the American Alliance for Health, Physical Education, Recreation and Dance on teaching students the conceptual background of physical education requires that prospective teachers understand the cognitive domain and strategies for teaching intellectual skills. The development of positive student feelings toward physical education is the key toward continued participation by students in physical activities outside of the school. Therefore, the affective domain should also be studied.

The text includes a number of learning aids to help students zero in on the concepts presented. Study stimulators at the beginning of each chapter are designed to introduce the main ideas of the chapter in a question format. A step-by-step approach helps students apply what is learned to actual school situations. Questions and suggested activities are provided for further review and expansion of learning. For more in-depth study of a topic, the student is directed to a number of suggested readings.

The book includes numerous practical examples in the areas of performance objectives, evaluation, preassessment, learning strategies, motivation, discipline, and classroom management.

Although the text is written on an undergraduate level, it can be used at the graduate level as well by supplementing the text with the suggested activities and readings at the end of each chapter. It is also suggested that graduate students actually form committees and design a resource unit and a school curriculum.

Acknowledgments

This text became a reality only through the encouragement and cooperation of many individuals, including students, colleagues, and friends. I wish to thank Elmo Roundy, chairperson of the Brigham Young University Department of Physical Education—Sports; Dwayne Belt, of the BYU Department of Secondary Education; and Marilyn Harding, Springville Junior High School, Springville, Utah; and many other colleagues for their support and encouragement throughout the development of the text. A special thanks goes to Berne and Miriam Broadbent for the many hours of borrowed time on the word processor and to Cheryl Skousen and Lisa Boyack for typing the figures and tables. I also wish to thank those authors and publishers who generously consented to have their work reproduced or quoted.

Finally, I wish to include a special word of appreciation to my parents, Loyd and Gladys Harrison, for convincing me that it was all possible.

In addition, I would like to express my gratitude to those colleagues who reviewed the manuscript and provided many valuable suggestions and comments: Gretchen Brockmeyer, Springfield College; Norma Carr, State University of New York at Cortland; Dorothy Deatherage, California State University at Long Beach; Doris Henderson, Illinois State University; Jeannette Scahill, University of Iowa; Neil Schmottlach, Ball State University; and Ruth E. Tandy, Texas Woman's University.

Instructional Strategies
for physical education

A Schematic of the Teaching World

This unit is designed to introduce you to the components of the educational system in which teachers function. Since physical education is a means toward the total education of the student, physical educators must be educators first and physical educators second.

The role of education in a democratic society is the focus of chapter 1. Past, present, and possible future purposes of education are reviewed. The characteristics of a successful school are also presented.

Chapter 2 stresses the importance of developing a philosophy of physical education and reviews the major philosophies of the twentieth century. Sample aims and objectives for physical education are presented; and the basis for selecting these goals are reviewed.

Chapter 3 emphasizes the importance of getting acquainted with students as individuals and presents some principles that must be considered when planning educational programs.

Four legal developments that directly affect physical education are reviewed in chapter 4, along with the implications of each one for the schools. Changes in the legal liability status and preventative measures are discussed. The Education for All Handicapped Children Act, Section 504 of the Rehabilitation Act, and Title IX are outlined and possible methods for implementing each of these programs are presented. The recent teacher accountability laws are also reviewed.

In chapter 5, the characteristics of effective teachers are presented and questions are asked to help you evaluate yourself with regard to these characteristics.

Understanding the Role of Education

Study stimulators

1. Is education synonymous with schooling?
2. Is the crisis in education real?
3. What similarities exist among the goals of education? Why might goals be different in the future?
4. Why are some schools successful and others unsuccessful?
5. How should education be different in the future?

Have you ever stopped to ponder the question what is education? As a high school or college graduate, do you feel "educated"? Do you think you will ever be truly educated?

Webster's New Collegiate Dictionary defines *educate* as "to provide schooling for."[1] How does this definition compare with your own definition of education? Do you think that education always results from, or even develops most efficiently, through formal schooling?

Someone once said, "Don't let your schooling interfere with your education." Have you ever been in a classroom in which the students were interested in an exhibit of frogs or snakes in the room, only to be told, "Come and sit down. We're going to have science now!"? How many times have you patiently made hot chocolate and cinnamon toast in home economics class when you could hardly wait to get home to prepare a gourmet dinner? Do you remember the time you listened to the driver education teacher talk about how to change a tire when the previous weekend you had rotated all five tires on the family car?

Education is a process of learning, not a place. In fact, historically education occurred in the home, on the farm, or in the craftsman's shop. Even today, much learning occurs on the job, in the home, or by way of the media. Today's advanced technological society demands continuous learning for effective living and working.

Aristotle said, "All men by nature desire to know." Have you ever mingled with a group of first-graders and attempted to answer their never-ending stream of questions? What happened to those children as they passed through the system of education? Some of them benefited from the formal education that occurred there. Others learned in spite of the programs of the school. Still others dropped out of the program, either officially or unofficially.

Where has the educational system gone wrong? Perhaps the public has erred in thinking of education as a product rather than a process. In an idealistic sort of way, we speak about education as a process of learning how to learn, of learning to apply certain commonly held principles of truth to whatever we do in our lives. But, in reality, educators test students on their ability to recite the names of the presidents or the proper height of the net in volleyball. We lead students to believe that their success in life is based on their ability to memorize and feed back information or perform skills rather than using those skills to solve life's problems.

The crisis in education

Teachers and students have become increasingly concerned about learning. Students report that classes are irrelevant and a waste of time. They speak of memorizing information to "hand back" to the teacher on a test—information that is promptly forgotten once the test has been taken. They view learning as something entirely disassociated from life itself.

Teachers, on the other hand, wonder how they can help students experience the excitement of curiosity and discovery. They are concerned with the students' image of them as lecturers, givers of assignments, and distributors of grades, rather than as real people who share in the learning process.

The taxpaying public too, is concerned about the schools. Academic and behavior standards decrease. Costs rise while budgets shrink. Enrollments rise where buildings are in short supply and decrease where they are plentiful. Discipline problems, drugs, crime, and vandalism are rampant. Apathy and disinterest among students are the norm. Teachers burn out and quit. Teacher strikes and union support for incompetent teachers have reduced teaching from a profession to just another job. Desegregation and forced school busing have resulted in increased racial turmoil and a removal of parental involvement in the schools. Is it any wonder that taxpayers in many areas have refused to provide the increases in funding essential during a time of runaway inflation or that teachers are constantly demanding increased pay and better working conditions? As Enochs said, in *The Restoration of Standards*

> It is time to admit it: In the last dozen years, educators have made a mess of
> things. The evidence against us is overwhelming. When children are safer on
> the streets than in their schools, when we are spending more on vandalism
> than on textbooks, and when we are clothing functional illiterates in caps and
> gowns, the time has come to start plea bargaining. We are guilty.[2]

Criticisms from all sides are becoming more vocal. In a recent *Newsweek* poll, 69 percent of the respondents wanted more stress on the basics and 60 percent expressed a need for a more orderly atmosphere for learning.[3]

There is some comfort in the fact that the crisis in education is a mirror image of the crisis of meaning and purpose in life itself.[4] Terrel H. Bell, Secretary of Education during the Reagan administration, suggested that pessimism about the schools is inevitable in view of our national mood. He said, "When we lack confidence in ourselves, when we are troubled and when we are not prospering, it reflects in the nations' attitude, respect and support for schools."[5]

Max Ways, journalist and social critic, indicated that in the nineteenth and the early part of the twentieth centuries we tended to perceive things optimistically. As a result, we ignored many of the realities of social injustice. Ways suggests that we have now reversed our perception to look on the dark side, thereby ignoring the progress that has been made. A society that used to perceive a bucket as half full now perceives it as half empty.[6]

In spite of criticism, American schools are graduating more students than ever before, with nearly half of them going on to college, including larger numbers of blacks and Hispanics.[7] In a poll conducted for ABC and *The Washington Post,* more than 70 percent of the respondents graded their community's public schools with an A, B, or C.[8] In a *Newsweek* poll, 60 percent of parents said their children's education is better than was their own.[9]

However, Silberman points out that to say that things are better than they were is not to say that they are as good as they should be. In part, he says

> . . . what Ways calls the 'Dark Perception' is simply a long overdue sensitivity to social ills that should have troubled us all along. . . . The test of a society, as of an institution, is not whether it is improving, although certainly such a test is relevant, but whether it is adequate to the needs of the present and of the forseeable future.[10]

We are living in a culture that consistently demands more and more sophisticated knowledge just to obtain a job. In such a society, any system that is not getting better is fast becoming worse. As Graham Down, of the Council of Basic Education stated, "What passed for competency in 1960 wouldn't pass for it in 1980 and cannot hope to pass for it in the year 2000."[11]

Can something be done? Yes! But only by facing up to these challenges and coming up with new and better ways to achieve learning. As Singer and Dick indicate, "The changes in the air should please and excite you."[12]

The purposes of education

How are the purposes of education determined? The following story by Krajewski should give you an idea:

> This is a story of civilization of some thousands of years ago. The people lived in the warm lands, covered by streams fed by glaciers far to the north. They supported themselves by spearing fish and by trapping tigers.
>
> The glaciers moved south. The lands became cold. The tigers left and sediment from the glaciers choked the rivers. Still, the people remained.
>
> Before the advent of the cold weather the people had prospered and in their prosperity they felt that they should embellish their society and they set up a school system. In that school system, quite logically, they taught the spearing of fish and the trapping of tigers. Then the cold came and the fish left and the tigers left. The people of this area now survived by snaring eel and hunting bear. And they prospered again. They went back to examine their school system. They asked the headmaster what he taught. And he said, 'I

Education is a process of learning, not a place.

teach spearing fish and trapping tigers.' And they said, 'Well, do you not teach snaring eels and hunting bears?' He said, 'Well, of course, if you want a technological education; but for a well-rounded education I prefer the classics.'

Krajewski continued:

Let us assume that by some highly selective catastrophe, all the schools and universities in this country were destroyed last night. Our task now is to build a new system.

Would we recreate the present educational system? . . . The answer is clearly 'No.'[13]

Why not? Because the school curriculum is a reflection of what the people in a given society think, feel, believe, and do. Whenever the curriculum deviates significantly from the purposes of education and the values held by the society, the people will force a change to occur to resolve the differences. In general, the purposes of education in any society include one or more of the following:

1. to preserve and maintain the desirable aspects of the society or culture by transmitting them to the young;

2. to teach the skills and competencies needed to function effectively as an adult member of our society, both socially and vocationally;

3. to help the individual function within society to the fullest extent possible, both currently and in the future, through intelligent self-direction, group deliberation, and action; and

4. to teach the individual to constructively evaluate societal issues and to influence the social order by contributing to ordered, purposeful change.

The purposes of education in America in historical perspective

Throughout history, a number of specific educational goals for secondary education have emerged. These are summarized in table 1.1.

In 1913, the National Education Association (NEA) appointed a committee known as the Commission on the Reorganization of Secondary Education for the purpose of developing fundamental principles through which the responsibilities of education for democracy could be met. After five years of work, one of the most influential documents in education emerged. It was based on the philosophy that the purposes of secondary education should be determined by the needs of society, the characteristics of adolescents, and a knowledge of the best available educational theory and practice. The worth of each subject area was to be evaluated on the basis of its ability to contribute to the attainment of the seven "Cardinal Principles" of education shown in table 1.1.[14]

In 1935, the NEA created an Educational Policies Commission to resolve the problems created in education by the Great Depression. The result of this commission was a set of four comprehensive educational aims as follows: (1) self-realization, (2) human relationship, (3) economic efficiency, and (4) civic responsibility.[15] The four aims of education were supposed to meet the ten "imperative needs of youth" as outlined in the table. [16]

Following World War II, the commission reacted to an obvious lack of implementation of these aims in the schools by producing a set of three volumes describing an ideal educational system in each of two supposedly typical settings—Farmville and American City. In 1964, the American Association of School Administrators appointed its own commission to identify the imperatives of education. This commission identified the nine imperatives shown.[17] These two lists were later combined into one list of fifteen needs of youth for the eighties by the Institute for Educational Management at United States International University at San Diego, California.[18]

In 1973, the Commission on the Reform of Secondary Education drew up a new set of goals for secondary education. It consisted of seven content goals and six process goals.[19] In 1978, Gross proposed seven new cardinal principles of education to make the original list more relevant to today's world.[20]

A quick glance at table 1.1 shows many similarities in the goals of education from 1918 to the current time. All of the original seven cardinal principles have been reemphasized in at least two of the other four sets of goals. The major additions have been in the areas of respect for the environment, appreciation of beauty and achievement, and economic understanding.

Table 1.1 A perspective of the national goals of education

Cardinal principles of 1918	Ten imperative needs of youth	Imperatives of education
Health (physical fitness)	Good health and physical fitness.	Deal constructively with psychological tensions.
Command of fundamental processes	Think rationally, express thoughts clearly, read and listen with understanding.	
Vocation	Develop salable skills.	Prepare for world of work.
Civic education	Understand the rights and duties of a citizen. Develop respect for others, live and work cooperatively with others.	Keep democracy working. Work with other peoples of the world for human betterment.
Worthy home membership	Understand the significance of the family.	
Worthy use of leisure	Use leisure time well.	Make the best use of leisure time.
Ethical character	Develop ethical values and principles.	Strengthen the moral fabric of society.
		Make intelligent use of natural resources.
	Know how to purchase and use goods and services intelligently.	
	Develop capacities and appreciate beauty in literature, art, music, and nature.	Discover and nurture creative talent.
	Understand the influences of science on human life.	Make urban life rewarding and satisfying.

*Process goals

The purposes of education in the future

Will the purposes of education remain the same as we move into a new century? Should they? The answer is "probably not." To understand the purposes of education in the future, we must study current trends and predicted future events as they might affect our educational needs.

Society, culture, and our American value system affect education in two ways—by direct intervention of parents and local citizens at the local or community level and indirectly by changes in the society around us.

National goals of 1973	Seven new cardinal principles
*Adjustment to change (mental health).	Personal competence and development.
Communication skills. Computation skills. Critical thinking.	Skilled decision making.
Occupational competence.	
Responsibility for citizenship. *Respect for law and authority. *Appreciation of others.	Civic interest and participation. Global human concern.
	Family cohesiveness.
*Clarification of values.	Moral responsibility and ethical action.
Clear perception of nature and environment.	Respect for the environment.
Economic understanding.	
*Appreciation of the achievements of individuals.	
*Knowledge of self.	

Haas indicated that we are faced with "a crisis of purpose such as we never faced in the past."[21] Shane identified a possible reason for that crisis as follows:

> To put it simply, change has confronted us so rapidly that we have been wrenched from *yesterday* and thrust into *tomorrow* without having been given an opportunity to adjust ourselves to *today*. As Alvin Toffler phrased it years before he published *Future Shock,* we are suffering from '. . . the dizzying disorientation brought on by the premature arrival of the future.'
>
> In effect, the crisis of transition has subjected us to new customs, changed behaviors, and strange mores and morals *in our own land and in our own time.* The transition has left us feeling alien—as if we were in a different

land—with one big difference! We never left home! Nor is there any place to which we can return. . . . Small wonder that our life and the times have sometimes failed to make sense to us.[22]

Lined up behind this crisis of values and purposes, Haas continues, "like so many planes on a runway, are other major contemporary problems: environment, the energy crisis, changing values and morality, the family, urban and suburban crises, equal rights, and other social problems."[23]

Environment

The naive use of our superindustrialized technology has resulted in a tremendous amount of devastation to our environment. The wise use of our technology to resolve these problems is needed within the next generation or irreparable damage will be done to the environment.[24]

Energy crisis

New ways of providing energy, coupled with a need for self-discipline in the use of our current energy resources, will be needed for our society to survive in the future.

Changing values and morality

Americans are becoming increasingly concerned about the decline in values of the younger generations. Our older citizens grew up in an America that seemed secure and stable as to what was "right" and what was "wrong." As Shane indicated, they knew the answers to what was "good taste, proper dress, and appropriate social behavior." He continued

> Today we have a value crisis because the certainties have been swept away. We are uncertain and indecisive with respect to such matters as drug abuse, the sale of pornography, the role of women, sexual mores, the emerging functions that the churches might perform, the publicized decline of the work ethic, and so on.[25]

In addition, we are increasingly at a loss as to whom we can believe with regards to these issues. Government, industry, and even parents, teachers, and ministers "have had their authority questioned, ignored, and threatened."[26] In response to these problems, Shane points to the changes that futurists expect to see

> Permissiveness in child-rearing, which has heretofore sometimes bordered on license, will be replaced by more firm (but not harsh) policies as today's youth evaluate some of the flaws in their own upbringing.[27]

The shift from the political and social apathy of the past is yielding to intense feelings about political and social concerns.[28] This was reflected in the 1981 Gallup poll in which 70 percent of those polled favored instruction in values and ethical behavior as part of the public school curriculum.[29]

The family

Traditionally, the two-parent family has been one of the most important institutions of society. Today, however, 20 percent of all students live in one-parent homes and that number is increasing daily. Fifty percent have no parent at home during the day.[30] The result is that the schools are expected to assume many of the duties formerly belonging to the family. As former Chicago school superintendent Angelina Caruso said, "We've gotten so far afield from education that we have little time or energy left to do what we're supposed to do."[31] The futurists warn that "women will continue to be a significant and growing part of the labor force, including more mothers of children of age ten and below."[32]

Equal rights

In recent years, equal rights has grown from a racial issue to one including women, the handicapped, the disadvantaged, the gifted, the very young, and the elderly. The futurists are concerned about what constitutes equity. They ask

> Is merely equal treatment fair and just, or does justice reside in *different* treatment for the gifted, the disadvantaged, the culturally different, the handicapped, the very young, or the elderly? Does special provision for special clusters of people discriminate against the persons who do *not* receive special attention and for whom there is relatively less to spend for education or job training? Are they disadvantaged by being 'average' or 'normal'?[33]

They are also concerned about the fact that many of our citizens are not just striving for an egalitarian society but rather to be equal with the top 10 percent of the population. Democracy is conceived of as a way of life better than one's parent's station in life. This leads to frustration and resentment on the part of young people who are not satisfied with being technicians, production workers, and sales personnel.[34]

The implication for education is to help young adults "develop a personally, socially, and vocationally satisfying self-image that will prove to be realistic as they grow older" and to take pride in one of a number of socially useful jobs rather than only in the prestigious professional roles.[35]

Other social problems

The urban-suburban crisis with an increasing gap between rich and poor mirrors the widening gap on a global scale between the "have's" and the "have not's."[36] Students in the inner city lose their identities in the dense, overpopulated slums and feel powerless to overcome their inadequacies in socially acceptable ways. For this reason, they often turn to crime and violence to achieve their goals. These urban students need the security of a well-planned and executed routine of learning that capitalizes on their strengths and provides the skills needed to survive in the larger society of which they are a part.

Other social changes have arisen from the increasing complexity of our society. Population shifts from rural to urban to suburban (and, in some cases, back to rural), along with increased mobility from job to job and state to state have created a lack of acquaintance and mutual concern of people for one another. Because of this lack of concern people feel that they have less influence on their schools and communities and become apathetic with regard to national politics. They are prone to let labor unions and other special-interest groups lobby for social action rather than get involved themselves. When they are unable to solve problems by reasoning together, emotional outbursts and demands occur. One result of this may be the increase in crime such as school vandalism and attacks on teachers. Another is the increase in lawsuits.

Technological changes, caused by tremendous knowledge gains in science and tens of thousands of new inventions each year, have resulted in sudden and sweeping changes in occupational and employment preparation. Just as increased numbers of youth are entering the labor force, many of their parents are being forced to reeducate themselves for jobs that require greater technological skill. At the same time, television, satellites, and other mass communication media have created a smaller world with a growing need to work with other peoples of the world for human betterment.

The futurists also indicate the potential advantages to education of cable television, videodisc and videotape recording, home computers, and the other promising media and electronic devices now being produced.[37]

Economic inflation, by robbing both individuals and institutions of their purchasing power, has forced a reexamination of priorities. Shane foresees that status in the future will be less closely related to material possessions.[38]

Implications for education

Can schools really accomplish what is being asked of them? What characteristics differentiate a successful school from a nonsuccessful one? In a study of successful schools across the United States, Benjamin zeroed in on the following characteristics, as outlined by Edmonds

1. Strong instructional leadership marshalling the school's resources toward common purposes.

2. A climate of high expectations in which no children are allowed to fall below minimum standards of achievement.

3. A clear, shared emphasis on the basic skills that takes precedence over all other school activities.

4. An orderly, but not rigid, school atmosphere conducive to instruction.

5. Frequent, careful monitoring of pupil progress.[39]

Leadership

Leadership in schools is dependent upon two very important groups—administrators and teachers. Benjamin emphasized and reemphasized the critical relationship between the principal's leadership and the quality of the school. Studies show that effective principals take the initiative in defining instructional goals and objectives. They serve as instructional leaders, spending a large amount of time in classrooms and halls. They employ teachers who set high expectations for students and put pressure on incompetent teachers to leave. Most effective principals are assertive disciplinarians.[40] Silberman emphasized the fact that successful schools also have "unusually able and dedicated teachers."[41]

High expectations

The second prerequisite for a successful school is, as Silberman indicated, "the teachers' unshakable conviction that their students *can* learn. . . . In every successful program in fact, a major reason for success is the fact that project directors and teachers expect their students to succeed, and that they hold *themselves*—not only their students—accountable if the latter should fail."[42]

Instruction in basic skills

In a review of research on classroom instruction and student achievement, Rosenshine concluded that "effective classroom teaching of basic skills takes place in an environment characterized by an emphasis on academic achievement. . . . Teachers who make a difference in students' achievement are those who put students in contact with curriculum materials and who find ways to keep them in contact."[43]

Time spent directly on tasks to be learned correlates significantly with achievement. Frequent, careful monitoring of student progress, with specific feedback to students is also an essential component of effective learning. Enochs wrote in *The Restoration of Standards*

> In the name of innovation and relevancy, we suspended our better judgment. Rather than be thought rigid in a period when flexibility was the highest virtue, we first relaxed our standards and then abolished them completely. We began to feel guilty and proceeded to pull up our roots and examine them for rot. Homework, honest grading, demanding courses, required courses, earned promotion—up they went and out they went. . . . It was all simply easier that way. If there were no standardized bench marks against which to be measured, there was no accountability. . . . Something called the 'affective domain' became the cloak of decency for lazy teachers and administrators. It was easier to make students feel good than to hold them accountable to the rigors of learning.[44]

School atmosphere

Directly related to academic standards are standards for behavior. Benjamin stated, "Kids want adults to act like adults. They want to know who's in charge. They want to know what's expected of them. They want to know what's right and wrong today will be right and wrong tomorrow."[45]

In his Modesto, California, schools Enochs established written conduct codes for students from kindergarten through grade twelve. The codes specify the rights and responsibilities of students and the consequences for infractions. A parent handbook outlining the codes is distributed to parents, who sign a receipt verifying they received it. Character and citizenship education programs complement the behavior codes, and students receive a grade for punctuality, preparedness, and other appropriate behavior. Various school privileges can be earned or lost on the basis of these grades. The entire Modesto plan is based on a system of mutual accountability between the schools and the community. The public schools hold the parents and community responsible for the behavior of their young people and the community holds the schools responsible for the academic achievements of the students.[46]

Monitoring of pupil progress

In addition to monitoring progress and providing continuous feedback during instruction, many districts and states are requiring minimum competencies for promotion and graduation. This is a result of a number of lawsuits claiming inadequate education for students. The accountability movement is discussed further in chapter 4.

Implications for education in the future

Toffler cites three goals for the education of the future.[47] They are—

1. to learn how to learn;

2. to learn how to relate with others—to make and maintain rewarding human ties; and

3. to learn how to choose—to make decisions in an environment of overchoice.

To learn how to learn

Students starting school now will be entering the labor force in about the year 2000. As Silberman expressed

> To be 'practical,' an education should prepare them for work that does not yet exist and whose nature cannot even be imagined. This can only be done by teaching them how to learn, by giving them the kind of intellectual discipline that will enable them to apply man's accumulated wisdom to new problems as they arise. . . . 'The qualities essential to employability and productivity,' Francis S. Chase, former dean of the Graduate School of Education of the University of Chicago, has written, with some exaggeration, 'are coming closer and closer to the characteristics that have long been attributed to the educated person.'[48]

Education must turn out men and women who are capable of educating themselves and their families as circumstances change. Silberman continued

'Merely to let children live free, natural, childlike lives,' as Carleton Washburne, one of the giants of American progressivism, warned in 1925, 'may be to fail to give them the training they need to meet the problems of later life.' Thus Washburne insisted on a dual focus. 'Every child has the right to live fully and naturally as a child,' he wrote. 'Every child has the right also to be prepared adequately for later effective living as an adult.'[49]

The "Back-to-the-Basics" and the accountability movements are an attempt to ensure that every student has the opportunity to learn the skills needed for effective living in the world of the future. The Council for Basic Education advances three propositions: (1) the primary purpose of education is academic, not social; (2) basic subjects are inherently more worthwhile than other subjects; and (3) all children can learn.[50] Basic subjects are identified as those that enable people to go on and learn whatever they need or want to in later life.

The basis for the back-to-the-basics schools is the growing realization that schools have been asked to assume social responsibilities, such as checking students' teeth and preparing them for family life, that they were not designed to accomplish. The increased demands overtaxed resources, thus forcing the schools to do many things poorly, including instruction in the basic subjects.[51]

A dominant educational trend in the 1970s was the use of "magnet" schools to "attract" students from all areas of a school district to schools no longer needed in their immediate neighborhoods. These magnet schools offered such programs as back-to-the-basics programs, nongraded instruction, and year-round schooling. The schools, most of which were in the inner cities, also accomplished voluntary desegregation by attracting many middle-class students from the suburbs.

In a survey by Doll, which asked students how schools should educate them in ways no other agencies could, the student responses could be summarized as follows:

1. Put what we learn in school into a framework or system that will help us understand it better. . . .
2. Teach us "fundamentals." Nowhere except in school are you likely to gain the tools you need for thinking and serving.
3. Give us opportunities and materials in school to help us inquire, discover, and probe meaning. Getting meaning is perhaps the most important thing schools can help us do.
4. Stop attempting to compete with and to destroy what we learn elsewhere. Instead, seek to coordinate what we are taught in school with what we learn outside school.[52]

In *Teaching as a Subversive Activity*, Postman and Weingartner suggest that education should equip students with skills that would enable them to process the vast amounts of material thrust at them by the media. This would require instruction in the techniques of inquiry, such as questioning and examining alternatives in order to arrive at truth.[53]

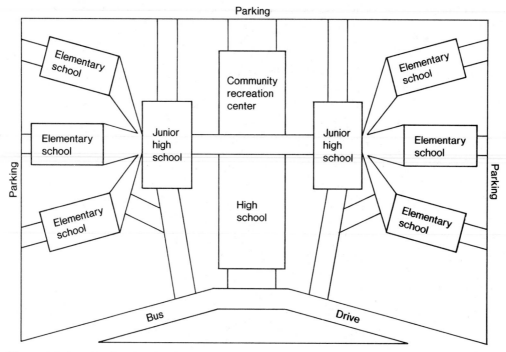

Figure 1.1 An educational park with a community recreation center.

Education in a constantly changing environment can *not* restrict itself to the young. It must be a lifelong process in which individuals can move into and out of the schools as needed. Shane suggested this concept in his theory of the "seamless curriculum." The curriculum would be nongraded, year-round, and directed toward the individual needs of the learner at any age level.[54] With this in mind, a number of alternative educational institutions and methods should be studied. Some alternatives to the traditional school include (1) the community-school, (2) the educational park, and (3) the nonschool. Some advantages of alternative schools are the opportunities for individualized instruction, community involvement in education, and increased student responsibility for learning.

The community-school

The community-school is a facility that houses educational, aesthetic, recreational, social, and political programs under the same roof. It shares its power with the community and bridges the gap between the community and the school through parent use of the school for recreational and social needs, parent involvement in school programs, and parent-school involvement in local community problems.[55]

The educational park

The educational park is a large school (5,000–20,000 students) that consolidates students of various educational levels and locations into a large facility as shown in figure 1.1. One purpose of such a park is to share underused facilities, such as an auditorium, swimming pool, or concert hall. A secondary purpose is school desegregation through busing large numbers of students from a wide area to a centrally located school. To be worthwhile, an educational park must provide a higher quality education than that available at smaller neighborhood schools.[56]

The nonschool

The nonschool is a learning center in which there is no campus. Students complete all work via telephone, television, computerized units of instruction, contracted work-study programs, and other similar processes.

To learn how to relate to others

One of the goals of American education is to facilitate the fullest possible growth and development of each individual regardless of race, religion, sex, or ability. If any person fails to develop his or her potential and to use it for worthy purposes, the educational system has fallen short of achieving its purposes.

To design educational programs that serve all students in ways adapted to their different capabilities and needs is a challenge to those who plan and conduct educational programs. The future success of America as a nation depends increasingly on the abilities of teachers to promote common concerns through cooperative problem solving that is based on fact, reason, and brotherly and sisterly love rather than authority or force. Mutual understanding and empathy for others are becoming essential in today's "pressure-cooker" American society. For this reason, skills in cooperation should be emphasized in physical education classes.

Another value traditionally held by American society is the freedom to interact with others while, at the same time, being responsible for one's own actions. Respect for the rights and feelings of others and sensitivity to one's actions on others are essential components of an individual's moral responsibility in society. Classroom management should be based on the principles of individual responsibility for one's own behavior. Chapter 18 describes how this can be done.

To learn how to choose

"Security is the best preparation for an insecure future," said Shane.[57] One of the keys to security for young people is to see secure adults interacting with their environment.[58] In the school setting, this occurs when teachers act like adults rather than as pals to their students.

Another key to learning security is discovering how to make choices. Coping with change demands that students explore possible alternatives for the future. Teachers can assist students in acquiring these skills by helping them look at ideas and skills that have helped people adjust in the past. They can also encourage students to search for generalizations or concepts that organize learning into meaningful wholes. Course subject matter should have wide application to everyday life, both now and in the future. Students need to be taught to think seriously about why they are doing what they are doing and to learn the consequences for the decisions they make.[59] Thus, critical thinking and problem-solving skills need to become important components of the educational program. The development of these skills is discussed in chapters 6 and 14.

Further purposes of education are to preserve and maintain the desirable aspects of society and to constructively influence the social order through ordered, purposeful change. The American Association of School Administrators summarized how the educational system of America has emerged as one of the greatest creations of humankind

> The vitality of the institution of public education and the force for human betterment that it exercises have emerged from experiences of people . . . reaching upward for something better than they now have. The cherished qualities of the institution of public education have been built into it by the painstaking care and skillful molding of people who believe deeply in the importance of education, by people who understand the basic principles of how learning takes place and children mature, and by people with a sense of responsibility for the institution of public education which Horace Mann long ago asserted was the greatest creation of mankind.[60]

Questions and suggested activities

1. Formulate your own definition of education.

2. Interview several community leaders to determine what they think the purposes of education should be. Compare their ideas with those presented in this chapter.

3. As a group of parents, teachers, and concerned citizens (or other selected roles), list the things that a graduate of a high school in your city should be able to *do* to receive a diploma from your district.

4. Identify factors in the American educational system that might hinder a student in achieving the items you listed in answer to question 3.

5. Write a description of the school of the future as *you* visualize it.

6. Study lists of educational goals published by state and/or district boards of education. Compare them with each other and with the goals listed in this chapter.

Suggested readings

Adler, Jerry, and Abramson, Pamela. "The School That Flunked." *Newsweek,* 6 October 1980, p. 86.
Bucher, Charles A. "What's Happening in Education Today?" *Journal of Health, Physical Education, Recreation* 45 (September 1974): 30–32.
Carlson, Gerald P. "Physical Education Is Basic." *Journal of Physical Education, Recreation, and Dance* 53 (January 1982): 67–69.

Cohen, Michael. "Effective Schools: What the Research Says." *Today's Education* (April–May 1981): 58GS–60GS.

Cooper, John M. "Random Thoughts on the Future of Educational Processes." *The Physical Educator* 34 (December 1977): 171–74.

Frymier, Jack R. *A School for Tomorrow.* Berkeley, Calif.: McCutchan Publishing Company, 1973.

Gross, Ronald, and Gross, Beatrice. *Radical School Reform.* New York: Simon and Schuster, 1969.

Koenig, Constance R. "New Directions: Back to the Basics?" *Journal of Physical Education, Recreation, and Dance* 52 (June 1981): 14.

Pierce, Kenneth M. "Trying the Old-Fashioned Way." *Time,* 9 March 1981, p. 65.

Scribner, Harvey B. and Stevens, Leonard B. *Make Your Schools Work: Practical, Imaginative and Cost-Free Plans to Turn Public Education Around.* New York: Simon and Schuster, 1975.

Toffler, Alvin. *Future Shock.* New York: Random House, 1970.

Tomlinson, Tommy. "Effective Schools: Mirror or Mirage?" *Today's Education* 70 (April–May 1981): 60GS.

Vayhinger, Harold P. "The Great Experiment: The American System of Education." *Phi Kappa Phi Journal,* (Winter 1977): 29–36.

Warren, Barbara Leonard. "May I Have Your Attention, Please." *Today's Education,* 70 (November–December 1981): 64.

Developing a Philosophy of Physical Education

Study stimulators

1. What is a philosophy? How do you get one?
2. What major philosophies have developed in physical education since 1900?
3. What four goals are usually included in physical education programs?
4. How are the goals of physical education developed?
5. Describe a physical education program of the future.

Physical education is the study, practice, and appreciation of the art and science of human movement. It is a part of the total process of education that begins at birth and ends at death. As you enter the profession of physical education, your ability to define and state your philosophy of physical education will be essential.

What is a philosophy?

A philosophy is a composite of the knowledge, attitudes, beliefs, and values that forms the basis for a person's actions and provides central direction or purpose to his or her activities. When an individual's personal philosophy is out of tune with the philosophies of associates, unhappiness and frustration result. For example, if you have a philosophy that a well-planned and organized instructional program can help students function more effectively in society and the physical education department in which you teach fosters a "throw out the ball" program, you can not be happy working there. Therefore, it is essential that your personal philosophy be consistent with the philosophies of your school and department.

Some people have a philosophy that whatever takes the least amount of work is best or that whatever everyone else is doing is okay. Such philosophies result in unplanned, incidental learning. Oberteuffer and Ulrich indicated that

> To understand anything one must relate all of the parts, episodes, or individual
> actions to the "grand plan," the overall purpose. This is sometimes called the
> point of view—or the philosophy underlying the effort. Without an overall
> plan, direction, or philosophy, a physical education program, or anything else,
> becomes nothing more than a series of disconnected and unrelated activities,
> having no unifying purpose.[1]

A sound philosophy of physical education is essential for both individuals and institutions if physical education is to result in the most effective benefits to students. A philosophy gives physical educators a basis for making the decisions inherent in creating and implementing physical education programs. It provides direction in the selection of the goals and objectives of the program, the curriculum pattern, and the coursework. It dictates what is taught, how it is taught, and how the work is graded.

A teacher whose philosophy stresses physical fitness will have a strong school physical fitness program. Another who believes strongly in student responsibility for learning will use many individualized learning methods. Because of a philosophy that emphasizes the totality of learning, a third instructor stops activity on a beautiful spring day to point out the awe-inspiring mountains capped with snow.

Every educational institution should have a written statement of its philosophy that can serve to guide the development of the curriculum. The following is a statement of philosophy published by the American Alliance for Health, Physical Education, Recreation, and Dance:

> Physical education is the study and practice of the science and art of human movement. It is concerned with why man moves; how he moves; the physiological, sociological, and psychological consequences of his movement; and the skills and motor patterns which comprise his movement repertoire. Through physical education, an individual has the opportunity to learn to perform efficiently the motor skills he needs in everyday living and in recreational activities. He can develop and maintain sound physiological functions through vigorous muscular activity. He may increase the awareness of his physical self. Through expressive and creative activities, he may enhance his aesthetic appreciations. Physical education provides situations for learning to compete as well as to cooperate with others in striving for achievement of common goals. Within the media of physical activity, concepts underlying effective human movement can be demonstrated and the influences these have on the individual can be better understood. Satisfying and successful experiences in physical education should develop in the individual a desire to regularly participate in activity throughout life. Only through enjoyable and persistent participation will the optimum benefits of physical activity be derived.[2]

Parents, school boards, administrators, teachers, and students all want to know where we are headed. Leland Stanford used to say, "The world stands aside for the man who knows where he is going."[3] Stanford was right. If an individual knows where he or she is going, people will pay attention. In the past, too many physical education teachers have not been able to state where they were going.

How do you develop a philosophy?

A philosophy is the result of continuously changing knowledge and experience. It is dynamic, always evolving, never static. The development of a philosophy of physical education involves the following steps:

Step 1. Study the philosophies of various leaders.

Step 2. Analyze your own feelings and experiences.

Step 3. Obtain feedback from others.

Step 1—Study the philosophies of various leaders

The first way to obtain a philosophy is to study the philosophies of various leaders in physical education, both past and present. During the twentieth century, three philosophies have emerged. They are (1) education *of* the physical, (2) education *through* the physical, and (3) the human movement approach.

Education *of* the physical

In the early history of physical education in the United States, the emphasis was predominantly on health and physical fitness—the development of the body as an end in itself. Programs consisted primarily of gymnastics and calisthenics. This philosophy was later dubbed "education of the physical."

The emphasis on physical fitness was resurrected during World War I and II and the Korean War. It was also emphasized following the report of the Kraus-Weber Tests in 1953. These tests showed that American children were inferior in strength and flexibility to European children. This report sparked a national interest in physical fitness and a number of conferences on youth fitness. It finally resulted in the formation of a National Council on Youth Fitness and various other efforts to support physical education in the schools.

The emphasis on physical fitness was championed by Arthur H. Steinhaus and Charles H. McCloy. McCloy stated, "For a profession that has glorified the physical side of man from before 500 B.C. until, shall we say, A.D. 1915, the physical education literature of today is strangely silent about the more purely body-building type of objectives."[4] Steinhaus emphasized that "all forms of education may develop the mind and spirit of man but only physical education can develop his body."[5]

Education *through* the physical

As early as 1893, Thomas Wood emphasized the need to replace physical training with physical education. He later wrote:

> Physical education must have an aim as broad as education itself, and as noble and inspiring as human life. The great thought in physical education is not the education of the physical nature, but the relation of physical training to complete education, and then the effort to make the physical contribute its full share to the life of the individual, in environment, training, and culture.[6]

Wood was accompanied in his effort by Luther Halsey Gulick and Clark W. Hetherington. Together they emphasized a "new physical education," consisting of sports and games, outdoor recreation, and educational gymnastics. This break with formal gymnastics was important in the move for physical education to become an accepted part of the educational curriculum.

Gulick, a prominent leader in the recreation and outdoor education movement, emphasized the social and play needs of youth. He stated:

> The first necessity . . . is to provide for the development and fashioning
> of out of school play and games that shall engage large numbers of
> children. . . . Gymnastics can never take the place of play, and upon play we
> must depend in the future, as we have in the past, for the fundamental
> conditions for the development of organic life and power.[7]

Hetherington emphasized the importance of educating the total person—physically, mentally, emotionally, and socially—by meeting the specific needs and interests of each age group. He attempted to "describe the function and place of general neuromuscular activities, primarily general play activities, in the educational process." He said:

> We use the term *general play* to include play, games, athletics, dancing,
> the play side of gymnastics, and all play activities in which large muscles are
> used more or less vigorously.
> The interpretation given might be called the new physical education,
> with the emphasis on education, and the understanding that it is "physical"
> only in the sense that the activity of the whole organism is the educational
> agent and not the mind alone.[8]

It was Hetherington who presented the four basic processes, or objectives, of physical education that have continued for more than half a century. They are: organic education, psychomotor education, character education, and intellectual education.[9]

It was some time before "education through the physical" became the dominant philosophy of physical education. This philosophy was a natural outgrowth of the broadening of the curriculum to reflect the life of the community as advocated by John Dewey. Jesse Feiring Williams defined once and for all the distinction between the two theories in his 1930 article, "Education Through the Physical:"

> No one can examine earnestly the implications of physical education
> without facing two questions. These are: Is physical education an education *of*
> the physical? Is physical education an education *through* the physical? . . .
> Education of the physical is a familiar view. Its supporters are those who
> regard strong muscles and firm ligaments as the main outcomes. . . .
> Modern physical education with its emphasis upon education through the
> physical is based upon the biologic unity of mind and body. This view sees life
> as a totality. . . . It sees physical education primarily as a way of living.[10]

Jay B. Nash joined with Williams to promote the social and moral aspects of physical education. He emphasized that "character is one of the desirable outcomes of education and hence is one of the desirable outcomes of physical education."[11]

No prominent physical educator in the past thirty years has deviated significantly from the philosophy of "education through the physical."

Human movement is an expression of the individual interacting with the environment.

The human movement approach

A relatively new physical education philosophy is the human movement approach to physical education developed by Rudolph Laban in England in the late 1930s. However, it did not appear significantly in literature in the United States until the late 1950s. One of the earlier advocates of the philosophy in the United States was Eleanor Metheny. She wrote:

> If we may define the totally educated person as one who has fully
> developed his ability to utilize constructively all of his potential capacities as a
> person in relation to the world in which he lives, then we may define the
> physically educated person as one who has fully developed the ability to utilize

constructively all of his potential capacities for movement as a way of expressing, exploring, developing, and interpreting himself and his relationship to the world he lives in. This is the part of education we have chosen as our peculiar task. Our job is to help him learn to move his body.[12]

The movement philosophy was adopted and promoted by Camille Brown and Rosalind Cassidy, who defined human movement as "the change in position of man in time-space as a result of his own energy system interacting within an environment. Human movement is expressive and communicative, and in the interactive process changes both the individual and the environment."[13]

The human movement philosophy attempts to help students understand the principles of efficient movement through participation in movement experiences. A combination of kinesiological and biomechanical concepts are combined with the four concepts of movement proposed by Laban—body, effort, space, and relationships. It also encourages self-expression and social interaction.

Today the human movement philosophy has been implemented primarily in the elementary school and in dance. Although there are many proponents of this approach, it has been difficult for many secondary school physical educators to adapt to this teaching style.

Step 2—Analyze your own feelings and experiences

Many philosophies reflect an eclectic approach, in which aspects from each of the preceding philosophies are merged into a personal philosophy of physical education.

Through reacting to what is going on around you and questioning why things are as they are and how they should be, you can get an idea of your own feelings regarding physical education, education, and even life itself. Through struggling to define your philosophy you will also gain valuable insight into what you really believe.

Step 3—Obtain feedback from others

In addition to self-analysis, stating your philosophy orally or in writing to others and defending it will help you to see areas that you have neglected to consider. You will then need to reconsider what you believe over and over again as you gain knowledge and experiences throughout your life.

The aim and goals of physical education

Directly related to a philosophy of physical education is the aim or purpose of a program. An *aim* is an ideal which acts as a compass by giving direction to the total program. It also provides a basis for evaluating curricular offerings. In view of the recent emphasis on accountability for instruction, care should be taken to avoid aiming at more than we could possibly accomplish. The following statement is an aim:

Physical education is that integral part of total education which contributes to the development of the individual through the natural medium of physical activity—human movement. It is a carefully planned sequence of learning experiences designed to fulfill the growth, development, and behavior needs of each student.[14]

Since an aim is a distant or ideal goal, it must be broken down into a number of smaller goals which, when achieved, will direct us toward the aim. These *instructional goals* are statements of the outcomes to be expected of all students in the school. The following statements are instructional goals for physical education:

1. To develop physical skills which will enable participation in a wide variety of activities.

2. To develop physical fitness and soundly functioning body systems for an active life in his/her environment.

3. To develop knowledge and understanding of physical and social skills, physical fitness, scientific principles of movement, and the relationship of exercise to personal well-being.

4. To develop social skills which promote acceptable standards of behavior and positive relationships with others.

5. To develop attitudes and appreciations that will encourage participation in and enjoyment of physical activity, fitness, quality performance, a positive self concept, and respect for others.[15]

These goals have generally been accepted by leaders in the profession as the basic goals of physical education.

Physical skills

The development of neuromuscular skill essential for efficient everyday movement (posture and body mechanics) as well as for efficient movement in a variety of activities leads to less energy wasted in skill performance and more enjoyment in activity. Fundamental skills, sports skills, and skills in rhythmic activities are all important.

Physical fitness

The development of physical fitness and health contributes to effective living and enjoyment of life. One aspect of physical fitness is health-related fitness, including such components as strength, flexibility, endurance and body composition. Motor fitness expands the definition to include such areas as balance, agility, coordination, and speed.

Knowledge and understanding

An understanding of the importance of physical activity and how it relates to one's health and well-being is essential. Such an understanding must include skills in designing and implementing a fitness or weight-control program, evaluating fitness, and safe participation in activity. Knowledge about game rules, strategies, and techniques of participation enhance participation in a variety of physical activities. Game play can also increase one's ability to solve problems in highly emotional situations. Students should also learn the processes for acquiring physical skills and the basic principles of movement (equilibrium, absorption of force, etc.) that are common to all activities.

Social skills

Desirable social values—such as cooperation, leadership, followership, sportsmanship, and courtesy—should be taught through participation in physical education activities.

Attitudes and appreciations

The attitudes a student has toward physical activity influence the student's future participation. Care should be taken to ensure that only positive attitudes and appreciations result from physical education classes. When participation occurs in a supportive environment, students can increase their feelings of self-esteem and develop initiative, self-direction, and creativity. Physical activity also provides an opportunity for releasing emotional tension through appropriate channels.

Each of these goals can be broken into short-term goals called *objectives,* which can be adjusted to meet the needs of individual students. The writing of objectives will be further discussed in chapter 10.

Although there is general agreement among the leaders of physical education on the goals to be achieved, there are differences in the priorities (or ranking) of these goals. Since physical education teachers cannot do everything, what should be emphasized? Rosentswieg conducted a study of 100 college physical educators in teacher-training institutions and found that organic vigor and neuromuscular skills were the most highly valued goals of physical education.[16]

The question that remains to be answered is whether or not the specified goals are being realized in actual practice. To be effective, both aims and goals must be worthwhile, be in harmony with educational and physical educational philosophy, and be attainable. The National Association of Secondary School Principals stressed the importance of physical education as follows:

> Today's physical education programs are aimed at helping students acquire constructive concepts and desirable habits regarding the preservation of our environment's most prized natural resource: the well-tuned, efficiently functional human body and all its healthy competitive components. . . .
>
> Furthermore, physical education has earned a role as one of the essential elements in any curriculum designed to educate the whole person, whether he be highly talented intellectually or otherwise, only average, or faced with the task of trying to cope with physical, mental, or emotional handicaps.[17]

How are goals for physical education developed?

Goals are a result of a step-by-step process of thought that considers (1) the relationship of physical education to the purposes of education, (2) the needs and interests of students, (3) the nature of the school and its community, and (4) the personal philosophies of the faculty.

Physical education and the purposes of education

Since physical education is a part of education, the curriculum in physical education must be based on a sound philosophy that, in turn, is consistent with the social and educational philosophies of the time and place in which it functions. This includes the role of education in American society and the more specific purposes of education expressed within the particular school in which the program operates. If each subject area were to pursue its own objectives, then the students would be deprived of a well-balanced education devoted to the development of the total individual. For this reason, the goals of physical education should be integrated with the purposes of education. For example, physical education contributes to health through the development of organic vigor, to the worthy use of leisure through the development of skills for use in leisure-time activity, and to ethical character through the development of sportsmanship. Many other correlations also occur.

The needs and interests of students

All teachers must be concerned about the needs and interests of students, but teachers in physical education should be particularly sensitive to the needs of students with regard to physical fitness and motor development and the intellectual, personal, and social needs that revolve around these important goals.

Well-planned and implemented physical education programs provide opportunities for *all* students to experience success in physical activity. This can only occur when the program provides a logical progression of developmental activities designed to challenge students to improve existing skills. This includes remedial activities for poorly skilled students, adapted activities for the handicapped, and activities to challenge gifted students. It includes fitness activities that challenge the highly fit and that also help the poorly fit to gradually increase their physical fitness. Students' interests should also be considered in the selection of activities for the program. Chapter 3 suggests some ways to study student needs and interests and some principles for planning educational programs to meet these needs and interests.

The nature of the school and community

A number of local factors must be considered when selecting the goals of physical education. These include the economic and cultural background of the community surrounding the school. Programs must be adapted to the needs and interests of the students and community. For example, in some communities, dancing may be prohibited by certain religious groups.

In inner-city areas, the costs of participation in golf would be prohibitive. Climate may dictate that many of the activities be conducted indoors. The resources of the school and community will also influence the activities and content of the program as outlined in later chapters of this book.

Personal philosophies of the faculty

The personal philosophies of the faculty have an important effect on the selection of goals and content for the physical education program. Daughtrey suggests that prospective teachers ask themselves the following questions:

1. Do I know where I am headed? What is my aim?

2. Can I scientifically justify the activities I wish to teach?

3. Am I willing to abandon the teaching of certain activities if they are shown to be educationally unsound?

4. Is my program self-centered or pupil-centered?

5. Are the activities safe?

6. Is my program a play program or is it a teaching program?[18]

A sound philosophy is the basis for a sound program. Is your philosophy such that your physical education program will be a justifiable addition to the school program?

Some principles for the future

Bookwalter and VanderZwaag define a principle as "a guiding rule for general action toward some goal . . . based on scientific fact or authoritative opinion."[19] Several principles have been included here as a basis for the direction of future programs:

1. Strong leadership will be the key to a successful physical education program.

2. The need for physical activity will be even more important than it has been in the past.

3. Programs must be designed to meet the needs of all people regardless of age, sex, race, or ability. This may necessitate the expansion of programs outside the traditional walls of the school.

4. Programs must stress a health-maintenance life-style and the ways in which students can evaluate and design their own fitness programs.

5. Students must be taught how to learn new skills and be gradually exposed to programs in which they can learn to be self-directing rather than dependent on teacher instructions.[20]

6. Research findings about the effects of exercise on individuals must be used to enhance personal development and improve our society.[21]

Questions and suggested activities

1. Write your philosophy of physical education. Try to keep this philosophy in harmony with your philosophy of education. Keep it short, concise, and written so the average parent can understand it. Include such areas as how you feel about students, how physical education can help them meet the goals of education, and the values of physical education for students and others in out-of-school situations.

2. As parents, concerned citizens, administrators, teachers, medical doctors (or other selected groups), list the things that a graduate of a successful physical education program should be able to *do* to receive a high school diploma.

3. What kinds of experiences might be needed in order to meet the objectives listed in activity 2?

4. Identify factors in our educational system that might hinder the teacher and/or the students in achieving the objectives you have listed.

5. List ways in which physical education meets the goals listed for education.

6. If curriculum content is a result of one's philosophy, how can we account for the "throw out the ball" programs that exist in many schools?

7. In considering students' needs on the high school level, if you had a choice of either having an elective program or a required program, which would you choose and why?

8. You have been asked to give a ten-minute talk on the value of physical education at a parent orientation night. What will you say?

9. Assume that you are the defense lawyer in a pretrial hearing in which the following complaint is expressed: School physical education classes fail to make a significant contribution to all students enrolled; therefore, (1) the required physical education program should be rescinded and (2) tax funds expended for physical education should be used for some other educational program. What will you do?

Suggested readings

Arnold, Don E., and Razor, Jack E. "Physical Education and Community Education: Extending the Scope of Physical Education." *The Physical Educator* 34 (March 1977): 20–23.

Beyrer, Mary K. "The College That Is HPER." *Journal of Physical Education and Recreation* 50 (June 1979): 20–23.

Burton, Diane E. "Shaping the Future." *Journal of Physical Education and Recreation* 47 (March 1976): 20–21.

Collingwood, T. R., and Engelsgjera, Mike. "Physical Fitness, Physical Activity, and Juvenile Delinquency." *Journal of Physical Education and Recreation* 48 (June 1977): 23.

Gallahue, D. L. "Aims of Physical Education." *The Physical Educator* 33 (December 1976): 170.

Kneer, Marian E. "Exit Competencies in Physical Education for the Secondary School Student." *Journal of Physical Education and Recreation* 49 (January 1978): 46.

Koehler, Robert W. "Can This Be Physical Education?" *The Physical Educator* 32 (October 1975): 151.

Melograno, Vincent. "Physical Education Curriculum for the 1980s." *Journal of Physical Education and Recreation* 51 (September 1980): 39.

Moore, Clarence A. "Future Trends and Issues in Physical Education and Athletics." *Journal of Physical Education and Recreation* 51 (January 1980): 20–21.

Razor, Jack E. "Elective PE Programs: Expansion vs. Limitation." *Journal of Physical Education and Recreation* 46 (June 1975): 23–24.

Soudan, Salem, and Everett, Peter. "Physical Education Objectives Expressed as Needs by Florida State University Students." *Journal of Physical Education, Recreation, and Dance* 52 (May 1981): 14–17.

Welsh, Raymond. "Futurism and Physical Education." *Journal of Health, Physical Education, Recreation* 44 (October 1973): 28–9.

Zeigler, Earle F. "Physical Education—Dead, Quiescent, or Undergoing Modification?" *Journal of Physical Education, Recreation, and Dance* 53 (January 1982): 51–53.

Getting to Know the Student

Study stimulators

1. What common characteristics do adolescents have? What differences do they exhibit?
2. What effect do student differences have on learning? What effect do their similarities have on teaching?

Ralph Waldo Emerson once said, "The secret of education lies in respecting the pupil." Respect comes from getting to know one another and appreciating the worth of the other person. In getting to know students, three areas need to be considered: (1) common characteristics of children and youth, (2) significant differences among students, and (3) educational programs that meet the needs identified in the first two areas.

Common characteristics of children and youth

Much research has been conducted in child and adolescent growth and development and is available in textbooks of educational and developmental psychology. Consult these references for specific data on specific age levels. However, caution should be exercised in defining all students in terms of these norms. Since students are continuously growing and developing, all students do not fit the norm for a particular grade level. In fact, students in one grade level may be as much as eleven months different in age, not counting older students who have been held back. Even students of the same age mature at different rates; therefore, there is seldom a time when all children of a given group will be at exactly the same stage of growth and development.

Obviously we cannot have a different school for each student. Therefore, common characteristics of children and youth serve as a general basis for making curriculum decisions for the school.

Significant differences among students

Fader reminded us that "We stopped looking at children. They no longer become salutary evidence in a statistical society. We don't look at children. We look at the statistics that represent them."[1] By learning to look at students as individuals, we can design our instructional programs to help them become successful, contributing members of our society.

Students differ significantly in many areas. Major differences occur in the areas of (1) physical growth and development; (2) intellectual development; (3) social forces that affect students; and (4) personality, attitudes, and interests.

Students differ significantly in physical and intellectual growth and development, social experiences, personality, attitudes, and interests.

Physical growth and development

Growth and development depend upon both heredity and environment. Because of improved nutrition and better health care, today's children grow up faster. Both boys and girls are taller, heavier, and mature earlier than children of previous generations. They can expect the longest life expectancy ever known in our society.

Chamberlin and Girona describe adolescence as a "clash between culture and biology," in which "adults try to cling to and pass on the values and mores of our culture to our children while they struggle with maturing bodies and childlike emotions."[2] Although adolescence begins earlier, the economic and educational requirements of a technological society force it to end later. As a result, curriculum activities that used to be reserved for older students are now handed down to younger students. This leaves older students frustrated by the fact that there is nothing new left for them to try, and yet they are not allowed to assume the privileges and responsibilities of adulthood. Teachers face the challenge of trying to help students cope with the physical and emotional changes that challenge them.

In addition, adolescents differ widely in physical growth and capacity. Some children are early bloomers and others mature much later. They vary widely in body build and physical capacity. Motor ability factors—such as agility, balance, coordination, flexibility, strength, and speed—predispose some students to success in some motor activities and others to success in other activities. Body build, muscle composition, and respiratory capacity help some students to be better long-distance runners and others to be better sprinters or jumpers. Other factors that vary include visual and auditory acuity, perception, and reaction time. Physical handicaps enlarge the differences among students.

Because of the wide variety of individual differences among students, physical education programs should include a variety of activities so that students will find some commensurate with their individual abilities. Different levels of activity should be provided so that students will be challenged to extend their abilities, yet experience success during the learning process.

Intellectual development

The youth of today are better informed than their counterparts of yesteryear. Nursery schools; television and other media, scores of books, newspapers, and magazines; and widespread travel have increased the information available to today's adolescents. As a result of these experiences, children and adolescents are not easily impressed. They've seen it all. However, the abundance of information causes what Chamberlin and Girona call "over choice."[3] Young people have so much information and so many choices provided in dress, life-style, courses, occupations, and values that they are confused as to what information to process and how to make the decisions that confront them. They must be helped to deal with problem-solving behaviors if the school is going to be of value to them.

Social forces that affect students

Rapid changes in our society have had a detrimental effect on the youth of our nation. The influence of the family deteriorated as divorce became more and more common. Increased mobility has taken families away from relatives and friends. Dramatic role changes for men and women have confused some young people as to what is expected of them. Values and morals change constantly and are no longer a stabilizing force in American society.

According to Margaret Mead, a noted anthropologist, adolescents today are expected to act like adults but are not allowed to accept the roles of adults.[4] They have been superficially exposed to so many adult activities and privileges that by the time they are in their mid-teens they are already bored and have nothing to look forward to. Many respond by escaping to drugs, delinquency, or religious cults.

The effects of social forces on individual students differ in terms of their various backgrounds and experiences. Students who come from upper and middle-class families often have more pressure placed on them to learn and to conform to school policies, while lower-class students have other values. Ethnic groups have different expectations regarding the value of education. Families differ in the cultural experiences they provide their members, as well as in their goals and interests. Friends, neighbors, and other social groups influence values and attitudes. Experiences of individual students can be so different that generalities are no longer of use in planning some educational programs.

Personality, attitudes, and interests

Various personality characteristics cause students to feel more comfortable in one activity than another. The aggressive, competitive, social student might prefer participation in a team sport, whereas the cooperative, passive loner might prefer engaging in a jogging or cycling program.

Self-esteem correlates highly with body image and skill in physical activity. A program that helps students develop proficiency in activity can increase self-esteem and enhance the development of positive attitudes toward physical activity.[5]

A number of different needs stimulate interest in physical activity. These needs may take the form of social affiliation, energy-release, health and well-being, or self-fulfillment. As needs change from time-to-time, so do interests. When students are allowed to select their own activities, motivation to learn is increased considerably.

Studying Student Needs

Getting to know students implies taking the time necessary to find out what the similarities and differences are among students in your particular school. Some of this information will be available in the form of school and student records. School records include data about the entire school population such as total enrollment, age and sex distributions, race or ethnic backgrounds, dropout rates, and other essential information needed for developing educational programs. Student records include health and medical status, intelligence and achievement test results, grades, results of interest and attitude inventories, and other information.

Parent-teacher conferences and back-to-school nights can be helpful in getting acquainted with family backgrounds. A drive through the area where students live can provide an idea of socioeconomic levels and cultural activity.

Observation of students in the school setting can be a valuable source of data. The following questions could be used to direct your observation of students in a selected class:

1. What would you guess to be the range in height in the class?

   Shortest boy _____   Tallest boy _____

   Shortest girl _____   Tallest girl _____

   In weight?

   Heaviest boy _____   Lightest boy _____

   Heaviest girl _____   Lightest girl _____

   Have you observed any students for whom size may be the source of potential problems? What problems do you foresee? Record ideas for dealing with these problems.

2. What is the age range of students in the class?

   Oldest boy _____   Youngest boy _____

   Oldest girl _____   Youngest girl _____

   Does it appear that age is a problem factor for any student in this class? Explain.

3. Identify the student whom you consider to be the most aggressive in the class; the least aggressive. List their names below:

_____   _____

As you think about these two and observe them, do you see a basic difference in the way they approach learning activities at school? Explain.

4. List below the name of the student who, in your judgment, comes from the most affluent home; the least affluent.

_____   _____

What implications do you see for instruction and learning?

5. What is the performance range of students in the class in a rhythmic activity?

_____

In a sport? _____

In a fitness activity? _____

How would you adapt the instruction to meet the needs of each level of performance?

6. Identify students who are handicapped physically, culturally, or otherwise.

_____   _____

What would you do to help them achieve success?

7. List as many other ways as you can think of in which students differ. Which of these do you consider to be factors that might affect the way a student learns? Try ranking them in order of importance.

Observation of students in nonschool functions can also provide an insight into student activities, interpersonal relationships, and leadership abilities. The following questions might be used as a guide:

1. Who was the group leader? How could you tell?

2. How did the boys react to the girls and vice versa?

3. Who directed the activities officially? Unofficially?

4. How was attention shown? To whom was it shown?

5. How were the student's behaviors different from their behaviors in school?

6. Did you see the "typical teenager"? Is there such a thing?

7. What motivating factors influence students when they are not in school?

8. What group or individual values were in evidence?

9. How did the group values influence the individuals?

10. How were decisions made among the students?

11. What learning was taking place?

12. What was the nature of the activity (constructive, destructive, social, religious, etc.)? How did this help determine the type of behavior considered appropriate for the situation?

13. Why were these particular students together?

14. Were the leaders in these activities also leaders in school activities? Why or why not?

15. What methods of influence did you notice being practiced?

16. How will knowing this information about students change *your* behavior in the classroom?

17. How do students behave differently in adult company? With different teachers?

Questionnaires can provide insight into the actual interests, attitudes, and values of students. Some possible questions are given here. Other ideas are included in chapter 11.

Questionnaire

Directions: Do not write your name on this paper. Answer the questions below in the best way you know how.

1. How do you feel about yourself? I am:

_____ too tall	_____ too short	_____ too fat
_____ too skinny	_____ just right	_____ popular
_____ unpopular	_____ okay	_____ average
_____ rich	_____ poor	_____ middle-income
_____ sharp dresser	_____ shabby dresser	_____ average dresser
_____ good in sports	_____ bad in sports	_____ average

2. How do you rate yourself as a student?

_____ fast learner	_____ outstanding student
_____ slow learner	_____ average student
_____ average speed learner	_____ poor student

3. Do you have a job? _____ What kind? _____

4. What do you do in your free time?

5. What are your favorite sports or activities?

6. Do you play a musical instrument? _____ Take private lessons in dance, music, sports, etc.? _____ If so, what kind? _____

7. Do you have a lot of friends? _____ A few friends? _____ Are they close friends? _____ Casual friends? _____ Both? _____

Of course, teacher-student interaction before, during, and after classes provides one of the best opportunities for teachers and students to get to know each other on a more informal basis.

Educational programs that meet student needs

Physical growth and development, intellectual development, social forces, and personality factors all affect the ways in which students learn. Therefore, various styles of learning should be provided for in the instructional program. Some principles that must be considered when planning educational programs include the following.

1. Each student is unique, a result of both heredity and environment.

2. Each student learns at his or her own rate regardless of how the teacher paces the instruction.

3. Students learn many things simultaneously.

4. Students learn different things from identical experiences.

5. Learning does not take place in a smooth, continuous process. It involves intermittent periods of growth followed by plateaus.

6. Students must learn for themselves. The teacher cannot learn for them.

7. Students learn best when:
   a. Learning is positively and immediately reinforced by praise, success, etc.
   b. The learning process involves experiencing and doing.
   c. A wide variety of meaningful learning experiences are provided at the appropriate level for the maturity of the student.
   d. Goals and objectives are set or accepted by the students and provide realistic standards for each student.
   e. Students can see the results of how well they are doing.
   f. Students experience many more successful experiences than failures.
   g. Learning is directed to the whole student.

h. The learning experience and evaluation are adapted to the individual differences of the student.

i. The learning environment is a comfortable place to make (and learn from) a mistake.

Each of these principles will be discussed in more detail in the following chapters. Doll suggests that "the challenge to education in a democracy appears much more prominently in the differences among children and youth than in their similarities."[6]

Some years ago, the members of the Educational Policies Commission summed up the purpose of education for all American youth, a purpose that still holds true today. They said:

When we write confidently and inclusively about education for all American youth, we mean just that. We mean that all youth, with their human similarities and their equally human differences, shall have educational services and opportunities suited to their personal needs and sufficient for the successful operation of a free and democratic society. . . . Each of them is a human being, more precious than material goods or systems of philosophy. Not one of them should be permitted to be carelessly wasted. All of them must be given equal opportunities to live and learn.[7]

Questions and suggested activities

1. Talk to children or youth. Show genuine interest in them. Ask them about where they live, their parents' occupations, their brothers and sisters, friends, interests, attitudes, etc.

2. Select one student and observe him or her very closely. Prepare an anecdotal record about the student over a period of several days or weeks.

3. Do one of the following:
   a. Go on a field trip to an Indian reservation.
   b. Observe for a couple of days in an inner-city school.
   c. Observe students in casual situations such as at dances, shopping centers, downtown, school parking lots, drive-ins, etc.
   d. Contact leaders of a youth group for permission to work with young people. Possible groups could be the YMCA, YWCA, scout troops, city athletic programs, church groups, etc.
   e. Observe the different age groups and activities of young people as they are waiting in lines (at theaters, athletic events, in the cafeteria, etc.).
   f. Spend a day with someone who is concerned with young people in a nonschool situation, such as a truant officer, social worker, juvenile court judge, police officer, camp counselor, etc. How do students react to these authority figures? Why? Are there some who have good rapport with students? Why?

g. Tutor a student over a period of more than a month. Try to become the student's friend. Does the student like you? How can you tell? Are you being successful as a tutor? Why or why not?

h. Select a student who appears to have a low self-concept and talk to him or her about home life, social life, success in school or other areas, etc. How could you help this student develop more self-confidence?

4. Read the article or watch the film, "Cipher in the Snow" (available for purchase from BYU Media Marketing or for rental from BYU Audio Visual Services, Brigham Young University, Provo, Utah 84602.) How do we go about turning a boy or girl into a cipher? How can a teacher somewhere along the way stop the slow eroding of students as persons of worth?

5. How can you meet the needs of all of the students in your classes? Must all instruction be individualized? What common learning needs do all students have?

Suggested readings

Danziger, Paula. *The Cat Ate My Gymsuit.* New York: Delacorte Press, 1974.

Decker, Sunny. *An Empty Spoon.* New York: Harper & Row, 1969.

Fader, Daniel. *The Naked Children.* New York: The Macmillan Company, 1971.

Forgan, Harry W. "Teachers Don't Want to Be Labeled." *Phi Delta Kappan* LV (September 1973): back cover.

Hayden, Torey L. *Somebody Else's Kids.* New York: G. P. Putnam's Sons, 1981.

Hentoff, Nat. *Our Children Are Dying.* New York: Four Winds Press, 1966.

Herndon, James. *The Way it Spozed to Be.* New York: Simon and Schuster, 1968.

Kaufman, Bel. *Up the Down Staircase.* Englewood Cliffs, N.J.: Prentice-Hall, 1968.

Knutson, Marjorie C. "Sensitivity to Minority Groups." *Journal of Physical Education and Recreation* 48 (May 1977): 24–25.

Kohl, Herbert. *36 Children.* New York: New American Library, 1967.

Kozol, Jonathan. *Death at an Early Age: the Destruction of the Hearts and Minds of Negro Children in Boston Public Schools.* Boston: Houghton Mifflin, 1967.

Mizer, Jean. "Cipher in the Snow." *NEA Journal* (November 1964): 8–10.

Rood, Ronald N. "Teacher to the President," *PTA Magazine* (May 1963): 21.

Van Slooten. "Four Theories of Development and Their Implications for the Physical Education of Adolescents." *The Physical Educator* 31 (December 1974): 181–86.

Physical Education and the Law

Study stimulators

1. What is "tort liability"?
2. How can you defend yourself in a tort liability case?
3. How can you keep from getting sued in the first place?
4. What is P.L. 94–142? What is Section 504 of the Rehabilitation Act? How do they affect physical education programs?
5. What is an I.E.P.? How is one created?
6. Define "mainstreaming" and "least restrictive environment". How are they different?
7. How can classes be adapted to provide equal opportunities for the handicapped?
8. How can the implementation of Title IX improve physical education programs?

A number of developments have taken place in recent years that dynamically affect instructional programs in physical education. These are primarily the result of society's reliance on the courts to resolve controversies and the intrusion of the federal government into areas previously considered to be the province of local governments or boards of education.[1] These developments include (1) changes in the legal liability status of the schools; (2) P.L. 94–142, The Education of All Handicapped Children Act, and Section 504 of the Rehabilitation Act; (3) Title IX; and (4) legislation requiring teacher accountability. Each of these developments will be discussed in this chapter. The discussion will be limited to the effects of these developments on the instructional rather than the extracurricular program.

Legal liability in physical education

Liability refers to a legal responsibility that can be enforced by a court of law in a *civil* action, which is an action involving a relationship between citizens or between citizens and an institution such as a school or district. A basic understanding of the laws governing liability in physical education is essential to the preservation of physical education programs in the schools.

A malpractice craze has literally swept the United States. From 1961 to 1970, the number of law suits in physical education doubled from those of the previous ten years.[2] Again in the decade of the seventies, the number of reported cases more than doubled.[3] Settlements now reach millions of dollars and a single case can wipe out the entire year's budget of a school district.[4]

It is common knowledge that over half of the accidents occurring in the schools are in physical education or related activities. Accidents in physical education are usually less severe than those in intramural and athletic activities.[5] However, even one accident involving a loved one is one too many. Through a knowledge of the law, accompanied by intelligent action, many of these accidents and law suits could be prevented.

What happens in a legal liability case?

The parents of a senior high school student filed a $1 million suit against her physical education teacher and the board of education for injuries the young woman suffered in a physical education class-related accident on a trampoline. In the suit, they complained that she was required to take the class in order to graduate and that reasonable safety precautions were not taken to prevent injury.

In the above incident, the injured girl and her parents were the *plaintiffs*—the person or group initiating the action against another party. The teacher and school board were the *defendants,* the person or group against whom the action is brought. The complaint summarized the reasons why the plaintiff felt she was entitled to compensation for her injury. As the legal process continued, the defendant filed an answer stating why she felt she was not at fault. After a period of time, the case came before the court.

The entire lawsuit is based on the assumption that a *tort* has been committed. A *tort* is a civil or legal wrong, an action that results in injury to another person or to that person's reputation or property. A tort can be caused by intentional interference, such as assault and battery, defamation, or negligent action.

An *assault* is a threat to inflict harm on someone. *Battery* is the unlawful use of physical force against another person. *Defamation* involves a malicious intent to injure a person's reputation through the spoken word—*slander*—or the written word—*libel.*

Most liability cases involving the schools are based on negligence. *Negligence* is the failure to act as a reasonably prudent person would act under the same circumstances. Negligence may be caused by nonfeasance, misfeasance, or malfeasance. *Nonfeasance* involves failure to do what is required, such as failure to instruct the students properly in the use of the trampoline or failure to administer first aid to an injured student. *Misfeasance* involves doing something incorrectly, such as moving an injured student when it is improper to do so, thereby injuring the young person further. *Malfeasance* involves doing something illegal, such as using corporal punishment in a state where it is against the law.

Negligence involves a comparison of the situation with an acceptable or established standard of conduct for persons in similar situations. In order to determine negligence, the courts generally ask four questions.[6] The questions are:

1. Did one person owe a duty to another?

2. Did that person fail to exercise that duty?

3. Was a person actually injured?

4. Was the failure to exercise due care the direct or proximate cause of the injury?

A *duty* is a legal responsibility to act in a certain way toward others to protect them from physical or mental harm. It includes the expectation that a teacher will provide appropriate instruction, supervision, and a safe environment in which students can learn. *Foreseeability* is involved when a teacher could have anticipated or foreseen a potential danger and fails to eliminate the danger. If a person is injured as a result, the teacher is liable. In the case cited above, the teacher could have seen that leaving a trampoline available for student use would result in students jumping on it even when advised not to do so.

In order to establish negligence, it must be demonstrated that the teacher's actions were the direct or *proximate* cause of the injury. In the case just cited, the fact that the trampoline was left out by the teacher could be considered to be the proximate cause of students jumping on it and, therefore, of the accident.

Defenses against negligence usually include (1) governmental immunity, (2) contributory negligence, (3) comparative negligence, (4) assumption of risk, or (5) an act of God.

Governmental immunity is based on the English common law premise that "the King can do no wrong" and is therefore immune from suit. In a few states, the government still enjoys this privilege. Therefore, even though the school district was negligent, no *damages* or money could be awarded. However, beginning in 1959, when an Illinois state court abolished governmental immunity in a school transportation case,[7] approximately 80 percent of the states have lost their immunity through legislative or court action.[8] Although boards of education were not previously liable for tort, individual administrators, teachers, or other employees of the district have never been immune from tort liability.

Contributory negligence occurs when the injured person directly contributes to the injury. In the case discussed earlier, the student contributed directly to her injury by jumping on the trampoline despite the fact that she knew she was violating the safety rules that were established by the teacher and repeatedly reemphasized. Participants must act for their own protection as a reasonably prudent person of that age level would act.

Comparative negligence happens when both the injured person and the defendant are jointly responsible for the accident. The court generally determines the percentage of responsibility held by each person and distributes the money accordingly. For example, in the case involving the trampoline, the student, the teacher, and a medical doctor could be held responsible for 50 percent, 25 percent, and 25 percent of the injuries, respectively. Although comparative legislation is fairly new, approximately one-half of the states have enacted legislation providing for it.

Assumption of risk occurs when a person understands and accepts the fact that participation in an activity involves a certain amount of risk of injury that a teacher or supervisor can not prevent. In spite of the risk, the person voluntarily agrees to participate. This applies particularly to activities that are potentially dangerous such as football, rappelling, and rock climbing. However, a person never assumes the risk of negligent behavior of another person in any activity.

An act of God (vis Major) is an unforeseeable or unavoidable accident due to the forces of nature. If a student were suddenly struck by lightning while playing softball, the accident would be considered an act of God. However, a teacher allowing students to remain in an outdoor swimming pool during an electrical storm is, undoubtedly, negligent.

Legal precedents are court decisions made previously in similar cases. They are used by both the plaintiff and the defendant to defend their particular points of view. Cases that follow often depend on these previous legal decisions for their solution.

Because of the large settlements occurring in court cases, more and more lawsuits involving physical education are being settled out of court. However, when they do come to court, the courts are showing less tolerance for mistakes by teachers and demanding greater responsibility than ever before.

Prevention

Negligence generally arises from one of five sources. They are: (1) the failure to supervise students properly, (2) the failure to instruct students properly, (3) unsafe facilities or equipment, (4) the failure to take proper first aid measures in an emergency, and (5) failure involving transportation. By increasing their awareness of these five areas, teachers can considerably decrease the chances of becoming a defendant in a lawsuit and the damages awarded if such a case does occur.

Supervision

More than 50 percent of all lawsuits involving physical education and sports are a result of improper supervision.[9] The quantity and quality of supervision needed is dependent upon the circumstances and should consider (1) the age and maturity of the students, (2) the amount of risk inherent in the activity, (3) the skill level of the students, and (4) the previous preparation of the students.

Age and maturity. Younger, less mature students need more supervision; older, more mature students generally need less. However, teachers should consider the tendency of older students to engage in horseplay.[10]

Amount of risk in the activity. Activities that involve greater risk—such as gymnastics, wrestling, swimming, and archery—need closer supervision and fewer students per teacher than activities with less risk.

Skill level. Students who are just beginning to learn a new skill need more direct supervision than advanced students.

Preparation of students. Students should be gradually prepared by the teacher to assume responsibility for their own behavior. Students should earn the opportunity to participate in the more student-directed styles of learning.

Administrators have the responsibility (1) to assign qualified teachers for each activity taught in the curriculum, (2) to communicate to teachers what is expected of them, and (3) to supervise the teachers to determine whether or not the expectations have been met. They also have the responsibility to regulate class size to meet the needs of the students.

Coeducational programs help students develop
social skills.

Teachers have a responsibility to remain with their classes at all times. When an emergency occurs, a student should be sent to the physical education office for help. The teacher should not leave the room to assist an injured student unless a second, qualified teacher is in the room. Classes should never be dismissed early or late. Teachers are liable for unsupervised students in the halls or on the school grounds.

Berryhill lists two basic questions frequently asked by the attorney for the plaintiff in a suit involving supervision:

1. If the supervisor had been present would the accident have occurred?

2. Did the supervisor perform his assigned duties or abide by the rules and regulations?[11]

If the above principles have been put into practice, there should be no major reason for concern. Appenzeller summarizes the area of supervision as follows:

Enough cases have been decided that help give a clear pattern for teachers to follow. Most courts do not expect superhuman effort by teachers in this area. No one can reasonably expect teachers to be everywhere at the same time. The court does expect teachers to remain in the general area of play, however, and will not tolerate teachers who leave the vicinity to gossip with fellow teachers. The teacher should also use common sense and stay in the locality in which the greatest risks are present.[12]

Instruction

Several principles apply when designing the instructional situation. They relate to (1) the selection of the activity, (2) safety precautions, (3) planning, (4) direct instruction, and (5) grouping.

Selection of the activity. Potential activities must be evaluated in terms of their educational value and their appropriateness for students. Educational value is determined by the ability of the activity to help students meet the objectives of physical education. Appropriateness for students is determined by the age, maturity, skills, and fitness levels of students. Students should be carefully screened for such high-risk activities as combatives and gymnastics and in fitness activities in which students might be compelled to push themselves beyond their normal limits.[13]

Health problems should be evaluated to prevent students from participating in activities that are beyond their abilities. Students should not be allowed to participate in activity following a serious illness or injury without medical approval. Particular care must be taken in the evaluation of activities when handicapped students are mainstreamed with regular students.

Safety precautions. Students should be warned of the possible dangers inherent in the activities in which they participate and be cautioned not to try things that they have not yet been taught. This is especially true in the area of gymnastics where the plaintiff has usually been favored in court cases.[14]

Safety rules and regulations should be carefully formulated and taught to students. They should be few in number and well-enforced. In order to ensure that students have learned the safety rules, they should be distributed to students, reviewed with students, and posted as reminders. Then, students should be tested to determine their knowledge of the rules before being allowed to participate in the activity. Failure to follow the rules should result in exclusion from that activity.

Safety equipment—such as eyeglass protectors, fencing masks and body protectors, catcher's masks and chest protectors, helmets, and other game-related safety equipment—should be required of *all* participants. Teachers should also check to make sure that *all* equipment is used properly and safely. Ground rules can be used to help students learn safety rules, such as requiring softball players to lay the bat in a marked area on the way to first base or be called out.

Students should be taught that they have a responsibility to be careful, to respect possible dangers, and to prevent them from occurring by using appropriate means of prevention. Instructors should provide a handout explaining the responsibility of participants to report bad equipment, to rest when fatigued, and to ask for help when experiencing difficulty in performing a new skill. Students should be reminded that the instructor can not be present at all times to help each individual and, therefore, they must accept some responsibility for their own safety.

Planning. Teachers should follow accepted procedures for instruction contained in a state, district, or school course of study or in a recognized text. Deviations from such procedures should be based on sound reasons. Unit and lesson plans can be extremely valuable in providing evidence that sound planning for teaching has occurred.

Direct instruction. Instruction in proper techniques and progressions should precede participation in any activity. Students should progress gradually from less-strenuous and simple tasks to more demanding, complex, and higher-risk activities. Instruction should include proper techniques for the performance of the activity, the proper use of equipment, the inherent dangers in the activity or the equipment, and information on how to avoid those dangers.[15]

Drowatzky provides several guidelines regarding instruction. His guidelines are:

1. The care exercised by the teacher must increase as the risks involved in the activity increase. . . . If the activity is compulsory because of a curricular requirement, the need to complete it for a grade, or the teacher insists that the student perform it, the amount of care required on the part of the instructor increases dramatically. When the dangerous and compulsory features are both present in a given situation, the instructor must be most diligent and careful.

2. Skill level of the students is an important consideration; beginners should have closer supervision and be placed in situations that can be controlled to prevent any injuries that may be caused by their inexperience.

3. Instruction must include proper techniques of performance, safety precautions, and pertinent characteristics of the equipment. The instructor must follow progressive, professional procedures and instruction should not be delegated to advanced students. . . . If students are used as spotters, they must be taught how to spot before they are given any responsibility.[16]

Grouping. To prevent unnecessary injuries in contact sports or combative activities students should be grouped for competition by similar characteristics such as skill, age-height-weight exponents, or sex.

Unsafe facilities, grounds, and equipment

Essential components of accident prevention are safe facilities, grounds, and equipment. Administrators should set policies and make plans for periodic inspection of facilities, grounds, and equipment to determine possible hazards and defects. The line of responsibility should be clearly delegated to a specific person.[17] Records listing the inspector, date, condition of the equipment, and recommendations for repair should be maintained.

Physical educators should inspect facilities, grounds, and equipment frequently and take note of any potential hazards. These should be reported promptly to the principal and followed by a written letter to the principal (and superintendent, if necessary), stating the date and the nature of the problem. A copy should be retained by the teacher. Administrators are responsible to see that the facilities and grounds are maintained and that defects are corrected.

While waiting for the defect to be corrected, the teacher should use temporary measures to protect students from injury. This can be accomplished by posting signs warning of the danger, warning students to stay away from the area, closing off or locking the area, or stationing a supervisor nearby to keep students away. No facility should be used while unsafe conditions exist. Appenzeller sums up one of the major problems with equipment as follows: "Too often teachers try to get by just one more day with obsolete and outdated equipment that should have been discarded years ago. These teachers are either indifferent to the needs of their pupils or are totally unaware of the serious consequences that may lay ahead."[18]

An *attractive nuisance* is a dangerous situation that attracts the attention of children or youth. Swimming pools, gymnastics apparatus, jumping pits, and excavation areas are all attractive nuisances. To prevent injuries, teachers and administrators have a responsibility to keep such areas and equipment locked up when not in use.

First aid vs. medical treatment

The law both requires and limits the medical treatment of students to first aid—the immediate and temporary care needed to preserve the student's life or prevent further injury until medical care is available. This legal duty is imposed because the teacher stands *in loco parentis,* or "in the place of the parent," and also because physical education teachers are expected to be qualified to administer this aid.

Two common errors occur in giving first aid—doing too much or doing too little. An example of doing too much is moving an injured student before medical help has arrived. Many cases of spinal injury and paralysis have resulted from this particular error. On the other hand, failure to obtain medical help for students suffering from heat exhaustion, a broken bone, or other injury can also be fatal. Students who have been seriously ill or injured should be required to obtain a doctor's release before resuming normal physical activity.

To help prevent accidents, proper medical examinations are often required of students at various school levels. Physical educators should take note of students who have medical problems or handicaps and may need close supervision or adapted instruction in order to meet their needs.

If an accident does occur, administer first aid while sending a student to summon medical help and inform the principal. An emergency plan should be formulated and reviewed frequently so that it can be followed quickly without further mishap. An accurate report of each accident should be kept, including a detailed report of the activity and the circumstances of the accident, the nature of the injury, the first aid treatment given, medical attention obtained, the names of persons rendering service, and the names of witnesses. A sample accident report form is shown in figure 17.10.

Appenzeller summarizes the expectations of the court regarding first aid as follows:

> As a coach, the court expects you to handle emergencies when they arise. The court will set a much higher standard of first aid for the coach than the average classroom teacher. The court will demand emergency treatment but nothing more. Do not go beyond the emergency stage; avoid attempting to treat your players; *let the professional do this!*[19]

Transportation and field trips

When transportation is necessary to and from off-campus facilities or during a field trip, school officials should approve all travel arrangements. The preferred arrangement is to use school buses or commercial vehicles. However, when these are unavailable, several precautions should be taken.

When teachers or adults drive their own cars, administrators should ensure that they have adequate liability insurance in case of student injury. They should also be aware that many automobile insurance policies do not protect the car owner who is paid for transporting passengers, even if the pay is only reimbursement for gas and oil. An insurance rider on the policy must be purchased to provide this protection.[20]

When students are used as drivers, administrators should examine the student drivers' reputations and records for safe and careful driving and the cars for freedom from defects that might make them unsafe. The drivers should also be cautioned to obey all traffic laws and not to overload their cars or to let students drive who have not been approved by the administration. The students' insurance policies should be checked for adequate coverage.[21]

School boards would be wise to protect their students by establishing rules and regulations for student transportation and by securing liability insurance for their employees who transport students. It is also good public relations to let parents know exactly what is and is not covered. Liability waivers or release forms are often sent home to parents before students are allowed to go on field trips. Although these waivers do not stand up in court, they serve a valuable purpose by informing parents and receiving their permission for the trip. They may also reduce the possibility of a lawsuit.

Protection

In addition to following the guidelines presented in this chapter, the wise physical education teacher will also obtain liability insurance to protect against catastrophic personal loss. Personal liability insurance is available from the American Alliance for Health, Physical Education, Recreation and Dance or the National Education Association. In some states, *save-harmless* legislation permits or requires districts to provide teachers with protection against the financial losses resulting from a job-related liability suit.

Implications of the changes in legal liability status

Because of the abrogation of governmental immunity, more students are now able to recover damages for injuries caused by the negligence of school employees. Although this is a positive outcome, it also means that teachers may be involved in more nuisance suits with resulting stress, professional embarrassment, and financial loss. School districts will also be involved in paying higher rates for insurance and sports equipment.[22] The result is a higher cost to the taxpayers for the support of their schools.

The fact that physical education teachers are held legally responsible for their actions should not cause prospective or practicing educators to "throw in the towel." Rather, it should make them take their responsibilities as educators seriously and use common sense in their interactions with others. Wise teachers will make a point of becoming acquainted with the tort liability laws as they apply in their particular states.

The Education for All Handicapped Children Act and Section 504 of the Rehabilitation Act

The Education for All Handicapped Children Act of 1975 (Public Law 94–142) came about through parental lobbying and court action, which pressured Congress into action. Two landmark court decisions (Pennsylvania Association of Retarded Citizens and Mills v. Board of Education of District of Columbia) resulted in a decree that all children of school age have a right to a free quality education, regardless of their handicap.

In November 1975, the act came into being and the final implementing regulations were approved 23 August, 1977. The basic purpose of the law is to:

> assure that all handicapped children have available to them . . . a free
> appropriate public education which emphasizes special education and related
> services designed to meet their unique needs, to assure that the rights of
> handicapped children and their parents or guardians are protected, to assist
> States and localities to provide for the education of all handicapped children,
> and to assess and assure the effectiveness of efforts to educate handicapped
> children.[23]

Physical education is the only subject area specifically referred to in the law. Every handicapped student must have access to a physical education program either within the regular program or in an adapted program as defined by the student's individualized education program (I.E.P.)

According to the law, physical education includes the development of (1) physical and motor fitness; (2) fundamental motor skills and patterns; and (3) skills in aquatics, dance, individual and group games, and sports (including intramural and lifetime sports). In addition, P.L. 94–142 specifies that students receiving special education and related services must have access to extracurricular activities, including athletics, that are comparable to those received by their nonhandicapped classmates.

Special care must be taken to meet the needs
of *all* students.

Related services—such as recreation and school health services—or supportive services—such as athletics, physical therapy, or dance therapy—*must* be provided if such services are required to assist a handicapped student to benefit from special education. The service can be provided directly by the district or school or contracted from some other agency.

The Individualized Education Program

Every student receiving special education and related services as part of the free, appropriate education guaranteed under the law must have an individualized education program (I.E.P.). This is a written statement that is developed and implemented in accordance with the regulations and includes the following:

1. A statement of the student's present levels of educational performance in such areas as academic, social, psychomotor, vocational, self-help, and adaptive behavior.

2. A statement of annual goals, including short-term instructional objectives.

3. A statement of specific special education and related services to be provided to the student and the extent to which the student will be able to participate in regular educational programs.

4. Projected dates for initiation of services and the anticipated duration of the services.

5. Appropriate objective criteria and evaluation procedures and schedules for determining on at least an annual basis whether short-term instructional objectives are being achieved.

Other appropriate inclusions are the activities to be learned, including sequences and progressions; appropriate class placement; methods and teaching strategies, including adaptations of equipment, methods, and activities; motivational techniques; assessment strategies and techniques, and opportunities for follow-up and use of activities.

The first step in the process of designing an I.E.P. is to identify those students who are handicapped and who also have special educational needs. This step can be accomplished through evaluation to determine current levels of functioning in educational, medical, psychological, sociological, or behavior areas. An eligibility committee can then determine the student's eligibility for the program.

Once the student has been accepted, a planning conference should be convened, consisting of the student's teacher, a second school representative such as the principal, one or both parents, and the student (if appropriate). Other individuals may be invited by the parents or the school. Since physical education is required by law, the physical educator should sit in on this meeting. When a handicapped student is evaluated for the first time, someone who is knowledgeable about the evaluation procedures used with the student must be present at the meeting.

This group develops the I.E.P. for that particular student. Because each student's needs are different from those of other students (even with the same handicap), each I.E.P. will be different from all other I.E.Ps. The student's interests should be considered along with such problems as "physical disability, transportation, facilities, class sizes, capabilities of teacher, and related services like physical therapist, occupational therapist, adapted equipment, etc."[24]

Review of each student's individualized education program must be done at least annually. Complete reevaluation must be carried out at least every three years. It should be noted that any agency, teacher, or other person *cannot* be held accountable if a student does not achieve growth projected in the annual goals and objectives of an individualized education program.

Mainstreaming vs. the least restrictive environment

Mainstreaming is the procedure whereby handicapped students are educated in the regular classroom along with their nonhandicapped peers, rather than in special education classes.

The *least restrictive environment* refers to the education of handicapped students with their nonhandicapped peers when that environment is conducive to helping students reach their full potentials. If a student cannot participate successfully in a regular class program, then that student should be placed in a special class or school. The law specifically states that all handicapped students must be "afforded the opportunity to participate in the regular physical education program available to nonhandicapped children *unless . . . the child needs specially designed physical education,* as prescribed in the child's individualized education program." [emphasis added]

The majority of handicapped students can be successfully integrated into the regular physical education program if the instructor considers their individual needs. Handicapped students who participate in the regular program generally have a more favorable attitude toward physical education, adjust more adequately to the real world, and do better both academically and socially.[25] Their nonhandicapped peers also learn to understand and appreciate them in spite of their handicaps.

The inappropriate placement of severely handicapped students into a regular physical education class, however, often results in a *more* restrictive environment because of the discrepancy between the teacher's expectations and the student's inability to perform as expected.[26] It was for this reason that adapted physical education classes were created in the first place—to provide for needs that were not being met in the regular program.

To integrate all handicapped students into regular classes or to segregate all students into adapted physical education classes is to violate the principles upon which the law was based. Placement in a least restrictive environment must be made on an individual basis. Failure to do so could result in a malpractice suit.[27] Physical educators must take the initiative to see that placement flexibility is maintained in individualized education programs so that each student participates in regular physical education activities where possible and in specially designed programs as necessary.

Alternative placement possibilities

Since schools are now required to enroll students who possess a wide range of individual abilities, a continuum of physical education services must be provided. This continuum ranges from the most restrictive environment to the regular physical education class as shown in figure 4.1.

Regular physical education

Students who can safely and successfully participate in the regular physical education program should be encouraged to do so.

Regular physical education with modification

Some handicapped students can participate with their nonhandicapped peers if appropriate modifications are made such as (1) a buddy system, which pairs a handicapped student with an able-bodied partner for specific activities; (2) peer tutoring; (3) circuit or station organizational patterns; (4) contract-learning techniques; (5) team-teaching, involving regular and adapted physical education teachers, resource teachers, or paraprofessional aides; or (6) preteaching certain activities to students with special needs.

Students with special needs might work on such needs a specified amount of time each period, with the remaining time being devoted to regular activities with other members of the class. Some activities are more readily adapted for the handicapped than other activities.

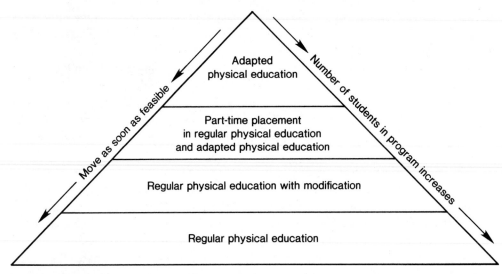

Figure 4.1 A continuum of physical education placement possibilities.

The best activities are those in which success or failure is not dependent upon the ability or performance of another person.[28] Since many secondary schools now offer selective or elective programs, all students have the opportunity to select the activities that best meet their needs.

Part-time placement

Part-time placement is an arrrangement whereby students spend specified days each week in an adapted physical education class where they concentrate on special needs as delineated in the I.E.P. and other days in regular classes. This type of placement may be especially useful in helping students gain the skills and confidence necessary to make the transition to a regular physical education program.

Adapted physical education

Students with severe or multiple handicaps may need to be placed in an adapted physical education class where they can receive corrective therapy or remedial help. Only in this setting can activities be adapted enough for students with severe handicaps to participate freely and successfully. Adapted physical education can occur as a separate class within the school, in a special school, in a home, or in a hospital.

Suggestions for teaching

Regardless of the placement chosen for each handicapped student, there are a number of suggestions that might be considered in teaching these students. First, teachers should get to know each student as a person of worth and dignity rather than as a handicap. Medical and educational needs—such as the need for rest periods, special motivational techniques, modified equipment, and resource persons—should also be considered. Second, the traditional demonstration/practice teaching strategy may not be appropriate for handicapped students. Teachers must learn to use a variety of teaching styles to meet the needs of all students. A style that is particularly appropriate for handicapped students is the inclusion style discussed in chapter 14.

Winnick suggested eight ways in which activities can be adapted so that handicapped students can participate effectively with their peers.[29] They are:

1. Modify activities to equalize competition by (1) creating "handicaps" for students, as in golf and bowling; (2) changing distance, height of basket, etc. [See the inclusion style in chapter 14.]; or (3) reducing skill complexity (i.e., kicking a stationary rather than a moving ball).

2. Permit "courtesy" runners (or partner runners for the blind) for students who need them.

3. Include activities in which contact is maintained with a partner, small group, or object (such as square dancing, wrestling, tug-of-war, a rail for bowling). Contact helps the blind, deaf, or retarded student know what is expected.

4. Modify the activity to require regular students to assume the impairment of the handicapped, such as in relays when all students have only one leg or in a game in which all players are blindfolded.

5. Assign positions according to the abilities of the handicapped persons. (Field hockey goalies and softball pitchers don't have to move as quickly and are good choices for individuals with one leg. Catcher can be a good position for persons with one arm because they don't have to throw as quickly.)

6. Change elimination-type activities, such as dodge ball, to permit students to exchange positions with the thrower or count the number of times hit rather than be eliminated.

7. Limit the size of the playing area by reducing the court size or increasing the number of players on a team.

8. Use audible goals, such as a horn or drum to allow blind students to compete in relays, basketball, archery, shuffleboard, or softball.

Section 504 of the Rehabilitation Act

A second federal law that affects physical education programs and facilities is Section 504 of the Rehabilitation Act of 1973 (P.L. 93–112). This law provides that "no otherwise qualified handicapped individual . . . shall, solely by reason of his handicap, be excluded from participation in, be denied the benefits of, or be subjected to discrimination under any program or activity receiving federal financial assistance."[30]

This law requires schools to provide equal opportunities for the handicapped to participate in *all* programs offered by the school, including physical education, intramurals, clubs, and interscholastic athletics. Accommodations, adaptations, and adjustments expected so that individuals with handicapping conditions can participate in regular physical education programs and activities include:

1. Accessible buildings and other facilities.

2. Appropriate transportation.

3. Appropriate curricular adjustments, such as changing competency requirements, eligibility requirements, and rules that discriminate.

4. Appropriate adaptations in activities, such as a bowling ramp, beeper balls, etc.

Implications for the schools

The major impact upon the schools as a result of the two laws dealing with the handicapped is to modify existing curricula to include a wide spectrum of activities for the handicapped. In addition, architectural, administrative, and instructional barriers must be removed to allow handicapped students access to all programs offered by the schools.

Title IX

Title IX of the Education Amendments Act of 1972 provides that "no person in the United States shall on the basis of sex, be excluded from participation in, be denied the benefits of, or be subjected to discrimination under any education program or activity receiving Federal financial assistance."[31]

Because coverage includes every program operated by a recipient of federal funds, enforcement can be effected by a withdrawal of federal funding to a school that does not comply with the law.

The law requires that all schools avoid discrimination on the basis of sex in such areas as course offerings, extracurricular activities, behavior, appearance, and student services. It also requires equal employment opportunities and compensation of faculty. Therefore, physical education departments, budgets, class schedules, activity areas, and requirements should not be designated by sex. Facilities such as toilet, locker rooms, and showers may be provided separately for each sex, but the accommodations must be comparable to those provided for the other sex.

With regards to physical education classes, the law provides that

1. Students may be grouped by ability using objective standards of individual performance developed and applied without regard to sex.

2. Students may be separated by sex *within* physical education classes during participation in contact sports—wrestling, boxing, rugby, ice hockey, football, or basketball.

3. Portions of classes dealing exclusively with human sexuality may be conducted separately for males and females.

4. When use of a single standard of measurement has an adverse effect on members of one sex, then appropriate standards may be used, such as in skill and fitness test norms.

Implications of Title IX

As a result of the implementation of Title IX in physical education classes, there have been both positive and negative results. The most frequently cited advantage to coed classes is the opportunity for social interaction among boys and girls. A second advantage is that it places sport participation into a more natural lifetime environment.[32]

Coed classes provide highly skilled girls with an opportunity to compete with others on a more competitive basis. They provide boys with an opportunity for instruction in a wider variety of activities than those formerly included in many of their programs.

Combining boys and girls departments into one can create greater communication between men and women teachers. This permits the use of facilities and equipment to the advantage of all students. Instead of purchasing duplicate sets of equipment, all students can use one set, thus providing money for the purchase of additional types of equipment.[33]

Two major problems have arisen with regard to Title IX. One is that many excellent physical education programs have gone downhill as women coaches devote more time and energy to their new assignments in coaching and less time to preparing for class instruction. Although athletic programs for girls are flourishing, students at the lower ability levels are being eliminated in the thrust for better athletic programs for girls and women. The second problem is that many programs have reverted to recreational programs in a variety of selected activities. Forced by law to integrate boys and girls and frustrated by how to teach in coed classes, many teachers have "given up" and assumed the role of supervisor of activity rather than instructor. When this occurs, physical education loses its educational purpose and becomes merely a recreation program in which physical education teachers could be replaced by lower-paid recreation leaders.

Selby cited three reasons for teacher frustration and insecurity with regard to coed classes. These included problems with (1) the physical contact and sexuality, (2) the differences in motor skill, and (3) the teacher's lack of knowledge or skills.[34]

Several respondents to Selby's questionnaire indicated a concern over touching students in demonstrations, while spotting gymnastics events, or when providing first aid for injuries. Locker room and shower supervision were also listed. A third area was concern about teacher-student communication regarding girls' menstrual cycles and activity.

With regard to motor skills, teachers were concerned that girls would be inhibited from participation when boys were present or that boys would play more aggressively, thus creating an unsafe environment for girls or denying them meaningful involvement. They also expressed concern that boys are not interested in instruction, learn faster, and need less practice, and would be held back by the lower skill level of the girls.[35] Teachers also worried about how to adapt boys and girls rules into rules that would be fair to both sexes.

One of the biggest reasons why men and women teachers have fought coed classes is that they have felt unprepared to deal with students of the opposite sex. Women are afraid they won't be able to maintain discipline with boys. Men are afraid they won't be able to handle the girls' emotional problems. Men and women both express a concern over teaching activities unfamiliar to them.

Many of these problems have been resolved quite easily once classes have been combined. If just one boys' class and one girls' class are scheduled each hour, there is always a teacher to supervise each locker room. Men have discovered that most girls can participate while menstruating with no effect on their performance. Appropriate contact between the sexes for instructional purposes has not been found to be a problem among those teaching coed classes.

Teachers have learned that there is a wider range of motor abilities within each sex than between sexes. Grouping students by ability can resolve the problems of students being intimidated or held back. Experimentation with rules can be done to find the best ones for both sexes. In fact, students can be challenged to experiment to find the best solution to the problem of appropriate rules. Instructors have learned to reach a happy medium with regard to too much or too little instruction and drill.

Discipline and emotional problems often resolve themselves when boys and girls are placed together. Boys tend to behave better in front of the girls and girls are challenged by the need to play harder.

For the most part, both teachers and students who have tried coed classes are overwhelmingly in favor of continuing them. In the study by Selby, 50 percent of the men and 86 percent of the women favored coed classes in secondary schools. All of the university faculty favored coed physical education, perhaps because of their successful experiences with coed classes for many years.[36]

In a survey of students in coed classes, 76.6 percent of the girls and 51.7 percent of the boys voted in favor of mixed classes. The most important factor in liking coed classes had to do with self-image. Girls who were good at sports and felt comfortable around boys enjoyed coed physical education. However, boys who felt they were highly skilled tended to vote "no" to coed activities. Students commented that they liked ability groupings and preferred both boys and girls to play by the same rules. They also expressed a need for more variety and more instruction in physical education classes.[37]

Recommendations for implementing coed programs

Kneer has expressed three ways in which the curriculum can be adapted to effectively implement coed activities.[38] The three are:

1. The *traditional class pattern* in which two coed classes are taught the same activity at the same time by their own teachers. Students can then be regrouped by sex rather than class for play involving contact sports. This arrangement also facilitates ability grouping and team teaching.

2. The *integrated pattern* consists of classes in which all students are integrated. When contact sports are played, students can be separated by sex *within* the class.

3. The *selective pattern* consists of placing all students into activities according to the interests of the students. Every few weeks, a new group of activities are offered for student selection. Activities can also be offered at beginning, intermediate, and advanced levels. Chapter 23 provides a more complete description of this scheduling pattern.

Kneer also suggested two methods for adjusting instruction for coed classes.[39] In *differentiated instruction,* students are introduced to new skills as a group but then provided different practice tasks and achievement levels. For example, some students might be working on right-handed lay-ups, others reverse lay-ups, and still others practicing lay-ups in a game situation. Students are grouped for play according to ability. In *individualized instruction,* students select different instructional programs to meet their various needs. Chapter 14 describes several strategies for individualizing instruction, as well as procedures for defining the tasks for differentiated instruction.

Game rules can be adapted to provide for students of both sexes. Some possibilities are as follows:

1. Players may only guard or block players of the same sex.

2. Players must pass the ball to a player of the opposite sex, or every player on the team must touch the ball before a goal is scored.

3. Females earn more points for a goal than males.

4. Players may choose the implement with which to hit and the object to be hit (softball type games).

5. The pitcher (in softball) must be a member of the team at bat.

Legislation requiring teacher accountability

Several lawsuits claiming inadequate education have forced state legislatures to pass laws requiring schools to be accountable for educating students. By 1980, thirty-eight states required students to pass minimum competency tests in order to graduate from high school.[40]

Accountability, according to the law, tends to be limited to accountability of teachers and administrators for learning by students. However, accountability is more than that. Schools have a responsibility to educate students. Parents and taxpayers have a responsibility for providing the resources necessary for adequate learning experiences. Students must be accountable for their own behavior.

Enochs set forth several principles for education in his Modesto, California, district. The principles included:

> The development of responsible adults is a task requiring community involvement. It cannot be left solely to the public schools. . . . Parents must consistently support the proposition that students have responsibilities as well as rights, and the schools have an obligation to insist upon both. . . . The full responsibility for learning cannot be transferred from the student to the teacher.[41]

Implications for physical education

Physical education programs are costly. Physical educators must face the possibility of their programs being eliminated if outcomes cannot be demonstrated. Therefore, administrators must be able to evaluate teachers' performance and to help teachers improve their effectiveness. Teachers must be able to state performance objectives, assess student achievement of objectives, and utilize strategies that help students achieve objectives. They must also learn to evaluate and remediate weaknesses in their own teaching and in their programs.

Questions and suggested activities

1. Define the following terms: legal liability, tort, plaintiff, defendant, attractive nuisance, *in loco parentis,* assumption of risk, negligence, contributory negligence, comparative negligence.

2. What percentage of suits are in physical education-related accidents?

3. Are suits increasing or decreasing in number? Why?

4. What is governmental immunity? What happens if a state does not have governmental immunity?

5. What can school districts do to protect themselves during a suit?

6. What can individuals do to protect themselves during a suit?

7. Explain negligence by omission, by commission.

8. Negligence generally arises from what five sources?

9. In what ways does negligence generally occur when giving first aid?

10. Legal defense of negligence is based on what three premises?

11. List some precautions that physical educators should take to prevent tort liability.

12. Talk to someone who has been through a tort liability suit to determine what defense was used and suggestions for preventing further suits.

13. Visit a school that has successfully integrated handicapped students into the physical education program. Study several individual education programs. How is the decision made for placement of students into the various physical education classes?

14. Put your dominant arm in a sling and use your other hand all day *or* borrow a wheelchair and get around as best you can for an entire day *or* blindfold yourself and let someone lead you around for an hour. How did the experience affect your self-concept? Did it change your feelings about handicapped persons?

15. Participation in a weight-training class in a senior high school was denied a male paraplegic even though he qualified for the activity. Can this be done?

16. You are teaching track and field and you have a girl who is asthmatic in your class. What will you do?

17. You are teaching volleyball and you have a boy with one arm paralyzed in your class. What will you do?

18. Visit a school that has a successful coeducational physical education program. What obstacles did they have to overcome to achieve success?

19. What other suggestions do you have for adapting games for use in coed classes? You may want to read Morris, G. S. Don. *How to Change the Games Children Play,* 2d ed., Minneapolis: Burgess Publishing Company, 1980.

20. You have just accepted a job in a physical education program that still has segregated classes for boys and girls. What might you do?

Suggested readings

American Alliance for Health, Physical Education, and Recreation. *Complying with Title IX of the Education Amendments of 1972 in Physical Education and High School Sports Programs.* Washington, D.C.: AAHPER, 1976.
———. *Practical Pointers: Individualized Education Programs.* Washington, D.C.: AAHPER, 1977, 1978.
American Alliance for Health, Physical Education, Recreation and Dance. Rules for Coeducational Activities and Sports. Reston, Va.: AAHPERD, 1980.
Appenzeller, Herb. *From the Gym to the Jury.* Charlottesville, Va.: The Michie Company, 1970.
Appenzeller, Herb. *Physical Education and the Law.* Charlottesville, Va.: The Michie Company, 1978.
——— and Appenzeller, Thomas. *Sports and the Courts.* Charlottesville, Va.: The Michie Company, 1980.
Arnold, Don E. "Legal Aspects of Off-Campus Physical Education Programs." *Journal of Physical Education and Recreation* 50 (April 1979): 21–23.

Auxter, David. "Equal Educational Opportunity for the Handicapped Through Physical Education." *The Physical Educator* 38 (March 1981): 8–14.

———. "Recreational Skills Through Individual Programs." *Journal of Physical Education, Recreation and Dance* 52 (June 1981): 32–33.

Carpenter, Linda Jean, and Acosta, R. Vivian. "Negligence: What Is It? How Can It Be Avoided?" *Journal of Physical Education, Recreation, and Dance* 53 (February 1982): 51–52, 89.

Dirocco, Patrick. "The Physical Educator and the Handicapped: Developmental Approach." *The Physical Educator* 36 (October 1979): 127–31.

French, Ron. "Direction or Misdirection in Physical Education for Mentally Retarded Students." *Journal of Physical Education and Recreation* 50 (September 1979): 22–23.

Klesius, Stephen E. "Measurement and Evaluation: The Neglected Element in Physical Education for the Handicapped." *The Physical Educator* 38 (March 1981): 15–19.

Long, Ed; Irmer, Larry; Burkett, Lee N.; Glasenapp, Gary; and Odenkirk, Benita. "PEOPEL." *Journal of Physical Education and Recreation* 51 (September 1980): 28–29.

Mallios, H. C. "Physical Educator and the Law." *The Physical Educator* 32 (May 1975): 61–63.

Margo, Ron, and Davis, Kenneth H. "Special Methods Aid Disabled Students." *Journal of Physical Education and Recreation* 52 (January 1981): 82–86.

Marsh, David B. "Competency Based Curriculum: An Answer for Accountability in Physical Education." *Journal of Physical Education and Recreation* 49 (November-December 1978): 45–48.

Megginson, Nancy L. "Regular vs. Specially Designed Programs: Use of Least Restrictive Environment in the Clarification of Physical Education Services to be Extended to Handicapped Children." *The Physical Educator* 37 (December 1980): 206–7.

Stewart, C. Craig. "Integrating the Physically Handicapped Child into the Physical Education Classroom." *Journal of Physical Education and Recreation* 51 (April 1980): 17.

Weber, Marie. "Title IX in Action." *Journal of Physical Education and Recreation* 51 (May 1980): 20–21.

Weiss, Raymond, and Karper, William B. "Teaching the Handicapped Child in the Regular Physical Education Class." *Journal of Physical Education and Recreation* 51 (February 1980): 32–35, 77.

Understanding the Role of the Teacher

Study stimulators

1. What teaching characteristics do effective teachers possess?
2. What responsibilities does a professional person have that a nonprofessional person does not?
3. What is a code of ethics? Of what value is it to a physical educator?
4. What is the purpose of a professional organization? What responsibilities does the teacher have to the organization?
5. How do you stack up as a potential teacher?

What is a teacher? In response to that question, a fourth-grade student replied, "A teacher is someone who knows that you can do what you never did before."[1] A good teacher not only has the vision to see what the student is capable of doing or becoming but also has the ability to help the student achieve that goal.

Although schools are full of those claiming to be teachers, many of them go through the motions of teaching without ever becoming involved with their students. They are subject-matter robots rather than teachers. Students take their classes without being able to recall having learned anything at all. Perhaps you will recall some of these teachers. On the other hand, you will undoubtedly recall one or two teachers who have influenced your life in some way. These are the great teachers. The sad truth is that some students never have the opportunity to sit at the feet of these great ones.

Characteristics of effective teachers

What makes some individuals effective teachers? Graham and Heimerer cite three groups of studies that have been done in an attempt to answer this question.[2] The first group attempted to discover common traits among successful teachers. The results failed to confirm any personal qualities possessed in common by effective teachers. These studies demonstrate the uniqueness of personal attributes among individual teachers. Therefore, we see effective teachers who are dictators and others who are like mothers and fathers to their students.

The second group of studies attempted to discover a common method of teaching among successful teachers. No such method was found. Since each situation may call for a different method, it is difficult to isolate any one method as being superior for all situations.

The third group of studies has focused on the process of teaching as it relates to student learning. An increasing number of systems for observing teacher-student interaction have emerged from these studies. These will be discussed in chapter 19.

From this research, investigators have concluded that most teacher behaviors are situation-specific; that is, they are directly related to the subject matter, environment, and characteristics of students. They have also pointed to a direct relationship between students' time spent working on specific tasks and teacher effectiveness. This concept has been further refined to include only on-task behavior in which students have a low rate of error (called academic learning time).

Further studies have attempted to determine what teachers do to create additional academic learning time. Since most studies of this type have focused on academic subjects and elementary school children, additional studies will need to be undertaken in secondary school physical education to validate the significance of these factors in the physical education field. At this point, however, the variables identified by Graham and Heimerer appear to be consistent with effective teaching in physical education and will be summarized here.[3]

Teacher warmth

One of the most important qualities of the great teacher is a genuine concern for the student. Postman emphasized this quality when he said:

> In spite of our attempts to make teaching into a science, in spite of our attempts to invent teacher-proof materials, and even in spite of our attempt to create "relevant new curricula" one simple fact makes all of this ambition quite unnecessary. It is as follows: *When a student perceives a teacher to be an authentic, warm and curious person,* the student learns. When the student does not perceive the teacher as such a person, the student does not learn. There is almost no way to get around this fact.[4]

This concern for the student is demonstrated through learning students' names, getting to know students as individuals, sharing experiences with students, and inviting students' responses. Students don't care how much you know until they know how much you care, or as Pullias said, "For teaching to be great, it has to be something like a love affair."[5]

It has been said that the mediocre teacher **tells,** the good teacher **explains,** the superior teacher **demonstrates,** and the great teacher **inspires.** Someone once said, "Your students deserve more than your knowledge. They deserve and hunger for your inspiration. They want the warm glow of personal relationship. This always has been the hallmark of a great teacher."

Communication of the subject also depends upon the teacher's ability to communicate interest or concern to each student. By creating a feeling of mutual respect and courtesy and avoiding criticism, ridicule, or embarrassment, teachers can encourage students to want to learn and achieve in school. Acceptance of individual differences in backgrounds, abilities, and personalities tells students you are interested in them as human beings and that they are essential to the success of the class. A willingness to listen to students and incorporate student ideas into the curriculum, when appropriate, are important factors in establishing student-teacher rapport.

Teacher expectancy

What teachers believe about students influences what teachers expect, and carries over into how the students perceive their own abilities. Calisch stated the following with regard to teacher expectancy:

> Most books I've read about teaching indicate that the prime requisite for a teacher is a "love of children." Hogwash! . . . What you must love is the vision of the well-informed, responsible adult you can help the child become.
>
> Your job as a teacher is to help the child realize who he is, what his potential is, what his strengths are. You can help him learn to love himself— or the man he soon will be. With that kind of understanding self-love, the student doesn't need any of your sentimentality. What he needs is your brains, and enabling him to profit from them calls for decisive firmness.[6]

Teachers who expect a lot from their students tend to spend more time working with students on on-task behavior and push students to work to their full capacity. These teachers can expect that their beliefs will be rewarded.

Task-oriented climate

Effective teachers establish a businesslike, but nonthreatening climate in which classes begin and end on time and are organized toward the achievement of specified performance objectives. Rules are generally firm but flexible. A balance between teacher-directed and student-directed activities allows students to develop intellectual and psychomotor skills as well as problem-solving behaviors. Management time in these classes is kept to a minimum so that academic learning time is maximized.

Effective instruction

The most effective teachers tend to use a more teacher-directed approach to instruction and to structure lessons so that students understand the objectives of instruction, the content to be learned, and the learning procedures to be used. These teachers also take time to outline lesson content, highlight important points, and summarize what has been learned.

Effective teachers provide immediate, task-related feedback to students with explanations of why a certain procedure is correct. Praise is given sparingly and is generally task-oriented rather than behavior-oriented. These teachers also evaluate students more frequently and ask students more questions to ascertain their understanding and to help them review what has been taught.

Lesson organization and methods of teaching should be varied for different purposes and different students. When teaching new information, effective teachers use large-group, teacher-directed instruction. When attitudes and appreciations are desired, student-directed, small-group instruction appears to be more effective. In either case, close adult supervision is utilized by the successful teachers. Graham and Heimerer conclude:

> No single teaching behavior by itself has been shown to consistently and highly correlate with student learning. More effective teachers employ a variety of appropriate behaviors, at appropriate times, and in appropriate situations.[7]

A professional code of ethics

A **code of ethics** is a statement of conduct that governs individuals within a profession. It refers to all of the relationships that occur among people and between people and institutions in the educational environment. The American Alliance for Health, Physical Education, Recreation and Dance endorses the code of ethics of the National Education Association. This code consists of the expected commitment of the teacher to the student, the public, the profession, and the employer.

Commitment to the student

The teacher must be committed to the optimum development of *every* student, regardless of skill level, sex, race, or handicap. Most physical education teachers are hired not only to teach physical education classes but also to coach at least one athletic team. These teachers need to remember that both areas are important to the welfare of the school and its students and that both demand time and effort. Neither area should be neglected. In order to accomplish these tasks, it is essential that men and women physical education teachers work cooperatively for the benefit of the entire program and help each other whenever difficulties arise.

A friendly but professional relationship should be established with students. When a student and teacher become too familiar, the teacher no longer has a student; he or she has a friend. This impairs the nature of the educational relationship. Information of a personal nature should be kept in strictest confidence and all students should be protected from unnecessary embarrassment.

Commitment to the public

All teachers must be committed to the principles of the American democratic heritage and the promotion of educational opportunities for all. Each teacher should participate in community affairs, promote good community-school relationships, and refrain from using school affiliation for personal gain.

Commitment to the profession

Teachers should make every effort to maintain relationships with other members of the profession based on mutual respect for one another.

A professional person is one who is dedicated to providing a service to other people. In the professions of medicine, law, and social work, the clients choose who to ask for service. An incompetent person in these areas is quickly weeded out. In education, more often than not, the students have no choice of which teacher to take. Moreover, many teachers have tenure and can be dismissed only for gross negligence, insubordination, or immoral conduct. Tenure laws, which originated to protect teachers, now protect incompetent teachers from being terminated.

Teachers have an obligation to be objective, honest, and fair; to respect and defend the rights of their associates; and to hold in confidence information shared by colleagues. However, professionals also have a responsibility to confront associates who are acting unethically or are incompetent. Moreover, they also have the responsibility to follow proper administrative channels and to be willing to listen to the other person's point of view.

Physical educators should never lose sight of the fact that they are **educators** and that the purposes of **all** programs in the school are to educate students. As such, physical education teachers and coaches should share the concerns of other teachers in the school and work together with them to promote total school unity. They can show their concern by attending general faculty meetings; serving on faculty committees; upholding school policies; and taking turns with hall, cafeteria, or bus duty. Cooperation with the school custodial staff is also essential because of the many and varied facilities necessary for physical education programs.

Professional organizations exist to help members of a given profession work together to achieve common goals. Some examples of professional organizations include local, state, and national education associations; and state, regional, and national affiliates of the American Alliance for Health, Physical Education, Recreation and Dance.

Members can share ideas with each other by speaking at conventions, writing articles in professional journals, serving on committees, holding an office; or by just attending, listening, reading, or helping. In any case, your failure to grow professionally cheats your students of the latest advancements within the profession and your colleagues of ideas that you have tried and found useful. Professional organizations also help with employment needs by publishing job openings and providing opportunities at conventions for potential employers and employees to get acquainted.

Commitment to professional employment practices

Once you have signed a contract with a school district, you are legally and ethically committed to complete the term of service specified with high-quality work and integrity in employment practices. If the contract must be terminated because of reasons beyond your control, then you and the district should arrive at a mutually agreed upon solution to the situation.

Professional development

Every teacher should develop a personal plan for professional development. Although some states or districts require attendance at in-service workshops or college classes for recertification or salary increases, the need for continuous updating of skills by each teacher should be a matter of professional pride, whether required or not. In addition to in-service workshops and college classes, other options include (1) reading professional books and journals; (2) participating in professional organizations; (3) doing research or writing books or articles; (4) traveling to observe programs, meet other professionals, and view facilities; (5) pursuing a graduate degree; (6) speaking at clinics or professional meetings; and (7) participating on professional committees.

Evaluating yourself as a teacher

Now that we have studied the qualities of the effective teacher, both in the classroom and as a professional, let's look at how well you measure up.

Teacher warmth

In order to establish a warm, supportive environment, teachers must feel positive toward themselves and have control over their own emotions. There are many policies and procedures in schools over which teachers have very little control. There are also frequent interruptions from students and colleagues. There are students, teachers, parents, and administrators who may be angry with you. In the face of these and other difficulties, can you be an example of the personal and social skills you will want your students to emulate? Rate yourself on the following questions to see how you stack up.

1. I like myself a lot.

2. I am teachable. I can take and utilize suggestions from others even when I didn't ask for them.

3. I adjust well to interruptions in my personal plans without resorting to anger.

4. I can stand up for what I believe without making others feel deflated.

5. I *actively* listen to what others say to me.

6. I treat other people as I would like to be treated, regardless of their race, sex, socioeconomic status, or occupation.

7. I enjoy working with other people.

8. I am sensitive to the needs and feelings of others.

9. I have a sense of humor.

10. I can admit when I make a mistake.

Teachers who expect a lot from their students spend more time working with students on on-task behavior and help students work to their full capacities.

Teacher expectancy

Before you can have a belief in the ability of your students to excel, you must have a belief in your own ability to achieve excellence. Rate yourself on the following questions.

1. I am aware of my strengths and weaknesses.

2. I am satisfied with my present skills and abilities.

3. I have and follow a personal plan for self-improvement.

4. I feel uncomfortable when I do not do well in something I promised to do.

5. I am willing to sacrifice for what I believe is right.

6. I learn from my mistakes.

Task-oriented climate

An effective teacher must be patient and understanding yet firm and unwavering when the need arises. Rate yourself on your ability to establish a task-oriented climate.

1. I can set a goal and stick to it until it is accomplished.

2. I can set limits on my behavior and maintain them in my everyday actions.

3. I can help others set and reach goals for themselves.

4. I can accept reasonable limits placed on me by others and can adjust my actions accordingly.

5. I can be firm in standing up for what I believe is right.

6. I do not procrastinate.

7. I am skilled in a variety of classroom management skills.

Effective instruction

Physical education teachers should attempt to develop excellence in knowledge, activity skills, communication skills, and research skills, and a knowledge of effective educational methods and procedures. By having a strong background in the subject, the teacher has the knowledge and skills needed for adequate preparation of the lesson. A knowledge of student characteristics, needs, and interests is essential in adapting lesson materials to help students reach their goals.

Teachers who command respect because of their knowledge, skills, teaching ability, and sincere interest in others are usually successful in helping students satisfy their personal needs, as well as to achieve group goals. Rate yourself on your background for effective instruction.

1. I am a positive example of personal appearance, personal hygiene, and cleanliness.

2. I am physically fit.

3. I can effectively demonstrate a wide variety of physical skills.

4. I can explain the basic concepts of physical education (i.e., exercise physiology, mechanical analysis, etc.)

5. I can use a variety of teaching methodologies.

6. I enjoy learning in many subject areas, such as art, literature, music, history, and science.

7. I can communicate well in both written and oral forms.

8. I am skilled in a variety of evaluation techniques.

9. I can set appropriate objectives for a wide variety of student needs.

10. I can provide effective feedback to students to help them improve their skills.

The professional teacher

There are some professional behaviors that you can engage in even before becoming a full-fledged member of the teaching profession. How do you rate?

1. I am a member of a professional organization.

2. I attend professional meetings.

3. I am actively involved in service to others in my school, community, church, or other organization.

4. I can confront others openly when I feel they have erred and the situation can be corrected.

5. I can abide by the decision of my employer or group even though I disagree with it.

6. I know what I want to accomplish as a teacher.

Now that you have rated yourself in each of the areas of effective teaching and have noted your strengths and weaknesses, make a plan to improve on the weaknesses you found. In the article, "The Secret of the Slight Edge," Meyer and Zadra sum up what it takes to be a great teacher:

> Sometimes the distance from the bottom to the top is shorter than we realize. For instance . . . if you spend just one full minute each day quietly planning your life . . . , then you will be building the same habit shared by the most admired and successful people on earth.

In sports and in life, the difference between "great" achievement and "good" achievement is often said to be about two per cent more study, practice, application, interest, attention and effort. . . . Each one is important, but the real secret is this: be consistent in all of them.

The key to great achievement is to give yourself the slight edge—that extra two per cent—time after time after time.[8]

Teacher stress

In most industrialized countries throughout the world, stress has become the main health concern of teachers.[9] Common symptoms include fatigue, nervousness, frustration, and sleeplessness. These can lead to many more serious illnesses, as well as to many psychological disorders.

In order to prevent stress, teachers need to plan, early in their careers, a personal life-style that can dissipate the stresses of teaching. Proper nutrition, exercise, and sleep are essential. Developing hobbies and interests totally separate from physical education is also important. Attending cultural events, interior decorating, woodworking, and many other activities can provide a release of built-up tension. Involvement with people from many other walks of life is also valuable.

Within the school environment, teachers should learn to use time efficiently so that they do not need to work longer than necessary. Careful planning and organizing in advance saves last-minute wear and tear on the nerves. Knowing school policies and procedures in advance of an emergency helps you to be calm in the face of adversity. Allowing students and paraprofessionals to help saves time and effort.

The Pareto principle is widely known in management circles. It indicates that by concentrating on a few of the most important tasks each day, most of the important results will be effected. An easy way to do this is to make a list of all the things you must do and number the items in order of importance. When you have a few minutes, begin with item one and work on it until it is finished. Then, begin item two, and so on. Even though you might never finish the entire list, you will know that the most important items are getting done.

Another rule is to never leave school for the day until your classes are prepared for tomorrow and, when you do leave, don't take anything home with you. Think, as LaMancusa said, "I have done what I can, and I have done what I must. Tomorrow will take care of some of it and, with a little bit of luck, time will take care of the rest."[10] Of course, during the first few months of teaching or when a crisis hits, stay a little late. However, don't make a habit of it.

Finally, find a copy of the following maxim, post it on your office wall, and try to put it into practice:

God grant me the serenity to accept the things I
    cannot change,
Courage to change the things I can,
And wisdom to know the difference.

Questions and suggested activities

1. List five teachers you have admired very much. What personal and/or professional qualities did they have that set them apart from other teachers?

2. What qualities would you like to concentrate on to help you become like these great teachers?

3. What special talents, attitudes, abilities, or knowledge do you now possess that you could offer to public school students?

4. What experiences might you need to help you acquire the qualities you desire?

5. What are you willing to give to acquire them?

6. What things do you do well? Why do you think you do them well? Has anyone or anything helped you learn them? In what ways?

7. Do you like to do these things so well that you often talk about them to others or do them with others? Does this help you learn them even better?

8. How can you help a student become a good learner?

9. What is the relationship between an ideal learner and an ideal teacher?

10. React to this statement: "A good teacher is born, not made."

11. In May, afraid of not getting a job, you signed a contract to teach at Podunk High School. In August, an offer comes from Centerville Junior High School where you prefer to teach and live. What will you do?

12. Create a self-development plan to help you become a better teacher. Include each of the areas discussed in this chapter.

Suggested readings

Austin, Dean A. "The Teacher Burnout Issue." *Journal of Physical Education, Recreation, and Dance* 52 (November–December 1981): 35–36.

Bach, Richard. *Jonathan Livingston Seagull.* New York: Macmillan, 1970.

Check, John F. "Wanted! A Humorous Teacher." *The Physical Educator* 36 (October 1979): 119–22.

Gallague, David L. "Excellence in Teaching: The Students' Point of View." *The Physical Educator* 31 (May 1974): 59–60.

Harkness, Jon. "Subcultures in the High School—Reconsidered." *Today's Education* 70 (September–October 1981): 37.

Ingram, Ann. "A Teacher of Physical Education Should Have These Attributes." *The Physical Educator* 34 (March 1977): 34.

"Job Satisfaction." *Today's Education* 70 (September–October 1981): 69.

Knutson, Marjorie C. "Sensitivity to Minority Groups." *Journal of Physical Education and Recreation* 48 (May 1977): 24–25.

Landsmann, Leonna. "Is Teaching Hazardous to Your Health." *Today's Education* (April–May 1978): 48–50.

Macy, Anne Sullivan. *Teacher.* Garden City, New York: Doubleday, 1955.

Mandino, Og. *The Greatest Salesman in the World.* New York: F. Fell, 1968.

Miller, David K. "The Effective Teacher." *The Physical Educator* 35 (October 1978): 147–48.

Williams, Dennis A.; Coppola, Vincent; Howard, Lucy; Huck, Janet; King, Patricia; and Monroe, Sylvester. "Teachers Are in Trouble." *Newsweek* (April 27, 1981) pp. 78–84.

Understanding the Nature of Learning

Physical education in today's world must do more than merely train students to perform activity skills. It must **educate** the total individual to solve those problems in society that relate to the physical well-being of people. The physically educated student must possess the following characteristics.

1. A working knowledge of:
   a. The effects of exercise on the body
   b. The processes of learning motor skills
   c. The processes of developing physical fitness
   d. The knowledges fundamental to activity and game performance, such as rules, strategies, terminology, among others
2. Competencies in:
   a. Physical skills
   b. Physical fitness
3. Positive attitudes and appreciations toward:
   a. Education
   b. Physical education and physical activity
   c. Himself or herself
   d. The body as an instrument of expression and learning

In order to achieve these goals, the various domains or areas of learning must be integrated into every aspect of instruction and curriculum planning in physical education. The learner then becomes the focus of the teaching-learning process as shown in unit figure 2.1.

The **cognitive domain** includes the learning and application of knowledge. The **psychomotor domain** incorporates the development of the physical body and neuromuscular skills. The **affective domain** involves the acquisition of attitudes, appreciations, and values. To influence any one of these areas will almost invariably affect the other two. Therefore, all three areas should be considered when planning the learning outcomes of instruction.

The learning outcomes in each area are often arranged into a hierarchy that shows the prerequisite, or simpler, knowledges, skills, and attitudes required for the performance of higher skills. A hierarchy is often called a taxonomy. A **taxonomy** is a system for classifying something. An educational taxonomy classifies the behaviors that students can be expected to demonstrate after learning.

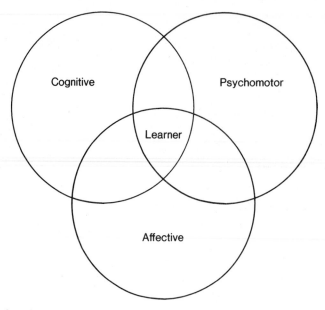

Unit Figure 2.1 Integration of the cognitive, psychomotor, and affective domains

A number of taxonomies have been developed. Perhaps the one most commonly known is that of Bloom and his associates shown in table 6.1.[1] The taxonomy for the affective domain, which is shown in table 8.1 on page 000, was developed later and has also been widely accepted, although rarely implemented in physical education.[2] Several efforts have been made to develop taxonomies in the psychomotor domain. The one proposed by Jewett and associates is shown in table 7.1.[3] Corbin has outlined a separate taxonomy for physical fitness,[4] and Singer and Dick proposed one for the personal-social area of physical education.[5]

The importance of a taxonomy is to encourage physical educators to include a progression of learning outcomes from those lower on the taxonomy through the higher order objectives listed at the top of each taxonomy. In this way the taxonomy also can be used as a checklist by teachers to make sure the entire range of behaviors is included in the curriculum or learning situation.

Corbin listed three common errors that result in failure to include the entire range of behaviors in the taxonomies. They are (1) trying to teach advanced skills and information without teaching essential prerequisites, (2) overemphasizing lower-order objectives, and (3) sacrificing higher-order objectives in the process of achieving lower-order objectives.[6] It is essential that we teach the higher-order problem-solving skills so that students can learn to apply their knowledge and skills to real-life problems. The challenge, then, is to help our students develop the capabilities to meet a full range of learning outcomes in each of the learning areas—cognitive, psychomotor, and affective.

Chapters 6, 7, and 8 discuss the cognitive, psychomotor, and affective domains in more detail and present a plan of action for organizing and incorporating research findings into the instructional setting. These plans can serve as a checklist for the instructional process to insure that all of the essential domains of education are included. Chapter 9 discusses motivational techniques for use with the various domains.

Suggested readings for unit II

Annarino, Anthony A. "Physical Education Objectives: Traditional vs. Developmental." *Journal of Physical Education and Recreation* 48 (October 1977): 22.
———. "Operational Taxonomy for Physical Education Objectives," *Journal of Physical Education and Recreation* 49 (January 1978): 54–55.
Howell, Jerry. "Exercise Science—Balancing Cognitive, Affective, and Psychomotor Objectives for Physical Education." *Journal of Physical Education and Recreation* 49 (January 1978): 49.

Understanding Cognitive Learning
The Learning and Application of Knowledge

Study stimulators

1. What is a taxonomy? Of what advantage is it to physical educators?
2. What does the cognitive domain include?
3. Why is perception important to learning?
4. Compare and contrast reception learning and discovery learning. When is each type of learning appropriate?
5. What does cognitive learning have to do with learning in physical education?
6. How can cognitive learning in physical education be improved?

The cognitive domain includes knowledge, comprehension, application, analysis, synthesis, and evaluation as shown in table 6.1. Each category on the taxonomy contains elements of the previous categories. Thus, "evaluation" may involve any or all of the categories preceding it on the taxonomy.

Some examples of physical education content that fit into the various levels of the taxonomy include:

    I. Knowledge
        a. of game rules and strategies
        b. of terminology
        c. of history and current events
        d. of body systems
    II. Comprehension
        a. of game rules and strategies in specific game situations
        b. of the effects of exercise on the body
        c. of the benefits of exercise
        d. of factors affecting exercise
        e. of social and psychological factors affecting sports participation
    III. Application
        a. of game rules and strategies
        b. of biomechanical principles to produce effective body movement
        c. of processes for learning new skills
        d. of techniques for relaxation and stress management
        e. of principles of safety
        f. of game etiquette

Table 6.1 The cognitive domain

Levels of behavior	Terms for objectives

1. *Knowledge*—Involves recognition and *recall* of:
   —specific facts, terms, definitions, symbols, dates, places, etc.
   —rules, trends, categories, methods, etc.
   —principles, theories, ways of organizing ideas
	Define
	Match
	Spell
	Recite
	Who, what, where, when, why

2. *Comprehension*—Involves ability to use learning:
   —translating, paraphrasing
   —interpreting, summarizing
   —extrapolating, predicting effects or consequences
	Translate
	Paraphrase
	Tell in your own words
	Summarize
	Compare or contrast
	Predict

3. *Application*—Involves ability to use learning in a variety of situations:
   —using principles and theories
   —using abstractions
	Solve
	Apply

4. *Analysis*—Involves breaking down the whole hierarchy of parts:
   —identifying or distinguishing parts or elements
   —discovering interactions or relationships between parts
   —relating organizational principles (parts to whole or whole to parts)
	Analyze
	Examine
	Break down
	Delineate
	Determine
	Identify

5. *Synthesis*—Involves combining elements into a new whole:
   —identifying and relating elements in new ways
   —arranging and combining parts
   —constructing a new whole
	Compose
	Write
	Design
	Invent
	Hypothesize
	Plan
	Create
	Produce
	Organize

6. *Evaluation*—Involves judgments of value of material and methods for a given purpose:
   —judgments in terms of internal standards
   —judgments in terms of external criteria
	Judge
	Evaluate
	Defend

Source: Concepts taken from Bloom, Benjamin S., ed. *Taxonomy of Educational Objectives, Handbook I: Cognitive Domain*. New York: McKay Co., 1956.

IV. Analysis
   a. of game strategies for effectiveness in specific situations
   b. of commercial physical fitness and recreation programs
 V. Synthesis
   a. of exercise programs to attain physical fitness
   b. of new games or game strategies
VI. Evaluation
   a. of the quality of sports-related consumer goods
   b. of exercise programs
   c. of rules and strategies and their effects on game play
   d. of how equipment affects game play

Perception

The basis for all learning is perception. **Perception** is the capacity for awareness, observation, or comprehension. Although many facts and experiences are presented to students, the ones they will remember are dependent upon their awareness of the words or ideas to be learned. Ideas and skills may be omitted, distorted, or only partially remembered because of the different perceptions of the learners. What the learners perceive is influenced by their attitudes, expectations, motivation, and previous experiences. Perception is enhanced by the five senses—sight; touch, or kinesthetic awareness; smell; taste; and hearing. The more senses used to teach something, the better the learner perceives the subject.

Cognitive learning

Two principal divisions of cognitive learning have emerged. Ausubel referred to these as reception learning and discovery learning.[1] **Reception learning** includes memorization, or rote learning, and meaningful verbal learning. **Discovery learning** includes concept learning and problem solving. Table 6.2 shows the relationship among the various kinds of cognitive learning.

In reception learning, the information to be learned is presented to the learner in its final form as in a rules presentation. The student then internalizes it for future use. In discovery learning, information—such as the principle of equilibrium—must be discovered by the learner before it is internalized. Each category of learning has its own advantages and disadvantages. While large amounts of information can be acquired through reception learning in relatively short periods of time, it is discovery learning that helps individuals solve many of life's problems. Some overlap exists, of course, in that reception learning supplies the knowledge needed to solve problems and discovery learning can be used to extend the information gained in reception learning.

Table 6.2 Relationship of the various types of cognitive learning

	Critical and creative thinking Applied practice	
Reception learning		**Discovery learning**
Rote learning (memorization)		Concept learning
Meaningful verbal learning		Problem solving
	Perception	

Most young children learn best through discovery learning. This is why the movement approach to teaching is so popular at the elementary school level. As children mature and their levels of abstract cognitive thinking are developed, they can often take advantage of the savings in time offered by reception learning.

The task of the teacher is to master teaching methods appropriate to each of these types of learning and then to select the one most beneficial in a particular instance. By using a variety of methods, the students' different learning styles can be accommodated. A discussion of each of the four kinds of cognitive learning follows.

Memorization, or rote learning

Once the learner has perceived the information to be learned, memorization is a result of (1) the organization of the material to be learned, (2) active practice of the verbal sequence, and (3) reinforcement or confirmation of the correct responses.

Organization of the material to be learned

Learning a series of things in order is a common method of organizing learning. For example, learning the components of motor fitness is done easily in alphabetical order—agility, balance, coordination, endurance, flexibility, speed, and strength. A second method is the use of a key word, phrase, or picture to remind the learner of the idea to be learned. An example is the use of a diagram like the one in figure 6.1 that explains the principles of equilibrium.

Active practice

Practice is essential to promote rote learning while eliminating the effects of interference on new information and information already learned. One common practice method is the progressive part method in which the student learns the first part, then parts 1 and 2, then 1, 2, 3, and so forth. For example, when learning the bones in the body, start with the foot, then add the ankle, then the leg, thigh, and so forth.

Another practice method is to respond to the entire task on each trial by using some kind of prompts or cues as needed to get through the material. One way to do this is to gradually cross out parts of the material as it is practiced until the whole sequence of material has been learned. This method has been used in the programmed learning sequence in figure 14.2. A third method is the use of questions spaced periodically throughout the practice phase to stimulate student attention to the material during practice.

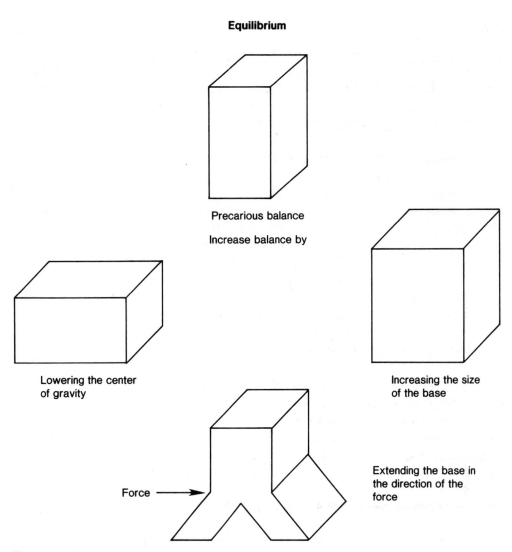

Equilibrium

Precarious balance

Increase balance by

Lowering the center
of gravity

Increasing the size
of the base

Force ⟶

Extending the base in
the direction of the
force

Figure 6.1 The use of a key organizer for memorization.

Reinforcement or confirmation of the correct response

Knowledge of results is essential so that the learner knows that the material has been learned correctly. The ability to provide meaningful feedback is one of the most important abilities a teacher possesses. Feedback can be either visual or verbal. Whether oral or written, feedback must be specific enough that the student knows whether the response is correct or incorrect and, if incorrect, how to change it to make it correct.

Visual feedback might be an approving nod or writing the answer on the chalkboard. Verbal feedback could be a comment on the response or a simple "thank you." Of course, visual and verbal feedback can be used simultaneously.

	Muscular Strength	Muscular Endurance
Physiological Processes	Ability to exert maximal force for one muscle contraction	Ability to perform repeated muscle contractions over a period of time
Measurement	One chin-up with weight attached to body One sit-up with weight held behind neck	Chin-ups to determine maximum number of repetitions possible Sit-ups to determine maximum number of repetitions possible
Training	Repetitions with near-maximum resistance	Many repetitions with light resistance

Figure 6.3 A comparative organizer for muscular strength and endurance.

Anchoring new ideas

In order to facilitate anchoring the new learning material to that previously learned, the teacher must (1) remind the learners of the total picture and help them to summarize the new material, (2) point out similarities and differences with the previously learned material, and (3) describe how the new material supports the previously learned material. Students should be asked to supply from their own experiences additional examples of the concepts learned.

Mastery of new ideas

Retention is enhanced by helping students to retrieve and use the information in some way. A written or oral quiz, a class discussion, or a problem-solving situation forces the student to retrieve the information by supplying cues that tell the context within which the information is normally used. These activities may, in effect, be "post-organizers."

Learning consists of new information or experiences that the learner discovers have personal meaning. This explains why schoolwork often goes over the heads of the students for whom it is intended. It never gets to their level. Studies show that meaningful verbal material is learned more rapidly and retained more readily with less interference than rote learning. However, this does not seem to hold true with less-able learners.

Concept learning

A **concept** is an idea or picture in the brain that helps to aid understanding. The origination of a concept is diagrammed in figure 6.4. Each concept consists of one's perceptions, the meanings given them, the feelings about them, and the words or symbols with which one discusses them. Most school learning takes the form of concepts or the rules and principles that are made when concepts are linked together.

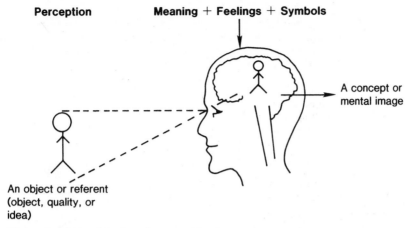

Perception   **Meaning + Feelings + Symbols**

A concept or
mental image

An object or referent
(object, quality, or
idea)

Figure 6.4 The origination of a concept.

Concept learning involves the identification of objects, experiences, processes, or configurations (often of widely differing physical appearances) into a class or category of elements that share certain essential characteristics. A concept has:

1. A name or label—a term given to a category or class of experiences, objects, processes, or configurations, such as aerobic activities.

2. Examples—instances of the concept that contain all of the essential attributes of the concept, such as jogging or walking.

3. Nonexamples—examples with none or only some of the essential characteristics, such as sprinting or calisthenics.

4. Essential or shared attributes—common features or characteristics of examples within a concept, such as the constant use of oxygen without incurring an oxygen debt.

5. Irrelevant attributes—features that often accompany, but are not a required feature of, an element to be included in the concept, such as where you run or when you run.

6. Definition—a statement specifying the essential attributes of the concept, "activities that develop oxygen transportation and utilization without incurring an oxygen debt are called *aerobic* activities."

Concept learning involves the ability to discriminate (1) essential characteristics from irrelevant characteristics and (2) essential characteristics of examples from essential characteristics of nonexamples, as shown in table 6.3. Concepts can be taught by the following sequence:

1. Present a variety of labeled examples that incorporate all of the essential characteristics of the concept (simultaneously or in close time succession). Jogging, stationary cycling, and walking are aerobic activities.

Table 6.3 Discrimination of various characteristics of concepts

	Examples	Nonexamples

Essential characteristics	Activities that use oxygen:
	
	    Jogging
	    Cycling
	    Swimming
		Activities that don't use oxygen or incur an oxygen debt:
		
		    Sprinting
		    Speed skating

Irrelevant characteristics	Where you exercise When you exercise What clothes you wear	Where you exercise When you exercise What clothes you wear

2. Compare examples and nonexamples to identify essential characteristics and develop a hypothesis. Within the examples and nonexamples, vary the irrelevant attributes. Start with examples that are least similar, with the fewest shared characteristics. Is this an aerobic activity?

    rowing—yes   sleeping—no   folk dance—yes
    swimming—sometimes

3. Verify the hypothesis by asking for several new examples of the concept. List several aerobic activities.

4. Have students state a definition of the concept in their own words.

5. Reinforce correct answers and hypotheses.

6. Apply the concept.

7. Test the concept. When the instructor wants to know if the students have acquired the concept, he or she must assess whether or not the students can generate examples with the essential characteristics and distinguish examples from nonexamples.

Concepts become more meaningful to students as they accumulate more experience with their objects, or referents. Laboratory experiences and demonstrations are important in helping students gain the experiences needed.

Concepts can be linked together in various ways to form rules or principles. Rules and principles can be taught best by applying them. Students who learn to say or write a rule forget it within a few weeks, while those who are able to apply them retain them easily. Rules and principles are best taught when the following procedure is followed.

1. Inform the learner of the performance to be expected at the conclusion of the lesson. It may later serve as a reinforcement to learning.

2. Recall the component concepts.

3. Provide verbal cues that explain the relationships of the concepts.

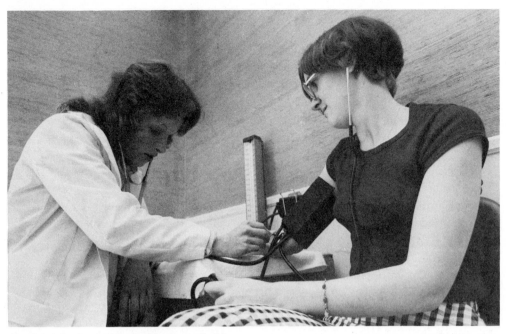

Students learn best when learning is applied to real-life situations.

4. Ask each student to demonstrate one or more instances of the rule (i.e., apply the rule).

5. Request that each student state the rule verbally.

Problem solving

Problem solving is the capacity to solve previously unencountered situations or problems by combining old rules and principles into new higher-order ones. Problems must be new to the individual, but not necessarily to society. A problem is solved when the individual's previous knowledge or behavior is put together into a new relationship or added to new information to form an *insight* that resolves the new situation.

The nature of the task determines the specific problem-solving behaviors, but certain general behaviors are essential. In order for a problem to be solved, the following must occur: (1) the student is presented with a problem that is worth solving; (2) the student recalls previously learned knowledge and behavior that relate to the problem; (3) the teacher provides assistance to channel students' thinking; and (4) the teacher reinforces both the problem-solving process and the solution.

Presentation of a problem

Recognition of a problem may occur as a result of teacher selection and presentation or student perception. Teachers often design problems to help students apply recently learned principles. There are two important elements of the problem, namely, that the teacher and the student see some worth in its solution and that the essential features of the solution can be inferred from the problem. Of course, the problem chosen must be one that can be handled within the limitations of time and the resources available.

The student should understand the problem and the performance expected. The essential features of the solution could be in the form of questions to be answered. A problem can be as simple as "What technique makes it possible for you to jump the farthest in the standing broad jump?" A more complex problem might be "Why are some people better performers in some activities, while others are better in other activities?"

Recall of previous learning

Students must possess the knowledge and behavior essential to the solution of the problem or be taught the information to be used in solving the problem. They often must be helped to identify and recall those knowledges and skills that relate to the problem.

Teacher assistance

Research has demonstrated that providing information about the method for solving a problem or the principles to be used leads to better problem solving by students. Teacher assistance may take many forms—from listening to students' exploration of possible alternatives to providing students with cues to direct or channel their thinking.[3]

One of the most important things a teacher can do is to establish an environment of acceptance and self-worth in which students feel free to explore alternative solutions to problems without recrimination. Problem solving cannot occur when conformity is the norm. Teachers should ensure that students have the time necessary to solve problems without being pressured.

Another help is to teach principles for analyzing and solving problems and helping students know when the problem has been solved effectively. Some techniques might include the scientific method, trial and error, and brainstorming. Group discussion and participation in problem solving appears to be superior to individual problem solving in assisting students to learn the problem-solving process and to use the principles learned to solve other problems.

Reinforcement

Teachers who use problem solving must have confidence in their students' abilities to solve problems whether or not they achieve the solutions the teacher considers to be most effective. Reinforcement of both the process and the product are important in encouraging students to continue to solve problems.

Students differ with regard to their abilities to attack and solve problems. Bloom and Broder discovered a number of differences in problem-solving behaviors of successful and unsuccessful problem solvers.[4] They are paraphrased as follows.

1. Unsuccessful solvers failed to understand the problem. It made no sense to them. Often they solved the problem only to discover that the problem they solved was not the one presented. These students also experienced difficulty with reading comprehension.

2. Unsuccessful solvers were unaware that they possessed the knowledge necessary to solve the problem, whereas successful solvers broke the problem down into manageable components and selected relevant knowledges and skills from their previously learned skills.

3. Unsuccessful solvers approached problems as if the problems had pat solutions. Successful solvers perceived the possibility of several solutions.

4. Unsuccessful students lacked confidence in their ability to solve problems and often introduced personal biases into the solution.

The greater the repertoire of previously learned knowledges and skills and the easier it is to recall and apply them, the greater are the chances of solving the problem. The main concern about problem solving is whether or not the problem-solving abilities can be transferred from the school to real-life situations.

Applied practice

Students should be encouraged to make a conscious effort to apply learning to life's problems. Homework assignments might be used to encourage the transfer of school learning to problems in the home or community.

Critical and creative thinking

Critical and creative thinking require a thorough background in subject content, mastery of intellectual skills, and practice in using problem solving, criticism, and research skills. They also demand considerable self-control and maturity. Although instructors should promote critical and creative thinking, care should be taken to help students be successful on small-scale projects. This opportunity for success is more effective than inviting shoddy or inferior performance and feelings of failure in using such processes.

Application of cognitive research

The following questions summarize the important components of cognitive learning and provide an advance organizer for the discussion of teaching strategies that follows. The remaining chapters of the book will provide further examples for implementing these components into physical education classes.

Consideration of factors within the learner

Do students have the facts, intellectual skills, and strategies that are prerequisite to the material to be taught?

Are students physically and emotionally ready for the material to be taught?

Consideration of factors external to the learner

Are the following factors provided for in the instructional situation:
(1) contiguity, (2) repetition, and (3) reinforcement?

Design of the instructional situation

Does the instructional situation provide for: (1) gaining attention,
(2) informing students of expected outcomes, (3) stimulating recall of
prerequisites, (4) presenting the stimulus for learning, (5) offering guidance
for learning, (6) providing feedback, (7) appraising performance, (8) making
provisions for transfer, (9) insuring retention, and (10) allowing students to
succeed or fail on their own merits?

Consideration of factors within the learner

Gagne identified the factors affecting learning as being internal, or within the learner, or
external to the learner.[5] Internal factors include the previously learned capabilities of the
learner such as **facts** and **intellectual skills.** Facts may be provided by the teacher at the time
of learning, recalled by the learner from previous learning, or learned just prior to the task
at hand. Intellectual skills must be recalled from previous experience. If both facts and intellectual skills have been mastered, the learner is said to have the appropriate readiness for
learning.

A third internal factor involves **strategies** for learning and remembering. These strategies are used to help the learner decide what past knowledges and skills are to be used and
how to implement them. During early learning experiences, the strategies are cued by the
teacher. As the student's experience increases, the strategies may be expected to be self-
activated by the learner.

Some other factors that affect learning include student health, both physical and emotional, and student interest. Because each student approaches learning with a different internal makeup, a preassessment of existing knowledge, skills, and strategies is essential.

Consideration of factors external to the learner

The external factors generally cited as affecting learning are contiguity, repetition, and reinforcement. **Contiguity** means that the stimulus for learning must occur almost simultaneously with the student's response in order for learning to occur. **Repetition,** or practice,
has long been considered essential for strengthening learned connections and to insure retention. Gagne cites several studies as evidence that repetition may not be necessary for the
initial learning experience if students possess the essential prerequisites for learning cognitive skills.[6] However, it is still necessary for retention. **Reinforcement** occurs when students
are rewarded for correct performance, whether by a tangible reward, a verbal signal, such
as "that's right," or a nod of approval. An even more desirable reward is self-reinforcement.
Extinction, or unlearning a response, can be achieved by omitting the reinforcement.

Design of the instructional situation

Instruction involves deliberate control by the teacher over the external events of the learning situation. Gagne listed nine events that are essential to learning.[7] They are discussed in the following paragraphs. Although they generally occur in the order listed, individual differences or differences in the learning tasks may allow the deletion or rearranging of one or two of them. The events cited here are often initiated and controlled through the use of verbal directions.

Gaining and controlling attention

Gestures, pictures, verbal statements, sudden movements, printed information pointing out something (such as an arrow, a circle, a box around information, a change in type styles, or color) can be used to get attention and direct it toward a learning stimulus.

Informing the learner of expected outcomes

Knowing what is expected is essential to the learning process. A demonstration of a skill, a verbal statement about what is to be learned, or the use of **advance organizers**—as advocated by Ausubel—all provide direction to the learning process.[8]

Stimulating recall of relevant prerequisite capabilities

Verbal directions or cues tell the learner to recognize or recall previously learned facts, skills, or strategies for use in current learning.

Presenting the stimulus inherent to the learning task

The stimulus must be presented in a way that is perceived by the learner. This may differ depending on what is to be learned. Reading, listening to a presentation, observing a demonstration, or doing an experiment all involve the presentation of a new learning stimulus.

Offering guidance for learning

Verbal, visual, or kinesthetic prompts and cues guide the discovery of concepts and solutions to problems. Often this guidance takes the form of questioning to channel the learner's thoughts in such a way that extremely incorrect hypotheses are eliminated and learning can be speeded up.

Providing feedback

Feedback is information about the learner's response. It may be provided by the learner or by the environment. Feedback may be verbal, such as "Right!" or "That's close," or it may be nonverbal, such as a nod, smile, glance, or merely continuing on to the next part of the lesson. In the early stages of learning, immediate feedback is important. Later on, more and more feedback is provided by the learner and the environment; consequently, teacher feedback decreases.

Appraising performance

Evaluation is a form of delayed feedback. The initial test should appraise exactly what the student has learned. Periodic appraisals facilitate retention and motivate students to continue learning, especially when they receive immediate feedback on each examination and must restudy the material they have missed.

Making provisions for transferability

Transfer can occur laterally, such as from a school situation to a real life situation, or vertically, such as from the learning of a concept to the use of that concept in problem solving. It can also occur proactively, affecting something learned in the future, or retroactively, affecting past learning. When transfer enhances the learning of another idea or skill it is called **facilitation.** Negative transfer is called **interference.**

The most important variable in promoting transfer of learning is a thorough learning of the original concept or principle. Pointing out occasions where transfer might be expected is also advantageous.

Insuring retention

Retention is facilitated by the meaningfulness of the concepts learned. Meaningfulness is enhanced by relating new verbal material to that which has been previously learned through the use of advance organizers or post organizers to help students anchor new ideas to a larger conceptual framework. Another factor facilitating retention is the use of periodic reviews to help students exercise their retrieval strategies. For example, a brief oral quiz each day can be effective in helping students avoid the deteriorating effects of time and the interference of other learning activities.

Student responsibility for learning

Although the design of instruction attempts to establish the conditions that will facilitate learning, it is up to the learner to take advantage of them. Teachers can not learn for their students.

Traditionally, physical education teachers have relied on the teaching of skills and activities as the components of physical education. The time has come when we must stop *training* students and start *educating* them. Unless we begin to apply the concepts learned in kinesiology, exercise physiology, and motor learning, physical education will never come of age.

Teaching the cognitive aspects of physical education is not easy. It requires extensive planning to integrate concepts with psychomotor activity. However, knowledge learned through relevant experiences is more lasting than that gained merely through reading or listening, and learning occurs faster when students understand the principles involved in skill performance.

Mohr emphasized the importance of integrating concepts with physical activity to enhance understanding and save time. She said:

> Our students do not have to stop motor activity in order to engage in cognitive activity. Students do not store their brains in their lockers along with their books and street clothes. Cognitive activity goes on during all of the hours one is awake, and perhaps even in dreams. To develop physical education understanding we need to guide these cognitive activities, just as we guide the motor activities. In other words, we can accomplish the intellectual, aesthetic, and social objectives without moving into the classroom. However, in some parts of the country, during inclement weather, physical education classes must be held in classrooms or other confined spaces. The resourceful teacher will take advantage of these times to plan worthwhile cognitive activities related to the body of knowledge in physical education and to the motor activities involved in the unit of curricular content. Modern audio-visual aids and numerous innovative teaching techniques are available to motivate and challenge the students to exciting cognitive achievements.[9]

Mohr provided some additional ideas for teaching concepts.[10] They are paraphrased here as follows:

1. Explain why one method of performance is better than another.

2. Omit some important feature of a skill, like stepping in the direction of the throw, to help the students see what a detrimental effect this has on the force of the throw.

3. Incorporate the learning of fitness concepts, such as exercise heart rate, recovery rate, and respiration rate, into rest periods between vigorous exercise.

4. Conduct informal experiments by comparing conditions, such as heat, cold, smog, etc., as they affect exercise on different days.

Mohr concluded with the following statement:

> In your undergraduate and graduate professional preparation programs you have learned many exciting and valuable concepts about principles of movement, how the body performs desired movements, the effects of activity on these wonderful bodies of ours, and the effects of numerous factors on performance. Why keep these learnings a *secret?* Why not let your students share these exciting understandings so that their lives will be enriched by them just as yours have been.[11]

Ley listed some concept areas that should be included in instruction. They include the following:

1. Statements of description that provide information about "what"—facts, knowledge, information
2. Statements of importance that answer "why"—simple reasons, values, justifications, worth
3. Statements of scientific analysis that answer "why it happens"—principles, relationships, laws
4. Statements of problem solving (what one can do about it)—application of facts, principles, and relationships.[12]

Simplified concepts can be taught in elementary school with more in-depth analysis of the same concepts occurring in the secondary schools.

Questions and suggested activities

1. What is a taxonomy? Why is it important?

2. Why is perception important in all kinds of learning?

3. What kinds of physical education content are included in the cognitive domain?

4. What similarities and differences exist in the four kinds of cognitive learning? With which kind do you learn best?

5. Is it important for students to memorize facts in physical education? If so, what ones?

6. In what content areas of physical education might the use of meaningful verbal learning be most valuable?

7. List some concepts that you might teach when explaining the rules of a sport or game.

8. Can you think of some examples of problem solving that might help students learn the principles of biomechanics in sport activities?

Suggested readings

American Alliance for Health, Physical Education, Recreation and Dance. *"Basic Stuff" Series.* Reston, Va.: AAHPERD, 1981.
———. *Knowledge and Understanding in Physical Education.* Rev. ed. Washington, D.C.: AAHPER, 1973.
Corbin, Charles B., et al. *Concepts in Physical Education with Laboratories and Experiments.* 4th ed. Dubuque, Iowa: Wm. C. Brown Company Publishers, 1981.
———. *Fitness for Life: Physical Education Concepts.* Palo Alto, Calif.: Scott, Foresman and Company, 1979.

DeSorbe, Brian M. "How Do You Get the Ball from *Here* to *There?* Teaching Children About Angles and Trajectories." *Journal of Physical Education and Recreation* 48 (June 1977): 35–36.

Edington, D. W., and Cunningham, Lee. "More on Applied Physiology of Exercise." *Journal of Physical Education and Recreation* 45 (February 1974): 18.

Joyce, Bruce R. *Selecting Learning Experiences: Linking Theory and Practice.* Washington, D.C.: Association for Supervision and Curriculum Development, 1978.

Lawson, Hal, and Lawson, Barbara. "An Alternative Program Model for Secondary School Physical Education." *Journal of Physical Education and Recreation* 48 (February 1977): 38–39.

Marlowe, Mike. "Motor Experiences Through Games Analysis." *Journal of Physical Education and Recreation* 52 (January 1981): 78–80.

Meyers, Edward J. "Exercise Physiology in Secondary Schools: A Three Dimensional Approach." *Journal of Physical Education and Recreation* 46 (January 1975): 30–31.

Rog, James A. "Teaching and Textbooks." *Journal of Physical Education and Recreation* 52 (February 1981): 45.

Seidel, Beverly L.; Biles, Fay R.; Figley, Grace E.; and Neuman, Bonnie J. *Sports Skills: A Conceptual Approach to Meaningful Movement,* 2d ed. Dubuque, Iowa: Wm. C. Brown Company Publishers, 1980.

Terry, James W.; Erickson, Charles; and Johnson, Dewayne J. "Changing Habits by Changing Attitudes." *Journal of Physical Education and Recreation* 48 (September 1977): 13.

Understanding Psychomotor Learning
The Learning of Physical Skills

Study stimulators:

1. What processes are included in psychomotor learning?
2. What implications do motor learning principles in the following areas have for instruction:
   a. specific vs. general motor ability?
   b. transfer?
   c. massed vs. distributed practice?
   d. whole vs. part practice?
   e. knowledge of results or feedback?
   f. retention and reminiscence?
3. What are the keys to the effective instruction of psychomotor skills?

Psychomotor learning deals with the learning of physical or neuromuscular skills. By watching a baby learn to walk, we can get an idea of how humans learn motor skills. Once the child gets an idea of what is required and has the prerequisite skills—strength, maturity, and so forth—the child makes crude attempts that are gradually refined through constant feedback from the environment—door, sills, falls, carpet textures, parents "ohing and ahing," etc. Finally, a skilled performance emerges that is unique to that particular toddler.

The taxonomy

The taxonomy for the psychomotor domain shown in table 7.1 follows the normal learning process just described. When learning psychomotor skills, people progress through three stages of development, namely, (1) generic movement, (2) ordinative movement, and (3) creative movement. Examples of each of these stages and processes are presented in table 7.2. An understanding of these stages of development is essential when planning the instructional sequence in physical education. Unless the teacher understands the higher levels of the taxonomy, the tendency is to stop too soon and omit several of the most important aspects of the learning process.[1]

Table 7.1 Proposed taxonomy of educational objectives: the motor domain

Learning behavior	Definition	Terms for writing objectives
1.0 Generic movement	Movement operations or processes, which facilitate the development of human movement patterns.	
1.1 Perceiving	Recognition of movement positions, postures, patterns and skills by means of the sense organs.	Identify Recognize Discover Discriminate
1.2 Imitating	Duplication of a movement pattern or skill as a result of perceiving.	Replicate Duplicate Pantomime
1.3 Patterning	Arrangement and use of body parts in successive and harmonious ways to achieve a movement pattern or skill.	Perform . . . pattern Demonstrate . . . pattern Execute . . . pattern Coordinate . . . pattern
2.0 Ordinative movement	Meeting the requirements of specific movement tasks through processes of organizing, performing and refining movement patterns and skills.	
2.1 Adapting	Modification of a patterned movement or skill to meet specific task demands.	Adjust Apply Employ Utilize
2.2 Refining	Acquisition of smooth, efficient control in performing a movement pattern or skill as a result of an improvment process, e.g., a. elimination of extraneous movements. b. mastery of spatial and temporal relations. c. habitual performance under more complex conditions.	Control Synchronize Improve Systematize Regulate Perform rhythmically (efficiently, smoothly)
3.0 Creative movement	Processes of inventing or creating skillful movements which will serve the unique purposes of the learner.	
3.1 Varying	Invention or construction of unique or novel options in performing a movement pattern or skill.	Alter Change Revise Diversify
3.2 Improvising	Extemporaneous origination or initiation of novel movements or combinations of movements.	Interpret Extemporize Improvise Anticipate
3.3 Composing	Creation of unique movement designs or patterns.	Design Compose Symbolize

Source: Jewett, Ann E., L. Sue Jones, Sheryl M. Luneke, and Sarah M. Robinson. "Educational Change Through a Taxonomy for Writing Physical Education Objectives," *Quest,* XV (January 1971): 35-36.

Generic movement

Generic movement includes the initial processes of receiving information and transforming it into a motor pattern. These processes are perceiving, imitating, and patterning. *Perception* was described in chapter 6 as the basis for all learning. The student must be helped to perceive, or zero in, on the important aspects of the skill to be learned. *Imitating* involves "trying out" a movement pattern or skill. *Patterning* is the process of acquiring a specific movement pattern such as throwing, catching, leaping, or galloping. Guided practice is essential in helping the learner achieve the desired psychomotor objective.

Ordinative movement

Ordinative movement involves the processes of organizing and refining generic movement patterns into skillful movement. *Adapting* consists of modifying a skill to meet the needs of a variety of conditions, such as shooting from different distances at archery targets or adapting to an opponent's movements on a basketball court. *Refining* a skill involves a process of practicing the skill until it becomes smooth, efficient, accurate, and automatic.

Creative movement

Creative movement includes the processes of creating or changing movement patterns to serve the unique needs of the individual performer. In order to be completely at home in activity, students need the experience of developing their creative skills in movement activities.

Varying occurs when the performer changes force, speed, effort, shape, or other variables in order to make the movement unique to the learner. *Improvising* utilizes spontaneous movements to create new or previously untried movements or combinations of movement, such as when a student must recover from an error in a gymnastics routine or when the ball must be saved from traveling out-of-bounds. *Composing* makes use of consciously planned movements to create a new movement or a movement unique to the individual performer. This occurs when a learner choreographs a dance or synchronized swimming routine, or creates a new game or movement skill.

Two examples of each of the processes just identified are presented in table 7.2.

Motor learning principles

A study of motor learning provides us with specific principles that form the basis for determining teaching methods. Without a knowledge of motor learning, teaching would be, at best, a trial-and-error situation. Only a brief review is presented here. For an in-depth study of each area, the reader is referred to the many excellent texts on motor learning that are available.

Specific vs. general motor ability

General motor ability implies that a person has an inherent ability to acquire proficiency in psychomotor skills. If this were true, people would tend to be good performers in all sports or poor performers in all sports.

Specific motor ability implies that the ability to learn motor skills is task-specific or that a person who has a high ability in one motor task may have a low ability in another task. For many years, physical educators believed in the concept of general motor ability and searched for the general qualities they assumed led to the "all-around athlete" and the lack of which led to the "motor moron." This belief led to the attempt by Brace, McCloy, Johnson, Cozens, and others to design tests to measure general motor abilities.

Since the 1950s, Henry and others rejected the concept of general motor ability and reintroduced the concept formerly espoused by some psychologists and physical educators that different movements require different abilities.[2] The fact that some persons seem to be more highly skilled than others may be because they have had the desire and the opportunity to develop proficiency in a large variety of specific movement skills.

The implication for teaching is that each student can achieve proficiency in movement skills if sufficient instruction, motivation, and practice are available. The problem is that units of instruction are often too short for many students to achieve proficiency even when adequate instruction is provided. The challenge is to design and implement a curriculum in which students have the opportunity to receive instruction and practice in the depth necessary for skill mastery. Motivation may also be increased when students have a choice of activities from which to select.

Transfer

Closely related to the topic of specific motor ability is the question of transfer. **Transfer** is the effect that learning one skill has on the learning or performance of another skill.

Transfer theories include (1) the theory that general elements such as balance, kinesthesis, or coordination carry over from one activity to another; (2) the theory that only identical elements (ie., specific elements common to both tasks) transfer; and (3) the theory that transfer occurs as a result of the ability to apply previously learned principles and insights or problem-solving strategies to new situations; and (4) combinations of the general and specific theories.[3]

Laboratory research shows that very little transfer is seen from one task to another, which tends to support the identical elements theory. However, the transfer of general problem-solving and learning strategies is supported when more complex tasks are studied. It is probable that transfer is a result of several factors, including those specific to the task and those inherent in the learning environment.[4]

An understanding of the conditions affecting transfer is essential for planning instruction. Singer listed five conditions that affect transfer. They include (1) the similarity between the tasks, (2) the amount of practice on the first task, (3) the motivation to transfer, (4) the method of training, and (5) the intent of transfer.[5] Cratty adds a sixth condition—the amount of time between tasks.[6]

Table 7.2 Two examples of the movement behaviors described in the taxonomy

Movement process	Balance beam	Soccer
Perceiving	The child walks on the balance beam hesitantly, stops frequently to maintain balance; may hang onto partner or teacher. Experiments with body and arm positions. Child may use a shuffle step or slide step.	After a demonstration, the student replicates a kicking pattern. A fundamental striking pattern (swing) with the foot is the goal of performance. Neither accuracy nor distance is brought into focus.
Patterning	Child walks on the balance beam using an alternating step pattern with a well balanced body position. Some hesitancy or slowness in performance may still exist.	The student executes a kicking pattern. The force, point of contact, and follow through is the focus.
Adapting	Child walks on a balance beam with an alternating step pattern. He/she walks over a wand and through a hula hoop. May lack smoothness in performance.	The student adjusts his/her kicking pattern to perform an instep kick.

Source: Gotts, Sheryl L., unpublished paper, Purdue University, 1972, 1976. Cited in Jewett, Ann E. and Marie R. Mullan. *Curriculum Design: Purposes and Processes in Physical Education Teaching-Learning,* Washington, D.C.: American Association of Health, Physical Education and Recreation, 1977.

Similarity between tasks

This is probably the most important of the six conditions. The greater the similarity between the tasks, the greater the transfer. If there were no similar elements, there would be no transfer (either positively or negatively). In many tasks, however, some elements will yield positive transfer and others will elicit negative transfer. Thus, Cratty indicated that "the degree to which negative or positive transfer is measured depends on whether the *summation* of the negative transfer elements equals, exceeds, or fails to exceed the total of the common elements likely to produce positive transfer."[7]

Movement process	Balance beam	Soccer
Refining	Each time the child walks on the balance beam, he/she performs the task smoothly with an alternating step pattern and good body position. He/she is able to move over the wand and through the hula hoop with no hesitation or loss of body control.	The student performs efficiently the instep kick in soccer. The pattern of the kick is performed smoothly with the same force and accuracy each time.
Varying	The child while walking on the balance beam varies the walk by adding a hop. The child is trying to perform a movement in a different way.	The student alters his/her kicking pattern to perform several variations. The student tries to perform the soccer kick from varying distances and positions from the goal.
Improvising	The child while walking on the beam uses a leap to go over the wand instead of a step.	The student in a game of soccer modifies the pass pattern to take advantage of his/her opponent's being pulled out of position.
Composing	The child designs and performs a series of moves on the balance beam.	The student will be able to design an offensive strategy, (kick at goal) responding to a set pattern of play developed with teammates.

Similar or identical elements can be found in the student's perception of the stimulus or in the response. Negative transfer occurs when the students are asked to respond to the same verbal or visual perception with a different response. For example, if students have practiced rebounding by batting the ball continuously against the backboard during practice, and then are expected to rebound the ball into the basket during a game, negative transfer will occur. Negative transfer may also result when the weight of an object changes, such as when changing from tennis to badminton, or when the speed of the object differs, such as in rallying a ball off a backboard rather than over a net. Similar movements, such as the overarm softball throw and the overhead volleyball serve, differ in that one is a striking skill and the other a throwing pattern.

Positive transfer occurs when there are a number of identical elements between the two tasks, such as the names of the players in softball and baseball. Some positive transfer occurs when the same response is expected to a number of related situations. Examples include shooting at different sizes of targets or different distances in archery, or throwing a ball fielded from many different directions to first base.

When two tasks have many elements that are similar, but not identical, negative transfer results. An example is in the rules and scoring of soccer, speedball, speed-a-way, and field hockey. Tennis, badminton, and racquetball have similarities in eye-hand coordination and agility. However, differences in wrist action and the weight of the object struck can cause negative transfer.

Amount of practice on the first task

Greater positive transfer occurs when the first task is well learned. Less practice on the first task may result in negative transfer. Therefore, skills involving similar movement patterns, such as tennis and racquetball, should not be taught at the same time if the learner is a beginner in both activities.

Motivation to transfer

When motivation toward the transfer of skill or knowledge to a new task is high, greater positive transfer occurs. Increasing the motivation of students should also increase the effects of positive transfer.

Method of training

The highest positive transfer occurs when the whole task is practiced rather than when the parts are practiced separately. For this reason, many current writers discourage the use of drills and progressions to teach skills.

Intent of transfer

When the teacher points out the common elements in the two tasks, the learner will probably make greater transfer to the second task of principles and skills learned in the first task. Often, general problem-solving and learning strategies will transfer to the new situation.

Amount of time between tasks

As the amount of time increases between the learning of two tasks, both negative and positive transfer decline until negative transfer disappears entirely. Since negative transfer decreases faster, there is a point at which positive transfer is at its optimum, before it too disappears. For this reason, skills may be best learned during distributed practice sessions.

The foregoing information reveals some other implications for instruction, especially in the areas of drills and progressions. Nixon and Locke stated:

> Progression is a near sacred principle in physical education, and is taken most seriously in teacher education. Evidence indicates that the faith . . . may be misplaced . . . progressions generally appear not to be significant factors in learning many motor skills.[8]

Progressions, however, are valuable when fear or danger are present. Unless well planned, drills may introduce elements that do not transfer to the game situation. Therefore, drills should be planned so that the environment and movement relationships are as gamelike as possible. Evaluation should also be in as gamelike settings as possible. No objective test has yet been able to replace the subjective opinion of the experts.

Massed versus distributed practice

Massed practice is a practice or a series of practice sessions with little or no rest time allotted between. An example is teaching one skill for the entire physical education period. **Distributed practice** is practice interspersed with rest or alternative activities. This can be done by practicing several skills for a brief period of time during each class session.

Research findings about the advantages of each type of practice are contradictory because of the inconsistency in terminology used. They show that while performance improves with distributed practice, there appears to be no significant difference in learning of gross motor skills between the two methods.[9] This is shown by the fact that the wide differences in performance at the end of practice fail to remain on later tests of retention.[10]

When boredom and fatigue are not factors, massed practice is equally effective with distributed practice, assuming that the number of practice trials is the same. Massed practice has the advantage of reaching the goal sooner under these conditions (i.e., Monday, Wednesday, Friday for 1 hour versus 3 hours on Monday).[11]

Distributed practice sessions in which several skills are practiced during a class period are usually preferred for beginners. This results in less chance of boredom, fatigue, and frustration with learning new skills. When students take turns practicing, a built-in rest interval also occurs.

Lawther listed several factors to consider when planning the frequency and length of practice sessions.[12] They include (1) the learner's age, skill level, and experience; (2) the type of skill to be learned; (3) the purpose of the practice; and (4) the circumstances in the learning environment.

The learner

Younger students and students with low ability levels fatigue easily and have shorter attention, or concentration spans, and lower interest levels. Shorter distributed practices lessen the negative feelings of students and produce the best learning. Older, more highly skilled students may possess high levels of concentration and motivation and, therefore, can tolerate longer practices with less fatigue.

The skill

Strenuous activities often must be scheduled for shorter periods of time due to the effects of fatigue. Complex activities can cause transfer interference resulting in confusion.

The purpose

An overview of an activity may require a different scheduling pattern than intense practice for competition or performance.

The circumstance

Weather conditions, such as heat, cold, smog, rain, and school activities, such as assemblies, may interfere with a practice session. With distributed practice less time is lost when one practice must be cancelled or interrupted than when a massed practice is cancelled.

When scheduling practices, one should remember that the time scheduled is not nearly as important as the amount of time spent in actual activity or the number of trials the learner attempts. Too often, instructors expect a beginner to learn an entirely new activity in a two-week unit (ten days at 30 minutes of instruction per day = 300 minutes) while they spend two hours every day for months coaching talented students in the same basic skills.

Whole vs. part practice

Whole practice is practice of a whole task as opposed to practice of its parts. For example, in the breast stroke in swimming, the whole method is to demonstrate the stroke and have the students imitate and practice it. In **part practice** the whole is broken down into parts, each of which is mastered separately before putting them all together into the whole. For example, the kick might be taught first until it has been mastered. Then, the arms and breathing are taught and practiced. Finally, the coordination of the entire stroke is demonstrated and practiced.

In order to overcome the difficulty experienced by the student when putting the parts together, the **progressive part** method was developed. It consists of learning part one, then learning and adding part two, then part three, and so on until the whole is completed. When learning the breast stroke, for example, the student begins with a glide, then adds the arm stroke, then breathing, and finally the kick.

In a review of thirty studies by Nixon and Locke, none showed the part or progressive part methods to be superior, and the majority found some variation of the whole method to be superior.[13] The basic problem seems to be in the definition of the "whole." Seagoe describes the characteristics of a whole as follows:
"(1) It should be isolated and autonomous, an integrated unity. (2) It must have "form" quality. (3) It must be more than the sum of the parts; it must be a rational structure in itself."[14]

Team and dual sports are not wholes from the practical standpoint of teaching and learning. They are made up of whole skills, such as throwing, catching, dribbling, passing, and shooting. The skills are then combined to form play patterns. In sports that require no interaction with others, such as in archery or bowling, the sport itself may be considered to be a whole for the purposes of instruction.

Implications for teaching are that the learner should begin with a whole that is large enough to be meaningful and challenging but simple enough for success to occur. Meaningfulness is increased when the skill approximates the final objective sought. Work to improve portions of the performance can occur readily during practice of the whole movement. When the complete action is too complex for the beginner to handle, such as in activities in which there is a chance of injury or the learner is afraid, it should then be broken into the largest subwhole that the learner can handle.

Knowledge of results or feedback

Information provided to the learner following a performance that tells about the quality of the performance is called **knowledge of results. Feedback** is information available during the performance. Studies show that little or no learning occurs without feedback or knowledge of results. In fact, Bilodeau and Bilodeau stated, "Studies of feedback or knowledge of results show it to be the strongest, most important variable controlling performance and learning."[15]

Feedback can occur from the performance itself, from the performer's kinesthetic awareness of body position, or from visual or verbal cues from the teacher. It should be matched to the individual learner's comprehension and ability to make use of it in subsequent practice.

Lawther summarized the research on knowledge of results as follows:

1. Learning is proportionally greater as the quality, exactness, and precision of this playback of knowledge of results increases.
2. When knowledge of results is not available, learners often can improve to some extent by setting up their own criteria from past experience, to help them subjectively approximate their results.
3. With a delay of knowledge of results, performance declines.
4. Performance deteriorates when knowledge of results is withdrawn.
5. Continuous and complete knowledge of results fosters much greater learning than discontinuous and incomplete knowledge of results.
6. Precise supplemental aids (graphs, films of action, etc.), which provide more precise knowledge or make apparent the differences between the learner's performance and those of better performers, seem to increase learning.
7. Feedback of incorrect information retards learning in direct proportion to the amount of misinformation.[16]

Application of motor learning research

The questions presented here draw together the principles of motor learning and the processes of psychomotor learning into a useable instructional system. Six keys for effective instruction in psychomotor skills are presented. The remaining chapters of this book will amplify and provide further examples for implementing the model in physical education classes.

Wise selection of activity

Is the activity challenging? Is it possible for students to be successful in the activity?

Are students progressing in skill development?

Appropriate instruction

Are students aware of the objective of the lesson?

Is there an appropriate model of the skill (with cues)?

Is student practice guided by appropriate feedback in an effective learning environment, with verbal, visual, and kinesthetic cues?

Is there an opportunity for students to overlearn the skill?

Is there an opportunity for students to apply the skill (in a gamelike situation)?

Is there an opportunity for creative expression?

Maximum student participation

Is teacher talk reduced to a minimum?

Is roll call and dressing time reduced to a minimum?

Are efficient class organization and equipment management used to minimize time spent in transition from one activity to another?

Do drills or games provide for maximum participation by (1) keeping groups or teams small to provide maximum contact with the equipment for each student, (2) changing rules if necessary to allow students to be active as much as possible, and (3) having several small fields or activity areas instead of one large one?

Equal opportunity for all students

Does instruction consider left-handed students, low-skilled students, highly skilled students, foreign students, socially unadapted students, and female and male students?

Safe participation

Are proper progressions followed?

Are students taught or reminded of safety rules?

Is equipment in good repair and used properly?

Motivation

Were students successful (i.e., did they achieve the objective)?

Did students have fun?

Were students encouraged for honest effort and praised for achievement?

Wise selection of activity

The selection of instructional activities should reflect a logical progression of developmental activities. When planning units and lessons, care should be taken to insure that the selected activities are ones for which students have the essential background knowledges or skills and are ones that challenge the students to improve existing levels of skill. Teaching the spike in volleyball to seventh-grade students who cannot set up the ball is obviously an incorrect choice of activities. On the contrary, teaching beginning volleyball year after year in junior and senior high school is also incorrect.

Instruction in selected activities will always need to be adjusted to challenge students who have a high level of skill or to correct deficiencies so that poorly skilled students can benefit from the instruction. The curriculum, as well as unit and lesson plans, should include a progression in skills from simple to complex.

Appropriate instruction

Objectives

Each unit or lesson should have one or more objectives, and students should be made aware of the objectives or goals to be achieved. Skills to be taught should be the largest possible wholes that the learners can handle.

A correct model of the skill to be taught is essential to successful performance by students.

Model

A correct model of the skill should be provided so that students will gain a correct perception of the successful performance they are trying to achieve. The model could be conveyed visually, verbally, or in written form. However, the visual form is preferred, especially with beginners. If you are unable to demonstrate, then a student or a loop film could be substituted.

Beware of verbalizing the skill. In some classes so much time is spent on talking about the skill that no time is left for practicing it. Remember that a good demonstration is worth a thousand words. Pick out two or three short verbal cues that will help the student perceive the key points of the demonstration without being distracted by nonessential portions of the movement. Too much verbiage or too many cues can be distracting to the learner. Adding cues one at a time can facilitate absorption by the learner. By thinking of potential problem areas for the learner and counteracting those problem areas with positive cues, the most important points will be reinforced. An example of cues for the set in volleyball might be (1) look through the triangle, (2) keep your seat down, and (3) extend. For the badminton clear, the cues might be (1) scratch your back, (2) reach for the shuttle, and (3) make the racket whistle.

The kinesiological or biomechanical analysis of a skill by the instructor is used as a basis for developing cues that focus the students' attention on relevant parts of the skill and provide feedback during the guided practice following the demonstration. In no case should the kinesiological or biomechanical analysis be presented to the student while in the process of learning a new skill. This overloads the limited capacity of the learner with irrelevant details that have no meaning.

Irrelevant elements should be eliminated as much as possible until learners have mastered the beginning stages of a skill. Since students can handle only small amounts of information at a time, "chunking" information can promote retention. For example, in teaching a folk dance, you could present the grapevine step as four separate movements—step to the side, step behind, step to the side, step in front. As soon as the student is familiar with the sequence it can be reduced to one piece of information, the grapevine. The same thing may be done with the entire folk dance. As the sequences of the dance become automatic, the entire dance becomes "chunked" under one piece of information, coded under the name of the dance.

Other factors that can interfere with the learner's attention on the model are visual, auditory, or internal. Visual difficulty takes the form of poor eyesight, sighting into the sun or against a similarly colored background, or other activities occurring in the background. These activities may also include yelling and talking that can interfere with the students' auditory perception. Internal factors include sleepiness, fatigue, boredom, or discouragement.

Guided practice

Following the demonstration, the student should practice the desired skill in the most appropriate environment. The learning environment should include as many of the situations as possible in which the student will actually use the behavior (i.e., a moving [rather than stationary] ball as close to the real speed as possible). In activities involving a ball, stress speed and accuracy rather than just speed or just accuracy. When the skill is too complex, work on speed first and then accuracy. In that way, the movement does not have to be changed from low speed to high speed.

Since most skills are learned best in an atmosphere of positive reinforcement and low muscle tension, care should be taken to avoid a stressful learning situation. Chapter 8 discusses the establishment of an appropriate environment for learning.

Feedback is the strongest, most important variable controlling learning and performance. Feedback from the environmental consequences of the movement performance (i.e., a "strike," "home run," etc.) help the student adapt the performance to meet the desired outcome. This type of feedback is augmented by feedback about the performance itself. The ability to provide meaningful feedback is one of the most important abilities a teacher possesses. Verbal feedback might make use of the verbal cues you used to accompany the initial skill demonstration. Feedback may also be structured by the teacher, such as a rope over a badminton net to encourage correct serving technique. Kinesthetic cues, such as moving a student's arms in the correct swimming pattern, can be useful with some students.

Another valuable feedback technique is a redemonstration of the skill following the initial skill attempts of the student. In all cases, the students' attention should be directed to the essential aspects of the skill and to relevant feedback that will help them to correct

Feedback is the strongest, most important
variable controlling learning.

initial attempts at skill achievement. Gradually, as the students' skills approximate the model, patterning is complete and the cues should be changed so that the skill performance will be more refined.

Repetitive practice

Once the skill can be performed correctly, repetitive practice of the skill in gamelike drills provides for retention and refinement of the skill. Often students can perform the skill upon leaving the class one day and return to the next class unable to repeat it correctly. Repetitive practice will insure that the skill has been learned well enough for retention.

Care should be taken to insure that students are practicing the skill correctly, since practice does not necessarily make perfect. It makes permanent. Interrupt incorrect practice for review and to provide time for forgetting the incorrect performance. Continue to provide feedback on skill performance, especially when the form of the skill is the essential component (i.e., diving or gymnastics). Students should begin to "feel" the correct movements through kinesthetic perception of their own body movements.

It is at this point that physical educators often make the mistake of introducing a new skill rather than refining the skill already presented. Students should be assisted in setting goals for accuracy, distance, speed, quality of movement, and reduction of errors. Practice situations can be modified to meet the needs of specific individuals as they work on their own goals.

Applied practice

Applied practice will, of course, differ for open and closed skills. **Open skills** are those skills in which the student must anticipate and make responses to a large number of environmental stimuli in a brief period of time. These activities require constant adaptations of the learned skill to various situations. In basketball, for example, the ball and the players are constantly moving to provide a changing environment, and skills must be learned to deal with the many possible situations in which the players find themselves. Therefore, drills and lead-up games should approximate the real game environment as closely as possible. Practice in the competitive situation can help students experience the interaction between the skill and the constantly changing environment.

Closed skills, such as archery and bowling, occur in a relatively stable environment. The practice goal here is the refinement of a specified sequence of responses for consistency of performance. Self-testing activities can be helpful in providing feedback to the learners about their performance. Videotape playback is also valuable.

Creative expression

The problem-solving approach presented in chapter 6 could be implemented at this stage of learning to provide students with opportunities for the creative application of psychomotor skills to the infinite possibilities that exist in the movement environment. Students can be challenged to develop game strategies, create new games, compose gymnastic routines, choreograph dances, and a host of other problem-solving behaviors.

Maximum student participation

Instruction should be provided in a way that allows maximum participation by each student. The organization of time, space, equipment, rules, and group size all affect the amount of time each student has to participate in the activity and, therefore, to achieve success.

Time

Because time is at a premium in most physical education classes, care should be taken to eliminate noninstructional activities as much as possible and to reduce the time spent in activities such as roll call, equipment distribution and collection, and unnecessary showering or time spent dressing for activity just to discuss the rules. Many physical educators could also reduce teacher talk to a minimum by using more effective demonstrations with cues, thereby increasing practice time for students. Well-planned lessons will also eliminate time spent in transitions from one activity to another. Other suggestions for increasing the actual student learning time are included in each of the areas below.

Space

Facilities in physical education have not always kept up with the demand, resulting in large classes in facilities built for few students. By making use of community and commercial facilities as well as hallways and multipurpose rooms, some additional space can be acquired. However, physical education teachers have often ignored the possibility of adjusting group sizes among themselves to fit the spaces available. For example, if two instructors have a class of eighty and only four tennis courts, it is possible to divide the students into one group of sixty or more to learn soccer so that the other twenty or so can be instructed in tennis. Another possibility is to offer two units simultaneously, such as badminton and jump rope. Students can also officiate, mark ratings on incidence charts, work on contracts or skill checklists, or rotate in every two minutes.

Equipment

Maximum participation requires appropriate quantities of equipment. Although one ball or bat may be appropriate for game play, individual dribbling practice requires one ball per student. Teachers should provide for maximum use of equipment within the limits of safety and practicality. Using training balls and balls of various sizes can increase the chances of success. Very small balls are difficult to catch. Very large balls may be too big for tiny hands to throw accurately.

Rules

By changing game rules, students can experience all of the facets of the game in a shorter period of time. For example, a seven-inning "one-swing" softball game can be played in one class period, whereas in a regulation game, some students will "sit" in left field for the entire period waiting for a turn at bat. Lowering the volleyball net allows players who have never been able to spike to enjoy that aspect of the game.

Group size

By keeping teams small, students will have the opportunity to play the ball more often. The use of many smaller teams, on smaller fields if necessary, provides the opportunities students need to apply skills to game situations.

Equal opportunity for all students

One of the most difficult things for a physical education teacher to do is to adapt class instruction to meet the needs of the wide variety of students who appear in classes. There are boys and girls, low-skilled and highly skilled, slow learners and gifted students, normal and handicapped, and a large number of different cultural and ethnic backgrounds, including many non-English-speaking students.

In order to meet the needs and interests of each student, programs should include a broad spectrum of activities, with occasional opportunities for students to select their own preferences. Activities should also be provided on various skill levels. Grouping students by ability level within classes can help low-skilled students experience success while, at the same time, it provides a challenge for the more highly skilled. Individual contracts or units can also be used to individualize instruction. A number of learning activities that can be used to individualize instruction to meet the differing learning needs of students are presented in chapter 14.

Most activities can be adapted to meet the needs of students of varying abilities by decreasing time periods, modifying courts, fields, and equipment and by changing the rules. Jones summarized some of the problems of inadequate equipment as follows:

> . . . having students practice with balls, striking implements, bows, or other equipment that is too heavy or cumbersome may be particularly deleterious to proper acquisition of skill. For example, a bowling instructor may furnish a perfect demonstration model of the four-step approach and delivery and use excellent teaching cues, but all of this will go for naught on a student who is struggling just to hang on to a fourteen pound ball. Other examples observed far too often in physical education classes include: tennis racquets too heavy for youngsters to handle properly, archery bows too heavy to be drawn correctly, balls too big or heavy and baskets too high for correct execution of skills by the students involved. In volleyball, a student may be reluctant to practice the forearm or bump pass correctly because it hurts his arms.[17]

By adapting activities to meet the needs of individual students, they will learn faster and experience positive attitudes toward physical activity.

Safe participation

Care should be taken to insure safe participation in activities. Teachers should inspect facilities and equipment daily and teach students to follow safety rules. Teaching skills in order of difficulty, from simple to complex, with appropriate practice and supervision also helps to prevent accidents.

Motivation

A variety of teaching techniques should be utilized to make learning fun and satisfying. By reducing boredom, motivation also increases the attention and, therefore, the perception of students. Chapter 9 discusses various techniques for motivating learning. The real key to motivation, however, is student success in the activity and its accompanying rewards.

Questions and suggested activities

1. How can an understanding of the processes of learning psychomotor skills be helpful to you as a teacher? As a performer?

2. What implications do each of the motor learning principles studied in this chapter have for you as a teacher of physical education? As a coach? Are they the same or different?

3. What are the six essential keys for effective psychomotor instruction?

4. How would you rate as a teacher in terms of your ability to use the keys of effective instruction in an actual teaching situation? Use the questions in the chapter as a guide.

5. What two principles can you use to help you select appropriate activities for students?

6. What can be done to maximize student learning in the following situations:
   a. You are teaching a basketball unit to forty-five eighth-graders. You have only one court and wish to let the students have the opportunity of playing a three-day tournament on a full-court. What will you do with the students who are not active in the game?
   b. You are teaching a badminton unit to forty-five ninth-graders. You have three courts. How will you provide for all players to practice fundamentals? How will you keep every student active and succeed in letting each student have the opportunity to play a regulation game?

Suggested readings

Annarino, Anthony. "Accountability: An Instructional Model for Secondary Physical Education, *Journal of Physical Education and Recreation* 52(March 1981):55–56.

Barrett, Kate R. "Observation for Teaching and Coaching," *Journal of Physical Education and Recreation* 50(January 1979):23–25.

Bertel, H. "Try What? Introduction of a New Activity in the Physical Education Class," *Journal of Health Physical Education Recreation* 45(May 1974):24.

Brown, Eugene W. "Visual Evaluation Techniques for Skill Analysis," *Journal of Physical Education, Recreation, and Dance* 53(January 1982):21–26, 29.

Chew, Richard A. "Verbal, Visual, and Kinesthetic Error Feedback in the Learning of a Simple Motor Task," *Research Quarterly* 47(May 1976):254–59.

Clumpner, Roy A. "Maximizing Participation and Enjoyment in the PE Classrooms," *Journal of Physical Education and Recreation* 50(January 1979):60–62.

Docherty, David and Les Peake. "Creatrad: An Approach to Teaching Games," *Journal of Physical Education and Recreation* 47 (April 1976):20–22.

Jones, Nancy Bondurant. "Show Students You Care!" *Today's Education* 70 (November–December 1981):44.

Klesius, Stephen E. "Wide-Width of Acceptability Games," *Journal of Physical Education and Recreation* 50 (April 1979):66–67.

Kulewicz, Stan. "The Children, Not the Games," *Journal of Physical Education and Recreation* 52 (April 1981): 67–69.

Larche, Harry E. and Douglas W. Larche. "Success and Excellence in Teaching: Reality Therapy for Physical Education," *The Physical Educator* 32(December 1975):194–98.

Lay, Nancy. "Practical Application of Selected Motor Learning Research," *Journal of Physical Education and Recreation* 50 (September 1979):78–79.

Morris, G. S. Don. *How to Change the Games Children Play*, 2d ed. (Minneapolis: Burgess Publishing, 1980).

Rink, Judith E. "The Teacher Wants Us to Learn," *Journal of Physical Education and Recreation* 52(February 1981):17–18.

Singer, Robert N. and Richard F. Gerson. "Task Classification and Strategy Utilization in Motor Skills," *Research Quarterly for Exercise and Sport* 52 (March 1981):100–16.

Understanding Affective Learning
The Learning of Attitudes, Appreciations, and Values

Study stimulators

1. What is affective learning? Is it a worthwhile goal for physical education?
2. What relationship exists between teaching physical education and affective learning?
3. What are the best methods for incorporating affective learning into the teaching of physical education?

Affective learning refers to the emotional aspect of learning. It deals with how students feel about the learning experience, how they feel about the subject, and how they feel about themselves. It considers their interests, appreciations, attitudes, values, and character.

Since attitudes and appreciations cannot be measured directly, we infer them by the tendencies of persons to engage in certain behaviors when they have positive attitudes and in certain other behaviors when they have negative attitudes toward some subject. For example, Greta has a positive attitude toward sports events. This attitude is demonstrated by the fact that she talks about sports, attends every sporting event she possibly can, and learns the names and characteristics of each of the players. Once she even took her radio to a club meeting so she could listen to a championship game.

In general, people who like something keep going back for more experiences with the subject. They seek opportunities to be involved with the subject in preference to other activities. The stronger their attraction, the more obstacles they will overcome to get involved and stay involved. On the contrary, people who don't like something choose to engage in something other than the subject. They go to great lengths to avoid it, by changing the subject, inventing excuses, or walking away from it. When forced to become involved in instructional situations that they dislike, they threaten never to have anything to do with the subject in the future. Once such an attitude has developed, the chances are slim that it will be reversed, since the opportunities to influence students become fewer and fewer as time goes by.

The taxonomy of affective behaviors developed by Krathwohl, Bloom, and Masia describes levels on a continuum of internalization of behaviors.[1] To illustrate with an example from physical education, Adam first becomes aware of what physical fitness is, begins to listen to material concerning fitness activities, and even selects and reads articles about fitness to the exclusion of other reading materials. Adam then responds to this information by forming an opinion about physical fitness, initially only by complying with a teacher-initiated fitness program. He participates voluntarily in a school-sponsored fitness program and begins to feel some satisfaction in doing so. Later, he can be seen trying to convince his

Table 8.1 The affective domain

Levels of behavior	Terms for objectives	

1. *Receiving:*—Involves passive attention to stimuli:
    —awareness of a fact, occurrence, event or incident
    —willingness to notice or attend to a task
    —selecting stimuli
	Notice
	Select
	Tolerate
	Be aware or conscious of
	Listen	

2. *Responding:*—Involves doing something about stimuli:
    —complying, following directions
    —voluntarily involves self
    —satisfaction or enjoyment
	Comply
	Follow
	Volunteer
	Enjoy
	Be satisfied
	Agree or disagree
	React
		Give opinion
		Sympathize with
		Appreciate
		Attend
		Read
		Accept responsibility

3. *Valuing:*—Places worth on something; involves display of behavior consistent with values:
    —expressing strong belief in something
    —expressing preference for something
    —seeking activity to further something and convert others to own way of thinking
	Prefers consistently
	Supports consistently
	Pursues activities
	Involves others
	Debates
	Argues
	Values
		Purchases
		Improves skills

4. *Organization:*—Organizes values into a system:
    —seeing how the value relates to other values held
    —establishing interrelationships and dominance of values
	Discuss codes, standards
	Formulate systems
	Weigh alternatives against standards
	Define criteria
	Base decisions on values	

5. *CHARACTERIZATION:*—acts consistently with internalized value system:
    —acting consistently in a certain way and can be described by others in terms of actions or values
    —developing a total *consistent* philosophy of life, integrating beliefs, ideas, and attitudes
	Demonstrate consistent behavior or methods
	Integrate total behavior or values	

Source: Concepts taken from Krathwohl, David R.; Bloom, Benjamin S.; and Masia, Bertram B. *Taxonomy of Educational Objectives, Handbook II: Affective Domain.* New York: David McKay Co., 1964.

friends of the importance of a fitness program. The young man then internalizes his conviction of the importance of physical fitness and incorporates it into his hierarchy of values. His own beliefs now guide his actions rather than the opinions of others. Adam becomes so committed to the importance of physical fitness that he may even decide on a career in or do volunteer work instructing others about the importance of physical fitness.

A close relationship exists between the affective domain and the other two. By learning about something (cognitive) or doing some skill (psychomotor), instructors can produce attitudinal changes in students. We can also motivate students to learn cognitive or psychomotor skills by increasing positive attitudes toward physical education.

Is affective education a worthwhile goal for physical educators?

As we look at the total educational setting, we can identify affective learning possibilities in almost every area. But, compared with cognitive and psychomotor learning, very little, if any, affective learning has been deliberately introduced into the physical education curriculum. What has been present in many cases is a preponderance of negative affect that is generated by such procedures as enforced group calisthenics or structured units with little or no personal relevance to the students.

There are several reasons for this negative effect. One reason for this may be that it is easy to teach cognitive facts and psychomotor skills, but it takes training to incorporate affective learning into the educational process. The widespread attitude that the students' beliefs and values are private and should not be tampered with in the schools is a second reason. Third, society fluctuates in the affective objectives it wants or doesn't want taught in its schools. The constant change makes many teachers and administrators wary of teaching any values at all and so they resort to those areas of the curriculum with which they are more comfortable—knowledge and skills.

It should be obvious that because students are thinking-feeling beings, no intellectual or psychomotor learning can possibly occur without some sort of feelings being involved—feelings about themselves, the subject matter, and the situation.

In each student's feelings and values are powerful forces that determine or control the individual and ultimately the society. Sometimes these forces block learning; on other occasions they enhance it. When a teacher is aware of the existence of students' feelings and their relationships to physical education, he or she can do a lot to insure that appropriate learning situations are provided.

Allport has stated that "If the school does not teach values it will have the effect of denying them."[2] By ignoring attitudes and values, we ignore the fact that students and teachers come to the educational environment with value systems already built in. They have interests, attitudes, and feelings learned from their homes, televisions, peer groups, churches, and other sources. We must start from where they are and carry on from there. School is more than just a place where academic skills are taught and learned. School is a miniature community where members interact and influence the behavior of each other.[3]

When schools ignore the affective domain and put pressure on students to learn apart from their feelings and interests, students often end up regarding learning as something to be tolerated or a "system to be beaten." Emotional tensions often result in antisocial or even criminal behaviors. Obviously, consideration of affective learning is essential to education. One's tastes, preferences, attitudes, values, and ideals will ultimately affect how one chooses to behave.

Any society has some values that permeate the entire society and, as an agent of society, the school is obligated to transmit them to the young. History demonstrates that many of the values imparted to us by others have been those cherished by the American people, including loyalty, self-discipline, honesty, and hard work. The recent emphasis on "doing one's own thing" results in selfishness and the destruction of many of the values we have traditionally held to be true.

Kahn and Weiss aptly summarized the conclusions of the proponents of affective education as follows: "Education cannot afford the luxury of having its most important affective outcomes occur as accidents or unintended effects of the curriculum and of school life in general."[4]

As physical educators, our primary purpose of teaching students in the affective domain is to help them learn how to deal with their emotions and attitudes towards physical education and towards others. Hopefully, we are helping them to develop some positive attitudes toward participation in physical activity. Society also places demands on individuals to develop character and values. These character traits are necessary to continue upholding society's standard.

Klausmeier and Goodwin have suggested that the following attitudes are worth fostering:

Liking for the subject being presented

Liking for teachers

Liking for classmates

Liking for school generally

Starting work promptly

Working with enthusiasm and vigor

Following directions

Taking care of property

Observing safety rules

Being courteous to others

Some students have said that the attitudes in this list smack of conformity. But few disagreed with the idea of fostering self-respect in pupils, respect for others, openmindedness, freedom from prejudice, and the promotion of individuality and self-actualization.[5]

Application of affective research

The following questions summarize the important components of affective learning. They will be discussed in detail in the pages which follow. Further examples will be provided in the remaining chapters of the text.

Be an effective model

Are you an example of the affective behavior you desire your students to acquire?

Establish an environment in which optimum learning can occur

Are aversive conditions in physical education kept to a minimum?

Is the student's contact with physical education followed by positive consequences?

Improve student self-esteem and confidence

Is the student treated as a unique, special individual?

Does each student have the opportunity to experience success in the program?

Do students have the skills for nurturing their own self-esteem?

Be an effective model

Since much of our behavior is a result of following the example of others, it is imperative that physical education teachers be examples of what they are attempting to teach. This is especially true in the realm of the affective. If the teacher demonstrates a negative attitude toward the subject, unsportsmanlike behavior, or dishonesty, the students can be expected to do likewise. Teachers should take pride in themselves and their teaching. Many teachers are not convinced that they are competent. They don't compliment themselves on doing a good job. Their students, therefore, like their models, see themselves as incompetent and develop poor self-concepts.

Students have models in parents, siblings, teachers, peers, or public figures such as sports, television, or movie stars. To serve as a model, the person must be someone the learner respects and with whom the learner identifies. Models are more effective teachers when their actions are viewed as leading to some type of reinforcement.

Research demonstrates that if we desire to increase positive attitudes and behaviors toward physical education in our students, we must exhibit those same attitudes and behaviors ourselves, including physical fitness, participation, and enjoyment in activity. Wise administrators would be advised to hire the kind of people they want their students to model. Teachers would be wise to also identify appropriate models within the students' peer group.

Establish an environment in which optimum learning can occur

One of the purposes of physical education is to promote the enjoyment of physical activity so that students will continue to engage in activity after they have left our immediate influence.

Since the teacher or coach may be one of the primary influences on student attitudes toward physical education and, since the likelihood of a student engaging in physical activity is influenced by his or her attitudes towards activity, it follows that an important objective of every teacher should be to have the student leave his or her influence with as favorable an attitude toward physical education as possible. Only in this way can you encourage the student to remember and use what you have taught and increase the chances of the student's learning even more about physical education in the future.

In order to accomplish this objective, it is imperative that we arrange our instructional system so that each time students are in the presence of any physical education instructional or extracurricular activity they are, at the same time (1) in the presence of positive conditions and consequences and (2) in the presence of as few aversive conditions and consequences as possible. This does not mean to imply that all physical education instruction should be fun, but rather that, given the appropriate conditions, students will work harder. In order to end on a positive note, let's consider the negative conditions first.

Eliminate the negative

An *aversive* condition is one that causes physical or emotional discomfort. It is anything that causes students to lose their self-respect or that diminishes the self-concept. When associated with a student's physical education experience, it results in the student's dislike for physical education and results in the avoidance of physical education in the future.

Although it is not always possible to determine whether a given condition is positive or negative for a certain student, Mager has suggested a number of conditions or consequences which are generally considered to be aversive.[6] They include the following general areas. In each case, specific examples related to physical education have been added.

Pain (physical discomfort)

1. Forcing students to overdo in a physical fitness program, resulting in nausea, sore muscles, etc.

2. Failing to provide adequate safety, with resulting injury.

3. Making students sit for long periods of time when dressed for activity.

4. Allowing the classroom to be too hot or too cold.

5. Forcing students to rush from one class to another or to dress more quickly than is reasonable.

6. Using subject matter as an instrument of punishment.

Anxiety (mental or emotional discomfort or anticipated unpleasantness)

1. Being unpredictable about what is expected or how it will be graded.

2. Expressing that there is no way the student can succeed.

3. Using vague, threatening punishment.

Frustration (interference with goal-directed activities)

1. Presenting information or skills faster or slower than the student can learn them or forcing all students to learn at the same pace.

2. Providing learning materials without regard for the students' abilities.

3. Teaching one thing and testing another.

4. Failure to provide immediate and/or adequate feedback.

5. Stopping an activity just as the students are beginning to enjoy and be absorbed in it.

6. Overemphasizing competition during class time.

Humiliation and embarrassment (lowered self-respect, pride, or painful self-consciousness)

1. Making a public spectacle of a student such as making the student do push-ups while the class watches or belittling the student's attempts to do well.

2. Repeated failure.

3. Labeling students—"special ed.," "handicapped" etc.

4. Wearing uniforms that are uncomfortable and ill-fitting, or immodest.

Boredom

1. Talking in a monotone.

2. Making students repeat instruction they've already had.

3. Failure to challenge students.

4. Failure to use variety in presenting course content.

Obviously, no teacher has control over all of the aversive conditions or consequences that students face. However, by analyzing your teaching behavior and environment, you can become aware of those aversive conditions or consequences over which you can have an influence. First, videotape one or more class sessions. Then, review the videotape in private. You may also need to review the materials used in your course and the administrative policies that affect your students. If you really want to know how students feel, talk to a few students and get their reactions to your teaching. For more information on teacher evaluation, refer to chapter 19.

Accentuate the positive

A positive condition or consequence is one that increases the students' self-esteem and confidence and increases the chances of a student repeating the activity in which he or she is engaged. Positive practices include:

Content-oriented conditions

1. Providing challenging instruction that leads to success most of the time.

2. Helping students know what the course objectives are and where they are in relation to the goal.

3. Preassessing students and individualizing instruction accordingly.

4. Providing instructional tasks that will help students achieve course objectives.

5. Providing immediate, specific feedback in a positive way.

6. Helping students to develop confidence in their performance by overlearning skills.

7. Relating new information to that already learned by the student.

8. Keeping verbal instruction to a minimum.

9. Using only relevant test items for the specified objectives.

10. Allowing students to select some learning activities.

11. Basing grades on each student's achievement, not on how well the other students performed.

Student-oriented conditions

1. Expressing genuine interest in the students and in their individual successes.

2. Treating each student as a person.

3. Acknowledging students' responses as legitimate learning attempts even when incorrect.

4. Allowing students to learn without public awareness of errors.

Environment

1. Providing an environment in which students feel accepted, supported, and trusted.

2. Providing a wide range of activities in which students can choose to involve themselves with appropriate counseling.

3. Increasing the ratio of positive to negative experiences of students by focusing on what students can do rather than on what they can't do.

Improving student self-esteem and self-confidence

Self-esteem and self-confidence have to do with a belief in one's own worth and positive attitudes towards one's own abilities. In order to understand and accept other people, it is essential that individuals first learn to understand and accept themselves. The foundation for self-esteem and self-confidence is laid in infancy. Love leads to trust and a sense of being acceptable and worthwhile. Children who are unloved develop a sense of being unworthy and inadequate. Children's associations outside the home modify or reinforce their self-esteem. Children often feel inadequate and make many mistakes. Adults need to overcome these negative influences by providing successful experiences for children in each area of their lives.

Once the self-concept is formed and internalized, we tend to nurture it by searching out experiences to validate it. For example, if John feels he is a failure, he will not try to learn. He will continue to fail, since that supports his image of himself. If he hates himself, he tends to hate everything else he does in life.

It is obvious, then, that positive feelings must be internalized before behavior can be changed. To change a student's self-concept, significant people in the student's life need to provide encouragement and acceptance over a long period of time. These significant people include family, friends, neighbors, and teachers. Because the self-concept is an enduring one, even minor changes for the better should be applauded.

Unless knowledges and skills are related to students' attitudes, feelings, and beliefs about themselves and their fears and concerns about the community that surrounds them, the likelihood is that education will have a limited influence on their behavior. If we, as physical educators, are able to discover the emotional forces that motivate students, we will be able to effectively involve students from any background in the learning experience, regardless of the instructional methods employed.

Instruction then becomes a matter of linking the cognitive and psychomotor aspects of the curriculum to the intrinsic feelings and concerns of the students. It is unlikely that students will learn anything without also developing attitudes toward the subject or toward themselves. It is also unlikely that they will develop self-esteem and self-confidence without learning some skills for which they feel rewarded. By validating these feelings and experiences, we tell students that they are worthwhile.

Combs stated:

> The student takes his self-concept with him wherever he goes. He takes it to Latin class, to arithmetic class, to gym class, and he takes it home with him. Wherever he goes, his self-concept goes, too. Everything that happens to him has an effect on his self-concept.

Are we influencing that self-concept in positive or negative ways? We need to ask ourselves these kinds of questions. How can a person feel liked unless somebody likes him? How can a person feel wanted unless somebody wants him? How can a person feel acceptable unless somebody accepts him? How can a person feel he's a person with dignity and integrity unless somebody treats him so? And how can a person feel that he is capable unless he has some success? In the answers to those questions, we'll find the answers to the human side of learning.[7]

A unique, special individual

Research has demonstrated a relationship between the extent to which teachers are interested in students as individuals and the extent to which students enjoy physical education classes and continue to participate in physical activities outside of class. When this interest takes the form of trusting and respecting the learner as an individual, the learning environment is enhanced. Someone once said, "One can survive in an atmosphere of acceptance, but only in the loving air of being *cherished* can one fully blossom."

An important part of this interest is communication, not just a communication of words, but a communication of feelings. The teacher realizes that within every student lies an inner self which can be reached only through invitation from the student. This invitation will never be issued until the student feels the sincere, unselfish concern of a warm and loving teacher. When this happens, openness and teachability result. It is only at the feeling level that people's lives are changed. This level is reached by active listening. To love is to listen. A teacher who listens to a student sends the student a message, "I love you. Your feelings are important to me." Listening is different from hearing. It involves putting yourself into the other person's shoes and listening with the heart.

Stephens wrote, "I have learned . . . that the head does not hear anything until the heart has listened, and that what the heart knows to-day the head will understand tomorrow."[8] It involves patience and compassion. Hanks added:

> The time to listen is when someone needs to be heard. The time to deal with a person with a problem is when he has the problem. The time to listen is the time when our interest and love are vital to the one who seeks our ear and our heart and our help. . . .
>
> Every human being is trying to say something to others, trying to cry out, "I am alive. Notice me! Speak to me! Listen to me! Confirm for me that I am important, that I matter."[9]

A teacher can be the one that confirms that the student matters. When talking to a student, take every opportunity to encourage the student to express feelings by asking such questions as "Would you explain that?," "How do you feel about that?," "What would you have done?," or "Why do you think it turned out like that?" Then, listen with understanding, by noting the student's facial expressions, posture, and tone of voice as well as what is said. Teachers are unable to give effective help unless they understand the problems and conflicts of their students.

Other ways in which you can show that you care about each student include calling each student by name and recognizing each student in some way each day. Learn something about each student—interests, achievements, hobbies, favorite subject, favorite sport, family life, etc. Get feedback from students on how they would like their class to be run.

A file card or dittoed form handed out at the beginning of the year or unit could solicit answers to such questions as:

1. Most of all, what do you like to do?

2. What is your favorite game, sport, or hobby?

3. What are your expectations of the class? The teacher? Yourself?

4. How would you like the class to be run? How will you help?

5. What would you like me to know about you?

A snapshot or photo of each student can also be helpful in learning names and helping to bring to mind specific needs of students in your classes.

Make it your business to be in strategic places at strategic times—such as the school play or a band concert when a student of yours is participating. Seek opportunities to say "hello" when you see them in the hall or on the street. Compliment students, and interact with them. Sit with them at football games or in the cafeteria. Notice their achievements in other curricular areas such as the school newspaper, home economics, wood shop, or in out-of-school service to the community. Share student successes with other teachers and administrators.

When teaching lessons, seek to adjust the content in light of student needs and interests. Encourage student involvement and sharing. Make it easy for students to ask questions and make comments. Counsel with individuals regarding fitness and skill test scores so students know where they stand with regard to class goals.

Become acquainted with parents, families, and friends of your students. Take opportunities to talk to each student. Compliment students when deserved and appropriate. Pat them on the back for a job well done. Emphasize their positive qualities. Move around the class so you can get a better feel for the accomplishments of each student. Focus your attention on both the skilled and the unskilled. All of them deserve equal time and attention. Avoid embarassing students by choosing-up teams, allowing some students to experience continual failure in competition, or requiring students to perform in front of their peers.

Give students an opportunity to accept leadership positions and rotate positions often so every student can participate. Don't do for students what they can do for themselves. Students can be assigned to greet visitors, demonstrate skills, give brief reports, lead exercises, and issue and set-up equipment. Know the current needs and interests of your students and work them into the program whenever possible. Provide each student with the opportunity for success and recognition.

Sigmund Freud's niece once recalled a mushroom hunt her uncle had during a family outing. By the end of the activity each child had a prize—for the biggest, oddest, smallest, first, last, or other mushroom. Similar awards or recognition could be given to students in physical education or intramural programs. Some possibilities include participant of the month, best equipment monitor, best sport, best official, most improved player or official, or best scorer. In most cases recognition before the class carries more weight than individual recognition because of the need for peer approval.

Gustafson suggested constructing a checklist listing your own personal strategies for enhancing self-esteem.[10] This could be used as a self-check to see how well you are doing in incorporating these items into your teaching routine.

Opportunity for success

Goethe once said, "If you treat an individual as he is, he will stay as he is. But if you treat him as if he were what he could and ought to be, he will become what he ought to be." The Pygmalion effect so dramatically portrayed in George Bernard Shaw's *Pygmalion* was later demonstrated to occur in the classroom in studies by Rosenthal and Jacobson, and many others as reviewed by Brophy and Good.[11,12] The studies found that students perform in agreement with the perceived expectations of their teachers. This was generally found to be more likely when the students were children than when they were adults and especially true of disadvantaged children in urban schools.

Although no studies of the self-fulfilling prophecy appear to have been done in physical education classes, the implication for teaching is still clear, that successful teachers are those who believe that their students are capable of success and communicate that belief to their students.

Students who enter school with a positive self-concept based on successful experiences are able to adjust to even the negative aspects of school. Students who enter with a poor self-concept tend to be "flattened" by the pressures that are heaped upon them.

Since self-esteem is linked to body image and skill in physical activities, a program that helps students develop physical fitness and proficiency in activity skills can increase self-esteem, as well as attitudes toward physical activity in general.

A challenge for every physical educator is to get each student on the avenue of success by planning situations in small, sequential steps so that all students can succeed as often as possible. Although this takes more time, it is rewarding because students progress more rapidly and there are fewer discipline problems. For a discouraged student, even a small success can be a boost, since often these students feel that they have never experienced success before. As skills are learned and small successes become big successes, self-esteem begins to increase.

Once students begin to experience success, they show a willingness to try new skills, they put forth greater effort, they obtain more success, and the circle continues as shown in figure 8.1. On the contrary, failure results in an unwillingness to try and little or no effort.

Plan a variety of activities so students can find at least one that interests them. Use a variety of teaching techniques to provide for differences in learning styles. Include noncompetitive activities in the curriculum.

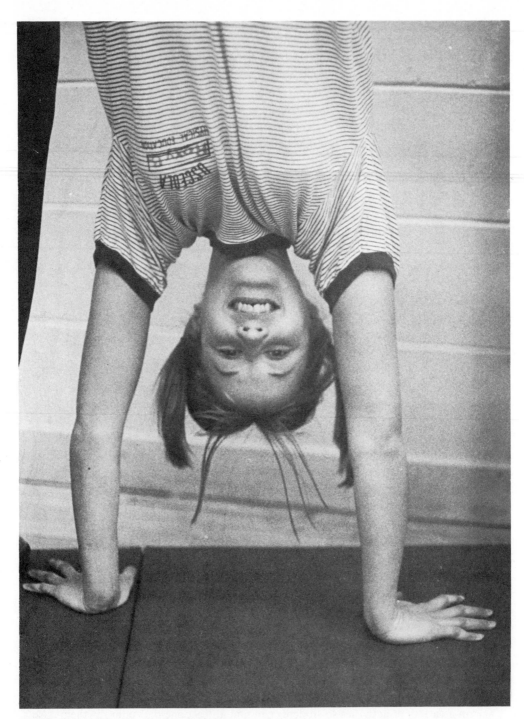

Success in physical activities increases self-esteem.

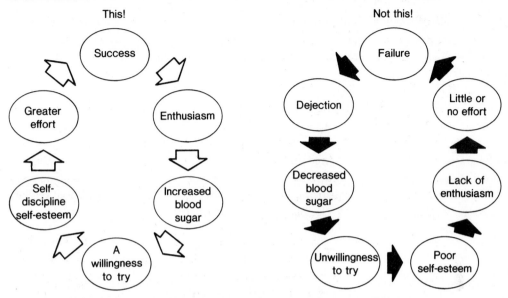

Figure 8.1 Failure and success cycles in students.
Source: Health, Physical Education and Recreation Newsletter, Utah State Office of Education.

Change grading policies to meet the needs of the students. "Learn three new skills" would challenge all students in gymnastics, while "perform a somersault dismount off the balance beam" might discourage all but a few. Consider a combination of factors rather than just skill alone.

Occasionally, you would do well to engage in skills for which you have little competence or expertise, thereby showing by your behavior that you know how difficult it is to learn a new and unfamiliar skill. This skill could be taught by a student or student teacher.

Harris emphasized the importance of students entering the "psychological door" through enjoyment in a specific physical activity that has meaning for them.[13] One of the main goals of physical education should be to get students to incorporate physical activities into their life-styles. Students must experience successful participation in physical activities in a warm, supportive, positive environment, with teachers who care if they are to continue to participate outside of the school setting.

Skills for developing self-esteem

Felker developed five keys for improving the self-concept based on helping students develop the language necessary to enhance and maintain the self-concept.[14] They include (1) adults, praise yourselves, (2) help students to evaluate realistically, (3) teach students to set reasonable goals, (4) teach students to praise themselves, and (5) teach students to praise others.

Praise yourselves

Because students learn by imitating a model, teachers must learn to praise themselves in front of their students. Begin by expressing how good it makes you feel that you accomplished such and so. Later, expand to praise of your personal qualities. Environmental situations can also be praised. Try to use a variety of different phrases for praising.

Help students evaluate realistically

Students need to learn to evaluate what was actually achieved and the level that can be considered to be a measure of success. Negative evaluations that are accurate can prove to be a catalyst toward behavior change that will result in success. When the student evaluates unrealistically, however, a performance change may still be regarded as a failure. One way of helping students evaluate realistically is to have them check off skills or grade and record test scores as they achieve them. See chapter 11 for examples of check-off charts and other useful techniques.

Teach students to set realistic goals

Research shows that students with poor self-concepts tend to set unrealistic goals (either too high or too low) and then perceive themselves as failures when they fail to achieve those goals or when they achieve a goal that anyone, even they, could reach. Students must be taught to set their own goals. When students set their own goals, their commitment to reaching them is increased. However, they must be helped to set realistic goals as compared to their own past performance and not in relation to the group. This is difficult to do when a norm-referenced grading system is employed. (See chapter 12.) Goals should be set slightly higher than prior performances for the most effective learning to occur. Students should then move step-by-step up the ladder toward a long-term goal that may be more compatible with the teacher's long-term expectations. Short-term goals are geared toward success and lend themselves to appropriate praise and reward for achievement.

Teach students to praise themselves

By teaching students to praise themselves, the teacher is released from the role of behavior-reinforcer and the students become the reinforcers of their own behavior. Teachers can help them do this by beginning with group praise, such as "Didn't we do well . . . ?" and then moving to "Don't you think you did a great job on. . . ?" Students can brainstorm a list of adjectives for praising themselves and others. An "I'm okay day" in which students write or tell something nice about themselves can also help students begin to understand the concept of self-praise.

Students could also be helped to evolve from self-encouraging statements such as "I am trying hard," or "I am improving," to self-praise, such as "I did a good job," or "I am a good sport." As students praise themselves, they attach the label of "worthwhile" to themselves and their behavior and their self-esteem rises.

Teach students to praise others

Felker points out that self-praise and praise of others are positively correlated. Praising others tends to result in satisfying responses from others, but students need to be taught how to handle the few negative responses that might result. They also need to be taught how to receive praise; sometimes by praising in return, sometimes by a simple "thank you."

Questions and suggested activities

1. Freud once said that "No one ever does anything unless he would rather." What does this statement suggest about affective learning?

2. How can you tell whether or not a student feels good about physical education?

3. How can you increase the chances of a student's feeling good about physical education?

4. You have been hired to teach physical education at an institution for juvenile delinquents. These students have had little or no experience with succeeding at anything. Your assignment is to provide instruction that will help them succeed. What factors will you consider?

5. It has been suggested that "Winning is not the most important thing. It is the only thing!" How does it feel to lose? Try the following activity:

   a. Have someone draw a diagram with squares or rectangles similar to the one shown here:

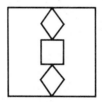

   b. Have the person *tell* you how to reproduce the diagram without showing it to you or answering any questions. Could you draw it? If you were successful, would you like to try again? If you failed, will you risk another try? Repeat the experience in competition with several others. Set a time limit. Then, try it working with a partner to complete the diagram. Which way did you like best? What did this experience tell you about winning and losing? About your self-concept?
   Source: Kneer, Marian E. "How Human Are You? Exercises in Awareness." *Journal of Health Physical Education Recreation* 45 (June 1974): 32–34.

6. Discuss the following statements:

Have you ever worked very hard at something you felt was not understood or appreciated? What was it? What was said or done that made you feel your effort was not appreciated?

Have you ever wanted to share things—ideas, feelings, something you've written, or made—but were afraid to? Were you afraid that people might put you or it down? What kinds of things might they say or do that would put you, your ideas, or your achievements down?

Source: Canfield, Jack and Harold C. Wells. *100 Ways to Enhance Self-Concept in the Classroom.* Englewood Cliffs, N.J.: Prentice-Hall, 1976, p. 67.

7. Circle the statements that describe you most of the time:

I am happy.	I'm a gossip.	I am sexy.
I am sick.	I'm neurotic.	I'm sad.
I am good.	I am a bore.	I'm a good teacher.
I am beautiful.	I'm a mess.	I am smart.
I'm a loser.	I'm cool.	I am a good person.
I'm okay.	I am successful.	I'm a slow learner.
I am bad.	I'm a failure.	I'm not okay.
I am clumsy.	I'm loveable.	

Of the twenty-six sentences, how many positive ones did you circle? How many negative ones? What kind of self-concept do you appear to have?

Source: Canfield, John T., and Wells, Harold C. "Self-Concept: A Critical Dimension in Teaching and Learning." In *Humanistic Education Sourcebook,* Donald A. Read and Sidney B. Simon. Englewood Cliffs, N.J.: Prentice-Hall, 1975, p. 460.

8. Do the following activity: Your name is Michael. Take a piece of paper and write the letters IALAC (I am loved and capable) on it. This is your self-concept. Then, read the following story and tear off a piece of your self-concept each time it is attacked.

A seventh grade boy named Michael is still lying in bed three minutes after his alarm goes off. All of a sudden his mother calls to him, "Michael, you lazyhead, get your body out of bed and get down here before I send your father up there!" (rip!) Michael gets out of bed, goes to get dressed, and can't find a clean pair of socks. His mother tells him he'll have to wear yesterday's pair. (rip!) He goes to brush his teeth and his older sister, who's already locked herself in the bathroom, tells him to drop dead! (rip!) He goes to breakfast to find soggy cereal waiting for him. (rip!) As he leaves for school, he forgets his lunch and his mother calls to him, "Michael you've forgotten your lunch; you'd forget your head if it weren't attached!" (rip!) As he gets to the corner he sees the school bus pull away and so he has to walk to school. (rip!) He's late to school and has to get a pass from the principal who gives him a lecture. (rip!)

How would you feel if you were Michael? How does putting yourself in Michael's shoes help you to be a better teacher?

Source: Canfield, Jack, p. 91.

Suggested readings

Blackmarr, Syd. "Every Child A Winner." *Journal of Health Physical Education Recreation* 45 (October 1974): 14–16.

Carlson, Judith B. "Fathoming Feelings in Physical Education." *Journal of Physical Education and Recreation* 52 (February 1981): 19–21, 54.

Check, John F. "We All Count—Or Do We?" *The Physical Educator* 31 (October 1974): 121–25.

Curry, Nancy L. "Self Concept and the Educational Experience in Physical Education." *The Physical Educator* 31 (October 1974): 116–19.

Danziger, Paula. *The Cat Ate My Gymsuit.* New York: Delacorte Press, 1974.

Glasser, William. *Schools Without Failure.* New York: Harper & Row, 1969.

Johnson, Sandy. "Personalizing Physical Education for Children." *Physical Education Newsletter* no. 129 (September 1981).

Kneer, Marian E. "How Human Are You? Exercises in Awareness." *Journal of Health Physical Education Recreation* (June 1974): 32–33.

Locke, Lawrence F., and Lambdin, Dolly. "Personalized Learning in Physical Education." *Journal of Physical Education and Recreation* 47 (June 1976): 32–35.

Martinek, Thomas J. "Pygmalion in the Gym: A Model for the Communication of Teacher Expectations in Physical Education." *Research Quarterly for Exercise and Sport* 52 (March 1981): 58–67.

Mood, Dale. "Evaluation in the Affective Domain? No!" *Journal of Physical Education, Recreation and Dance* 53 (February 1982): 18–20.

Raths, Louis E.; Harmin, Merrill; and Simon, Sidney B. *Values and Teaching: Working with Values in the Classroom,* 2d ed. Columbus, Ohio: Charles E. Merrill Publishing Co., 1978.

Snodgrass, Jeanne. "Self-Concept." *Journal of Physical Education and Recreation* 48 (November-December 1977): 22–23.

Stevens, Carla. *Pig and the Blue Flag.* New York: Seabury Press, 1977.

Stoner, Lela June. "Evaluation in the Affective Domain? Yes!" *Journal of Physical Education, Recreation and Dance* 53 (February 1982): 16–17.

Understanding Motivational Techniques

Study stimulators

1. Explain Maslow's motivational hierarchy.
2. Define extrinsic and intrinsic motivation. When is each one usually used?
3. What is the key to intrinsic motivation in education?
4. What methods can be used to enhance classroom management? Fitness activities? Public relations?

According to Joe Cybulski, a ten-year-old at Ballwin Elementary School in Ballwin, Missouri, motivation is "to convince someone he always wanted to learn something he never even knew he wanted to learn." One of his classmates defined it as follows: "Motivation is like when a person has never jumped backward because he thinks it's a silly thing to do. Then, he comes to a curb and there is a mud puddle in front of him. A car is coming around the corner. The rest is motivation."[1]

Motivation is an urge or desire to achieve a specific goal. It involves both intensity of activity and direction toward the goal. Students who are motivated engage in approach behaviors toward the activity or subject involved. Unmotivated students engage in avoidance behaviors and do not perform the desired responses; therefore, they do not learn. The process of learning is more rapid when students are motivated. It works somewhat like a mathematical equation, in which skill = performance $\times$ motivation. Learning increases geometrically as motivation increases.

Motivation is an inner urge to do one's best, to surpass one's previous performance, or to exceed the performance of another. It is part of the desire of humankind to improve and to excel. Achieving one's best under trying or even disappointing circumstances is a part of living one's life to the fullest. Great moments in sport, as with great moments in life, are not so much those of winning or losing but of doing one's best.

Motivation plays a role in effective learning, self-discipline, and classroom management.

Maslow's Hierarchy of Needs

Maslow identified a hierarchy of needs that has come to be accepted as the basis for all motivation.[2] These needs include (1) physiological needs, (2) safety (and security) needs, (3) love (or social needs), (4) esteem needs, and (5) the need for self-actualization. He proposed, in general, that lower order needs must be satisfied before the next higher need can be activated. Thus, when the physiological needs have been met, the individual is concerned

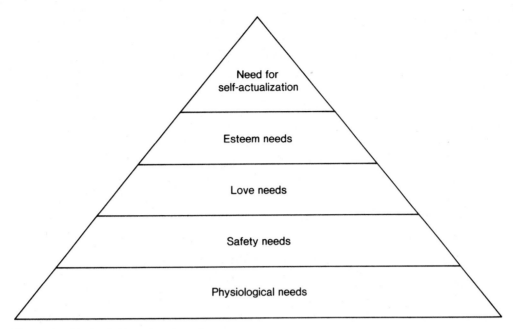

Figure 9.1 Maslow's hierarchy of needs.

with safety and so on up the hierarchy until another physiological need must be attended to. Occasionally, a certain need can take precedence over all other needs regardless of its position in the hierarchy. Such is the case when a mother risks her life for her child.

Another variable is the range of need satisfaction within a given level of the hierarchy. For some persons, minimal satisfaction of a need is enough to progress upward to the satisfaction of another need. For others, the satisfaction must be at a higher level before continuing.

Physiological needs

Certain physiological needs such as food, water, sleep, exercise, and bodily elimination are essential for survival. When these needs are not met, students can not learn effectively. Teachers can see evidence of this effect on classes that meet right before lunch, on students after a morning of taking achievement tests, or on a student who is ill. Students who are concerned about physiological needs can not pay attention to learning. Since perception is distorted, learning suffers accordingly.

Safety (and security) needs

Both physical and psychological safety are essential within the school environment. The threat of physical violence in some schools prevents effective learning, as does discrimination on the basis of race, sex, or ability.

In physical education, students who are afraid of learning a new skill due to possible failure or ridicule will be concerned about security. It should be noted that some students have a high level of tolerance for mental or emotional stress or physical risk while others have a low level of tolerance and react strongly to situations in which their security is threatened.

In order to solve this problem, Kehres suggests that curricular activities should provide for a safe progression of activities so that students develop self-confidence and skill in basic movement skills and are, therefore, secure enough to try activities requiring higher levels of skill.[3] Students should never be forced to try activities which they feel are dangerous. Standards for measuring performance should allow for differences in skill level.

Love (or social) needs

Once the need for safety and security is met, the student seeks to fulfill the need for love. This need can be met in part through social approval. Approval may come from adults or peers in varying degrees, but it must come in order for students to be successful in school. Most dropouts are students who lack acceptance from one of these sources. Kehres lists four guidelines for teachers to use in planning group interaction experiences for students. They include:

1. Games and activities should allow for both competition and cooperative interaction among students.

2. Games and activities should at times be structured so that low-skilled individuals are not at a disadvantage.

3. Opportunities should be provided for experiencing both individual success and success as a member of a group.

4. Students encountering social rejection by peers should be given special assistance in developing acceptable social behavior and physical skills so that their status in the group may be improved.[4]

Esteem needs

Everyone needs to feel capable as an individual; therefore, it is essential that each student have some activities in which he or she feels success. Gagne emphasizes the need for teachers to arrange the learning environment in such a way that students experience success and thereby develop self-esteem. He said:

Achievement, successful interaction within the learning environment, and mastery of the objectives of an educational program can themselves lead to persisting satisfaction on the part of the learner and can therefore become a most dependable source of continuing motivation. Something like this conception must evidently be a strong component in the development of a "continuing self-learner"; and such development is often stated as one of the most important goals of education.[5]

Teachers should arrange the learning
environment in such a way that students
experience success and thereby develop self-
esteem.

This fact underscores the value of adapting activities to meet the needs of students
with a wide range of abilities so that each student experiences success and enjoyment. Students can also be counseled to select those activities best suited to their individual needs and
interests.

The need for self-actualization

Once the other four categories of needs have been satisfied, the individual can move on to
self-actualization. Self-actualizing persons are motivated from within and have an intense
desire to explore, discover, and create. They are aware of their own strengths and weaknesses
and those of the environment that surrounds them and resolve to improve themselves and
their environment in a consistent, orderly manner. Maslow felt that only a small percentage
of the population would become self-actualized.

The role of the school, then, is to create an environment in which students can strive
to satisfy their basic needs so that they will be free to move on to self-actualization. With
regard to physical education, Kehres emphasized the following principles:

1. The relationship of vigorous movement to health and well-being
   in adulthood should be taught to students.

2. Each student should be placed in a position of leadership and responsibility, during which time his decisions influence the behavior of others.

3. Participants in both physical education and athletic programs should be allowed to make decisions; the teacher or coach should not be the sole authority.[6]

Extrinsic and intrinsic motivation

Two types of motivation exist—extrinsic and intrinsic. **Extrinsic motivation** is external to the learner and is result-oriented—a good grade, peer recognition, or teacher approval. **Intrinsic motivation** is internally perceived and controlled by the learner. It includes the pleasure derived from participation in the activity itself, self-confidence, self-discovery, pride, or a knowledge of personal progress.

Recent studies have demonstrated that when intrinsic motivation is present, the use of extrinsic rewards can actually decrease satisfaction in the activity. Deci isolated two kinds of rewards, only one of which results in a deterioration of intrinsic motivation. Rewards that intend to make students do what the teacher wants, when and where the teacher wants it done, are called *controlling* rewards. *Informative* rewards are those that provide students with feedback about their competence and self-determination. They include comments such as "good work" written on a student's paper. Deci's results showed that when teachers stressed the informative nature of rewards rather than the controlling nature, students were more intrinsically motivated, had more positive attitudes toward themselves, and were more self-directing. He concluded that "rewards, communications, and other external events can be expected to decrease intrinsic motivation only when the controlling aspect is salient for the recipient.[7]

Many educators question the use of extrinsic motivators in the classroom. However, for those students who have a relatively low level of intrinsic motivation, the use of rewards can be especially significant, just as a paycheck is occasionally motivating to an adult who is working on a particularly nonsatisfying task. In any case, the use of extrinsic motivation is certainly better than having to rely on disciplinary techniques to achieve the same goal.

Intrinsic motivation is increased by the selection and implementation of appropriate learning experiences. Classroom management, on the other hand, often makes use of extrinsic motivational techniques.

Enhancing the learning experience

Physical educators should help students to experience fun and enjoyment in physical activity so that they will have an intrinsic motivation to continue in physical activity.

Challenging activities

Activities that are meaningful to the students and have carry-over value to daily living should be chosen. They should be challenging and yet at a level that permits students to experience success as early in the learning experience as possible. Success is one of the keys to effective motivation, therefore, great care should be taken in lesson and unit planning to insure a logical progression of activities from simple to complex and to choose activities for which students have the prerequisite skills. Students who are successful usually enjoy the activity and no one wants to sit out when the activity is fun. On the other hand, activities that are too easy or are repeated year after year are not challenging and students will lose interest and stop trying to excel. Students like to work hard at worthwhile and challenging tasks as long as success is possible.

Motivation does not automatically increase with success and decrease with failure. The difficulty of the task and the anxiety level of the performer can influence the motivation of the student. Ambitious and relatively successful people tend to raise their level of aspiration after success and have the confidence to try harder after periodic failure. Students with poor self-concepts and histories of failure, however, will soon quit trying when their chances of success seem doomed. For this reason, it is important that teachers teach for success and that teachers help students to develop self-confidence and respect for their own abilities and to find activities in which they can be successful students. By helping students set realistic goals and achieve them, students can increase their motivation or desire to learn.

A well-rounded program of activities provides students with the opportunity to acquire skills in a variety of activities. This contributes to the students' enjoyment of physical activity and the development of positive attitudes toward the body.

Clearly stated objectives

After an activity has been chosen, students should be told the purpose of the activity, what is expected of them (i.e., the objectives), and why it is important. Students need to understand the goals of the course and to receive periodic feedback so that they are aware of the progress they are making toward the successful completion of the objectives. Make students aware that they are welcome to look at your records to keep track of their progress toward objectives. Also, take time to explain the overall goals of physical education to students.

Variety of learning activities

A variety of interesting, well-planned learning experiences presented by an enthusiastic teacher, and the opportunity to participate in learning situations in an active manner result in success in school and a minimum of student disruption. Attractive and applicable learning aids and bulletin boards can focus student attention on learning. Often students can be allowed freedom to select or create their own materials or methods of study. An attempt should be made to place more and more of the responsibility for education on the learners. One seldom observes signs of friction or disorder in a classroom where the students are interested and actively engaged in meaningful school activity related to their needs and interests, and especially if that schoolwork is a part of their own planning.

By utilizing the element of surprise, the teacher can have students excited to see what might happen next. Unusual warmups, exercises to music, unique or gamelike drills, films, fun tournaments, and holiday themes can spark youthful enthusiasm. A Christmas tree pyramid tournament in badminton or pumpkin targets in an archery class might be just the thing when students are excited about an approaching holiday. Novelty games, such as archery bingo, or game adaptations, such as blind volleyball (with a sheet over the net) or indoor baseball (with a plastic bat and ball) can be helpful on a rainy day, while still providing maximum participation in the activity currently being taught. Participation in extraclass activities—such as interclass competition, playdays, or sportsdays—parent-teacher organization programs, and clubs can heighten interest in intraclass activities as well. Field trips to a bowling alley or a university athletic event or classes "on location," such as skiing, horseback riding, or canoeing, can reach students often unreachable with other activities.

Competition can be effective when students have a reasonable chance of winning. On the other hand, cooperation should also be used to help students learn new skills. Coeducational activities often have a motivating effect on achievement of course objectives.

Maximum participation

In order to experience success, each student must have an adequate opportunity to practice. Success results only from opportunities to work with the sport-related equipment on a one-to-one basis. Therefore, adequate time and equipment are essential if students are to be successful in an activity. In drills and games, an attempt should be made to *decrease the number of participants* interacting with each piece of equipment and to *increase the number of pieces of equipment.* Relay teams should be kept to a few players to avoid waiting for a turn. Soccer and football teams should be reduced to six or seven players instead of eleven. Students should rotate from one piece of equipment to another when few pieces are available.

Instant involvement in challenging learning activities not only contributes to the opportunity for success but also keeps students busily engaged in positive behavior with little or no time or incentive for irrational, unruly behavior. Talking rather than doing contributes to boredom, inattention, and deviant behavior. Bertel suggested an excellent way to obtain maximum participation and increase the fun of an activity. It involves starting an activity just like it might have been played by its inventors and then adding rules, skills, and strategies as the need arises. Once the students become involved, they will want to learn more. For example, basketball can be played with peach baskets or the old rules of three dribbles before passing or shooting.[8]

Feedback

Evaluation techniques, including preassessment and diagnostic techniques, should be designed to give immediate feedback to students on where they stand in relation to the instructional objectives and to help students recognize when they have achieved the objectives. Students who know where they stand at all times in the learning experience are more secure and can work longer on their own without difficulty. An oral quiz, a written quiz, a handout to be filled in during a rules discussion, or a timed trial in baserunning help students learn accountability for their time in class while, at the same time, becoming aware of what is expected of them by the teacher. Evaluation techniques also help the teacher adjust to individual differences in rate of learning and/or previous experience.

Individual and group coaching, encouragement by the teacher, and indications of progress toward successful achievement of the objectives help students to maintain interest even when objectives are difficult to achieve. Students should also be encouraged to help each other achieve the course objectives rather than competing among themselves for the best grade. Grades should be indicative of success in achieving the course objectives and "good grades" should be within the realm of possibility for all students. Sadly, many students who get poor grades do so, not because they are poorly skilled but because the teacher has been unable to teach them. Is it fair to grade the student on the basis of the teacher's inabilities?

Praise

Probably the most reinforcing of all behaviors is appropriate praise or recognition for positive achievement. The effects of praise or criticism vary with the experience, personality, and previous successes and failures of the students. Some students find praise embarrassing; others encourage and even elicit praise from teachers. Teachers should be careful to use praise only when it is sincere. It should be noted that ignoring a student is less motivating to many students than either praise or criticism.

By rewarding positive behavior and ignoring negative behavior, students will work to earn a desired reward. Opportunities for student leadership may be given to students who attempt to demonstrate proper behavior and to reward students who change their behavior from bad to good. Encourage students to read and discuss books or articles about handicapped athletes who never gave up.

In summary, students who are taught by well-prepared teachers who love their students and their subject and who have the ability to organize learning so that students can successfully achieve the goals of instruction are motivated to do so.

Enhancing classroom management

The components of an effective system of classroom management are discussed in chapter 17. Effective class discipline techniques are reviewed in chapter 18. The discussion here is limited to those aspects of classroom management that relate directly to motivation.

Some teacher behaviors that can be used to enhance classroom management include:

1. Be efficient, while keeping the emphasis on the activity rather than on the organization.

2. Keep distractions to a minimum.

3. Begin lessons promptly. If activities offer personal advantages to students, they will settle down immediately.

4. Be alert for boredom or inactivity.

5. Be consistent with respect to requirements.

In addition to these behaviors, norm-setting and classroom management games can be effective in many situations. Norm-setting involves students and teacher in setting rules for the health, safety, and mutual welfare of all concerned. When students participate in setting rules they are generally more responsible for implementing them. For a complete explanation of norm-setting, refer to chapter 18.

Management games are generally based on Grandma's Law, which states, "First clean up your plate and then you may have your dessert."[9] Translated into physical education terminology, it states, "By accomplishing certain classroom management tasks quickly, you will have more time for free play." Clearly specify a few rules that tell what is expected in order to earn the reward. The reward may be based on the behavior of the entire class or of each squad. For example, all squads quiet, sitting in place, and ready for roll call within five seconds from the teacher's signal, earn a point. A stopwatch can be used to record the amount of time used. Can you think of some ways to save time?

Use a variety of reinforcers to reward appropriate behaviors. Since some events or things are rewarding to some students and other events or things are rewarding to others, you should attempt to discover what things function as rewards for your students. Some suggested ideas follow.

Tokens or points

Tokens or points can be exchanged for other reinforcers. Two examples of the use of tokens or points follow:

1. Award extra-credit points for participation outside of school hours in each ten hours of physical education activities, from archery to water skiing. Have students keep a log of dates and hours spent in each activity.

2. Award tickets for events in track and field according to the height jumped or distance thrown or place of finish in sprints and relays. Award a different ticket for jogging a lap on the track. Students will work hard to earn tickets when they would otherwise just sit around. See figure 9.2 for an example of this system.

Contingent activities

Contingent activities should always be positive, *never* negative, such as using running or push-ups as punishment for the losers of a game or for inappropriate behavior. Some possible activities include:

1. Reward students who have completed a predetermined score on a drill or learning activity by allowing them to play the game sooner. "Getting to play" is a tremendous motivator, but it should be used to reward correct performance of the skill and not just any performance. Work with students who are having difficulty so that they can soon play also.

Name _____ Period _____ Total score _____

INDIVIDUAL TRACK RECORD

Staple tickets below:
Blues on top, reds
next, etc.

	Blue	Red	White	Yellow	Green	Orange	Ticket totals for each event
High jump	4	2	3	2	1	1	13
Standing long jump							0
Running long jump		2	1	2	1		6
All dashes (50-75-100)	2	2	1	1	✕	✕	6
All relays (440 and Shuttle)	2	1		1	✕	✕	4
Total number of tickets for each color	8	7	5	6	2	1	29

To calculate your total score:
   Count 10 points for *each* ticket. _290_
   Count 3 more points for each *blue* ticket. _24_
   Count 2 more points for each *red* ticket. _14_
   Count 1 more point for each *white* ticket. _5_

Total score [333]

Figure 9.2 Individual track record.
Source: Kathryn Alldredge and Mary Taylor.

2. Reward class effort by letting students play novelty games or make up their own games.

3. Allow students who complete assigned tasks early to help set up equipment, run errands, or collect materials.

Social approval

Activities that can be used to show social approval of students include:

1. Award team points for sportsmanship, courtesy, games won, and number of students dressed for activity.

2. Post a "player of the week" type award on the bulletin board for any specified behavior such as leadership, sportsmanship, effort, or skill performance.

3. Award a lollipop or piece of Halloween candy to the winners of a "move-up" tournament. The tournament is played by having winners move up one court, lane, or target, and having losers move down except on the first court where winners stay and on the last court where losers stay.

4. Award fun prizes for unusual accomplishments, such as the golden arrow (an old arrow sprayed gold) or the belle of the ball (a tennis ball dressed in a gown).

Enhancing fitness

Motivating students to achieve physical fitness can be achieved in a variety of ways. Several ways follow.

Be an example

Keep yourself physically fit! Exercise with the students, not just in front of them. Point out how other prominent people, such as movie stars and astronauts stay physically fit.[10] Be enthusiastic about physical education.

Involve students in their own fitness

Teach "why" physical fitness is important and provide guidelines for choosing activities. Then, let students choose their own fitness activities. Use several exercise leaders and rotate often so all students have the opportunity to lead warm-ups. Let students invent or name their own exercises, bring their own music, and develop aerobic dance or other exercise routines. Use obstacle courses, circuit training, follow the leader, partner exercises, and other fun variations for developing fitness.

```
              Fitness Frolics--Information Sheet

  1. All faculty, staff, and students are eligible and encouraged to
     participate.
  2. The program is conducted each semester for fourteen weeks.
  3. Decide the distance you want to jog, cycle, or swim during the se-
     mester or term and indicate your goal on the entry form. Changes in
     goals may be made until midsemester or midterm. The distance goals
     are:


                          MILES PER DAY

            Jogging     Cycling    Swimming
              0.5         1.0         0.25
              1.0         2.0         0.50
              1.5         3.0         0.75
              2.0         4.0         1.00
              2.5         5.0         1.25
              3.0         7.0         1.50
              4.0        10.0         1.75


  4. Upon entering and stating your goal you will receive a logbook for
     recording your daily distances.
  5. Every Monday submit your logbook to the Physical Education office
     indicating the past week's distance.
  6. Certificates will be awarded to those who attain their goal.
  7. In addition, special awards will be given to those participants
     who complete designated distances by the end of winter semester.
     These include:
     100 miles--T-shirt
     300 miles--Nylon windbreaker
     500 miles--Trophy
```

Figure 9.3 Fitness Frolics Information Sheet.
Source: Brigham Young University Intramurals.

Award certificates to students who achieve their own predetermined goal in jogging, bicycling, or swimming. A minimum of one-fourth-mile per day is required as a goal and logs of daily activity must be submitted each Monday for the previous week. See figures 9.3 and 9.4 for an example. Award ribbons for jogging five, ten, fifteen, twenty, or twenty-five miles and post a chart of those achieving each distance.

Have a team jogging meet to motivate jogging. Divide the class into teams of two or three people. Set a timer for a given time period, such as fifteen or thirty minutes. Team members alternate laps, one runner at a time, and report to a scorer at the conclusion of each lap. Joggers are allowed to walk, skip, run, or move as they wish, but the team with the most laps completed within the time period wins the meet.

Have competition among classes to see who can run the farthest in one month's time. Students record their laps each day. Average the scores to determine the winning class. Also, give awards to the individuals with the highest distance in each class and to all students who completed the goal.

FITNESS FROLICS--ENTRY AND RECORD FORM

Please print.

Name _____ Date _____
           Last   First

Address _____ Phone _____

Semester _____ Weeks in program _____

I commit myself to complete the following goal: _____ Miles _____
                                     Goal   Color

_____
                Signature

RECORD OF COMPLETED MILES

Week	Miles	Total to date	Week	Miles	Total to date
1	_____	_____	9	_____	_____
2	_____	_____	10	_____	_____
3	_____	_____	11	_____	_____
4	_____	_____	12	_____	_____
5	_____	_____	13	_____	_____
6	_____	_____	14	_____	_____
7	_____	_____	15	_____	_____
8	_____	_____	16	_____	_____

      Total Miles _____   Total Miles _____

Reminder letter sent _____
                  Date

Goal attained ( ) Yes ( ) No

Certificate awarded ( )

Figure 9.4 Fitness Frolics entry and record form.
Source: Brigham Young University Intramurals.

Have a treasure hunt in which students run from point to point as directed by a series of clues. Students can pick up a marker at each point to show that they covered the entire course.

Sundberg suggested participation races in which students run to a given point and back, picking up a marker at the midpoint. Students are encouraged to pace themselves so they do not have to stop and walk. Students who walk have their markers taken away. Only the finishers count. This type of race should be used at the end of a fitness unit after students have learned to pace themselves and have the endurance to last the entire distance. To compare classes or teams, divide the number of finishers by the number of starters. He emphasized that those who finish first count no more than those who finish last.[11]

Corbin suggested prediction races in which students attempt to run as close as possible to their predicted times. Individuals or teams can be used. The individual or team coming closest to its predicted time wins.[12]

Stein described a "Run for Fun" in which students run a specified distance and then record their overall finish place and category on a card. Awards are given to those finishing first in each category. Although he suggested age and sex for the categories, many other categories could be selected—such as eye color, color of tennis shoes, birth month, etc.[13]

Provide fitness feedback

Give periodic fitness tests using the American Alliance for Health, Physical Education, Recreation and Dance Youth Fitness Test, the AAHPERD Health-Related Fitness Tests, or state or local fitness tests. Provide feedback to each student in the form of fitness profiles, individual counseling, and letters to parents. A computer can be used to track students and provide individual feedback.[14]

Reward progress

AAHPERD and the Presidential Fitness Awards or local awards, such as certificates, t-shirts, or patches, may be used to reward progress.

Enhancing the environment

A pleasant, attractive environment that is conducive to both physical and emotional well-being can help students feel free to experiment and learn without pressure.

With regard to the physical environment, temperature, lighting, and sound should be adjusted to meet the needs of the activity being conducted. Loud music not only injures students' hearing but also tends to create discipline problems among students.

A variety of interesting and thought-provoking displays help to capture students' attention and direct it toward physical education. Student-designed graphics posted or painted on walls, plaques for records by students in class events, sports figures, and other appropriate visual aids can promote a warm, positive feeling toward activity. Bulletin boards that capture students' attention can arouse interest in a new activity, convey knowledge, clarify ideas and meanings, and summarize what has been taught. Bulletin boards can also be used to make announcements; post fitness and tournament results; and display articles, pictures, cartoons, and quotes. Students should also be encouraged to bring materials for display and to assist in creating bulletin boards. Bulletin boards should be attractive and changed often, usually every few weeks. A sloppy, unattractive, outdated bulletin board can be worse than no bulletin board at all. The most important part of the environment is the warm, personal feeling created by a teacher who really cares about the students' well-being and success.

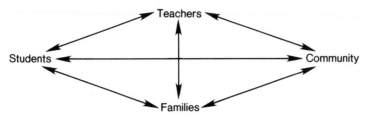

Figure 9.5 The interrelationships among the various publics of the school.

Enhancing public relations

Since motivation is contagious, it is worth taking some time to promote a cycle of motivation among the various school publics. Figure 9.5 shows the interrelationships among these groups. Some ideas for motivating students, families, teachers, and community are presented here.

Students

Students are our most important public. They are the only ones we see from day to day. When students experience a sound instructional program, they will "sell" it to their parents through their enthusiasm. We should remember also that students grow up into community and school leaders and will have an influence on physical education in the future. Students who have a positive experience in physical education now will be more supportive of it in the future.

We have already discussed a number of ways to enhance student learning. Some other events that can promote public relations within the school include demonstrations of physical activities in school assemblies, interdisciplinary units with teachers of other subject areas, field days, and contests for the entire school. Implementing interdisciplinary units with teachers of mathematics, foreign languages, home economics, health, and physiology can be effective in promoting student and faculty interest in physical education activities.

A fun type of field day for students at the elementary or middle school level is a "Super Kids' Day" in which students compete in partners, rotating about from one event to another.[15] Each student has a "Super Kids' Day" certificate (see figure 9.6) on which the event and place—first or second—is recorded at each station.

Tenoschok listed a number of schoolwide contests that might be conducted during National Physical Education and Sport Week or at another appropriate time. He included a physical education essay contest; a poster coloring contest; a sports-in-action drawing contest; a physical education slogan contest; an invent-a-game contest; and a sports safari contest, which asks students to identify athletes by their animal nicknames. These activities can stimulate an overall school awareness of the objectives of physical education while encouraging students to achieve in other areas in the curriculum.[16] All-school activity days or weeks, in which contests are scheduled in all academic areas, can be both fun and profitable to students and faculty alike.

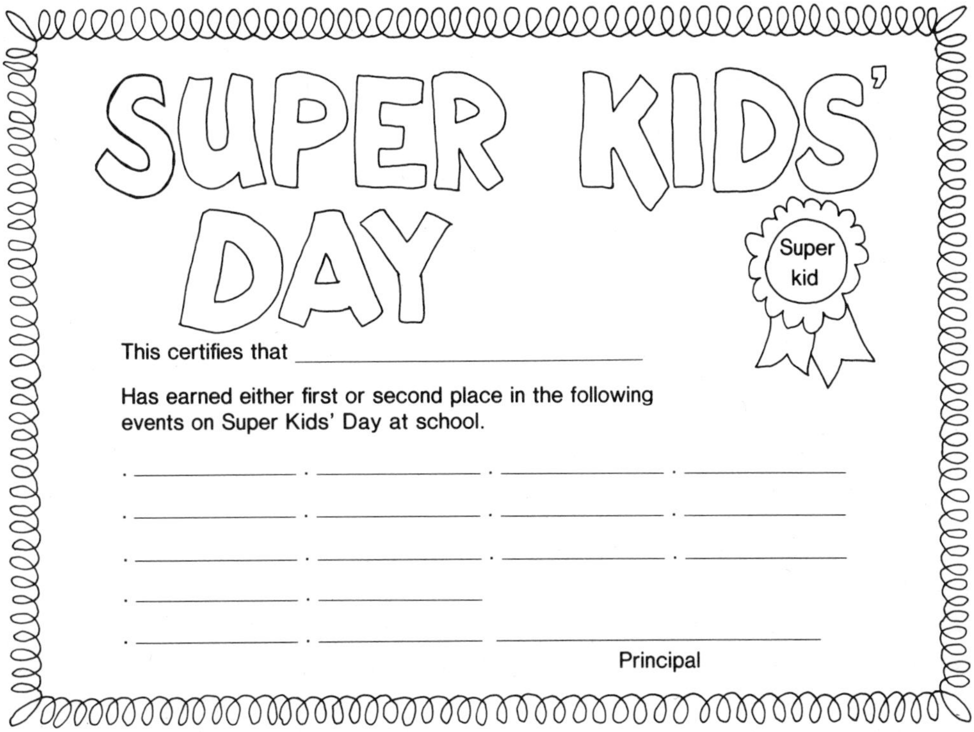
SUPER KIDS' DAY

Super kid

This certifies that ______________________

Has earned either first or second place in the following events on Super Kids' Day at school.

. __________ . __________ . __________ . __________

. __________ . __________ . __________ . __________

. __________ . __________ . __________ . __________

. __________ . __________

. __________ . __________ ______________________

Principal

Figure 9.6 A "Super Kids' Day" certificate.
Source: Pat Sawley, Woods Cross High School, Woods Cross, Utah.

Homework

Homework can play an important role in informing the family about physical education and can even involve them directly in physical education activities. Homework can be used to practice skills, to learn or apply concepts, to increase physical fitness, to solve problems, and to develop self-discipline.

French listed a number of possibilities for homework in physical education.[17] They include:

1. Practicing skills using task sheets.
2. Attending sports events or watching them on television.
3. Coaching or officiating youth sports.
4. Tutoring another student in a skill.
5. Watching films or other media in a learning resource center.
6. Studying for tests and quizzes.
7. Interviewing well-known sports figures.

8. Reading books on sports and physical activities and writing book reports.

9. Reporting on current events.

Another possibility is working on individual physical fitness programs. Since one of the objectives of physical education is to encourage people to exercise on their own, why not reward our students who make a habit of self-directed fitness activity.[18]

Students can also be asked to solve problems, such as creating a gymnastics routine, a modern dance composition, strategies for a sports event, or a new game.

Administrators, faculty, and staff

Far too often, physical education teachers divorce themselves from the total school environment. Effective teachers will make the effort to emerge from the gymnasium to share experiences with the rest of the faculty. Take time each year to discuss the physical education program with the principal, including an overview of the program, goals for the year, changes that have been implemented, achievements, and new trends or ideas. Try to make sure the administrator understands the importance of your program.[19] Volunteer to serve on faculty committees. You will gain new ideas from the discussions and have a positive effect on the rest of the school. Be aware of opportunities to integrate physical education concepts with other subject areas in the curriculum. Invite administrators, faculty, and staff to participate in faculty fitness programs, clinics to learn new skills, tournaments, and free play activities.[20] Sell yourself and your program by your personal appearance, manner of speech, and enthusiasm about your own program and that of the entire school.

Promoting parent and family participation and interest

A number of methods can be used to help parents understand what is happening in physical education classes. A "back-to-school night" is held in many schools. Teachers should take this opportunity to point out the objectives of physical education and provide an outline of activities in which students will be involved. Samples of the students' work and mini-demonstrations by students could also be provided along with a schedule of future events. Parents should also be invited to visit classes during a back-to-school day or week.

Parent-teacher conferences are helpful in discussing mutual problems and goals for individual students and for the program as a whole.

Demonstrations are valuable in showing what students are learning and are generally well attended when all of the students participate in some way. These can be as simple as two teams playing speed-a-way or team handball during halftime at a football or basketball game or as complex as a demonstration night for parents in which every student in the school participates. The important thing to remember is to let everyone participate regardless of skill level or handicap. Each class can be asked to demonstrate some aspect of the program. This provides parents with a realistic view of physical education in contrast to that of athletics.

It is essential that each student have some activities in which he or she feels success.

Figure 9.7 "Spring into Fitness" program.
Source: Artwork by Marjorie Ann McClure.

Posters in downtown stores, notices to parents, and announcements in the local paper can be used to invite the public. A public-address system should be used. The principal should welcome parents and introduce the physical education faculty, who can take turns introducing the various numbers. A simple mimeographed program such as the one in figures 9.7 and 9.8 can be handed out at the door.

Parent or family participation in student homework can stimulate families to become more involved in outside activities, such as bike riding or jogging, and to be more supportive of student involvement in completing extraclass assignments or activities. Inviting families to participate in contests in which students earn points by participating in family recreational and fitness activities has also been very effective in some areas.

McLaughlin reported a "Chip-N-Block" bowling tournament in which a parent and student form a team and compete against other teams.[21] Parent-student participation nights can include everything from movement education to sports to fitness activities. Aerobic activities have become increasingly popular in recent years. Other possibilities include mother-daughter, father-son, father-daughter, and mother-son activities. Parents can also be involved as paraprofessional aides in the physical education program.

EASTMONT MIDDLE SCHOOL
PRESENTS
Spring into Fitness

1.	Tumbling	1st Period--7th Grade
2.	Pyramids	5th Period--8th Grade
3.	Lummi Sticks	2d Period--7th Grade
4.	Gymnastics Exhibition	Special Team
5.	Square Dancing	6th Period--6th Grade
6.	Tinikling	2d Period--7th Grade
7.	Jump Rope Routine	3d Period--7th Grade
8.	Parachutes	7th Period--6th Grade
9.	Dance Aerobics	4th Period--8th Grade

Acknowledgements

Principal	Mr. Glayde Hill
Vice-principal	Mr. Tom Hicks
Cover Design	Mrs. Marge McClure
Girl's Physical Education Department	Miss Robyn Graham
	Mrs. Karen Quinn
	Mrs. Bell Breen

Figure 9.8 "Spring into Fitness" program.
Source: Karen Quinn, Bell Breen, Robyn Johnson, Eastmont Middle School, Sandy, Utah.

A brief newsletter to parents or an article in the district newsletter several times a year can be valuable in describing school and community programs and promoting parent and family involvement in these programs. The newsletter might contain a description of the physical education program, objectives, evaluation and grading; physical fitness goals and achievements; extraclass programs; programs for handicapped students; and special events for parents. A portion of the newsletter could provide tips for better performance in a particular activity such as tennis, bowling, or physical fitness. See figure 9.9 for an example.

Newsletters should represent the best effort of the department in terms of spelling, grammar, layout, use of pictures, etc. Poorly written materials cast a poor image on the profession of physical education, as well as on the teachers involved. Consult with the English faculty for help if needed. In some locales the newsletter should be printed in both English and Spanish.

In addition to newsletters, letters can be sent to parents describing the specific fitness test results of their children and what they mean, or progress in learning other skills. Schuman mentions sending home red, green, or yellow cards each week for extremely unmotivated students. Green means "great work," yellow means "caution," and red says "stop and change your work habits." On the cards she lists all tasks completed during that week. Parents are asked to sign the cards and return them each Monday. When students know that they will be "paid" each week, they seem to work harder. Cards are stopped when students no longer need them.[22]

PHYSICAL
EDUCATION
NEWSLETTER

Dear Parents:

May I take this opportunity to tell you about our new physical education program at Podunk High School. During this past summer the members of our Physical Education Department, with the help of several students, completely updated our curriculum. We are very excited about the new course of study that will be implemented this Fall. Let me tell you about it!

The program is lifetime sports-oriented. That is, we have decided to teach a wide variety of sports that may be played throughout life. For example, tennis, golf, bowling, badminton, archery, skiing and other sports with high carryover value are now included in the curriculum. In addition, at grades 10 and 11, students may select those sports which they enjoy the most. Instruction will be given at beginning, intermediate and advanced levels so that students may become highly skilled in the sports they have selected. It is our opinion that unless boys and girls acquire a fairly high skill level they will not participate during the adult years.

At the 10th and 11th grade levels, the curriculum is completely elective in nature. It is also coeducational in non-contact sports. We see no reason why boys and girls can not learn sports skills together. We are hopeful that this change will produce better socialization and lead to increased understanding among young people.

We are still very much concerned about physical fitness but our approach to it has changed. In brief, the new program requirements call for a "gentle" approach to exercise. That is, we hope that students will become physically fit through participation in enjoyable activities. We still plan to give fitness tests twice a year but we are not trying to condition your son or daughter the way we prepare our athletes for interscholastic sports competition.

In the very near future we plan to hold "open house" so that you may come to school and see our program in operation. At that time you may ask questions, participate yourself if you like, and meet the members of our physical education faculty. We look forward to meeting you at this function.

Sincerely yours,

William F. Straub
Director of Physical Education

Figure 9.9 A physical education newsletter.
Source: William F. Straub, THE LIFETIME SPORTS-ORIENTED PHYSICAL EDUCATION PROGRAM, © 1976, p138. Reprinted by permission of Prentice-Hall, Inc., Englewood Cliffs, N.J.

Letters or phone calls to parents can also be used to point out student's accomplishments. The following story is told about a boy who hadn't had much success in school. The teacher sent home a letter to the boy's parents commending something he had done. Later, the teacher asked, "Did you give the letter to your mother?" "Yes," the boy responded. "What did she say?" "Nothin'," he replied. "Nothing? Why, it was a lovely letter—and your mother said, *nothing*?" The child nodded, "She didn't say nothing! She just bawled."[23] Generally, such parents make such a fuss over these students that they wouldn't dare do anything to get in trouble with such a teacher or principal.

Herman suggested another practical way of gaining the support of parents—have a junk day, in which parents can contribute old tennis racquets, golf clubs, shuffleboard sets, etc. Parents get rid of these space-wasters and the school gains some usable equipment. Be sure to gain the approval of your principal and send a note home on which parents can list what is being donated and sign it so they know what their children are contributing.[24] One school asked for old brooms for broom hockey and were surprised to discover that many parents went out and purchased new brooms just so they could help out.

Including the community

Two factors are involved in community-school relations. They include (1) getting the school involved in the community and (2) getting the community involved in the school.

Getting the school involved in the community

Teachers can take the lead in community involvement by participating in institutional, civic, and neighborhood activities or projects. Educators often participate in local business-education exchanges by touring various commercial institutions.

Students can also be encouraged to participate in community-oriented projects and in work-experience programs. Youth sports provide an excellent opportunity for service in the community.

In order to carry out a lifetime sports curriculum, many schools must rely on resources within the community. The first step is to survey the community to see what is available and whether it is appropriate for an instructional situation. The cost of the facility and the cost of transportation must then be determined. Once permission from the school and district administration is obtained, a specific legal agreement should be drawn up to clarify the dates and times the facility is to be used; the cost; the roles of the school and the institution with regard to the instructional situation, legal liability, etc. The legal implications of transportation to and from the facility must also be considered. The use of community facilities is one more way in which schools and community can develop a better understanding of one another.

Getting the community involved in the school

Passive involvement of the community in the schools generally occurs through the mass media, speeches, and exhibits.

PEPI—the Physical Education Public Information program developed by the American Alliance for Health, Physical Education, Recreation and Dance—has performed a great service by producing materials and sharing techniques for use in the public relations effort.[25] Another organization that has played a prominent role in public relations is the President's Council on Physical Fitness and Sport. Both groups have produced films and television spots that have been well-received.

Publishing articles in school and local newspapers about intramural activities, fitness projects, and class activities can stimulate community interest in physical education just as it has in athletics. All news articles should be approved by the administration to prevent embarrassment to the school from improper timing or undue controversy. Whenever possible, action photos should accompany the articles. Another way to inform the community about the physical education program is by speaking to parent-teacher organizations and civic groups. Talks can be accompanied by slides, videotapes, or actual performances by students. Exhibits in local stores, the public library, or other community buildings can be used to draw attention to special events.

Some more active methods of involving the community include community-school programs, community involvement in curriculum planning, and the use of community sponsors and paraprofessional aides.

The use of school facilities for adult education and family-oriented recreation programs is increasing in many areas. Programs range from supervised recreation to instructional programs in physical fitness and skill development. They may be sponsored by the city recreation department and/or the school district. Adults who become involved in these programs appear to be more supportive of school programs.

Another possible service to the community is a fitness fair in which booths are set up to show what the students have learned in the various areas of physical fitness.

Citizens can provide valuable input to school advisory committees, curriculum committees, and as resource persons. Many districts are realizing the importance of these committees in discussing school problems and making recommendations, serving as "sounding boards" for new ideas or programs, and reviewing films and books for adoption into the school curriculum. Whenever these committees are used, sound policies should be established as to the purposes of the committee and the role to be played by each member.

Just as many community groups contribute to athletics through booster clubs, a number of service clubs, commercial institutions, and government agencies, along with many lay citizens, contribute to school programs either financially or by donating their time and resources. Demonstrations, health and fitness fairs, safety clinics, and many other programs have been sponsored by these groups. Clay described an "adopt-a-school" program in which various businesses have each adopted a specific school and helped them with facility and equipment needs.[26]

Government and other public-service agencies have donated innumerable hours teaching first aid, safety, and health skills to students.

Invitations of prominent athletes, sportscasters, sports journalists, and commercial recreation leaders to speak in physical education classes, parent-teacher organization meetings, and other school groups can extend the relationship. A file can be kept on citizens who possess skills needed by the department. Foster grandparent programs provide a double service by helping senior citizens to serve in useful endeavors and through the many services they can provide to the schools. Parents and other lay citizens can also serve as paraprofessional aides.

With regard to motivation, it is readily apparent that no one technique works for every situation. By understanding a variety of techniques, the best one can be found for you, your students, and the situation. Gray suggested a number of rules that might be helpful:

1. Borrow, steal, or gain inspiration any way you can, but mainly by sharing ideas freely with teachers within your own school.
2. Never stick with a losing game plan any more than a basketball coach would.
3. "Carrot-and-stick" your classes to the limit. Reward whatever assists student progress; discourage whatever does not.
4. Don't be trapped by rules for motivation; keep them flexible.
5. Change your approach often, even when things are going well.[27]

Questions and suggested activities

1. What is the relationship between discipline and motivation?

2. Give examples of Maslow's Hierarchy of Needs from your own life. Do you think this is a valid explanation of motivation?

3. Watch the film, "John Baker's Last Race," (available for purchase from BYU Media Marketing or for rental from BYU Audio Visual Services, Brigham Young University, Provo, Utah 84602). List as many extrinsic and intrinsic forms of motivation as you can.

4. Why is it important to teach the "why" along with the "how" of physical activity?

5. View the film "Eye of the Storm" (an ABC production) with a view toward discrimination caused by being labeled a failure (instead of racial discrimination).

6. Obtain some PEPI materials from your local AAHPERD leaders. How could you utilize them to promote physical education?

7. What publics are important in a public relations program? Which group is the most important?

8. Make a bulletin board and evaluate it in terms of its effect on the viewers. Consider such items as the following: technical presentation, effectiveness in getting the idea across, and integration with the unit of instruction. How could it be improved?

9. Begin a bulletin board file of sketches, ideas, newspaper and magazine clippings, cartoons, pictures, objects, color book ideas, etc.

Suggested readings

Austin, Dean A. "Physical Fitness Reporting: A Method of Improving School/ Community Relations." *Journal of Physical Education and Recreation* 51 (February 1980): 83.

Ellis, Deca B. "Using the Community to Enhance Your Physical Education Program." *Journal of Physical Education, Recreation and Dance* 53 (March 1982): 77.

Hardy, Rex. "A Parcour With New Dimensions." *Journal of Physical Education and Recreation* 50 (November–December 1979): 27.

———. "Guidelines for the Physical Education Volunteer." *Journal of Physical Education, Recreation and Dance* 53 (March 1982): 72–73.

Hollifield, John H. "Research Clues—Does Teacher Praise Improve Students' Performance." *Today's Education* 70 (November–December 1981): 59.

Klappholz, Lowell A. "Securing Public Support for Physical Education." *Physical Education Newsletter* (March 1975).

Levitt, Stuart L. "Fitness On Your Own Time." *Journal of Physical Education and Recreation* 51 (November–December 1980): 79–80.

Marsh, David B.; Smith, John L.; Jenkins, David; and Livingstone, Edward. "Program Promotion." *Journal of Physical Education, Recreation and Dance* 52 (June 1981): 24–26.

Marquardt, Ron. "Voluntary Jog-a-Thon." *Journal of Physical Education and Recreation* 49 (November–December 1978): 68.

Michelin, Donald L. and William Albrecht. "Super-Star Physical Fitness Program." *Journal of Physical Education and Recreation* 50 (September 1979): 74.

"Motivating Today's Students: A Symposium." *Today's Education* 70 (November–December 1981): 33–50.

Smith, Nancy W. "Community Involvement Through a Curriculum Study Project." *Journal of Physical Education, Recreation and Dance* 52 (June 1981): 16–17.

Stewart, Michael J. "Eloquent Bulletin Boards." *Journal of Physical Education and Recreation* 51 (November–December 1980): 80–81.

Taylor, John; Williams, Martha; and Long, Lester. "Letting Parents Know What's Happening." *Journal of Physical Education and Recreation* 50 (January 1979): 52–53.

Wagenhals, Joseph G., III. "Involving Parents In After School Activity Programs." *Journal of Physical Education and Recreation* 51 (October 1980): 13.

Watkins, William. "Administrative Guidelines for Community Use of Physical Education and Recreation Facilities." *Journal of Physical Education and Recreation* 49 (October 1978): 32.

Willet, Loyce. "Physical Education: Alive, Well, and Growing." *Journal of Physical Education, Recreation and Dance* 52 (June 1981): 18.

Planning the Instructional Program

There once was a teacher
Whose principal feature
Was hidden in quite an odd way.
    Students by millions
    Or possibly zillions
    Surrounded him all of the day.

When finally seen
By his scholarly dean
And asked how he managed the deed,
    He lifted three fingers
    And said, "All you swingers
    Need only to follow my lead.

"To rise from a zero
To Big Campus Hero,
To answer these questions you'll strive:
    Where am I going,
    How shall I get there, and
    How will I know I've arrived?"[1]

This poem emphasizes the importance of planning the instructional program. Planning is essential in creating an environment in which each student can successfully reach the goals of physical education.

Planning is most effective when it follows an organized system or model like the one shown in unit figure 3.1. Just as a traveler uses a map to reach a certain destination, teachers can use the model to plan the best route toward their destination. By following the model, you can be sure you don't leave out an essential part of the planning process.

The model begins with a set of clearly defined learning objectives. When learning goals are clearly stated, it is possible to choose the most effective learning activities to meet the goals. Chapter 10 explains the process of writing objectives.

The second step is to develop materials and techniques to evaluate when the students have achieved the objectives stated in step one. A variety of techniques that can be used for evaluation, as well as the procedure for selecting the best technique, are described in chapter 11. Chapter 12 will explain how these techniques can be combined into a grading system.

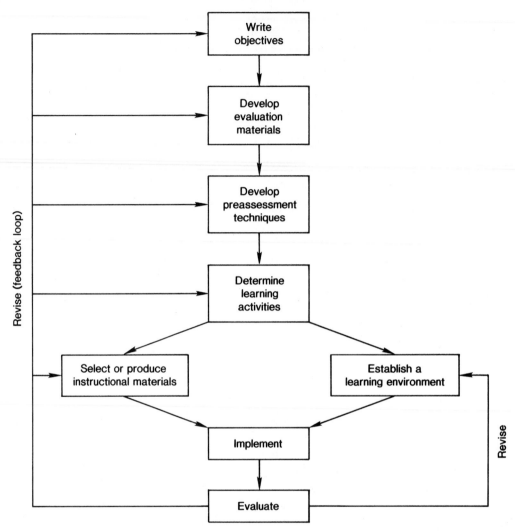

Unit Figure 3.1 A model for planning instructional programs.

The third step is to develop techniques for preassessing where the students are at the beginning of instruction. Chapter 13 discusses a variety of preassessment activities.

Learning activities must be selected to take students from where they are at the beginning of the instructional process to the achievement of the objectives of the unit or lesson. A number of learning strategies that can be used for this purpose are presented in chapter 14.

Chapter 15 describes the process for selecting or producing instructional materials to supplement the learning activities described in chapter 14.

In unit 4, the procedures for establishing an effective learning environment will be described.

One of the purposes of an instructional model is to provide a structure for reviewing and analyzing instruction so that it can be improved. Once the program has been implemented, an evaluation should be conducted to determine weaknesses in each of the preceding levels of the model. (Chapter 26 details the methods of program evaluation.) Feedback loops indicate revisions that might need to be made in the various steps of the model following the evaluation process.

In order to make the learning meaningful, it is suggested that you choose an activity and write an instructional unit that includes the following for each domain—cognitive, psychomotor, and affective.

1. Performance objectives
2. Evaluation materials and techniques
3. Preassessment techniques
4. Appropriate instructional materials
5. Appropriate grading and reporting procedures
6. Lesson plans for each day of instruction

Writing Performance Objectives

Study stimulators

1. Define and give an example of a goal, an objective, and a performance objective for each of the instructional domains. Why are both goals and objectives important?
2. What three elements must be included in a performance objective? How do these differ when evaluating affective objectives?
3. What is the difference between open and closed objectives? For what purpose are each used?
4. What are process objectives? What are they used for?

An **instructional goal** is a statement of a broad, general outcome of instruction. It expresses the common learning expected of all students in the school. Goals are used as a basis for curriculum planning and for summarizing the purposes of the school to the public. The following examples are instructional goals:

1. Students will be physically fit; have a desire to maintain physical fitness; and possess an understanding of how to assess, develop, and maintain physical fitness.

2. Students will develop skills sufficient to participate in several recreational activities of their own choosing, understand how to learn new skills, and have an appreciation for the value of participating in physical activity.

An **objective** is a relatively specific outcome of instruction which can be achieved within a short period of time. Objectives are derived logically from goals and serve as "stepping stones to the achievement of a broader goal."[1] Objectives can be used to personalize learning for individual students. The following are examples of objectives:

1. The student will achieve cardiovascular fitness.

2. The student will develop skill proficiency in an activity of his or her own choosing.

A **performance objective** is an objective that is attainable and is stated with enough specificity that it is possible to determine whether or not a student has achieved the goal. The following are examples of performance objectives:

1. The student will achieve the "good" or "excellent" category on the 1.5 mile run given two opportunities for doing so.

2. The student will hit three out of five tennis serves into the correct service court (given a racquet, balls, and an official tennis court).

You will note from these examples that a performance objective is a statement of (1) *what the learner will be able to do* at the conclusion of instruction, (2) *the conditions* under which the learner will perform the task, and (3) *the criteria* for successful performance.

Because learning is most often defined as a change in behavior, the results of effective instruction should also be defined in terms of student behavior. Since our only means of evaluating behavior is through the five senses, evaluation primarily includes observable behavior or an observable product of the behavior.

The advantages of performance objectives

The development of performance objectives serves as a basis for the entire process of instructional design. Without objectives, no effective evaluation techniques could be prepared, no preassessment would be necessary, and learning activities would be like a map without a destination. Expressing objectives in terms of performance provides us with the criteria for selecting and organizing the content and learning activities for the program of instruction.

Objectives also increase teacher accountability by focusing on specific behaviors that can be evaluated. Objectives convey to the teacher, student, parent, and administrator exactly what is to be accomplished. Teachers are more secure because they know that what they are teaching has been carefully planned and that evaluation is appropriate and specified. Students are more secure because they know what is expected and can spend more time on the important items and less time on unimportant items. Parents are assisted in their understanding of school programs and their ability to gauge the progress of their children.

With clearly defined objectives, it is possible for the teacher to preassess student behavior in relation to the objective, to evaluate progress toward the objective, and to determine the extent to which the objectives have been achieved by the learners.

Clearly stated objectives help the students to evaluate their progress toward the instructional goals and therefore serve as a motivating factor toward success. Students who know they need to shoot 200 points in five ends on a forty-eight-inch target at a given distance in archery are much better able to evaluate their own progress in class than students who are told only to shoot a round each day.

When you have written performance objectives for a lesson or unit of instruction, you will discover that you have already determined how to evaluate students participating in the lesson or unit, you know exactly what you will be teaching, and you can remove nonessential items from your lesson, thus providing more time to achieve what you consider to be the most important objectives. In addition, students will be able to evaluate their own progress and direct their efforts in the most effective direction.

Types of objectives

Performance objectives are generally divided into three types—cognitive, psychomotor, and affective. Cognitive objectives deal with the learning and application of knowledge (table 6.1). Psychomotor objectives deal with the learning of physical or neuromuscular skills (table 7.1). Affective objectives are concerned with interests, attitudes, appreciations, and values (table 8.1).

Since the general principles of writing objectives apply to both cognitive and psychomotor objectives, we will consider these two types simultaneously. Affective objectives will be considered later in the chapter.

Steps in writing performance objectives (Cognitive and psychomotor)

Writing performance objectives involves a statement of behavior, conditions of performance, and the criteria for successful performance. The following steps will help you write properly stated performance objectives.

Step 1. Define the area of instruction.

Step 2. Define what the student will be able to do at the conclusion of instruction.

Step 3. Describe the conditions under which the student's performance will be evaluated.

Step 4. Specify the criteria for acceptable performance.

Step 5. Evaluate the objective.

Step 1—Define the area of instruction

Choose a lesson or unit of instruction that is relevant to the student population in terms of real-world utility or preparation for future educational needs. Specify the target population in terms of age, sex, and previous experience in the unit. Some examples are:

1. Archery—seventh-grade boys and girls, no previous experience.

2. Volleyball—ninth-grade boys and girls, two years experience.

3. Physical fitness—high school, coed, varied experience.

Step 2—Define what the student will be able to do at the conclusion of instruction

In clear and concise terms, state what the student will be able to *do* at the conclusion of instruction. Be certain to include only those behaviors or products of behavior that you can observe through one or more of the five senses. Observable behaviors are always represented by action verbs, such as shoot, write, or attend, and never by verbs such as know, feel, or understand. Some examples of behaviors are:

1. Archery
   a. The student will *define* archery terms.
   b. The student will *pass* a test on the rules, etiquette and basic skill techniques of archery.
   c. The student will *shoot* with correct form.

2. Volleyball
   a. The student will *serve* a volleyball.
   b. The student will *volley* a volleyball.
   c. The student will *write* a paper on the history of volleyball.

3. Physical fitness
   a. The student will *create* an aerobic dance routine.
   b. The student will *improve* his or her 1.5 mile run score.
   c. The student will *engage in* a strength and flexibility program.

Step 3—Describe the conditions under which the student's performance will be evaluated

Include where, when, and with what equipment or materials and what set of rules. In informal units (i.e., those not programmed or written out for student use), some conditions may be implied and are not stated. Some examples of conditions follow:

1. Archery
   a. *Given a list of definitions* of archery terms, the student will write the correct terms.
   b. The student will pass *a multiple-choice test* on the rules, etiquette, and skills of archery. (Implied conditions are that the student will have a copy of the test, a pencil, an answer sheet, and that the test will be closed-book, etc.)
   c. The student will shoot using correct form *as rated on the rating sheet by the instructor.* (Implied conditions are the use of a bow, arrows, target, etc.)

2. Volleyball
   a. *Using an overhand serve,* the student will serve into the back half of the court. (A regulation ball and court are implied.)
   b. Using a legal volley, the student will volley a volleyball continuously *against the wall so that it touches above a line marked seven feet from the floor.* (A regulation ball is implied.)
   c. The student will write a *one to three page* paper on the history of volleyball. (Handwriting is implied, since typing has not been specified.)

3. Physical fitness
   a. *Given twenty minutes of class time daily,* the student *will join with two or three other students* to create an aerobic dance routine to *any music provided by the student or teacher.*
   b. *Given 10 minutes of daily practice time for jogging,* the student will improve his or her 1.5 mile run score. (A track or running area is implied.)
   c. *Given twenty minutes three times per week of class time,* the student will engage in a strength and flexibility program.

Step 4—Specify the criteria of acceptable performance

State the criteria in such a way that a qualified person could use it to successfully choose students meeting the standard. Describe the performance or the result of performance in terms of the number of trials, the number of successful completions, the number of repetitions within a given time allotment, improvement on a given scale, percent or percentile achieved, raw score, or other observable standard. Describe a subjective performance in terms of the degree or quality of performance required. The following objectives are now complete objectives with behavior, conditions, and criteria:

1. Archery
   a. Given a list of definitions of twenty-five archery terms, the student will write in the correct term with *fewer than four errors.*
   b. The student will pass a multiple-choice test on the rules, etiquette, and skills of archery with a *score of 80 percent or better.*
   c. The student will shoot using effective form as rated on the rating sheet by the instructor with a *minimum of two errors.*

2. Volleyball
   a. Using an overhand serve, the student will serve *eight out of ten* serves into the back half of the court.
   b. Using an official volleyball, the student will volley *fifteen consecutive times* against the wall so that it touches above a line marked seven feet from the floor.
   c. The student will write a one to three page paper on the history of volleyball which *includes origin, early rules and changes in the game, recent changes in the style of the game, and indications of current interest in volleyball.*

3. Physical Fitness
   a. Given twenty minutes of class time, the student will create with two or three other students a *two-minute* aerobic dance routine to any music provided by the student or by the teacher, which includes activities which will raise the heart rate to at least *150 beats per minute.*

b. The student will improve his or her 1.5 mile run score *by at least one level or will maintain his endurance at the "good" or "excellent" level.*

c. Given twenty minutes three times per week, the student will demonstrate participation in a strength and flexibility program *three times a week for six weeks by turning in a log of activities* on the form provided by the instructor.

Step 5—Evaluate the objectives

Evaluate the objectives by asking yourself the following questions: (1) Is the expected behavior attainable as a result of learning in the unit of instruction? (2) Is the objective important to success in the unit of instruction or is it included merely because it is easy to state in terms of performance? (3) Are good objectives omitted because they are difficult to state in performance terms? (4) Can another competent person understand my objective well enough to use it to evaluate learners in the unit of instruction? (5) Are both short-range and long-range objectives included for the unit of instruction?

Closed and open objectives

Burns identifies closed objectives as performance objectives that demand a single correct response of all learners.[2] An objective which asks the student to name the thigh bone has only one answer—the femur. Open objectives are performance objectives for which each learner might have a different response and yet meet the behavior specified in the objective. An example of an open objective might be to perform three new skills on a chosen piece of gymnastics equipment.

Experience, or process, objectives

By this time, you may have noted that there are some objectives which are important to your instruction but for which you see no need for students to develop a certain level of competency. The criterion for mastery may be that the student has engaged in the activity or experienced what the activity is like. In these cases, you need only note how you will determine when the student has completed the objective. For example, "The student will be present on the day the film is shown and participate in the discussion." This is called a process, or experience, objective.

Care should be taken to insure that objectives include all of the levels within each domain. An example of objectives for each level of the cognitive and psychomotor domains is shown in tables 10.1 and 10.2.

Table 10.1 A sample of objectives for each level of the cognitive domain

Knowledge

1. Match bowling terms and definitions on a written test at the 80 percent level.
2. Given a diagram of the human body, list the names of the bones and muscles shown.
3. List the six basic rules of archery.

Table 10.1—*Continued*

Comprehension

1. Given ten game situations in a specified sport, select the correct referee's decision.
2. Describe in writing the meaning of "intensity" in a physical fitness program.
3. Diagram a 2-1-2 zone defense in basketball.

Application

1. Buy a quality tennis racquet based on the characteristics emphasized in class.
2. Describe when to use a zone defense and when to use a man-to-man defense in basketball.
3. Write a physical fitness program for a specified individual that includes intensity, duration, and frequency.

Analysis

1. Analyze ten exercises in a magazine article to determine the muscles used and whether they are for strength or flexibility.
2. Analyze a basketball offense on videotape and determine which defense might be used against it.

Synthesis

1. Create five new plays for flag football.
2. Choreograph a new dance.
3. Create a gymnastics routine that includes at least five new stunts.

Evaluation

1. Evaluate various fad diets to determine whether or not they meet minimum nutritional standards.
2. Judge whether or not a specific behavior is sportsmanlike based on the recognized values of society.

Table 10.2 A sample of objectives for each level of the psychomotor domain

Perceiving

1. Watches the teacher perform a skill.
2. Asks a question to help "zero in" on how a skill is performed.

Imitating

1. Tries a skill demonstrated by the teacher.
2. Imitates a skill seen on television.

Patterning

1. Performs a gallop.
2. Dribbles a soccer ball.
3. Performs a forward roll.

Adapting

1. Dribbles a basketball while being guarded.
2. Shoots at three different distances in archery.
3. Bats to right, left, and center field.

Refining

1. Bowls with a smooth approach and release, meeting the criteria listed on the checklist.
2. Throws with accuracy at a target on the wall, scoring fifty points in ten throws.
3. Performs a series of three forward rolls in a straight line from standing to standing.

Table 10.2—*Continued*

Varying

1. Does a straddle, pike or other variation of a forward roll.
2. Modifies the bowling stance to increase the speed of the ball.

Improvising

1. Improvises a new soccer strategy because of an opponent's unanticipated moves.
2. Does the steps to an aerobic dance while improvising arm movements.

Composing

1. Creates a routine on the balance beam using at least five stunts already learned.
2. Invents five new flag football play patterns.

Self-check on performance objectives

Directions: Classify the following statements as (A) properly stated performance objectives or (B) improperly stated performance objectives. If the objective is classified as (B), identify the part of the objective that is incorrect or missing.

1. To teach the student to bat correctly. _____
2. The student will list five historically prominent persons in physical education. _____
3. The teacher will cover the rules of badminton. _____
4. The student should learn the reasons for using correct safety procedures in archery. _____
5. The Red Cross standards will be the model for student performance in swimming the five basic strokes. _____
6. The student will compute the percentage of body fat. _____
7. Given the specific data needed, the student will be able to solve six out of seven problems on body composition. _____
8. The course will provide the student with an understanding of physical fitness. _____
9. Given a pencil and paper, the student will pass a true-false quiz on the rules of bowling. _____
10. The student will appreciate the value of physical activity. _____
11. The student will shoot free throws from the foul line. _____
12. The student will understand basketball strategy. _____
13. The student will learn the overhead clear in badminton. _____
14. The student will demonstrate progress in weight training by keeping a progress log. _____
15. The student will demonstrate the serve in racquetball. _____

Answers to self-check

1. B, not stated in terms of observable performance.

2. A

3. B, not stated in terms of observable performance.

4. B, not stated in terms of observable performance.

5. B, not stated in terms of observable performance.

6. B, no stated conditions or criteria.

7. A

8. B, not stated in terms of observable performance.

9. B, no stated criteria.

10. B, not stated in terms of observable performance.

11. B, no stated criteria.

12. B, not stated in terms of observable performance.

13. B, not stated in terms of observable performance.

14. A

15. B, no stated conditions or criteria.

If you had difficulty with the self-check, review the preceding pages in this chapter before proceeding. Practice writing objectives until you feel that you have mastered the art of writing objectives. Have two of your classmates analyze your objectives in terms of the questions in step 5 and the three criteria for writing objectives.

Steps in writing affective objectives

Performance objectives in the affective domain differ from cognitive and psychomotor objectives in that attitudes, appreciations, and values cannot be measured directly but must be inferred by the behaviors of students toward or away from the desired behavior. These behaviors are called approach or avoidance behaviors. Lee and Merrill have provided us with a method for writing affective objectives.[3] Their ideas have been incorporated into the following steps for writing affective objectives:

Step 1. Describe the attitude you want the student to acquire.

Step 2. List specific student approach or avoidance behaviors.

Clearly stated performance objectives help students evaluate their progress toward instructional goals.

Step 3. Describe the conditions under which the approach or avoidance behaviors will occur.

Step 4. Specify the criteria under which the approach or avoidance behaviors will occur.

Step 5. Evaluate your objectives.

Step 1—Describe the attitude you want the student to acquire.

Write a descriptive statement describing the attitude, including interests, desires, or appreciations. For example, "The student will have a desire to maintain physical fitness."

Step 2—List specific student approach or avoidance behaviors.

Approach behaviors

List the behaviors that students will most likely be expected to *say* or *do* that bring them into closer contact with the subject. These behaviors are called approach behaviors. Some examples of approach behaviors are:

1. Physical fitness:
   a. Reads fitness books, articles, etc.
   b. Exercises daily.
   c. Tells everyone how exercise can improve their lives.
   d. Is always checking own heart rate during activity.
   e. Tries to get others to engage in fitness activities.
   f. Attends lectures about fitness.

2. A sport or dance activity:
    a. Reads the sports page of the newspaper.
    b. Subscribes to *Sports Illustrated.*
    c. Buys sporting goods equipment.
    d. Knows the names and performance characteristics of professional athletes or performers.
    e. Watches sport or dance events on television.
    f. Attends all local sport or dance events.

3. A desired attribute (sportsmanship, leadership, etc.):
    a. Volunteers to officiate intramural basketball.
    b. Joins a service club that helps with track meets, swim meets, etc.
    c. Calls own fouls during a tournament.
    d. Helps a friend learn a difficult skill.

Avoidance behaviors

List the behaviors that students will most likely do that will take them away from the subject. These behaviors are called avoidance behaviors. Some examples of avoidance behaviors include:

1. Physical fitness:
    a. Tries to convince physical education teacher that he or she is not supposed to run, but plays basketball later in the period.
    b. Teacher overhears student say, "It's no use, I'll never be able to lose weight."
    c. Asks to substitute marching band for fitness unit.

2. A sport or dance activity:
    a. Says, "This is a dumb activity."
    b. Tells the teacher this is the only time the counselor is available and asks to be excused.
    c. Fails to dress for participation.
    d. Is often tardy to class.
    e. Often fails to attend class.
    f. Fails to study for quiz or turn in paper, etc.

3. A desired attribute:
    a. Gives up smoking (i.e., avoids cigarettes).
    b. Joins the choir rather than be with students who are known to be on drugs.

In most school-related activities, approach behaviors are adequate for evaluating affective objectives and can be used exclusively if desired.

Observable behaviors

Eliminate activities that cannot be observed either directly or indirectly. Direct observation includes student activities that you actually see. For example, during homeroom reading time each day a student always has a sports magazine to read. Indirect observation includes student activities that are reported to you, such as the math teacher complaining about a student who listens to baseball games on a transistor radio during math class.

High-probability behaviors

Eliminate activities that are not commonly expected to occur among students or are inappropriate. Behaviors that are commonly engaged in by the students who like or dislike a subject are called *high-probability* behaviors. Behaviors that are *not* high-probability behaviors might include:

1. Stealing money to buy a ticket to a baseball game.

2. Talking parents into buying a universal gym for the family room.

The easiest way to know what kinds of behaviors are high-probability behaviors is to observe persons who have a known interest in the subject. The more you know about the subject, the easier it will be to define high- or low-probability behaviors.

Step 3—Describe the conditions under which the approach or avoidance behaviors will occur.

Stating the conditions or circumstances under which the behavior will take place is the hardest part of writing an affective objective. Only when the conditions are known can you interpret the behavior as a true approach or avoidance behavior. The testing situation must include a set of alternatives presented to the student that allow the student to make a free choice, unhindered by what the teacher may want the student to do. Two types of alternatives may be used:

1. Students can be asked to choose between two approach behaviors, such as "Each student may choose to play badminton or join the square dance group." This type of alternative will give you some feedback as to students' interests or preferences.

2. Students can be asked to choose between an approach behavior and a neutral activity, such as "Each student may join the square dance or sit out."

Of course, the third possible set of alternatives would be to ask the student to choose between an approach or an avoidance activity, such as "Each student can choose to play basketball or fail the course." In this situation, no one would feel free to sit out. *Free choice* is an essential component of the testing situation. Teachers must do as little as possible to influence the alternative chosen by a student in the testing situation. Some other examples of teacher influence might include extra credit, praise, special privileges, etc. Although these might be appropriate in a learning situation, they are completely inappropriate in a testing situation because they cause the student to approach the subject because of the teacher rather than because of a favorable attitude toward the subject.

When using questionnaires or other direct-observation techniques, care should be taken to make students feel free to express their true feelings, such as through anonymity, assessing feelings after the course grades have been submitted, etc.

Step 4—Specify the criteria under which the approach and avoidance behaviors will occur.

The criterion statement indicates how well, how often, or how much of the approach or avoidance behavior must occur for the objective to be achieved. Two types of criterion statements can be used:

1. At least one-half of the students will participate in intramural basketball. This kind of criterion statement indicates the number of *students* who will demonstrate the specified behavior.

2. Each student will engage in a fitness activity at least three times a week for one semester. This kind of criterion statement indicates the number of *activities* in which each student will participate.

One advantage to using the number of activities as a criterion is that it allows students with several interests or extenuating circumstances to demonstrate approach behaviors that might not occur in a single instance. For example, a student with a large number of sports-related behaviors had her tonsils out and could not participate in intramural basketball.

In either kind of criterion statement, the number indicates how much of the behavior will occur in order for the objective to be achieved. This number should be based on some realistic goal in terms of what is already known about students, perhaps through a preassessment of student behaviors. Teachers should not expect miracles to occur by stating numbers that are impossible for students to achieve.

In addition, teachers should avoid using numbers so large that it is impossible to tabulate the responses for the number of students or activities involved. Teachers can get a general idea of achievement of the objectives by selecting only one class to evaluate each semester. Words such as "several," "most," or "often" should also be avoided since they are too vague to demonstrate goal achievement.

Because behavior in the affective domain is evaluated on the basis of inferred behavior, teachers should avoid telling students what the performance objective says. A knowledge of the general objectives in the affective domain are usually sufficient for students.

An example of objectives for each level of the affective domain is shown in table 10.3.

Table 10.3 A sample of objectives for each level of the affective domain

Receiving

1. Listens attentively to an analysis of the volleyball spike.
2. When asked (following a demonstration), identifies the position of the feet in a tennis serve.
3. Selects a position to play in soccer, given a choice of three positions. . . .

Responding

1. Voluntarily assists in setting-up apparatus equipment before a gymnastics class.
2. Responds to a request to work on a subject-related project, such as designing and organizing a football bulletin board.
3. Remains after a class in wrestling takedowns for additional instruction or practice. . . .

Valuing

1. Attends an optional class session to practice high jumping for the Spring meet.
2. Risks being late for the next class by continuing a discussion concerning a certain defensive strategy in basketball.
3. Volunteers to organize an intramural swimming meet during his or her free time. . . .

Organization

1. Volunteers to play for the opposing softball team so that there are an even number of players on each team.
2. Following instructional units in judo and karate, organizes and supervises a self-defense club for girls.
3. Proposes alternative safety and spotting techniques to be used when gymnastics equipment is available during a free-time activity period. . . .

Characterization by a value or value complex

1. Requests additional information on ways to improve physical skills following each instructional unit.
2. Volunteers free time on Saturday mornings to coach an elementary-school basketball team.
3. Participates in all intramural events either as a player, team representative, council representative, official, scorekeeper, or equipment manager.

Source: Melograno, Vincent J. "Evaluating Affective Objectives in Physical Education," THE PHYSICAL EDUCATOR, 31 (March 1974):8–12.

Step 5—Evaluate your objectives.

Directions: After writing several objectives, check your objectives by referring to the following checklist which incorporates each of the steps described by Lee and Merrill.[4]

Attitude

Is there a descriptive statement of interest, desire, or appreciation?   Yes   No

Behavior

a. Is a student approach or avoidance behavior specified?   Yes   No
b. Can the behavior be directly or indirectly observed?   Yes   No
c. Is the behavior a high-probability behavior?   Yes   No

Conditions

a. Is a situation described in which the approach or avoidance behavior may occur and can be observed?   Yes   No
b. Are at least two alternatives presented to students?   Yes   No
c. Is the situation a *free-choice* situation in which the teacher does not directly influence the student's choice?   Yes   No
d. Are cues eliminated that might indicate the expected behavior?   Yes   No
e. Do students feel free to express their true feeling if direct observation is used?   Yes   No

Criteria

a. Is a number of students or approach behaviors specified?   Yes   No
b. Are indefinite words avoided?   Yes   No
c. Is the criterion a realistic estimate of changes that can be expected in the students?   Yes   No
d. Will the results indicate a trend or pattern of approach or avoidance?   Yes   No

Concerns about performance objectives

It would not be fair to leave the subject of performance objectives without relating some of the concerns that accompany their use. These are identified below.

It is easier to write performance objectives at the lowest levels of the taxonomies; therefore, there is a tendency to leave out many worthy objectives that cannot be easily evaluated. Often these objectives are among the most important ones.[5] Often just by knowing this is the case, teachers can be careful to avoid this deficiency by using the taxonomies to check their objectives.

Some teachers complain that writing objectives in advance of instruction prevents them from taking advantage of "the teaching moment." This is especially true in the affective domain in which it is impossible to schedule the teaching of such behaviors as good sportsmanship at a scheduled time and place.[6] These unintended effects of education may be as important or more important than many of the specified objectives.[7]

The specification of the objectives of instruction does not tell the teacher when it is to be taught. It can, however, make the teacher aware of the need to teach the behavior when the opportunity arises. The good teacher will continue to take advantage of the "teaching moment" to assist students in their learning rather than limit themselves to only those behaviors that will be evaluated.

Innovative efforts can be frustrated by an attempt to specify objectives too early in the program because the range of exploration is limited.[8] Teachers should specify minimal objectives and then add new objectives as they are discovered to be worthwhile.

In some fields, such as dance and the other arts, it is difficult to specify measurable student behaviors. However, teachers do have criteria which they use for evaluation and it is only fair that students be told the criteria on which they will be evaluated.[9]

The use of performance objectives has been said to dehumanize learning. Actually, for many students, performance objectives serve to humanize learning by telling students what is expected. The use of the open forms of objectives can also be used to individualize learning.

Questions and suggested activities

1. Write three or more performance objectives for a lesson or a unit of instruction that are clearly stated and include the three essential components—behavior, conditions, and criteria. Include the cognitive, psychomotor, and affective domains.

2. Discuss the advantages and disadvantages of performance objectives from your point of view. How can some of the disadvantages be overcome?

3. Write a performance objective for each level of the taxonomy in each of the three domains for a specified unit of instruction.

4. The recent emphasis on accountability has emphasized the use of performance objectives and the specification of competencies for graduation. What problems might arise because of this emphasis?

Suggested readings

Annarino, Anthony A. "Physical Education Objectives: Traditional vs. Developmental," *Journal of Physical Education and Recreation,* 48 (October 1977): 22–23.

Gagne, Robert M. "Behavioral Objectives? Yes!" *Educational Leadership,* 29 (February 1972): 394–396.

Heitmann, Helen. "Curriculum Evaluation," *Journal of Physical Education and Recreation,* 49 (March 1978): 36–37.

Kneller, George F. "Behavioral Objectives? No!" *Educational Leadership,* 29 (February 1972): 397–400.

Mager, Robert F. *Developing Attitude Toward Learning,* Palo Alto, California: Fearon Publishers, 1968.

―――. *Measuring Instructional Intent: or Got a Match?* Belmont, California: Fearon Publishers, 1973.

―――. *Preparing Instructional Objectives,* Palo Alto, California: Fearon Publishers, 1962.

Polidoro, J. Richard. "Performance Objectives: A Practical Approach toward Accountability," *The Physical Educator,* 33 (March 1976): 20–23.

Quinn, Lee W. "Generic Competencies in Physical Education," *Journal of Physical Education and Recreation,* 50 (April 1979): 68–69.

Singer, Robert. "A Systems Approach to Teaching Physical Education," *Journal of Health Physical Education Recreation,* 45 (September 1974): 33–36, 86.

Developing Evaluation Materials

Study stimulators

1. What is the difference between norm-referenced and criterion-referenced evaluation as they relate to test construction, test evaluation, and learner performance? Which type of evaluation is preferable?
2. Why is evaluation an important part of instructional design?
3. Define the following terms.
   a. Reliability
   b. Validity
   c. Objectivity

Student evaluation is a process designed to determine whether or not a student has achieved the objectives of instruction by comparing the student's behavior with the standard of behavior specified in the instructional goal or objective. It includes measurements of quantity, such as written and skills tests; and evaluations of quality, such as rhythm and form of movement in dance.

Types of evaluation

Two types of evaluation materials are norm-referenced and criterion-referenced evaluation. Norm-referenced evaluation refers to how well a student performs as compared with others in the class, grade level, or school. Standardized tests such as the American Alliance for Health, Physical Education, Recreation and Dance Fitness Tests are norm-referenced and provide important information regarding the general school population as it relates to national norms.

Norm-referenced evaluation is based on the normal curve that assumes that achievement is in fact normally distributed around the *average* class performance. When the distribution of student performance deviates from the normal curve, which is often the case, it is assumed that something was wrong with either the test (i.e., it was too hard or too easy) or the sample population tested. Therefore, the teacher is left to make a subjective evaluation as to the "true" performance of the students.

A common mistake in norm-referenced evaluation is comparing students with a norm from a different group of students. For example, students at one school may not fit the norm for students at another school. Students in a class one semester may not fit the norm for students in the class during a different semester. A class taught by one teacher will not fit the norm of the same class taught by a different teacher. In fact, one class taught by a teacher will not necessarily fit the norm of another class taught by the same teacher. Test scores from small classes or select populations (i.e., all athletes, all boys, or all girls) will not result in normal distribution scores.

Norm-referenced evaluation is often used for summative evaluation. Summative evaluation takes place at the end of a unit or course.

Criterion-referenced evaluation refers to how well a student performs in comparison with a predetermined and specified standard of performance. Ideally, given enough time for each student to learn the materials, each student should pass most of the items on the test. Failure to pass often indicates that the student has not had adequate time for preparation and needs more time or instruction to achieve the objective.

With increasing frequency, educators are using criterion-referenced evaluation materials to demonstrate the achievement of their students. This is because they show the extent to which a student has achieved competence in a given area of instruction (instead of what the student doesn't know). However, the complaint of grade inflation often prevents educators from adopting criterion-referenced systems.

One type of criterion-referenced evaluation is called a mastery test. A mastery test is used during a unit of instruction or course to determine whether or not students have mastered the content or skills presented. This type of evaluation is often used for formative evaluation because it helps the teacher formulate or revise learning activities while the course is in progress. Students should normally pass a mastery test with at least 80 percent accuracy.[1] Grades on mastery tests are usually "pass" or "fail." Students who fail are often given a chance to try again.

Purposes of evaluation

In spite of common thinking to the contrary, the primary purpose of evaluation should be to improve instruction. Teaching, learning, and evaluation are interdependent, each presupposing the others.

Evaluation, therefore, plays an important part in instructional design. At the beginning of instruction, it provides the teacher with information concerning those students who have already achieved the objectives of the course and those who have or do not have prerequisite skills for achieving the objectives. At the conclusion of instruction, it informs the teacher as to whether or not each student has achieved the course objectives and provides information as to the effectiveness of learning activities utilized in the instructional process.

Second, evaluation serves as a technique for informing the students of the course objectives and of their progress toward the objectives. In many cases in the past, students have been forced to guess the objectives from the nature of the evaluation techniques used and their progress toward the objectives from their grades on a written or skills test. In effective instruction, students have been prepared for the test in advance and there are no surprises in terms of what will be required. In such cases, a well-constructed test with a broad coverage of class content serves as a challenge for students to "put it all together" and as a summarizing experience that gives students a feeling of accomplishment by helping them realize how much they have learned.

Third, evaluation serves as a learning activity by arousing the student's interest, motivating study and class attendance, and finally requiring the learner to use or apply information and/or skills in a real or simulated situation.

Last, evaluation provides information to the teacher on which to base grades. Because evaluation is so important, it should be an on-going process. One of the important roles of the present-day physical educator should be that of evaluator.

Validity, reliability, and objectivity

Proper use of evaluation techniques requires an awareness of the strengths and limitations of the test. Although the focus of this book is not tests and measurements, several terms need to be reviewed before proceeding with a discussion of test construction because each is essential to a well-constructed, efficient test.

Validity is defined as the extent to which a test measures what it is intended to measure. Content validity is increased by creating a test "blueprint" so that the test items directly reflect course content. In order to determine the validity of any test, ask yourself the following question, "Are the student behaviors asked for by the test the same as those called for in the course objectives?" A common error made by teachers is testing the easiest things to write questions on or adopting the easiest skills test to give rather than testing on the content and skills they desire the students to know. Both approaches destroy content validity.

Face validity is defined as the ability of a test to measure what it is supposed to measure. When evaluating face validity, the teacher should ask the questions, "What might cause the student to get the wrong answer on the test when the student knows the answer if asked orally?" or "What might cause the student to perform poorly on a skills test when the student performs very well in a game situation?" Some reasons might be that the test is written on an inappropriate reading level, has vocabulary or instructions that are too difficult for the student to comprehend, or has a question type that confuses the student (such as the situation question that asks for the official's response). Skills tests might require skills different than those in the game situation, such as in the tennis backboard test where the ball returns at a rate much faster than in a regular tennis game. Tests given to foreign or bilingual students often create problems when given in written form, but they can be easily answered in oral form. Demonstrating what is required in skills tests helps to overcome some of these deficiencies.

A *reliable* test is one on which a student obtains similar scores on different trials of the same test. Reliability on norm-referenced tests is enhanced by increasing the number of test questions or trials or the number of students taking the test. For example, if only two questions or trials appear on the test and one day the student has a perfect score and another day misses one, the difference is 50 percent versus 100 percent. If 100 questions or trials appear on the test, missing one would only make the difference of 99 percent versus 100 percent. In the same way, if ten students take the test, our student might change from ninth to tenth place, whereas with 100 students, the difference in rank might be from ninety-ninth to one-hundredth place. Because objective tests are easier to score, they lend themselves to increased reliability over essay tests.

Criterion-referenced or mastery tests are designed for all students to achieve 80 percent or higher; therefore, the range of scores on the test is reduced and it is very difficult to obtain a high coefficient of reliability. Reliability is not usually checked in teacher-made tests.

An *objective* test is one in which a student obtains an identical score on the test regardless of who administers or scores the test. The objectivity of essay-type tests can be increased by making up a scoring key before administering the test.

Although evaluation in education cannot always be as precise as some statisticians would like it to be, it can certainly be much more precise than many teachers have supposed it could be. The examples on the following pages are designed to at least make it somewhat practical and objective for you.

Steps in developing evaluation materials

Step 1. Determine what to evaluate.

Step 2. Determine specific evaluation techniques.

Step 3. Construct written tests.

Step 4. Construct skill evaluation techniques.

Step 5. Construct affective evaluation techniques.

Step 6. Evaluate the evaluation techniques.

Step 7. Try out the evaluation techniques you have selected.

Step 1—Determine what to evaluate

If you have not already done this, refer back to the chapter on writing performance objectives. Each performance objective states the specific performance that is to be observed.

Step 2—Determine specific evaluation techniques

Decide how you will know when the behavior specified in each objective has been achieved. If the objectives have been correctly written in terms of performance, the verb should describe what the student will be expected to do to demonstrate achievement of the objective. For example, if the objective is to throw a softball, swim a distance, shoot free throws, or improve time in running, some type of skills test to determine skill in throwing, swimming, shooting, or running would be involved.

However, if the objective is to define bowling terms, score an archery round, or recognize correct rules of etiquette, some type of written test would be necessary. Some objectives—such as writing a paper on the history of tennis or passing a multiple-choice test on the rules of badminton—are evaluated exactly as specified, by writing a paper or passing a test. Some examples of various general objectives and appropriate evaluation techniques follow:

badminton short serve	skills test
archery form	rating checklist
swimming skills—dive, tread water, etc.	checklist
knowledge of rules	written test
dance composition	subjective evaluation by teacher using specified criteria

Many objectives would be more accurately evaluated by using several techniques:

lifesaving	skills test, essay test, personal interview
feelings about fitness	anonymous questionnaire, observation of participation in fitness activities
tennis serve	skills test on accuracy, teacher evaluation of form

Each of these techniques will be discussed in detail in the following pages.

Step 3—Construct written tests as needed

An example of a test construction "blueprint" is illustrated in figure 11.1. To help you learn to construct a test, each item will be discussed briefly.

Item 1. Decide on the course or unit to be tested; in this case, racquetball has been selected.

Item 2. Summarize the course objectives, including skills, knowledges, and other goals. Decide which objectives can best be evaluated by written test items—objectives A and B have been included in this test.

Item 3. Outline the course content based upon the list of objectives. Use your rules study sheet or text to make certain that all important rules have been included. Use your class notes, text, or study sheet for other areas of instruction. Occasionally you will discover that you have failed to note an important objective that you plan to evaluate. Go back and include it before continuing.

Item 4. Decide on the number or percentage of test questions to be included in each area of course content. The percentage of items on each content area should usually reflect the emphasis placed on that area during class instruction or in study materials, or the most common problems experienced by students (such as illegal serves in racquetball).

RACQUETBALL

1. Objectives
   A. To use the following skills successfully in game play as rated on a rating scale by the teacher: power serve, lob serve, kill shot, passing shot, lob or ceiling shot, drop shot, backwall play.
   B. To demonstrate a knowledge of the rules, history, and strategy of racquetball by passing an objective test at the 70 percent level or above.
   C. To participate in tournament play.
2. Course Content
   A. Skills (15)
      a. Power serve--1
      b. Lob serve--1
      c. Kill shot--1
      d. Passing shot--1
      e. Lob or ceiling shot--1
      f. Drop shot--1
      g. Backwall play--1
      h. Grip--1
      i. Skill breakdown--6
      j. Ready position--1
   B. Rules (49)
      a. Game--2
      b. Match--1
      c. Court and equipment--6
      d. Serving--9
      e. Illegal services--13
      f. Return of serve--2
      g. Hinders--6
      h. Ball hitting players--4
      i. Rallying the ball--6
   C. History (1)
   D. Strategy (10)
      a. On the serve--3
      b. Home base--1
      c. Shots to use when--2
      d. Double's play--2
      e. General--2

TOTAL   75

Figure 11.1 A test construction "blueprint" for racquetball.

Rule	1	2	3	4	5	6	7	8	9	10	Etc.
1.1	✓										
1.2		✓									
1.3	✓	✓									
2.1			✓								
2.2				✓							
2.3					✓						
Etc.											

Figure 11.2 A comparison of test questions with course objectives to determine content validity.

Item 5. Write or collect test items on cards or slips of paper and check to see that each area of course content has been evaluated. Check questions for defects by referring to common errors of construction in a tests and measurements textbook. An easy way to check test items with the blueprint is to put the rule number or content area in parentheses at the end of each question. For example:

1. In a match that goes three games, the winner of the second game serves first in the third game. (Rule 4.1)

2. In singles, it is considered desirable to return to the mid-court position after each play. (singles strategy)

Another way to check test items with course objectives is to list the content or objectives in a column on the left and the number of the test question at the top. This is shown in figure 11.2.

Item 6. Arrange questions by groups according to item types and add appropriate test directions. Slips of paper can be taped on sheets of paper or cards can be arranged in order for typing.

Item 7. Select or construct an answer sheet and make an answer key from a copy of the test. Proofread the test while making the answer key and correct any errors on the test. Then, make sufficient copies for class use. Number each copy if you wish to make certain that none has been taken during the administration of the test.

Item 8. Administer the test. Make certain that you have sufficient copies of the test and answer sheet, extra pencils, the answer key, and a red pencil or pen to use in correcting the tests. To minimize the temptation to cheat, seat students in alternate seats or ask them to spread out in the room. Review the testing procedures and the test directions orally to avoid needless questions. Include how to fill out answer sheets, how to get help if needed (i.e., raise

Written examinations reinforce important
concepts of physical education.

hand or come to front desk), what to do when finished, etc. Assign a student assistant to correct tests (if it is an objective test) as students complete them. Then, instruct students to review incorrect answers as time permits. In this way, the test serves as a learning activity as well as a means of evaluation. Make sure to collect all tests and answer sheets before dismissing the class.

Item 9. Evaluate your test by looking for and eliminating factors that might decrease its validity. Look for items such as unclear directions, complex vocabulary, poor sentence structures, poorly constructed questions, and materials that do not test course content as stated on the test "blueprint." Listen to students' questions as they attempt to take the test and note problems with the directions or test items on a master copy for use when you revise the test. Record the amount of time needed to complete the test by indicating when the last student finished.

Some variations of the written test include:

1. *The crossword puzzle* (figure 11.3). The crossword puzzle can be created by printing the terms in the squares on a piece of graph paper and working out interlocking words. Then, use a ruler to transfer the squares to a ditto by drawing around the squares on the graph paper that has been placed over the ditto master. Write in the numbers. (Don't forget to remove the tissue paper on the ditto master.) Be certain to proofread the test for accuracy before giving it to your classes. Answers can be listed alphabetically. These can be used by students who have difficulty spelling, or they can serve as practice assignments.

By using two answer keys (across and down), the puzzle can be scored as a test. Punch out the holes with a long-handled hole punch by clipping a copy of the puzzle over a piece of manila folder and then write in the answers beside the holes.

2. *Pyramid* (figure 11.4). Another puzzle-type test can be created by placing the longest terms at the bottom and building upward to the shortest terms. This type of test works well for testing a knowledge of rules or terminology.

3. *True-false test.* Develop a true-false test in which the answers are all true, all false, or half true, and half false. Instruct the students that one of the three conditions will exist.

4. *Multiple-choice test.* By labeling options of a multiple-choice test with letters other than the usual a, b, c, or d, the answers can spell out a phrase appropriate to a given holiday or activity.[2]

Instructions: Fill in the puzzle using the list of possible answers given below.

Across

2. The amount of force required to pull the bow to full draw.
4. The practice of shooting with bows and arrows.
9. An arrow that strikes the scoring area and bounces off the target.
10. The third ring outside the gold, counting four or three points.
11. To sight for hitting the target with the left eye closed for right-handed archers.
12. To pull the bowstring back to the anchor point.
14. Plastic "feathers" on an arrow.
15. A device that provides force for shooting arrows.
16. Six arrows shot in a row.
17. The fiberglass, aluminum or wooden portion of the arrow.
18. A term for archery equipment.
21. The second ring outside the gold, counting six or five points.
22. Two feathers on the arrow shaftment that are not at right angles to the nock and are the same color are called _____ feathers.
23. To place the tip of the index finger of the string hand on the anchor point and hold it steady until the release.
27. The outer ring on the target face, counting two or one points.
28. A certain place on the face to which the index finger of the string hand is brought consistently (every time) on each draw (two words).
30. The round object, marked with circles, at which the arrows are shot.
31. The side of the bow away from the string.
34. The upper and lower parts of the bow, divided by the handle.
35. Colored stripes used for identification that are placed near the feathers on an arrow.
37. The plastic portion of the arrow into which the bowstring is fitted.
39. A leather protection worn on the forearm to keep the string from hurting the arm (two words).
40. The arm, the hand of which holds the bow during shooting.
41. A device for holding arrows.
42. A leather piece worn on the shooting hand to protect the fingers (two words).
43. The center of the target, counting ten or nine points.
44. The side of the bow toward the string.

Down

1. The edge of the target face beyond the white ring, counting 0 points, sometimes marked "P" on the scorecard.
3. The center part of a bow that the archer grips with her hand.
5. The first ring outside the gold, counting eight or seven points.
6. To shoot the arrow from a position of full draw by straightening the fingers of the string hand.
7. Vanes are substitutes for this material.
8. The feather on an arrow that is set at right angles to the nock; usually of a different color from the hen feathers (two words).
13. To stand ready to shoot.
19. The middle section of an arrow.
20. Archery "games."
21. The string of the bow.
24. The part of the bow on which the arrow rests while shooting.
25. The line upon which the archer stands while shooting at a target.
26. The metal point of an arrow, on the forward end.
29. To brace the bow.
32. The object that is shot.

Figure 11.3 An archery crossword puzzle.

33. A method of recording hits and the total score on a score card.
36. The thread wrapped around the bowstring to keep the arrow or the fingers from wearing out the string where the arrow is nocked.
38. An archery ground.
40. To string a bow.

Possible Answers

Address	Belly	Crest	Hen	Red	Shooting line
Aim	Black	Draw	Hold	Rest	String
Anchor	Blue	End	Limbs	Rounds	Target
Anchor point	Bow	Face	Nock	Release	Tackle
Arm guard	Bowarm	Feathers	Rebound	Quiver	Tip
Archery	Bowstring	Finger tab	Petticoat	Serving	Vanes
Arrow	Brace	Gold	Pile	Scoring	White
Back	Cock feather	Handle	Range	Shaft	Weight

Pyramid Volleyball Quiz

Name _____

Period _____

Date _____

Instructions: Fill in the pyramid with the appropriate word or words to complete each sentence.

1.

2.

3.

4.

5.

6.

7.

8.

9.

10.

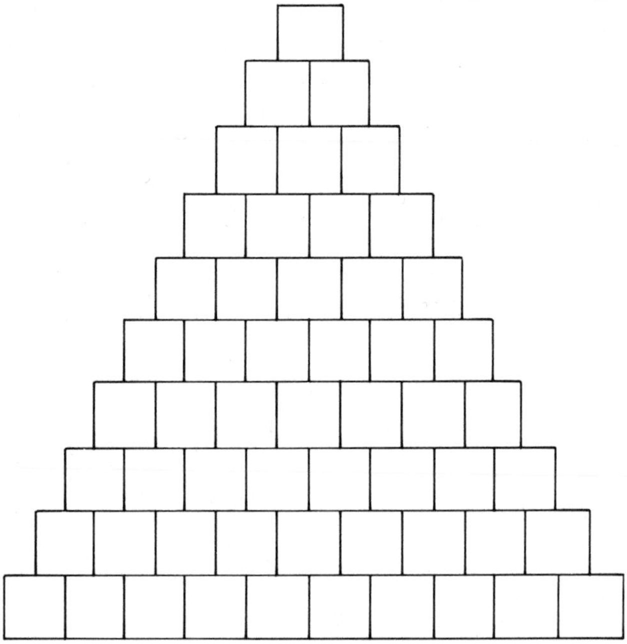

1. The winner of an official game must have at least a _____ point lead. (number)
2. The player in the _____ _____ position is the server. (initials)
3. An official team has _____ _____ _____ players.
4. A ball that lands on a court line is _____ _____ _____ _____ .
5. Except on a _____ _____ _____ _____ _____ the ball may be played out of the net.
6. To _____ _____ _____ _____ _____ _____ , is the moving of all players into position to begin serving.
7. _____ _____ _____ _____ _____ _____ _____ is called when the serving team loses turn of service.
8. The plan of attack used by a team to score points is called _____ _____ _____ _____ _____ _____ _____ _____ .
9. When the _____ _____ _____ _____ _____ _____ _____ _____ _____ team loses the rally, a point is scored.
10. In playing the ball, a player may step on but not over the _____ _____ _____ _____ _____ _____ _____ _____ _____ .

Figure 11.4 A pyramid test.

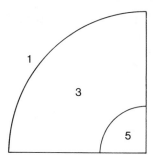

Figure 11.5 A target for the badminton short-serve skills test.

Step 4—Construct skill evaluation techniques

Review the course objectives and select those involving the performance of psychomotor skills. Look to see if appropriate tests can be found in tests and measurements books or professional books and journals. The American Alliance for Health, Physical Education, Recreation and Dance has skills tests for many activities. These tests generally cite coefficients of reliability and validity. *Always* check to see if the norm group is appropriate for your students or make your own norms.

If no tests appear for the objectives you are evaluating or if the tests cannot be used in your teaching environment, you will be forced to create your own. In this case, list the behaviors demonstrated by an outstanding player in the activity you are testing. For example, in badminton, an A student should be able to:

1. Hit a short serve as close to the corner of the service court as possible.

2. Hit an overhead clear that lands as close to the back boundary line as possible.

3. Hit an effective smash.

4. Hit an underhand drop shot that lands as close to the net as possible.

Next, devise a means of testing for the behavior specified. Try to keep the test as close to the game situation as possible.[3] For example, for the short serve, make a target (paper, plastic, or cloth) to place in the corner of the service court. This target should give higher points to players serving closest to the corner. (See figure 11.5.)

Continue to formulate the tests in a similar manner, keeping the tests as simple as possible. Try out the tests with a few students to see how they work and revise them as needed. For example, a review of the short serve test showed that students often hit the shuttle too high to achieve an effective short serve. A rope placed twenty inches above the net provided a solution to this problem. Also, the number of serves was reduced from twenty to ten to facilitate testing an entire class within one class period.

BADMINTON SKILLS TEST CARD

Name _____ Period _____ Date _____

SHORT SERVE:
Equipment: Rope--20" above net
Target--yellow, as shown

Directions: Serve 10 birds to the right court.

Scoring: Liners count higher number. (Serve must go between ropes. Must repeat illegal serves.) (Shuttle or racket above waist.)

5 or 3	Scored depending on area on target.
0	For hitting net.
0	For passing *over* rope.
1	For hitting in service area but not on target.

1. _____ 2. _____ 3. _____ 4. _____ 5. _____
6. _____ 7. _____ 8. _____ 9. _____ 10. _____
Have partners score as you serve.

Total _____

Figure 11.6 A skills test scorecard.

Before giving the tests to the class or classes involved in the activity, devise some method of scorekeeping and a management system. A sample scorecard for the badminton short serve is shown in figure 11.6. Administer the test and note any problems involved.

You should be aware of the disadvantages of grading on a single administration of a skills test. A student might be ill, anxious about the test, or just not able to perform as well some days as others. This can be remedied to some extent by allowing the student to take the test several times and use the highest score achieved. In this way, it also serves as a learning activity.

When administering the skills tests, it is best to demonstrate each test, read and explain the directions on the card or test sheet, and answer any questions students might have. Carefully explain trials, scoring, and recording. Make certain you have marked areas and set up equipment for all tests in advance.

SWIMMING	Sculling	Ch. direction	Turn over	Jump--waist deep	Jump deep	Level off	Dive	Bobbing--25 times	Rhythmic breathing	Tread H_2O for 1 minute	Ch. position	Elementary rescues	Feet first surface dive	Pike or tuck surface dive	
Mark	✓	✓	✓	✓	✓	✓	✓	✓	✓	✓	✓	✓	✓	✓	A
Gregg	✓	✓	✓	✓	✓	✓	✓	✓	✓	✓	✓	✓	✓	✓	A
Tracy	✓	✓	✓	✓	✓	✓	✓	✓	✓	✓	✓	✓	✓	✓	A
Gary	✓	✓	✓	✓	✓	✓	✓	✓	✓	✓	✓	✓	✓	✓	A
Lance	✓	✓	✓	✓	✓	✓		✓	✓	✓	✓	✓			B

Figure 11.7 A checklist.

Criterion levels the first time the unit is taught may have to be norm-referenced because you may not know how many points students can be expected to achieve. The results can then be used to determine criterion levels for future units.

Many physical education activities can be more appropriately evaluated through techniques other than written or skills tests. Some suggestions are presented here as a basis for your planning. You will probably be able to think of other techniques that could be used.

1. *The checklist.* A simple way to use the checklist is to determine those skills that cannot be effectively graded on a quality or quantity basis but which need to be performed at a minimal level. List the skills at the top of the card and the students' names in a column at the left. Then, simply check off the skills as they are achieved. The grade may consist of the number of skills completed. Examples of checklists are shown in figures 11.7 and 11.8.

2. *Scores.* Activities such as bowling and track lend themselves to direct forms of individual measurement because the score or time is the best indication of success in the activity. An example is shown in figure 11.9.

ARCHERY FORM CHECKLIST

Date _____

NAMES

Address	Feet not positioned properly	
	Weight unbalanced	
	Body twisted	
Nock	Arrow not perpendicular to string	
	Fingers grip nock	
	Archer's feet move to get arrow	
Draw	Fingers uneven on string	
	Finger or wrist curl	
	Grip on bow too tight	
	Forefinger above arrow rest	
	Forearm, wrist, hand not even with line of arrow	
	Bow canted	
	Bow elbow rotated downward	
	Head or body moves to meet anchor	
Anchor Aim	Incorrect eye closed	
	Unsteady bow arm	
	Not holding long enough to aim	
	Inconsistent anchor--no anchor	
Release	Body or head moves	
	Bow arm moves	
	String hand jerks	
Follow Through	Not holding form until arrow strikes target	

SCORE

Figure 11.8 A form checklist.

3. *Converted scores, percentiles, etc.* In some activities, such as archery, raw
   scores cannot be averaged because of differences in the rounds shot. In
   these cases, norms of some kind may be used to convert the raw scores
   into a standard score that can be compared with scores on other rounds or
   averaged to get a composite score. You can learn to calculate converted
   scores or percentiles by referring to any standard tests and measurements
   text. Grades on each round can also be used as converted scores and can
   be averaged. An example of converted scores is shown in the Archery
   Progress Record in figure 11.10.

BOWLING	Game 1	Game 2	Game 3	Game 4	Game 5	Final average	Form	Scoring quiz	Written final	Grade
Glen	134	134	148	140	144	140/A	B⁺	B	C	B
Jean	122	128	110	112	122	118/B	B	D	B	B⁻
Jim	150	168		120	168	151/A	A⁻	C	A	A⁻
Steve	121	83	114	112	104	106/C⁺	B	C	D	C
Lois	141	150	149	166	124	146/A	B⁺	C	B	B⁺

Figure 11.9 Grading with actual scores.

ARCHERY PROGRESS RECORD

ROUND	GRADE											TOTAL POSSIBLE
	Boys	A	A−	B+	B	B−	C+	C	C−	D+	D	
	Girls	A	A	A−	B+	B	B−	C+	C	C−	D	
NAA 900*		600	510	480	460	430	400	340	280	230	150	900
Columbia		500	410	360	330	300	280	240	220	180	140	648
Jr. Columbia		500	450	410	380	350	330	310	270	240	210	648
Scholastic		330	260	230	210	190	170	150	130	110	100	432
Jr. Scholastic		380	340	320	310	300	280	260	240	210	180	432

*Others listed are noncompetitive rounds.

Figure 11.10 Grading with converted scores.

4. *The rating sheet.* The rating sheet is a form of checklist used to evaluate
   (rate) some ability. It can be constructed from a list of expected
   behaviors. The teacher places a check mark beside the correct or incorrect
   item. Examples of rating sheets include the "Evaluation of Individual
   Presentation Rating Sheet" and the "Tumbling Routines Rating Sheet"
   shown in figures 11.11 and 11.12.

EVALUATION OF INDIVIDUAL PRESENTATION
RATING SHEET

Student presenting _____

Subject _____

CRITERIA	Excellent 5	Good 4	Satisfactory 3	Fair 2	Poor 1
I. Preparation					
A. Depth of material					
B. Breadth of material					
C. Accuracy of information					
D. Research information cited and reliability of sources					
II. Procedure					
A. Organization-- Logical Development of ideas					
B. Interesting, stimulating, provocative					
C. Visual aids, examples, and illustrations ..					
D. Level of class participation ..					
Column scores					

Highest possible score = 40

Highest possible average = 5.0

Total score ____

Average total / 8 ____

Figure 11.11 A rating sheet for evaluating an individual presentation.

5. *The incidence chart.* The incidence chart is a list of skills performed in a given activity. The "Badminton Incidence Chart" shown in figure 11.13 is an example. The number of times each stroke is utilized is tallied during a specified time period. Incidence charts can assist the teacher in describing game performance to the student.

TUMBLING ROUTINES RATING SHEET

Rating to be given in each area: 4 = Very Good; 3 = Good; 2 = Fair; 1 = Poor

Group number	Entrance	Team work	Original-ity	Quality of skill	Stage poise	Exit	Evidence of prepara-tion	Comments
1								
2								
3								
4								
5								
6								
7								
8								
9								
10								

Period _____   Date _____   Signature of evaluator _____

Figure 11.12 A rating sheet for tumbling.

6. *Subjective evaluation of performance.* Subjective evaluation by the teacher is one of the best methods for evaluating performance. However, several principles should be kept in mind. It is easier to evaluate some students each day and then to average the students' scores at the conclusion of the term rather than to evaluate all of the students at the same time. Figure 11.14 shows a sample of scores from a badminton class.

A skill or activity can sometimes be divided into convenient parts for evaluation. In the example shown, the students were graded in badminton as follows:

D or 1—Correct use of clear or serve

C or 2—Correct use of clears and serves

B or 3—Correct use of clears, serves, and smash or drop

A or 4—Correct use of all strokes

BADMINTON INCIDENCE CHART

| Name | SERVE | | | | | | SMASH | | | CLEAR | | | |
| | Short | | | Long | | | | | | | | | |
	Out-of-court	Into net	Too high	Out-of-court	Too short	Too low	Into or below net	Out-of-bounds	Missed bird	Too low	Too short	Out-of-court	Out-of-position
Diane White			/	///	/				///		////// ////	//	
Gregg Charlton				//////					//////		//////// ////// ///	////// //	///

Figure 11.13 An incidence chart.
Source: Rudy Moe, Brigham Young University.

NAME	9/17	9/19	9/24	9/26	10/1	10/3	10/8	10/10	10/15	AVERAGE
Judy	2		2			2+		2-		2
Sally	3+			4			4-		4	4-
Vickie	2	3-			3		3	3		3
Bonnie	1		2-	2		2+				2
Kay				4				4		4

Figure 11.14 Subjective evaluation of performance.

In swimming, each stroke can be divided easily into arms, legs, breathing, and coordination and one point can be assigned to each, the highest grade possible being A or 4. Never use a scale that is so detailed that you cannot interpret the difference between adjacent points on the scale to your students. For sport skills, a description of each point on the scale would contribute to a more objective and reliable grade. An example might be as follows:

Points	Rating	Definition
5	Excellent	Technique and form mastered. Effective, polished, confident in execution of skills and strategies.
4	Above Average	Good technique and execution of skill but not highly effective or efficient. Some minor errors. Good use of strategy.
3	Average	Basic skill performed but not refined. Accuracy and effectiveness consistent enough to permit some use of strategy.
2	Fair	Executes skill with many errors that result in inconsistency, inaccuracy, and ineffectiveness. Lacks confidence and timing.
1	Poor	Basic mechanics in performance of skills lacking. Experiences very occasional success. Fails to apply strategy.

Subjective evaluations in dance can often be made more objective by defining the factors to be considered, as in the "Modern Dance Composition Evaluation" shown in figure 11.15. This also helps the student to discern what is to be included in the composition.

7. *Tournament results.* Placement in a class singles tournament is generally a good indication of the playing ability of individual students. Otherwise, care must be taken to avoid grading one student on his or her partner's ability or lack of ability. Several kinds of tournaments that can be used to

MODERN DANCE COMPOSITION EVALUATION

Period _____ Grade _____

Names	Floor pat-terns (2)	Coordination of movements (3)	Variations (3)	Performance (2)
Janice				
Betty				
John				
Jerry				

Figure 11.15 Subjective evaluation in dance.

determine playing ability include: (1) a ladder tournament; (2) a chess tournament; (3) a challenge tournament; and (4) a round robin tournament.

The *ladder tournament* is a familiar type that involves challenging the player one or two places above one's own position and then exchanging positions if the lower person wins. A general rule is that a person must accept a challenge from someone on a lower rung of the ladder before challenging someone on a higher rung.

The *chess tournament* is most easily conducted by recording each participants' scores on an individual record card as shown in figure 11.16. The tournament begins by having the students pair off and play one game or match. Record the opponent played and the score on each player's card as follows. Under "round," indicate whether the player won (1–0) or lost (0–1). Under "total," indicate the total number of games or matches won. In the next round, assign students with an 0–1 record to play each other and students with a 1–0 record to play each other. Record scores and opponents. In round three, those with 2–0 records will play each other, those with 0–2 records compete, and those with 1–1 records are paired. Continue matching up the students as closely as possible until a winner is obtained. The winner is the student with the highest number of wins and the fewest losses. In case of a tie, the number of games won by each opponent is recorded in the "top" column and the student playing the hardest opponents (i.e., the highest score in the "top" column) wins.

The *challenge tournament* is played by having each student challenge as many other students as possible within the class and then keeping a record of the difference between the points scored by the student and the points scored against each student. An example of a challenge tournament is shown in figure 11.17.

The *round robin tournament* is played by having each player compete against every other player. The victor is the player who wins the most games and loses the fewest.

Name				
	SCORE			
Round	*Round*	*Total*	*Opponent*	*Top*
1	0-1	0-1	Sally Sales	
2	1-0	1-1	Jim Jenkins	
3	0-1	1-2		
4				
5				
6				
Place _____			Total points _____	

Figure 11.16 An individual record card for a chess tournament.
Source: Valentine, Ann. Brigham Young University.

8. *Accumulative tournament.* This tournament (see figure 11.18) is one in which a cumulative record is kept of student performance. For example, the distance swum by each student is recorded daily in the "Swim and Stay Fit" program of the American Red Cross. In basketball, a student can shoot ten free throws each day and record the total number made on an accumulative record. This type of tournament is most valuable as a motivational technique, but it is also a general indication of such factors as skill, endurance, and effort.

9. *The unit summary sheet.* A unit summary sheet tells students exactly what grade was earned in a unit by describing the grade or score earned on each activity. See figure 11.19 for an example.

Step 5—Construct affective evaluation techniques

Because affective evaluation techniques are generally used to assess ourselves as teachers rather than individual students, they can be somewhat less precise in terms of evaluation practices than tests on which individual students are graded. However, these evaluation techniques can be used in determining student progress toward course objectives in the affective domain and in assisting students through individual conferences, etc.

In general, we are attempting to assess (1) whether or not students appear to be as willing to approach physical education as readily at the end of our influence as when they entered our influence and (2) whether student attitudes are positive or negative toward physical education.

In order for students to answer honestly on affective evaluation instruments, they must trust that you will not use the results against them. Utilizing questions that require checking or circling the responses instead of writing, telling students not to put their names on the papers, having students collect the papers and tabulate the responses, or asking for papers

Student name _____ Point grand total _____

Telephone _____ Address _____

Brigham Young University
Round Robin Grade Tournament

P.E. _____ Sec. _____ Course name _____ Location _____ Days _____ Time _____

Instructor _____ Office _____ Ext. _____ Office hours _____
(and by appointment)

PLAYERS Men	TELEPHONE (Call for games outside of class.)	GAME SCORES (Record your scores first.)				DIFFERENCE OF SCORES							
		Singles	Doubles	Mixed Doubles	Cutthroat	Singles		Doubles		Mixed Doubles		Cutthroat	
						+	−	+	−	+	−	+	−

Figure 11.17 A racquetball challenge tournament.

Source: Copyright by Cryer, Walter. Brigham Young University.

Women									
Total of Scores									
Total Games									
Average Per Game									

Each game or match in Singles, Doubles, Mixed Doubles, or Cutthroat shall consist of _____.
  In Singles, record the scores of the games after your opponents' names. Record the difference of the scores in the Plus or Minus columns.
  In Doubles or Mixed Doubles, record the scores of the games and the difference of scores in the proper columns after your partners' names.
  In Cutthroat, record the scores of the games in the proper columns after each of your opponents' names. Signify by letter (a, b, c) after each of the two scores of the same game. These two scores must be counted as one game.
  You must play _____ matches or games. You may play more and count the best _____ scores. *Circle the scores of the _____ games which you are counting.* Remember, for each cutthroat game there will be two scores.
  This form must be completed with the "point Grand Total" figured and returned to the instructor on the last day of class.

Jogging Record

Name	¼	½	¾	1	1¼	1½	1¾	2	2¼	2½	2¾	3	3¼
Gail	■	■	■										
Lois	■	■											
Karen	■	■	■	■									
Penny	■												

Figure 11.18 An accumulative tournament.

to be placed in a box outside your office may help to convince students that you are sincere. At the beginning of the course, students can be told that their answers are needed to help organize the course to best meet their needs; at the conclusion of the course, they can be told that they are helping to improve instruction for following classes.

Two types of techniques can be used—direct and indirect. Direct techniques use quantitative data in the form of statistics, questionnaires, checklists, rating scales, inventories, ranking, and paired comparison. Indirect techniques use qualitative data such as teacher observation, interviews, and sentence-completion.

Statistics. A comparison of student approach or avoidance behaviors during the first quarter of the course versus their approach or avoidance behaviors during the last quarter provide a general idea of student affect.[4] Items for analysis might include:

Avoidance behaviors
   a. Dropouts
   b. Tardiness
   c. Absences

Approach behaviors
   a. Nonrequired club, intramural, or extramural participation
   b. Unassigned library books on physical education topics checked out
   c. Number of students volunteering to help with physical education-related activities
   d. Number of students desiring to major in physical education in college
   e. Amount of money spent on sports equipment

Questionnaires. From the following possible items, select (or invent) those that you feel are essential in giving you the evidence you need to make the instructional changes suggested by the student response:

Student goals and interests

   1. Indicate your interest in physical fitness *before* taking this class: highly interested/ interested/ neutral/ less interested/ highly uninterested.

UNIT SUMMARY SHEET

Name _____

CLASS _____

ROLL NUMBER _____

Fourth-Term Grade
Sheet
Physical Education

	Possible	*Points Earned*	*Total Possible: 100*
OBSTACLE COURSE TIME _____	35	_____	
TRACK AND FIELD SCORES			
50-yard Dash _____	10	_____	
Standing Broad Jump _____	10	_____	
Running Broad Jump _____	10	_____	*Your Total* _____
Jogging _____	5	_____	
TRACK AND FIELD QUIZ	5	_____	*Your Fourth-Term Grade* _____
WRITTEN TEST	10	_____	First _____
			Second _____
ATTITUDE Participation and sportsmanship	<u>15</u>	_____	Third _____
			Fourth _____
Total 100		*Total* _____	*Final* _____

Figure 11.19 A unit summary sheet.

2. How long do you plan to continue your present exercise program? throughout life/ throughout school years/ until school is out this year/ this term only/ I don't plan to continue.

3. Circle the subject you would be most interested in teaching. English/ physical education/ math/ science/ music/etc.

4. I took this class for the following reasons:

I was curious	_____	It was required	_____
I needed the challenge	_____	I've always liked it	_____
I wanted to learn something new	_____	I needed some easy credit or an easy A	_____
Nothing else was available and I needed an elective	_____	I don't know	_____

5. If you were asked to give a short talk about your favorite school subject, which subject would you talk about?

6. If someone suggested that you take up physical education as your life's work, what would you reply?

Student's perception of teacher and/or methods of instruction

1. If I had it to do all over again, I (would/ would not) have taken this course.

2. To what extent will you use the things you have learned in this class? often/ sometimes/ seldom/ never

3. What are the two most important things you have learned in this class?

4. Which of the following helped you most in meeting your course goals? teacher/ practice drills/ playing games/ study sheet/ individual work on skills

5. The study sheet was helpful in preparing for the test. strongly agree/ agree/ neutral/ disagree/ strongly disagree

6. The homework assigned was a useful part of the course. yes/ no

7. The present system of grading is appropriate. strongly agree/ agree/ neutral/ disagree/ strongly disagree

8. What things would you have liked more help with in this unit?

Students' perceptions of the curriculum

1. I learned more this semester because I was able to take the activities I wanted. yes/ no

2. I like being able to select the teacher I want. yes/ no

3. There should be a limit on the number of times a student can take a given activity. yes/ no

4. I enjoy coed classes _____ just boys _____ just girls _____

5. With regard to activities, I wish we had a class in _____ .

6. In which of the following did you participate?
   intramurals _____
   extramurals _____
   varsity sports _____
   none of these _____

Sport	Spec-tator	Occasional partici-pant	Frequent partici-pant	Low skill	Aver-age skill	High skill
Chess	(S)	(OP)	FP	(LS)	AS	HS
Archery	S	OP	FP	LS	AS	HS
Badminton	S	OP	FP	LS	AS	HS
Basketball	S	OP	FP	LS	AS	HS
Bicycling	S	OP	FP	LS	AS	HS
Others (list)						
_____	S	OP	FP	LS	AS	HS
_____	S	OP	FP	LS	AS	HS

Figure 11.20 An activity checklist.

7. By which method do you prefer intramural teams be picked?
   homerooms _____
   physical education class _____
   personal selection _____

8. If physical education were not required, would you still have taken it this
   year? yes/ no

Checklists. Checklists involve lists of activities or questions with brief responses that can be checked by students. Although they are relatively crude instruments, they can provide valuable data if they are carefully constructed. Checklists also run the risk of students "helping out" the result by marking what they think you want. An example of a checklist is shown in figure 11.20. To score the checklist, total the responses for each symbol and activity.

Rating scales. Rating scales provide a numerical value for each level of intensity on a scale. They can be used to provide information about the rater or the object of the rating. The danger in using rating scales is that they give the illusion of accuracy. There is also an implication that a high score on one factor can compensate for a low score on another. If a student scores low in skill, can this really be counterbalanced by high scores for attendance, attitude, and cooperativeness? Frequently, in practice, ratings tend to cluster on the high side with this system.

Labels used on the scales may not mean the same things to different people or to the same person on different occasions. It is essential, therefore, that ratings or labels are defined as to the frame of reference that students are expected to use. Otherwise, students will be influenced by what they think is the purpose of the scale, and since their guesses will be different from each other, ratings will diverge more than might be expected.

Rating scales usually include from three to nine choices. The number should be based on the complexity of the information required. Fewer choices yield more reliable data. More choices provide more information. Generally, an odd number is used so the midpoint will be a neutral category. Several types of scales exist. One form of scale is the continuum on which the rater places a mark as shown in this question:

Has positive attitudes toward self:

| / | / | / | / |

Very positive Positive Neutral Negative Very negative

Another type has boxes to check:

☐   ☐   ☐   ☐   ☐

Very positive   Positive   Neutral   Negative   Very negative

Several scales for rating behavior have been developed. In the Blanchard Behavior Rating Scale, the rater rates the frequency of observation of such traits as leadership, self-control, cooperation, and other personal and social qualities.[5] Cowell has developed a Social Adjustment Index to measure similar qualities, and a Personal Distance Scale to measure social acceptance.[6] Another test of group status is Breck's Sociometric Test of Status.[7] Fox has developed a tool that can be used to screen out students with low self-concepts.[8] An example is shown in figure 11.21. Results of all of these scales will be influenced to some extent by the amount of trust that has been developed between teacher and students. Teachers should be aware of the possible lack of validity and reliability in using these measures. Therefore, extreme caution must be exercised when using them.

Inventories. Inventories are rating scales designed to yield two or more scores by grouping items in certain prespecified ways. Many personality tests take the form of inventories. The Thurstone, Likert, and Osgood scales are some of the best known of the attitude inventories. Although each of these inventories has a carefully specified technique for formulation, teacher-constructed versions can provide useful information.

Several attitude inventories have been created to appraise student attitude toward physical fitness, exercise, and physical education. They are referred to in a number of tests and measurements textbooks. Attitude inventories generally contain three types of questions. The first type is based on the work of Thurstone and uses the following type of question:

	Agree	*Disagree*
1. Physical education is a waste of time. (2.00)	_____	_____
2. Physical education is helpful in one's life. (8.00)	_____	_____
3. Physical activity is important to my mental, physical and emotional fitness. (9.00)	_____	_____
4. Physical fitness is no longer essential in today's world. (3.00)	_____	_____

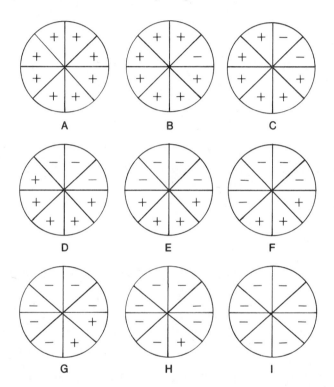

Date _____

Your Number _____

Class _____

How They See Me

Just as each part of the day is filled with positive, neutral, and negative things, each person is made up of things we like and things we do not like so much. Below are a number of circles showing persons with different amounts of positive (+) and negative (−) things about them. Which of these circles comes closest to the way you see yourself? Write the letter of the circle which most resembles you right here: _____ .

In the blank following each question, write the letter of the circle that you think each of the persons mentioned would pick for you.

1. Which circle do you think your closest friend would choose to describe you? _____
2. Which circle would the teacher in this class choose? _____

Figure 11.21 A self-concept scale.
Source: *Diagnosing Classroom Learning Environments* by Fox, Luszki and Schmuck. © 1966, Science Research Associates, Inc. Reprinted by permission of the publisher.

The student's score is an average of the scale factors (in parentheses) for all of the questions marked "agree."

The second type of question is based on the Likert scales. An example of this type looks like this:

	Strongly agree	Agree	Uncertain	Disagree	Strongly disagree
1. I need a lot of exercise to stay in good physical condition.	( )	( )	( )	( )	( )
2. Following game rules helps me be a better citizen in the community.	( )	( )	( )	( )	( )
3. I prefer to engage in activities that require a minimum of physical activity.	( )	( )	( )	( )	( )

The third type of question is based on Osgood's semantic differential technique. An example of this type of question follows:

Physical education is:

Pleasant	: : : : : : : :	Unpleasant
Good	: : : : : : : :	Bad
Active	: : : : : : : :	Passive

Another type of inventory is the interest or valued activities inventory. An example is shown in figure 11.22. To score the inventory, simply tally the responses for each activity.

Adjective checklists differ slightly from inventories. Students select those adjectives which apply to themselves or others from a list of those provided, as shown below:

Circle each of the words that tell how you feel about physical education:

interesting	dull	boring
fun	useful	very important
too hard	exciting	too easy
useless	tiring	

Ranking. Ranking involves arranging items on a list in order of personal preference or some other specified quality. Items to be ranked should be limited to about ten items. Two examples of ranking are shown here:

Example 1: List all the subjects you are now taking and then rank them in order from most interesting to least interesting. (1 is best)

Instructions: Circle the symbol representing your interest in each of the following activities.

	Strong interest	OK	Neutral	Don't like
Archery	SI	OK	N	DL
Badminton	SI	OK	N	DL
Basketball	SI	OK	N	DL
Bicycling	SI	OK	N	DL
Bowling	SI	OK	N	DL
Others (list)				
_____	SI	OK	N	DL
_____	SI	OK	N	DL

Figure 11.22 An interest or valued activities inventory.

Example 2: Rank order the following activities by placing a 1 by the activity you like to play best, 2 next and so on down to number 10:

Archery	_____	Folk dance	_____
Badminton	_____	Golf	_____
Basketball	_____	Gymnastics	_____

Do you dislike the activity you rated last? Yes   No
If yes, why?

To score, total the ranks from all students. The rank with the lowest score is indicative of the highest interest. One major disadvantage of ranking is that there is no way of knowing how much difference exists between items in adjacent ranks. Group scores, however, can provide valuable data.

Paired comparison. A relatively quick method for determining attitudes toward a subject or activity is the paired comparison technique.[9] To construct it, do the following:

1. List school subjects or physical education activities in the boxes as shown below:

Archery	Swimming
Badminton	Social dance
Bowling	Racquetball
Tennis	Square dance

2. Keeping the top left box stationary, rotate all other boxes as shown in the arrows until each box has returned to its original location. List each rotation separately.

3. Ask the student to consider each pair that results by indicating which one he or she would prefer to learn, or play, or likes best, etc.

4. To avoid a student's changing responses to insure consistency, use numbered flashcards with each pair and have the student note A or B, or put the pairs on separate pieces of paper stapled together.

5. Sample question: Circle the subject you like best in each pair (if on paper) or write the activity beside the question number on your answer sheet.

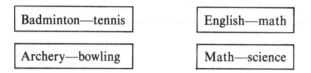

| Badminton—tennis | English—math |
| Archery—bowling | Math—science |

6. To score, count the number of times each subject has been circled or written. When used with school subjects, the paired comparison can be used as a pretest/posttest to indicate how physical education stacks up with other school subjects. If the second score is at least as large as the first, you can infer that attitude hasn't been seriously impaired. When used with physical education activities, it can tell you the rank order of activities preferred by your students.

Teacher observation. Teachers have almost unlimited opportunities to observe the students they teach. The fact that teachers have so many opportunities for observing student behavior and attitudes does not necessarily mean their judgement will be objective and informed. If the assessment is to be thorough and truly useful, teachers should systematically plan both data collection and procedures for recording information. If teachers do not consciously identify the behaviors to be observed and take time to gather and record information, their impressions are more likely to be formed on the basis of extreme incidents and behavior patterns, rather than by a less-biased sample of the behaviors of interest.

Ideally, teachers should take the time to devise a system of recording individual student behavior. Rating scales, frequency counts, or anecdotal records can all be useful in achieving this.

Interviews. Interviews can be structured or unstructured. Much valuable information about student feelings toward physical education can be acquired through informal discussions with individuals or groups of students. Structured interviews involve asking students questions that have been predetermined. The effectiveness of the interview technique hinges on the trust between teacher and students.

```
SELF-EVALUATION FOR _____

INSTRUCTIONS: Answer the following questions by circling the best
              response or filling in the blank.

 1. My attendance in class was: good     fair     poor.
 2. My participation in class was: good     fair     poor.
 3. I feel really good     good     ok     bad  about myself and what I
    have done.
 4. I accomplished all     almost all     most     some     none  of
    my contracted objectives.
 5. I completed _____ elective objectives.
              (number)
 6. My efforts on the objectives would be considered: good     fair
    poor.
 7. My efforts in helping others would be considered: good     fair
    poor.
 8. The grade that I contracted for was _____.
 9. The grade I have earned is _____.
10. If you were to grade yourself on a ten-point scale for each of the
    following items, what score would you give yourself on:
    a. Frequency of participation: _____
    b. Your current skill level: _____
    c. Your skill improvement: _____
    d. Your attitude toward the class: _____
    e. Your physical fitness: _____
11. How can you improve in the following areas in this class?
    a. Achievement _____

    b. Effort _____

    c. Citizenship _____
```

Figure 11.23 An attitude or effort inventory.

Sentence completion. Open-ended questions completed by students can provide information unobtainable in direct techniques because the teacher is completely unaware of the student's viewpoint. Questions might include such questions as "I wish this class . . ." or "I really like this class when . . ."

Student self-evaluation. Student self-evaluation can be helpful in assisting students to focus on their personal effort and involvement in physical education and to learn to evaluate themselves realistically. Often students will have a different feeling about their effort and progress than their teacher. Teacher-student conferences can be used to discuss these discrepancies and gain a better understanding of what goals each is trying to achieve. An attitude or effort inventory such as the one shown in figure 11.23 could be used for this purpose.

Step 6—Evaluate the evaluation techniques

Ask yourself the following questions about each of your evaluation techniques:

1. Does the evaluation agree with the performance objective stated for the activity (content validity)?

2. Are the directions and vocabulary simple enough for the student's maturity and are the test items carefully selected or constructed (face validity)?

3. Is the technique formulated so that another person with similar experience can use it for evaluation and get the same results (objectivity)?

4. Does the technique consistently result in the same score or grade for a student even when given on different occasions (reliability)?

5. Does the technique contribute to improved teaching-learning practices by enhancing teacher-pupil relations, encouraging students to devote attention to all areas of instruction, and serving as a fair and useful measure of achievement of outcomes emphasized in instruction?

Step 7—Try out the evaluation techniques you have selected

After or while using the evaluation techniques with one or more classes, note how you implemented each one, whether or not it was effective, and why. Then, make plans to remedy any problems and to increase the efficiency, validity, and reliability of the test. Remember, evaluation is a means to an end, not an end in and of itself.

Questions and suggested activities

1. Define and discuss norm-referenced and criterion-referenced evaluation and tell when each one should be used.

2. Obtain a copy of a standardized test—cognitive, psychomotor, or affective. What validity and reliability coefficients does it have? What do they mean? What norm group was used? Analyze the test in terms of its validity for your situation.

3. Select or develop evaluation materials in each of the three domains for the performance objectives specified in a unit of instruction.

4. Evaluate the tests given in a local school physical education program. Do they meet the criteria specified in this chapter? What shortcomings do they have? How could you improve them?

Suggested readings

Barrow, Harold M., and McGee, Rosemary. *A Practical Approach to Measurement in Physical Education,* 2d ed. Philadelphia: Lea & Febiger, 1971.

Barton, Grant E., and Gibbons, Andrew S. *Test Questions: A Self-Instructional Booklet,* 3d ed. Provo, Utah: Brigham Young University Press, 1973.

Baumgartner, Ted A., and Jackson, Andrew S. *Measurement for Evaluation in Physical Education.* Boston: Houghton Mifflin Company, 1975.

Bayless, John. "Conflicts and Confusion Over Evaluation." *Journal of Physical Education and Recreation* 49 (September 1978): 54–55.

Busch, William M. "Look! Instructors, Let's Improve Our Standards to Meaningful Objective Measurement." *The Physical Educator* 31 (October 1974): 129–30.

Coulson, Ronald R. "Using the High-Speed Computer for Knowledge Test Construction." *Journal of Physical Education and Recreation* 46 (June 1975): 28–29.

Gabbard, Carl. "Task Sheets—A Report Card That You Can Live With." *The Physical Educator* 37 (March 1980): 42–43.

Griffin, Patricia S. "Second Thoughts on Affective Evaluation." *Journal of Physical Education, Recreation and Dance* 53 (February 1982): 25, 86.

Johnson, Barry L., and Nelson, Jack K. *Practical Measurements for Evaluation in Physical Education,* 2d ed. Minneapolis: Burgess Publishing Company, 1974.

Mager, Robert F. *Measuring Instructional Intent: or Got a Match?* Belmont, Calif.: Fearon Publishers, 1973.

McGee, Rosemary. "Measuring Affective Behavior in Physical Education." *Journal of Physical Education and Recreation* 48 (November–December 1977): 29–30.

———. "Uses and Abuses of Affective Measurement." *Journal of Physical Education, Recreation and Dance* 53 (February 1982): 21–22.

Melograno, Vincent J. "Evaluating Affective Objectives in Physical Education." *The Physical Educator* 31 (March 1974): 8–12.

Safrit, Margaret J. *Evaluation in Physical Education: Assessing Motor Behavior.* Englewood Cliffs, N.J.: Prentice-Hall, Inc., 1973.

"Self-Evaluation—A Key to Learning for Both Students and Teachers." *Physical Education Newsletter* (December 1, 1973).

Shick, Jacqueline. "Written Tests in Activity Classes." *Journal of Physical Education and Recreation* 52 (April 1981): 21–22, 83.

Wiese, Cynthia E. "Is Affective Evaluation Possible?" *Journal of Physical Education, Recreation and Dance* 53 (February 1982): 23–24.

Grading and Reporting

Study stimulators

1. What is the purpose of giving grades in physical education?
2. What is the process for determining grades in physical education?
3. What kind of grading system is best?

Grading is perceived as one of the most bothersome of all teaching duties. Perhaps this is because there appears to be no consensus by members of the profession as to how or why it is to be done. In fact, many grading practices seem to be educationally unsound. Dressel points out:

> A grade (is) . . . an inadequate report of an inaccurate judgment by a biased and variable judge of the extent to which a student has attained an undefined level of mastery of an unknown proportion of an indefinite amount of material.[1]

The purpose of grading

Grades seem to have very little to do with success in real life. Why, then, do we continue to give grades? Because parents, teachers, and administrators demand them. The primary purpose of a grade is to inform students, teachers, and parents concerning the progress of students toward program objectives. Grades tend to promote positive public relations with colleges, universities, professional schools, and employers, who depend on them for admission and hiring. Grades may also serve as a motivator for both teachers and students to improve teaching-learning processes. Finally, if used properly, grades help to evaluate the effectiveness of instruction.

Principles of grading

In spite of the fact that educators have never been able to agree on how to grade, certain principles have emerged in the selection of a grading system.

1. The grading system should be developed cooperatively by parents, students, teachers, and school personnel.

2. Grades should reflect educational aims and promote educational outcomes. The stress placed on marks in conventional practice tends to cause the student to believe that getting good marks is the aim of education and, therefore, the end of education.

3. The grading system should be consistent with that used by other subjects in the school.

4. The grading system should be established cooperatively by all physical education teachers and be applied consistently to all physical education classes in the school.

5. Grades should be based on achievement of all of the objectives of physical education, such as skills, physical fitness, knowledge, social skills, and attitudes and appreciations.

6. Students should be informed in advance of the criteria and procedures used in assigning grades and receive adequate feedback on their progress toward objectives.

7. A variety of evaluation instruments, both objective and subjective, should be utilized in the evaluation process.

8. Evaluation should be an on-going process.

9. Evaluation procedures should foster positive student attitudes toward physical education.

10. A grading system should be detailed enough to be diagnostic, yet compact enough to be practical in terms of time, understandability, ease of recording, and accuracy as a uniform measure of achievement.

11. Evaluation procedures should consider individual differences such as physical characteristics, maturity, background experiences, and ability.

The process of grading

The process for determining grades in physical education involves the following steps.

Step 1. Select objectives and determine the emphasis to be placed on each objective.

Step 2. Select evaluation instruments for each objective.

Step 3. Measure the degree of achievement of each objective.

Step 4. Determine the grade based on the original percentage specified for each objective.

Step 5. Communicate the grade to the student.

Step 1—Select objectives and determine the emphasis to be placed on each objective

List each of the objectives of physical education and determine the percent of emphasis for each one. Consistent with the unique status of physical education, skill and physical fitness should be emphasized in the weighting.

Step 2—Select evaluation instruments for each objective

A comprehensive review of evaluation techniques was presented in chapter 11. Appropriate instruments should be selected to evaluate each objective. A sample plan for steps 1 and 2 is shown in table 12.1.

Step 3—Measure the degree of achievement of each objective

Student progress should be reported in terms of individual achievement of the objectives specified in each unit of activity. Care should be taken to record the data for each of the objectives. This information can be extremely valuable in interpreting student progress and grades to students and parents.

Step 4—Determine the grade based on the specified percentage for each objective

Based on the example shown in table 12.1, if a student achieved a B+ on skill, C on fitness, A on knowledge, and A on social skills and attitude, the grade would be averaged as follows:

$$
\begin{array}{lll}
\text{If} \ \ A+ = 12 & 35\% \ B+ \ = .35 \times \ 9 = 3.15 \\
\quad \ \ A \ \ = 11 & 35\% \ C \ \ = .35 \times \ 5 = 1.75 \\
\quad \ \ A- = 10 & 15 + 10 + 5 = \\
\quad \ \ B+ = \ 9 & 30\% \ A \ \ = .30 \times 11 = \underline{3.30} \\
\quad \ \ B \ \ = \ 8 & \qquad\qquad\qquad\qquad 8.20 = B \\
\quad \ \ B- = \ 7 \\
\quad \ \ C+ = \ 6 \\
\quad \ \ C \ \ = \ 5 \\
\quad \ \ C- = \ 4 \\
\quad \ \ D+ = \ 3 \\
\quad \ \ D \ \ = \ 2 \\
\quad \ \ D- = \ 1 \\
\end{array}
$$

Step 5—Communicate the grade to the student

Several days before the end of the grading period, the teacher should arrange a private moment with each student to communicate the grades earned as well as the reasons for each grade. Students can average the grades themselves, if desired. By doing so, many problems are eliminated and students are helped to see their own progress toward objectives instead of what the teacher "gave me."

Table 12.1 A sample grading plan

Objectives	Emphasis(%)	Instruments
Skill	35	Teacher observation checklists Rating scales Skills tests Student self-evaluation
Physical fitness	35	Objective physical fitness tests
Knowledge	15	Written tests Assignments Oral discussion Teacher observation of application in activities
Social skills	10	Teacher observation Student self-evaluation Anecdotal records

Attitude
  Attendance
  Punctuality
  Participation
  Dress
  Effort
	5	Attendance records
		Teacher observation
		Student self-evaluation

Grading systems

In the selection of a grading system or combination of systems, care should be taken to consider the advantages and limitations of each. No one method is superior in all situations; hence, some compromises must be made.

Several possible combinations of the systems have been proposed. In the first arrangement, grades should be calculated based on the extent to which the student has achieved each of the objectives of the course. Then, adjustments in the calculated grade can be made according to the student's effort or improvement in course objectives, thus preventing a student from flunking a course in which satisfactory achievement may be possible. The second arrangement is to group students according to skill and fitness levels and grade each group according to different criteria.

Norm-referenced evaluation ("Grading on the curve")

Norm-referenced evaluation is a measurement of individual performance as it compares to group or class performance. Student achievement is described according to a normal probability curve distribution, usually *A, B, C, D,* or *F.*

Norm-referenced evaluation is usually used for summative evaluation, that is, evaluation that takes place at the end of the unit or course. However, it can also be used to place students into ability groups for instruction. A third use is to establish the norms for criterion-based grading. Cognitive objectives in other school subjects are usually graded using this system of evaluation.

Norm-referenced evaluation is easier for beginning teachers not yet familiar with appropriate mastery levels for a given activity or content unit. A second advantage is that students are not penalized for poor instruction.

Several disadvantages of norm-referenced evaluation exist. First, it tends to assess the rate of learning of students rather than the ability to learn, therefore, the fastest learners get A's. Second, students in different classes or different semesters differ widely, as does the instruction, yet some students must always get A's or F's. The mark of C in one class may be the same as an A or F in another class. A third disadvantage is that grading on the curve is not consistent with evaluation based on performance objectives. It fails to tell whether or not the students have mastered the skills. In fact, some skills cannot be graded on a curve, such as "treading water" in swimming.

Criterion-referenced evaluation ("Mastery grading")

Criterion-referenced evaluation is a measurement of individual performance as it compares with a preestablished standard of performance, such as a score, number of tasks completed, or difficulty of tasks completed. It is often expressed in percentage scores, although it can be expressed in letter grades. Mastery grades are usually expressed on a pass-fail basis.

Criterion-referenced evaluation can be used for evaluating cognitive, psychomotor, or affective objectives. Before this system can be used, the teacher must be able to set appropriate standards. This system of evaluation is generally used for formative evaluation, that is, for evaluation measures that occur during a unit or course of instruction rather than at the end.

Criterion-referenced evaluation has many advantages. It allows all students to achieve a good grade. Grades are not influenced by the high skill levels of others or by the differing instructional abilities of teachers. The system is easy to apply once the standards have been determined. Criterion-referenced grading is consistent with evaluation based on performance objectives. It also facilitates program evaluation based on student achievement of objectives. Pass-fail grading solves the problem of distinguishing between performances in cases where distinctions are not needed, such as in "jump into deep water."

Criterion-referenced evaluation facilitates the use of student-paced programs, competency-based programs of instruction, and contract grading. Contract grading specifies the performance and criteria (quantity and quality) for which a student will receive a given grade. An example of contract grading is shown in figure 12.1. In individual contracts, each contract specifies the performance and criteria for that student and whether the student or teacher or someone else will determine when the criteria have been met.

Mastery learning places the emphasis on the mastery of the subject matter. It is based on the assumption that all students can master the material, but that some students need more time than others. As soon as students can pass a specified level of mastery on the subject matter, they proceed to the next content area. Students who fail a mastery check, practice or study some more and then take it again. A "pass" grade is awarded when all of the subject matter has been learned. In some instances a computerized printout shows all of the units that have been "mastered" during a certain term or school year. In many mastery learning systems, students are allowed to choose their own learning styles with the teacher serving as a facilitator and resource person.

Criterion-referenced grading reduces student anxiety and decreases subjectivity in grading. This is especially true of contract grading and mastery grading, which communicate to the student exactly what is expected in terms of performance, quantity, and quality. When students know what the objectives are, they are much more likely to achieve them.

The major disadvantage of criterion-referenced evaluation is that standards cannot always be specified before the activity or unit has been taught. Grades may become a reflection of test difficulty rather than of failure to achieve. For example, if no one got ninety or above on a test, that means the students didn't learn or the test was too difficult. In mastery grading, it is often difficult to draw the line between what is passing and what is failing. Standards may vary from one teacher to another. When pass-fail grading is used, students may lower their achievement to the level of the standard for passing, and motivation to excel is decreased.

Pass-fail grading does not differentiate between students of different abilities, except at a minimum level. In some systems, an A-pass-fail system is used to distinguish those students who wish to do more than achieve the minimum specified level of performance.

Pass-no credit grading eliminates the need for students to cheat in order to pass because there is no stigma on failure. It encourages students to try new activities that they might be afraid to fail. However, students still have to repeat the experience if they wish to receive credit.

Blanket grading (All *a*'s)

Blanket grading is when all students who attend class and participate in class activities for a specified number of periods each term receive an *A*. It is used in programs that are recreational rather than instructional in nature or with teachers who need an excuse to avoid evaluating students and providing feedback. The advantage, of course, lies in the ease of administration of such a system. The disadvantage is that students who are not challenged to learn new knowledges, skills, and attitudes often fail to do so. Grades in this system are meaningless in that they do not differentiate on the basis of any kind of achievement.

Improvement

Grading on improvement is supposed to reflect individual progress, demonstrated by performance on a posttest compared with performance on a pretest. It is used primarily for fitness objectives where high reliability exists and in individual sports where improvement is not based on the performance of others. It can also be used when student motivation is high enough to minimize students' purposely scoring low on the pretest.

TENNIS CONTRACT

A GRADE

I, _____ , contract with AFJH physical education instructors for an A grade. In return for this grade I will complete the following requirements on or before May 26.

_____ 1. Twenty-five forehand ball bounces.
_____ 2. Twenty-five backhand ball bounces.
_____ 3. Twenty-five alternating ball bounces.
_____ 4. Twenty-five consecutive forehand strokes against the gym wall.
_____ 5. Twenty-five consecutive backhand strokes against the gym wall.
_____ 6. Rally with a classmate at least six forehand and backhand strokes.
_____ 7. Serve ten consecutive serves to each court.
_____ 8. Play a match with an *experienced* player.
_____ 9. Write a two-page report on the four most popular tennis tournaments and the history of the game.
_____ 10. Pass a quiz on scoring.

B GRADE

I, _____ , contract with AFJH physical education instructors for a B grade. In return for this grade I will complete the following requirements on or before May 26.

_____ 1. Fifteen forehand ball bounces.
_____ 2. Fifteen backhand ball bounces.
_____ 3. Fifteen alternating ball bounces.
_____ 4. Rally against the gym wall fifteen consecutive strokes using forehand and backhand strokes.
_____ 5. Serve seven consecutive serves to each court.
_____ 6. Play one game with a classmate.
_____ 7. Write a *short* report on the history of tennis and scoring.

C GRADE

I, _____ , contract with AFJH physical education instructors for a C grade. In return for this grade I will complete the following requirements on or before May 26.

_____ 1. Ten forehand ball bounces.
_____ 2. Ten consecutive backhand bounces.
_____ 3. Ten alternating ball bounces.
_____ 4. Serve five consecutive balls over the net to the correct court.
_____ 5. Read the tennis information in Mrs. Anderson's workbook and answer the corresponding questions in the test booklet.

Figure 12.1 A contract for grading.
Source: Dona Anderson, American Fork Jr. High,
American Fork, Utah.

Procedures for Evaluation

1. All tests must be taken on or before May 25. An appointment must be made with one of the instructors to take the test either during class or before or after school. The appointment must be made at least twenty-four hours before the desired testing time.
2. All written reports and papers must be handed in to the instructors on or before May 25.

It's main advantage lies in the motivation of lower-skilled students, especially when they are included in classes with students who have high levels of ability.

Grading on improvement favors the less-skilled students over the highly skilled students because improvement at the higher levels is smaller. For example, a student who runs 1.5 miles in fifteen minutes can easily improve upon his or her time by several minutes, while the individual who runs it in nine minutes may be able to improve it by less than one minute. Because improvement scores are often quite small in comparison with achievement scores, they are quite unreliable. Therefore, a statistical error may be interpreted as a gain in achievement. Another disadvantage is that many activity units do not permit adequate time for improvement to occur. When students know you are grading on improvement, they will purposely score low on the pretest. Another reason against grading on improvement is that real life demands achievement, not improvement.

Impressionistic method

The impressionistic method is the practice of assigning grades based on the impressions of the teacher rather than on behaviors that are related to the specific objectives of the particular unit or course.[2] This often results in a grade based on such traits as attitude, attendance, sportsmanship, effort, dress, showers, and citizenship. Since there is generally a lack of sophistication of test instruments for measuring these traits, grades tend to result from the whims and casual impressions of teachers. Such grades tend to be punitive in nature in that they may be based on points subtracted for failure to dress, shower, etc., rather than on the achievement of course objectives. Personality becomes a factor in such a grading system and skilled performers may be penalized because it takes less effort to perform at higher levels of skill.

Descriptive methods of grading provide a
detailed analysis of pupil progress toward
course and program objective.

Descriptive methods

Various descriptive techniques of reporting have emerged over the past few years. They include (1) a form or profile showing test scores, performance data, and/or strengths and weaknesses of the student, (2) a student-teacher conference, (3) a checklist of achieved objectives, or (4) a letter to parents. Descriptive methods are most commonly used in elementary schools, although they often appear in competency-based programs, individually prescribed programs, or accompanying other forms of grading.

The advantages of descriptive reporting are that they can provide a detailed analysis of pupil strengths and weaknesses and show student progress toward course and program objectives. Because they are descriptive, they can also be more meaningful than letter grades and more helpful to students. From the teacher perspective, they encourage teachers to think of each student as a person rather than as a set of numbers.

The disadvantage of these techniques is that they are often too time-consuming to be practical. When teachers resort to the use of trite or vague phrases in describing student achievements, they may be confusing to students and parents as well. Written evaluations also allow teachers to rely on their own feelings about students rather than on actual performance.

Student-assigned grades

Because some teachers perceive grades as destroying student-teacher rapport, they favor student self-evaluation and grading. Students might be asked to write out their goals, criteria for evaluating goal achievement, ways in which the goals were achieved or not achieved, and the appropriate grade. Teachers may then add their own comments, negotiate with the student for a mutually acceptable grade, or average the student's and teacher's grades to arrive at a course grade.

Student-assigned grades are most frequently used in individualized learning programs when time is available for individual student-teacher conferences, although they can be used in a group situation if students are provided with some type of form for self-evaluation.

In order for this type of evaluation to be used effectively, students must be taught goal-setting techniques and techniques for evaluating their own strengths and weaknesses. Often, teachers will discover that students are harder on themselves than the teacher would be. However, honest self-evaluation is tough because of the intense pressure on students to get high grades.

Grading in coed and mainstreamed classes

With the introduction of Title IX and PL 94–142, the range of abilities within each class has widened considerably. This requires new insight into grading in order to provide equal opportunities for students to reach success.

Stamm discussed three possible approaches to grading in coeducational and mainstreamed classes. These include (1) grading on improvement, (2) using separate performance standards, and (3) mastery learning.[3]

Grading on improvement

The lack of reliability of improvement scores, accompanied by students purposely scoring low on the pretest, and the difficulty in equating improvement for students with different skill levels generally eliminates this type of grading.

Using separate performance standards

The practice of using separate standards of performance for boys and girls is common. For example, in order to get an *A* grade in bowling, boys may be required to obtain 130 points, while the girls' standard for an *A* mark may be 120. While this method is useful, it may result in a perpetuation of the stereotype that boys are capable of better performances than are girls. As girls receive more opportunities to develop skills at earlier ages, the differences in performance between the sexes may begin to decline. Perhaps a more equitable arrangement would be to group students by ability rather than by sex and then set the standards in terms of the abilities of each group. This plan might also prove more valuable in meeting the needs of the handicapped students in the class.

Mastery learning

Mastery learning appears to be the most promising method of evaluation for coed and mainstreamed classes, according to Stamm.[4] It works very well in activities such as lifesaving and Water Safety Instructor courses, which require a minimal standard of performance for all students regardless of sex or handicap. However, before mastery learning can be implemented, problems must be resolved regarding the validity and reliability of the standards established for mastery.

Whatever system is used, physical education teachers who are willing to experiment with the various methods of evaluation will undoubtedly arrive at a solution to this problem.

Questions and suggested activities

1. You have just been hired as a physical education teacher at Small Junior High School. It is your first year of teaching. What are some of the principles you will use in evaluating your students?

2. Discuss the pros and cons of grading on improvement. What might you do to individualize evaluation without the disadvantages of grading on improvement? Be specific.

3. One day during a rather dull department meeting, the department chairperson mentions that several parents and the school's principal think the grading system for physical education is too vague and subjective. The principal has asked that your group propose some alternative methods to the present impressionistic system. Include the advantages and disadvantages of each system.

4. Have a debate or panel discussion with each person or group defending a specific system of grading.

5. Are letter grades really indicative of achievement in physical education? Should physical educators insist on using letter grades just because the rest of the school uses them? What alternatives might you propose?

6. Role-play the following incident: The English teacher, Mrs. Frankel, gives her class a research assignment in which students choose their own topic and write a report. Dave, your outstanding receiver on the football team, fails to turn in a report and receives a failing grade. You need Dave to win the football game with Clearwater High on Friday and if he fails English, he will be unable to play.

7. Complete the following individual unit on grading, which was created by James Tyrrell and Rudy Moe of Brigham Young University and is used with permission.

CRITERIA FOR GRADING

Directions:
1. Choose the criteria you will use in grading by checking either the "Yes" or "No" column.
2. Give a brief explanation for your selection or rejection of each item.
3. Indicate the items from the class roll that you will use to determine the score or grade for each criterion.
4. Indicate the total number of points representing each criterion.
5. Indicate the percent of the total points for each criterion. (This must total 100%.)
6. Under "Comments" explain how you will determine the letter grade for each student.

Criteria	Yes	No	Explanation	Items on Class Roll to Be Used in Criteria	Points	Percent
Attendance						
Attitude						
Participation						
Fitness						
Improvement						
Skill Tests						
Written Tests						
Other						
				Total		100%

Comments:

Figure 12.2 Criteria for grading.
Source: Moe, Rudy. Brigham Young University.

Performance objective

Given the information provided on the class roll,
(1) complete the form entitled "Criteria for Grading,"
(2) calculate and assign a final grade to each student on the class roll, and
(3) justify in writing for Mrs. Robins the grade her son received by answering the attached letter.

Learning activities

1. Read the suggested readings at the end of the chapter.

2. Discuss your philosophy of grading with classmates and others in the teaching profession.

3. Schedule a meeting with the instructor, if needed, to discuss grading.

OFFICIAL CLASS ROLL

NAMES	Absent	Tardy	Improper Uniform	Suit-Cut	Discipline	No Shower	Improvement	Fitness test	VB Serves	VB Spike	VB Set	Wall Volley	VB Written test	VB Total Skill Pts.	Long Serve	Short Serve	Clear	Drop	Smash	Written test	Total Skill Pts.	Total Written Pts.	Total Skill Pts. - bad.	Total Skill Pts.	COMMENTS	TOTAL POINTS	FINAL GRADE
Adams, J.	2	0	0		✓		76	33	37	38	28	40	136	37	30	29	34	34	48	83	164	83	164	300	Average		
Alder, C.	0	3	0	✓✓	✓		68	38	40	41	33	41	152	42	36	42	38	37	37	78	198	78	198	350	Disrupts class continually		
Bennett, A.	1	0	0		✓		73	30	31	39	26	38	126	40	34	40	39	35	73	179	304	Average		
Boyle, D.	0	0	0	2	✓✓		57	38	35	36	27	40	130	34	28	32	27	44	84	162	292	Tries hard		
Butler, N.	3	4	3	✓	✓		59	28	35	32	19	37	114	28	33	36	34	38	75	154	277	Dirty gym clothes often		
Cannon, R.	2	2	0	✓✓✓	✓	1	64	29	34	37	25	38	125	36	34	28	26	40	78	154	277	Refuses to follow directions		
Evans, W.	0	1	0		✓		15	31	34	36	31	35	134	32	35	24	39	36	71	157	289	Above-average ability		
Garrick, S.	4	3	2	✓✓	✓		63	36	31	39	29	30	136	28	31	29	20	34	64	139	214	Lazy		
Jensen, T.	1	2	0		✓		78	40	38	33	20	37	141	35	30	37	36	175	73	316	Hardly ever notice student		
Jones, W.	0	0	2	✓✓✓	✓		68	37	33	30	39	139	32	36	36	24	34	73	154	283	Talks continually		
Madsen, G.	2	1	0		✓	-	76	33	36	41	28	37	138	30	33	34	39	59	76	197	So-so		
Nielsen, A.	0	2	1	4	-		70	30	27	28	20	38	105	26	30	38	18	44	148	82	253	Overweight - teased often		
Price, P.	0	0	0		+		89	43	41	38	36	37	158	43	44	46	28	39	43	246	803	Leader of class		
Pyne, K.	0	3	2	✓	✓		72	34	37	36	27	34	134	30	26	40	36	30	64	170	304	Comes from poverty area		
Reed, N.	4	0			-		80	40	57	36	41	143	37	37	30	28	34	57	171	304	Tries to impress me		
Rice, V.	1	0	0		✓		93	46	41	39	34	46	160	43	39	41	43	46	39	212	85	372	Highly skilled		
Robins, E.	1	2	0	✓ ✓	+		82	28	31	34	17	37	100	29	30	30	22	19	31	130	68	225	Parent comes in+gripes often		
Robinson, H.	2	0	0		✓		93	30	30	33	25	39	116	-	-	-	33	0	72	116	Always asks how he's doing		
Sandberg, B.	1	2	1	2 ✓✓	-	+	64	34	37	29	24	36	134	31	31	29	38	170	74	244	Bully		
Saunders, P.	2	2	0	✓✓	✓		86	43	31	29	26	43	119	41	35	36	31	48	177	91	296	Very conscientious		
Schwartz, R.	3	1	0		-		77	28	28	29	27	44	112	27	32	28	19	30	40	136	84	240	Shy and hesitant		
Simons, J.	0	1	0		✓		79	27	33	36	30	39	126	33	37	38	28	40	33	176	72	362	Average		
Snow, C.	0	0	0		-		30	30	31	34	17	46	112	27	22	30	18	19	42	116	88	228	Very uncoordinated		
Taylor, L.	1	0	0		+		85	29	33	30	20	40	122	24	23	36	18	20	41	166	81	288	Great improvement in skill		
VanBuren, T.	2	0	0		-		74	30	35	34	25	41	135	31	31	29	30	41	165	75	289	So-so		
Wilcox, B.	0	3	3	✓✓✓	✓		71	33	28	27	29	39	119	32	36	37	30	27	39	162	78	291	Foul language		

Figure 12.3 Official class roll.

Source: Moe, Rudy. Brigham Young University.

EXPLANATORY NOTES FOR OFFICIAL CLASS ROLL

1. *Absent*--Number recorded indicates the number of times the student was missing from class for an entire class period.
2. *Tardy*--Number recorded indicates the number of times the student was not present for roll call but attended class.
3. *Improper Uniform*--Number recorded indicates the number of times the student was not dressed in the full regulation uniform.
4. *Suit Cut*--Number recorded indicates the number of times the student was present but failed to dress for class.
5. *Discipline*--Each check mark (✓) indicates one incident in which the student was involved in a disciplinary action in class.
6. *No Shower*--Number recorded indicates the number of times the student failed to shower after class.
7. *Improvement*--The following marks were used:
   - (-) = Little or no improvement
   - (✓) = Adequate improvement
   - (+) = Great improvement
8. *Fitness Test*--The figure represents a *Composite Percentile Score.*
9. *Volleyball*--Each student was tested on the following:
10. *Badminton*--Each student was tested on the following:

	Attempts	Points	Total Points Possible		Attempts	Points	Total Points Possible
Serves	10	1-5	50	Long Serve	10	1-5	50
Spike	10	1-5	50	Short Serve	10	1-5	50
Set	10	1-5	50	Clear	10	1-5	50
Wall Volley	No./30 Seconds	No. Made	No. Made	Drop	10	1-5	50
Written	_____	_____	50	Smash	10	1-5	50
			_____	Written	_____	_____	50
			200 +				_____
							300

Figure 12.4 Explanatory notes for official class roll.

Source: Moe, Rudy. Brigham Young University.

Evaluation

Complete "Criteria for Grading," class roll, and answer the letter from a parent.

Letter from a parent

Dear Mr. or Mrs. _____ ,

I'm Mrs. Robins, the mother of Eddie Robins. I would like to know why my son received the grade you gave him for P. E. He has come home every day so excited about his badminton and volleyball class and has been quite conscientious about practicing both sports out in the back yard.

I would like to know what you based his final grade for the class on, and how you came to that decision.

Sincerely yours,

Mrs. Edward G. Robins

Mrs. Edward G. Robins

Suggested readings

Davis, Myron W., and Hopkins, Vicki L. "Improving Evaluation of Physical Fitness and Sport Skill Performance: A Model Profile." *Journal of Physical Education and Recreation* 50 (May 1979): 76–78.

Kirschenbaum, Howard; Simon, Sidney B.; and Napier, Rodney W. *Wad-ja-Get? The Grading Game in American Education.* New York: Hart Publishing Company, 1971.

McCraw, Lynn W. "Principles and Practices for Assigning Grades in Physical Education." *Journal of Health Physical Education Recreation* 35 (February 1964): 24–25.

McDonald, E. Daron, and Yeates, Marilyn E. "Measuring Improvement in Physical Education." *Journal of Physical Education and Recreation* 50 (February 1979): 79–80.

Safrit, Margaret J., and Stamm, Carol L. "Reliability Estimates for Criterion-Referenced Measures in the Psychomotor Domain." *Research Quarterly for Exercise and Sport* 51 (May 1980): 359–68.

"Self-Evaluation—A Key to Learning For Both Students and Teachers." *Physical Education Newsletter* (December 1, 1973).

Shea, John B. "The Pass-Fail Option and Physical Education." *Journal of Health Physical Education Recreation* 42 (May 1971): 19–20.

Solley, Wm. H., et al. "Grading in Physical Education." *Journal of Health Physical Education Recreation* (May 1967): 34–39.

Wickstrom, Ralph. "Ruminations on Grading." *The Physical Educator* 30 (October 1973): 118–20.

Developing Preassessment Techniques

Study stimulators

1. What is preassessment? Why is it important in the instructional setting?
2. What is a task analysis? Why is it important? How do you determine what tasks go where in the hierarchy?
3. What methods can be used to get to know your students?

Preassessment is any technique used at the beginning of instruction to determine where the learner is in relation to the instructional objective. Preassessment techniques can be used to determine:

1. Whether the learner or learners can or cannot already perform the behavior of the instructional objective and, therefore, whether or not the objective is appropriate for the learner or group.

2. Whether the learner possesses the concepts or skills necessary to succeed in learning the behavior of the instructional objective.

Why is preassessment important? It gives the teacher information needed to individualize instruction by identifying where each learner is in the learning process in relation to the objective. Students who have already achieved the objective should be allowed to perfect the behavior by practicing for accuracy, by practicing an advanced form of the skill, or by working on other activities. For example, if the objective states that the student will perform the lay-up shot in basketball successfully and with correct form, the teacher can quickly identify those students who can already perform successful lay-ups with correct form. These students can be sent to a separate court to work on consecutive lay-ups, left-handed or reverse lay-ups, or lay-ups in a game. In team-teaching situations, or when individualized instruction is available, students can move on to other objectives.

If the student can *not* perform the behavior specified in the objective, then the preassessment technique should tell the teacher which students lack the skills necessary to begin learning the specified behavior. These students should be given help in order to develop the prerequisite skills. For example, students who do not have the hand-eye coordination necessary to hit a badminton shuttle are not ready to learn the overhand and underhand clears. Special help must be given to help these students learn to connect with the shuttle before instruction can take place on the strokes.

Preassessment techniques are essential for grouping, for individualized programs, and for diagnosis or screening. They can also be helpful in clarifying objectives to the student, especially when the pretest is the same as the posttest.

Preassessment techniques can also be helpful in the evaluation of instructional objectives and methods of teaching. For example, suppose that the class average (mean) on a pretest is fifty-five and the mean on a posttest is sixty. This might indicate that the objectives need to be revised upwards, since students are apparently not being challenged to achieve higher levels of knowledge or skill.

In another example, Teacher A brags that all of her archery students can shoot 200 points at forty yards and, therefore, she is an excellent teacher. Without some other information, no judgment of her teaching ability can be made. Since 200 points at forty yards is a good score for a beginning student, we can assume either that she taught the class well or that she began the class with students who were already highly skilled in archery. Teacher B, on the contrary, indicates that in his class no student scored 200 points or better on the pretest at twenty yards, yet now all students can shoot 200 points at forty yards. Because of the pretest scores, we know that Teacher B can be pleased with the results of his teaching.

Preassessment can also assist students to increase their self-awareness with regard to their own skills, knowledges, and attitudes, and to reevaluate their own abilities through a knowledge of diagnostic procedures.

Preassessment can be done formally through written or performance tests or informally through observation, asking questions, or analyzing student records of previous work. The result of a previous test or evaluation can also be utilized to determine student skills and knowledges. Whatever the method, the preassessment should precede each new objective in the lesson or unit.

Note that some preassessment techniques fall within the realm of instruction (i.e., some can occur following the demonstration of the skill). Because of the safety factor in some cases, students should not be allowed to take a pretest until a certain level of fitness or skill has been achieved. For example, students should not be asked to take a twelve-minute run without engaging in a cardiovascular endurance program that gradually develops the ability to run that long without incurring adverse physical effects. In gymnastics, students should not be preassessed on higher level skills until they have demonstrated the ability to perform prerequisite skills.

The information that follows is designed to help you develop practical preassessment techniques for instructional situations.

Steps in developing preassessment techniques

Step 1. Write down how you will know if some or all of the students have achieved the objective.

Step 2. Analyze the objective into its component parts.

Step 3. Write down how you will know if students have the prerequisite skills to begin working on the objective.

Step 4. Decide how you will get to know the students.

Step 1—Write down how you will know if some or all
of the students have achieved the objective.

The preassessment technique utilized to determine how the students have achieved the objective will often be the same technique as that used for evaluating the objective. However, other less formal techniques will be useful when formal evaluation will be administered to the total group at the conclusion of a short unit of instruction or when preassessment is utilized for a single lesson. An explanation of some of the more common forms of preassessment is given here. Refer to chapter 11 for detailed instruction on each technique.

Pretest

A written test may be utilized to preassess knowledge or a skills test to check on skill achievement. These tests may be equivalent forms of a posttest or a simplified version if time is a factor. If a student passes an equivalent of the posttest, the student should not be asked to repeat the evaluation.

Teacher observation

Students are asked to perform a skill as they have previously learned it and the teacher observes to see which students can already perform the skill according to the criterion established in the instructional objective. This can be done while students are engaged in a learning activity.

Question or questionnaire

A formal questionnaire or an informal question asked of the student by the teacher is often sufficient to tell the teacher which students at least think they have achieved the objective. For example, "How many of you can do a feet-first surface dive?" If no one thinks he or she can, then it is probably a waste of time to utilize a more formal preassessment technique.

Step 2—Analyze the objective into its component parts

An analysis of each performance objective into its component parts is important for several reasons:

1. It can identify prerequisites to learning. Although we often have no control over acceptance of a student into our classes, this information is essential when writing individualized units of instruction or dividing classes into beginning, intermediate, or advanced levels.

2. It keeps you from leaving out important components necessary for success in instruction.

3. It assists in the formulation of an appropriate sequence for course instruction.

A pretest helps this teacher individualize a
fitness program for the student.

Analyze the cognitive components required by the objective. Analyzing cognitive objectives involves breaking down the objective into what the student will have to know in order to achieve the objective and then listing those statements in an appropriate order for learning to take place.

One way to analyze the objective is to create an outline consisting of the complex idea with more specific ideas listed under the general areas. The following example is the "Ideas To Be Learned" section from an individual unit entitled "How to Make A Bulletin Board."

1. A bulletin board is a visual form of an idea.
    a. It should include only one major idea.
    b. It may include subideas to the major idea.

2. A bulletin board has many uses. It can:
    a. Catch the student's attention
    b. Arouse interest
    c. Introduce a unit
    d. Clarify ideas and meanings
    e. Visualize problems of concern
    f. Tell a story dramatically
    g. Convey knowledge
    h. Summarize work that has been done
    i. Keep students informed of tournament results

3. A bulletin board must be:
    a. Simple—"When in doubt, leave it out."
    b. Relevant to classwork
    c. Attractive
    d. Interesting
    e. Eye-catching
    f. Changed often

4. Students can often learn from working together to plan and create bulletin boards.

Many cognitive objectives are composed of various concepts. After listing the concepts, define each as briefly as possible and list as many examples and nonexamples of the concept as you can. For example, if your objective states that the student will define physical fitness, an analysis might look like this:

1. Physical fitness
    a. Definition—the ability to tolerate stress
    b. Examples
        1. Staying up nights with a sick baby without becoming sick oneself
        2. Dashing into the street to rescue a toddler from an oncoming car
        3. Surviving and recovering quickly from surgery
        4. Working all day and having energy left to go out for an evening of entertainment

c. Nonexamples
1. A clean bill of health from an M. D.
2. Succumbing to a heart attack at age forty-five
3. Sleeplessness
4. Chronic fatigue
5. Irritability, tension, worry
6. Frequent illness

Other cognitive objectives can be more easily analyzed by writing the general idea or objective and then listing the principles that you want the student to learn. The principles may also have examples and nonexamples of correct application. For example, if the objective is that the student in a swimming class will discuss why a swimming rescue should or should not be attempted, the analysis of the objective might have the following principles as ideas to be learned:

1. Never attempt a swimming rescue unless you are a qualified life guard who has been *extensively* trained in lifesaving procedures.

2. If you are a qualified life guard, use a swimming rescue only if there is *no other means* of assistance.

Some cognitive objectives involve a sequence of problem solving designed to reach the learning goal. The easiest way to analyze these objectives is to state the problem and then list the steps or operations leading to the solution of the problem. For example, if the objective states that the student will write a program for strength and flexibility for a given person, the analysis appears as follows:

Problem statement

Given areas of the body that need strength and flexibility, the student will write a strength and flexibility program adjusted for personal choice of weight training, timed calisthenics, and flexibility options.

Operations

1. Choose weight training or timed calisthenics.

2. Refer to the appropriate exercise chart.

3. For each body part listed, choose one exercise and write it under the column entitled "exercise preference" on the work sheet.

4. On your work sheet, write in the appropriate number of sets and repetitions as indicated on the appropriate exercise chart.

5. Indicate the days on which you will exercise.

6. Determine the resistance necessary for overload.

7. Determine rest periods.

8. Plan warm-up activities.

Result

An appropriate program for strength and flexibility.

Analyze the psychomotor skills required by the objective. Most psychomotor skills consist of a series of basic psychomotor movements. The analysis is merely a list of *how* you would tell someone to perform the movement if the person were blind and could not see your demonstration. Note that each statement begins with a command (a verb). For example, if the objective were that the student will demonstrate the correct use of a life jacket, then the skill statements might be as follows:

1. Put on the life jacket.
   a. Turn the jacket so the ties are away from you.
   b. Slip the jacket over your head so the ties are in front of you.
   c. Place your arms through the straps on the sides of the jacket.
   d. Tie the ties and snap the waist band around you.

2. Jump into the water.
   a. Cross your arms over your chest and jacket with your hands pointing toward the opposite shoulders and pull the jacket downward.
   b. Keeping your arms crossed, jump into the water.

The psychomotor skills could also be stated as errors in performance and by isolating each one of the errors you might have a negative version of the above list. For example:

1. In putting on the life jacket, the student fails to:
   a. Turn the jacket with the ties outward.
   b. Slip the jacket over the head with the ties in front.

By using the list, the teacher or student can evaluate why the performance objective has not been achieved. If all of the skill statements are performed correctly, the learner has achieved the objective. An easy way to check your skill analysis is to have a friend read it and perform the skill exactly as stated. Any omissions or incorrect sequences can then be corrected or rewritten.

Step 3—Write down how you will know if students have the prerequisite knowledges or skills to begin working on the objective

Most objectives require some type of knowledge or skill in order to benefit from instruction designed to reach the objective. For example, to achieve most knowledge objectives, a student is asked at some time to *read* certain information either in the learning process or in the evaluation process. Other objectives might require the ability to perform simple *arithmetic* functions. An officiating objective might have a prerequisite of knowledge of the *rules* of the game. Before students can apply knowledge, there must be some knowledge to apply.

Psychomotor objectives also require a certain level of maturation or previous skill learning. It is impossible to teach diving safely if a boy cannot handle himself in deep water. A girl who cannot bounce a ball with control will be unable to dribble and keep her eye on her opponent.

The key to a determination of prerequisite knowledges and skills is the question: "What will the students have to be able to do in order to perform the objective?" For example, if the objective of the course were, "The students will be able to play tennis at a beginning level," then what will the students need to be able to do to play tennis. We would probably agree that the students will be able to use (1) a forehand stroke, (2) a backhand stroke, and (3) a serve; that they would know how to (4) score, and (5) follow game rules; and (6) like tennis.

The three taxonomies can assist you in placing the tasks into the hierarchy. See chapters 6, 7, and 8. The lowest, most easily learned tasks are placed at the bottom, with the higher level tasks at the top of the hierarchy. This is called a task analysis. An example of a task analysis for beginning tennis is shown in figure 13.1.

Obviously each of us might analyze the activity differently. That is what makes teaching as much an art as a science. However, by writing out a task analysis, we can pretest our students to determine at what point they are in the hierarchy. Knowing where our students are helps us to choose activities that are challenging, yet still within the realm of success for them. It eliminates the need for starting over with beginning basketball each year. By deciding on prerequisite knowledges and skills, students who are deficient in these areas can be diagnosed and remedial help provided.

Step 4—Decide how you will get to know the students

Some prerequisities other than skills which may affect instruction include student interests and attitudes, health status, family background, and goals. Some examples of ways to get to know students include (1) the student information sheet, (2) the self-introduction, (3) the peer interview and introduction, (4) the name game, (5) name tags, and (6) photos.

The student information sheet. A student information sheet can be very helpful to teachers who have not had an opportunity to become acquainted with students prior to instruction. A sheet similar to the example shown in figure 13.2 could be used at the beginning of the school year or at the beginning of an activity unit to help students communicate their feelings to the instructor.

The self-introduction. Students might be asked to share their names and something they like to do, such as a hobby, skill, special interest, etc. It is a good idea if you share first to put the students at ease as to what is wanted. Use a stopwatch to limit the introductions if necessary.[1]

The peer interview and introduction. Students can be asked to pair up with a student they don't know and interview their partners for a specified period of time, usually four or five minutes, then take one minute or less to tell something that impressed them about their partners.[2]

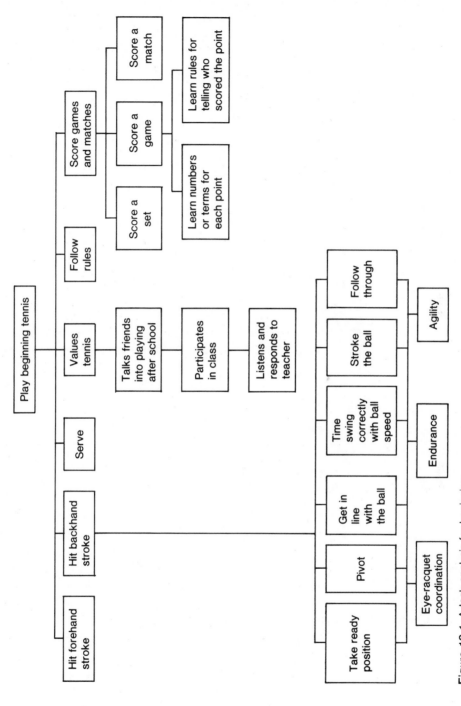

Figure 13.1 A task analysis for beginning tennis.

```
             STUDENT INFORMATION SHEET

Name _____

Address _____

Year in school: (circle one)
     Freshman      Sophomore      Junior      Senior

Brothers:      Ages:

Sisters:       Ages:

How many different schools have you attended since kindergarten?
_____

Do you have a job after school or on weekends? _____

If so, where? _____

What do you do? _____

If not, what do you do with your free time? _____

What are your favorite sports or activities? _____
What previous experience have you had in this sport or activity?
(circle one)

          None          Some          A lot

Do you have any special problems (physical disabilities, etc.) that
might affect your participation in this activity? If yes, explain. ___
_____

What are your goals for this activity? _____

What do I need to know about you to help you achieve your goal? _____
_____

List any areas in which you desire to receive special consideration
in this class. _____

Tell anything you feel would help your instructor to get to know you
better. _____
```

Figure 13.2 A student information sheet.

The name game. Students sit in a circle. You introduce yourself as *Jumping* Miss Jones, filling in the blank with an adjective that begins with the letter of your name. Each student repeats the names of the previous persons and adds his or her own. For example, "Jumping Miss Jones, Singing Sally, Typing Terry, and I'm Caroling Carolyn."[3]

Name tags. Students are asked to create a name tag that will help you get to know them. Some ideas include a collage representing oneself,[4] a personal coat of arms,[5] or a self-commercial, such as a guitar for a student who plays the guitar, a basketball for a member of the team, or an outline of a country for a foreign student.[6]

Photos. Take a picture of each student and post the photos on a bulletin board for quick reference.

Let the students know you want to learn their names and you want them to help you learn them. Jot down identifying characteristics in your roll book. Talk to the students to learn something about their personal lives. When all else fails, assign students to a given court or team and walk around learning the names of one group each day. Many other ideas can be created by both teachers and students to help class members get acquainted with one another.

Questions and suggested activities

1. For a chosen objective in each domain, design a *formal* preassessment procedure.

2. For a chosen objective in each domain, design an *informal* preassessment procedure.

3. Select a topic for a daily lesson. Include a psychomotor skill and related knowledge and affective objectives. Write terminal objectives and do a task analysis of each objective.

4. In your class or some other group of which you are a member, try out one or more ways of getting acquainted with other members of your group.

Suggested readings

Geiger, William, and Kizer, David. "Developing a Teaching Awareness." *The Physical Educator* 36 (March 1979): 25–26.

Selecting Teaching Styles and Learning Strategies

Study stimulators

1. For each of Mosston's styles of teaching, describe at least one learning activity with which you are familiar.
2. Tell how you would determine which teaching style or learning activity to use in a given situation.

Have you ever watched a talented chef throw in an ingredient here and an ingredient there and come up with a delightful casserole, while another person's efforts result in a dismal failure? The truly successful chef uses a recipe to obtain the correct ratio of ingredients and then enhances the interaction with personal experience in cooking procedures or processes.

In many ways instruction is like cooking. It involves the interaction of many factors in an organized arrangement or plan enhanced by experience and that "personal touch." Without a plan, even the most dedicated teacher would not know the destination; but without the warm, personal touch in the implementation of the plan, the proper interaction fails to occur and learning suffers. The goal of instruction then is to maximize the efficiency with which all the students achieve the desired objectives of the program.

Selecting teaching strategies

One of the elements of teaching that makes it more an "art" than a "science" is the large number of different teaching strategies that share the characteristic of successfully imparting desired knowledges, skills, and values to students. The best physical educators develop a large repertoire of strategies from which to select the appropriate activity for the occasion.

The selection of a teaching style or learning activity is dependent upon a thoughtful evaluation of the learning situation including such factors as (1) a philosophy about how students learn, (2) the subject matter to be taught, (3) the teacher, (4) the learning environment, and (5) time.

Philosophy

The first consideration in choosing a learning activity is an underlying philosophy about the teaching-learning process—a belief about how students learn. The method should consider the total educational needs of students—physical, intellectual, emotional, and social. The method may be very structured for younger children, with the teacher directing most of the

The best teaching strategy is one that "pulls" the learner toward greater capacity without overstressing the capabilities of the learner.

activities. Sooner or later the teacher should encourage students to take the initiative for their own learning. Since it is the individual student who does the learning, consideration must be given to the different ways in which students learn best. Different personalities, aptitudes, experiences, and interests combine to make each learner unique in the way he or she responds to a given style of teaching.

Joyce and Weil provided us with a formula for tailoring learning environments to individual student learning styles. They translate student characteristics into two dimensions: "a need for and tolerance of structure, and a need for and tolerance of task complexity." They define structure as "the degree of prescription in the environment;" and task complexity as the complexity or intricacy of the task, with more complex tasks demanding higher levels of skill.[1]

Hunt suggested striving for an "optimal mismatch" between the present capacity of the learner and the strategy chosen, so as to "pull" the learner toward greater capacity without overstressing the capabilities of the learner.[2]

Hawley suggested that by using a variety of teaching styles it is more likely that the learner will find one suited to his or her own learning style and will be more motivated toward achievement of the goals of the class. He also suggested that many students are only familiar with the more traditional styles of teaching and will need to be taught that learning can occur in a variety of ways.[3]

Subject matter

A second consideration in planning instruction involves the specific ideas or skills to be taught. Obviously, some methods work best for some activities while others prove better with other activities. For example, teaching an idea or skill at the lower levels of the taxonomy might utilize a more structured approach than helping students experience the creativity and problem-solving experiences at the upper levels of the taxonomy. Affective behaviors suffer with some teaching styles and blossom with others. A knowledge of concepts and skills in activities can be a valuable aid to the physical education instructor in the selection of teaching strategies.

Teacher

The teacher is the third consideration in the selection of learning activities. Anyone knows that some methods work better for some teachers than for others. Each teacher should select a comfortable teaching style in terms of his or her own personality and talents. The best teachers, however, experiment with many styles until they are comfortable with a wide range of styles, from which they can choose as the learning environment changes. They must also learn to be sensitive to feedback from the students and the learning environment and use that feedback to modify their teaching behavior.

Learning environment

The fourth consideration is the learning environment. Each teaching style establishes a unique social environment with a specific group of learners. The social system becomes a part of the learning experience along with the subject matter to be taught. Students learn competitiveness, cooperation, democratic processes, and other social skills as environments change within the school. The teaching style influences the way students react to each other, to the teacher, and to others outside of the class environment.

Time

Time is the fifth consideration. Early in the school year or in a new unit of activity, the teacher may choose to use a more structured teaching style. Later on, as the teacher gets to know the students' capabilities and learning styles, the teacher may choose a more informal approach.

The spectrum of teaching styles

A useful approach for classifying teaching styles and learning activities is Mosston's "Spectrum of Teaching Styles."[4] The concept of the spectrum of styles proposes a number of alternative styles of teaching that provide teachers with a knowledge of the roles of teacher and learner and the objectives that can be achieved with each style. This permits teachers to move back and forth along the spectrum as needed to meet the changing needs of students, environments, and subject matter. The seven styles are summarized in table 14.1, with accompanying descriptions and possible examples of teaching strategies.

Mosston described teaching behavior as "a chain of decision making." He identified the decisions as preimpact (before instruction), impact (during instruction), and postimpact (after the initial instruction). Together, these decisions make up what he calls "the anatomy of a style." A new style is created each time some of these decisions are shifted from the teacher to the student.

The following pages present a description of many of the teaching strategies that have proven effective as teaching and learning activities in physical education classes. An attempt has been made to define each activity, to delineate the uses, advantages and limitations of each; and to provide guidelines for effective use. It is up to you to select those strategies that are most comfortable for you and employ them to meet the varying needs of the students in your classes.

The teacher should move freely along the spectrum of styles, selecting one or more applicable styles for use during a particular lesson or unit of activity. An attempt should be made to involve the students as much as possible in the selection of methods that affect them and in the application of methods on the higher cognitive levels. The use of a variety of methods provides students with different learning styles the opportunity to find their "niche" in the learning experience. It also prevents boredom from overuse of a single style. Tying the method to an experience as close as possible to the real-life experience will facilitate the transfer of learning skills to real-life experiences.

Table 14.1 The spectrum of teaching styles

Style and characteristics	Teaching/Learning strategies
A. *Command* 　　Teacher makes all decisions. 　　Subject-centered.	Lecture and verbal presentation modes. Demonstration. Drills. Homogeneous grouping. Instructional games.
B. *Practice* 　　Learner makes implementation 　　　decisions—pace, order, place.	Skill checklists. Study guides, workbooks, journals. Progress charts.
C. *Reciprocal* 　　Partners teach each other designated 　　　skills or ideas. 　　Small groups help each other achieve 　　　common goals.	Peer tutoring.
D. *Self-Check* 　　Teacher-designed program with 　　　opportunity for self-assessment, self- 　　　pacing, self-motivated learning.	Testing activities as learning activities. Programmed learning. Individualized learning packets. Contract learning.
E. *Inclusion* 　　Students select the level of performance 　　　for each task assigned by teacher.	Inclusion skills checklist. Reaction and opinion papers. Goal setting.
F. *Guided Discovery* 　　Students' responses are directed by 　　　teacher's clues toward solution of a 　　　common problem.	Questioning strategies. Experiments, projects, and simulation activities. Inquiry learning. Discussion. Role playing.
G. *Divergent* 　　All decisions are made by the student 　　　except the design of the problem.	Brainstorming and buzz sessions. Problem-solving strategies.
H. *Going Beyond* 　　Student choice of problem and solution.	Quests.

　　　As a physical education instructor, the way is clear for you to be creative and design "new" methods of teaching in the future. You are limited only by the evaluative criterion of your method—is it successful in teaching students?

Teaching affective behaviors

It should be noted that affective behaviors can be learned during actual situations that arise during classroom interaction or during planned activities. The preferred method in physical education is through actual experience in situations as they arise. However, affective activities can be used on rainy days, during assembly schedules, and on other days when time does not permit dressing for activity.

Developing attitudes toward activities necessitates knowing something about the activity; therefore, the instructional sequence should begin with the learning of skills and knowledges relevant to that activity. By pairing a new skill or bit of knowledge with a preferred or rewarding activity, students may acquire a liking for the new skill or knowledge. Gagne generalized that *"success* in some learning accomplishment is likely to lead to a positive attitude toward that activity."[5]

A number of techniques for learning affective behavior have been included within the teaching strategies. Their use will be more effective in a democratic classroom environment.

The command style

In the command style, the teacher makes all of the decisions on what, where, when, and how to teach, and on how to evaluate learning and provide feedback. The command style capitalizes on the expertise of the teacher through such teaching/learning strategies as lecture and other verbal presentation modes, demonstration, and drill. Homogeneous grouping can be used advantageously during drills to individualize learning. Instructional games can also be used to "drill" students on such items as terminology and rules. Students are expected to respond as they have been "commanded" to do. This style generally is restricted to objectives at the lowest levels of the taxonomies. It is especially applicable when safety, efficient use of class time, and teacher control are essential.

Lecture and verbal presentation modes

Definition

A verbal presentation of a defined segment of information by one or more persons to an audience. This includes special reports, outside speakers, and panel discussions.

Examples

1. A talk on the dangers of drugs by a police officer.

2. A rules presentation by the teacher.

3. A discussion on fad diets by a panel of students.

Uses

1. To present material to a large group in a short time span.

2. To introduce, summarize, or explain.

3. To create interest in a topic.

4. To utilize the expertise of resource people or exceptional students.

Advantages

1. It saves time by imparting large amounts of information to large numbers of students in a short period of time.

2. It presents material with authority.

3. It provides in-depth study of a topic.

Limitations

1. It depersonalizes learning by eliminating student-student and sometimes student-teacher interaction.

2. It creates numerous opportunities for misunderstanding the information presented due to the large amount of information covered in a short amount of time with limited assessment of student learning.

3. It is limited to the acquisition of lower-level cognitive learning.

Procedures for lecture

1. Know your material.

2. Define the segment of material to be presented.

3. Organize the material to fit the time available and to proceed from simple or familiar to complex or abstract.

4. Present the information in a motivational way.
   a. Use visual aids to support the topic.
   b. Relate the lecture to real life.
   c. Use humor.
   d. Tell them what you will say, say it, tell them what you said.
   e. Pace the material at the middle-level student.

5. Speak clearly and succinctly.

6. Be sensitive to feedback from listeners and modify the delivery accordingly.

Procedures for special reports or outside speakers

1. Use tiny reports from students with questions based on quotes or excerpts.

2. Make assignments well in advance to someone who is an authority on the subject and can present the material in a meaningful way at the level of student understanding.

3. Define the assignment clearly. Explain the topic and information wanted (and the ages and background of the class for outside speakers).

4. Help students make reports interesting.

5. Thank the speaker.

Procedures for panel

1. Select and define the problem.

2. Choose and prepare panel participants in advance. All class members can be assigned to prepare and the panel chosen extemporaneously or panel members can be assigned in advance.

3. Select a moderator who can stimulate questions and guide the discussion.

Materials needed

1. Chalkboard or overhead projector.

2. Other pertinent media.

3. Anecdotes, stories, etc.

Demonstration

Definition

A visual presentation accomplished by *doing* something.

Examples

A model of a sports skill, safety skill, etc.

Uses

1. To show how something is done.

2. To create interest.

Advantages

1. It provides a visual referent or model, thereby avoiding misconceptions.

2. It heightens interest.

3. It increases retention.

Limitations

1. It may require considerable time for planning and setting up.

2. It involves only a few people.

3. Close-range vision is limited to small groups.

Procedures

1. Choose a demonstration that will be meaningful for the audience involved.

2. Practice the demonstration or acquire a good demonstrator. When demonstrating sport skills, remember to use the mirror-image technique— that is, say "right hand" to the students and use your left hand, etc.—or face away from the students so they will see the image as they will be doing it.

3. Assemble and set up equipment and the seating arrangement so all can see and hear.

4. *Briefly* explain the purpose of the demonstration.

5. Demonstrate using key points to enhance perception.

Materials needed

1. Models.

2. Equipment.

3. Chalkboard.

4. Films.

5. Loop films.

6. Videotapes.

Drills

Definition

Repetition of a learning activity until a desired level of skill has been achieved.

Examples

1. Everyone dribbles a basketball the length of the floor and back.

2. Partners volley a ball back and forth.

3. Three-person weave in basketball.

Uses

1. To learn skills.

2. To review skills.

Advantages

1. It uses time efficiently.

2. It provides a large number of practice trials.

Limitations

1. It is boring.

2. It generally limits learning in the cognitive and affective domains.

Procedures

1. Demonstrate and/or explain the learning activity.

2. Keep groups small for maximum participation.

3. Make drills as gamelike as possible.

4. Provide continuous feedback to ensure correct learning of skills.

5. Adjust or change drills to provide for individual differences in student learning.

Materials needed

1. Space.

2. Sports equipment.

Homogeneous grouping

Definition

A division of students into smaller groups of homogeneous ability levels.

Examples (Lay-ups):

1. Demonstrate lay-ups to the class.

2. Have all students go to baskets to practice the lay-up progression.

3. As soon as you see that a student can do successful lay-ups, have the student put on a pinnie, but continue to practice.

4. As soon as enough students are wearing pinnies, start a half-court game with these players and move players left at those baskets to other baskets.

5. Continue with 3, 4, and 5 until all players are successful.

Examples (Archery)

1. Have all students shoot at twenty yards and score the best five consecutive ends.

2. Have students who score 200 points at a given distance move back five yards.

3. Students will soon be shooting at various distances. The students at the closest distance need the most help.

Uses

1. To preassess students needing help with skill development.

2. To enrich the learning of advanced students.

3. To enhance safety.

Advantages

1. It permits the teacher to work with students who need the most help.

2. It permits advanced students to move on to new objectives.

3. It increases motivation and student effort.

4. It rewards student effort.

Limitations

1. It necessitates advance planning.

2. It is difficult to supervise many groups doing different things at the same time.

Procedures

1. Write objectives for each skill.

2. Preassess students on one skill.

3. Group together the students who pass the preassessment to apply the skill in an advanced situation (i.e., game play), to work on accuracy, or to work on advanced skills in an individual program.

4. Work with all of the other students until another group can pass the evaluation. Send them to do the same thing as the first group.

5. Continue working with less-skilled students and regrouping until 90 to 100 percent of the students can pass the evaluation.

6. You are now ready to begin teaching the next skill.

Materials needed

Depends on the activity.

Instructional games

Definition

A game that can be used to promote learning.

Examples

1. Soccer Scrambled Words (figure 14.1).

2. Football Terms (figure 14.2).

3. Hidden Terms (figure 14.3).

4. Bingo Lingo (figure 14.4).

5. Sports Bowl (figure 14.5).

6. Crossword Puzzles. (See chapter 11.)

7. Baseball (figure 14.6).

Soccer Scrambled Words

Instructions: Unscramble the following words. The circled letters will give you a message.

1. L Y E A R P S
2. N R U
3. N W I
4. C R O E S
5. B H A C A L F K
6. I K C K
7. T N P U
8. R E E F I K K C
9. S S A P
10. B B E L I R D
11. R E O S C C
12. L A O G
13. S L U O F
14. D F I L E

Figure 14.1 Soccer Scrambled Words.

```
┌─────────────────────────────────────────────────────────────────┐
│                         Football Terms                          │
│  Instructions: Answer the following questions. The answers will be football terms. │
│                                                                 │
│      1. To walk up a mountain.          _____  │
│                                                                 │
│      2. Something a boy feeds a girl.   _____  │
│                                                                 │
│      3. Not up.                         _____  │
│                                                                 │
│      4. Baby's first toy.               _____  │
│                                                                 │
│      5. What material is measured in.   _____  │
│                                                                 │
│      6. To finish.                      _____  │
│                                                                 │
│      7. Half of 50¢.                    _____  │
│                                                                 │
│      8. Fishing equipment.              _____  │
│                                                                 │
└─────────────────────────────────────────────────────────────────┘
```

Figure 14.2 Football Terms.

Uses

1. To encourage learning by drill in a motivational setting.

2. To promote learning when regular lesson plans cannot be used due to inclement weather, scheduling changes, or facility inavailability.

Advantages

1. It can be used individually or in groups.

2. It is fun.

3. It reduces discipline problems.

Limitations

1. It takes teacher time for development of the games.

2. It can lose instructional effectiveness if used too often.

Procedures

1. Design games to meet course objectives.

2. Keep activities on the students' learning level (i.e., vocabulary, spelling, etc.).

Materials needed

1. Dittoed sheets.

2. Pencils.

Hidden Terms—Track and Field

Instructions: Circle the terms that have to do with track and field. Words may read horizontally, vertically, or diagonally and forwards or backwards.

```
B R A K O S T S H O T A R T A L B U F A
T A R T A N B A U V A B A T O N A L I L
S T R O M M I N R A V E N D S Y L V N C
T J A V E L I N D U L I L I T A L S I R
E L S T R O M B L I A E X S R W S U S O
E X R I S T A H E F I I S C O N T N H S
P I T A N D R O S F H U L U N U A D A S
L E V A B E L D D A M O F S P R I N T C
E R I K M A D N U M C I T A O S D T R O
C I A M A M A D I K B A T L L I Y U I U
H U A N A K I L O L R O R O E L A T P N
A H S O C I T R O T K O N F V A R T L T
S T I A X L V Y E F H G N F A D D A E R
E L R E L A Y R G H J K L I U N S W J Y
B T A P E X S T V U O L N C L R T E U H
G N I R U S A E M Y N L O I T U T I M E
M E T E R U S P O U N D S A P S T G P J
D A M A R K E R N U O D F L A Y D H M D
S K C O L B G N I T R A T S R L C T D U
```

Bar	Pit
Baton	Polevault
Clock	Pounds
Cross Country	Relay
Discus	Runway
Distance	Shot
Finish	Sprint
Hammer	Starter
High Jump	Starting Blocks
Hurdle	Steeplechase
Javelin	Tape
Kilo	Tartan
Long Jump	Time
Marker	Track and Field
Measuring	Triple Jump
Meter	Weight
Officials	Yards

Figure 14.3 Hidden Terms.

Bingo Lingo—Diving

Instructions: The teacher draws a card one at a time and reads the definition. The first student to circle five terms in a row—either vertically, diagonally, or horizontally—wins.

Approach	Back Dive	Backward Take-off	Cutaway Dive	Degree of Difficulty
Entry	Forward Dive	Header	Hurdle	Free
Inward Dive	Jackknife	Layout	Lift	Opening
Pike	Press	Rotate	Somersault Dive	Spin
Swan	Straight	Takeoff	Tuck	Twist Dive

Figure 14.4 Bingo Lingo.
Source: Romine, Jack and Joyce M. Harrison. Brigham Young University.

Sports Bowl

Instructions: Follow the procedure below to play "Sports Bowl."
1. Divide class into two teams of equal size.
2. Read a question.
3. The first person to raise his or her hand gets to answer the question. If the question is answered correctly, a bonus question is directed to the answering team; if it is answered incorrectly, the other team may attempt the answer (and the bonus).
4. There is a thirty-second time limit on questions.
5. The scoring is as follows:
   Correct answer—10 points
   Correct bonus answer—5 points
   Incorrect bonus—no penalty

Questions can be created from sports, history, current events, game rules, etc. Typical questions and bonus questions might be:

Q. Who holds the record for lifetime home runs?

B. What is the record?

Q. How many points can be scored on a penalty bully in field hockey?

B. When is a penalty bully awarded?

Figure 14.5 Sports Bowl.

Baseball

Instructions: Follow the procedure below to play "Baseball."

1. Mark a diamond on the floor of a classroom or locker room area or use a magnetic board.
2. Write a list of questions about a sport.
3. Divide the class into two teams—designating one as the batting team and the other as the fielding team.
4. Ask the first batter a question. If correctly answered, the batter moves to first base. If incorrectly answered, the fielding team is allowed to answer. If the fielding team answers correctly, the batter is out. If not, the batter sits down and the next batter is up.
5. Continue until three outs are made or all batters have been up, then exchange teams.
6. Points are scored as runs are "batted" in.

Figure 14.6 Baseball.

The practice style

In the practice style, the teacher determines what is to be taught and how the activity will be evaluated. The students are then given a number of tasks to practice and each learner decides which task to begin with, where to do it, when to begin and end the practice of a particular task, how fast or slow to work, and what to do between tasks. Students are encouraged to clarify the nature of the tasks by asking questions as needed. The teacher moves around the class, offering feedback to each individual.

By using a variety of tasks, including fitness activities and testing activities, teacher and students can make use of all of the available space. Skill checklists; study guides, workbooks, and journals; and progress charts are some of the teaching/learning strategies that can be employed within this style.

Social interaction among students is increased with this style.

Skill checklists

Definition

A list of skills or tasks to be checked off when performed correctly with instructions for performance, such as quantity, quality, use of equipment, etc. Task checklists are of three types:

1. A checklist of skills in which the grade is determined by categories.

2. A checklist that is not divided into categories but merely specifies the grade from the number of items passed. For example, checking off ten items is a *C*, fifteen items is a *B*, etc.

3. A checklist that is not graded.

SKILL REQUIREMENTS FOR MAJOR TENNIS

Rally Rascals--"C" Grade   Name _____

Exercises

_____ 1. Fifty down bounces using forehand grip.

_____ 2. Fifty up bounces using forehand grip.

_____ 3. Twenty-five reverse bounces using forehand grip.

Wall or Backboard Practice

_____ 4. Return at least ten consecutive forehands. One bounce only from baseline.

_____ 5. Return at least five consecutive backhands. One bounce only from baseline.

Tossed Balls

_____ 6. Return five moving forehands in a row from no man's land to no man's land without an error. Repeat three times.

_____ 7. Repeat above for backhand.

_____ 8. Return eight out of ten moving forehands from baseline to baseline.

_____ 9. Return five out of eight moving backhands from baseline to baseline.

_____ 10. Return five out of eight moving forehand volleys to no man's land.

_____ 11. Return five out of eight moving backhand volleys to no man's land.

Self-Tossed Balls

_____ 12. Put ten consecutive forehands into play from the baseline to the baseline.

_____ 13. Put five out of ten backhands into play from the baseline to the baseline.

_____ 14. Serve five out of ten fast serves into either court.

Rally Practice

_____ 15. Short court rally for at least ten times.

_____ 16. With an experienced player, play a pro set.

Figure 14.7 A Skill Checklist—Tennis.
Source: Ann Valentine, Brigham Young University.

Examples

1. Tennis Checklist (figure 14.7).

2. Swimming Class Record Sheet. (See chapter 11.)

3. Badminton Skill Checklist (figure 14.8).

Uses

1. To motivate students to practice tasks.

2. To record preclass activities.

3. To allow some student control and responsibility for learning.

```
                    BADMINTON SKILL CHECKLIST

Name _____

_____ Twenty consecutive underhand drop shots in a rally with a part-
        ner.

_____ Eight out of ten short serves between short service line and
        white line.

_____ Score twenty-five short serves on court with rope twelve-
        inches above net and target in right court.

_____ Eight out of ten long serves on court with target in right
        court.

_____ Score twenty long serves on court with target in right court.

_____ Eight out of ten smashes with partner setting up (shots that can
        be returned with some effort by the partner cannot be counted).

_____ Eight out of ten clears (overhead) with partner setting up
        (must land between the two back boundary lines).

_____ Eight out of ten clears (underhand) with partner setting up
        (must land between the two back boundary lines).

_____ Read the handout on scoring and score one game.

Complete the following play patterns with a partner (you should be
player A and player B in each case).

_____ Player A--Serve
               B--Clear to deep backhand
               A--Drive down sideline
               B--Clear to deep forehand
               A--Clear to deep backhand
               B--Drive cross court

_____ Player A--Serve
               B--Clear to deep backhand
               A--Drop to the forehand
               B--Clear to the deep forehand
               A--Clear to the deep backhand
               Repeat
```

Figure 14.8 Badminton skill checklist.

Advantages

1. It motivates preclass activity and skill practice.

2. It involves students in worthwhile practice and eliminates standing around or "goofing off."

3. It encourages student initiative for some aspects of learning.

4. It requires students to reap the consequences for their learning decisions.

Limitations

1. It requires extra preparation time.

2. Some students will require extra help in order to succeed in working on their own.

Procedures

1. There are two ways of using the checklist method.
   a. A dittoed checklist can be issued to each student and items can be checked off by partners, team captains, student assistants, or the teacher.
   b. A check-off card, which lists each student in the class and the skills to be performed, can be maintained by the teacher.

2. Checklists may form part of the grade for a unit or may be used as a motivational device.

Materials needed

1. Checklists.

2. Pencils.

Study guides, workbooks, journals

Definition

A student guide to learning in hand-out or workbook format.

Examples

Archery Study Sheet (figure 14.9).

Uses

To provide for individual study of information.

Advantages

1. Can be used outside of class for learning or review.

2. Can focus attention on important instructional points.

Limitations

1. It is often boring.

2. It is often difficult to understand.

ARCHERY STUDY SHEET

INSTRUCTIONS: Briefly answer the following questions.

1. List *two* important factors about each of the following:

   Stance:

   Nock:

   Draw:

   Anchor:

   Aim:

   Release:

   Follow through:

2. Discuss aiming techniques with a bowsight, including how to correct errors.

3. Review scoring methods and procedures briefly. Include what to do in case of the following: liners, rebounds, pass-throughs, perfect end, shooting seven arrows.

4. Fill in the necessary information for the arrows shown below.

Figure 14.9 Archery study sheet.

Procedures

1. Use appropriate vocabulary and reading level for students.

2. Eliminate nonessential items.

3. If possible, write so that the student is actively involved in learning by filling in the blanks or working through the material to be learned, or so that the material is programmed with immediate feedback.

4. Answers to study guides can be provided through class instruction, programmed or individual units, "A Rule a Day" bulletin boards, or individual study of text materials or loop films.

Materials needed

1. Dittoed sheets or printed materials.

Progress charts

Definition

1. A chart for recording the progress of a student in a class.

Examples

1. Personal Bowling Record (figure 14.10).

2. Accumulative Tournament Chart. (See chapter 11.)

Uses

1. To increase student awareness of progress at all times throughout the course.

2. To record preclass activities.

3. To increase student awareness of the objectives of the course.

Advantages

1. It increases student motivation and achievement.

2. It facilitates grading.

Limitations

1. This approach demands more preparation and/or record keeping by the instructor.

Procedures

1. Progress charts can be kept by the instructor and made available during class time, or they may be kept by the students.

2. The use of progress charts should be based on the objectives of the course as communicated to students.

Materials needed

1. Progress charts.

Name: _____

Period: _____

								Test	Scores
Week	2	3	4	5	6	7	8	Score	Grade
Monday									
Tuesday									
Wednesday									
Thursday									
Total									
Average									
Class Rank									

Average--Total divided by the number of games bowled

Week	1	2	3	4	5	6	7	8
200+								
190-199								
180-189								
170-179								
160-169								
150-159								
140-149								
130-139								
120-129								
110-119								
100-109								
90-99								
80-89								
79-79								
60-69								
50-59								

Figure 14.10 Personal bowling record.

The reciprocal style

The reciprocal style involves students in providing the feedback for each other. One student performs while the other observes and provides feedback. Then, the students exchange roles. The teacher decides what tasks are to be accomplished and how they will be evaluated, gives the assignments to the students, and helps the observers improve their ability as observers and their ability to communicate with their partners. Socialization between students is an inherent part of the reciprocal style.

Peer tutoring

Definition

1. Peer tutoring is when one partner helps another learn a skill.

2. Team learning is when a team works together to help its members achieve a certain goal.

Examples

1. Partners helping each other to learn check-off skills in swimming.

2. Partners or groups of students working together and progressing only as all members have achieved each skill or passed each quiz.

Uses

1. To help reinforce learning that has already occurred.

2. To help slower learners progress.

3. To increase student involvement in the learning process.

4. To develop group participation and leadership skills.

5. To adapt to the learning styles of individual students.

Advantages

1. It saves the teacher's time to handle special cases and to provide enrichment materials.

2. It promotes learning by students who seem to learn better from their peers than from the teacher.

3. It encourages individual creativity and contributions.

4. It motivates some slower learners to work harder.

5. It promotes learning or retention by tutors.

6. It increases student social interaction.

Limitations

1. It necessitates preplanning for or with tutors and groups.

2. It can involve increased record keeping.

3. It is ineffective unless tasks are relevant to group members.

4. It is time-consuming.

5. It can discourage faster students if they are always asked to tutor.

6. Interpersonal conflict may occur between students.

Procedures

1. Select appropriate instructional objectives.

2. Preassess to find learning problems.

3. Select activities in terms of objectives and learning problems.

4. Create task sheets that include:
   a. A description of the tasks, including diagrams or sketches.
   b. Specific points to look for in the performance.
   c. Samples of possible feedback.

5. Make sure that students understand the purpose of the tasks and the criteria for correct performance.

6. Facilitate tutoring by helping tutors improve their skills of:
   a. Observation.
   b. Comparison of the performance with the criterion for correct performance.
   c. Communication of the results to the performer after the completion of each task.

7. Check for mastery.

8. Readjust groups often to avoid one student holding another student back or incompatible groupings.

The self-check style

In the self-check style, the feedback is provided by the individual learner instead of by the teacher or another student. The selection of tasks is important so that students can evaluate their own performance. Events that provide external feedback—such as making baskets, kicking a football over the goalposts, or hitting a target with an object—facilitate student self-evaluation. The role of the teacher is to help the students become better self-evaluators.

The self-check style can increase student self-esteem for students who are comfortable working independently. One disadvantage of this style is that student interaction with the peer group and with the teacher are at a minimum. A computer can be used to monitor student progress in the self-check style.

A number of different teaching/learning strategies can be employed within the self-check style, including the use of testing activities as learning activities, programmed learning, individualized learning packets, and contract learning.

Testing activities as learning activities

Definition

> The use of tests to stimulate or evaluate learning when not used as a grading device.

Examples

1. Self-administered and/or scored tests.

2. "Repeatable" skills tests. (See chapter 11 for examples.)

Uses

1. To motivate students to practice skills.

2. To help students evaluate their own learning.

Advantages

1. It can stimulate learning.

2. It can help students evaluate their own learning.

3. It can be used as preassessment activities.

Limitations

1. It can create a management problem.

2. It can encourage cheating if grades are given.

Procedures

1. Self-administered and/or scored tests
   a. Some tests can be self-administered from a handout or a posttest in an individualized unit, or students can sign up a day in advance to check out the test. All instructions appear on the test; therefore, no teacher direction is needed.
   b. Self-tests can be scored by checking out the "key" from the teacher, scoring the test, and then reviewing the missed questions to clear up misconceptions. This type of test generally shows the students whether or not they are ready for the final test on that unit.

2. "Repeatable" skills tests
   a. There are several ways of administering these skills tests:
      1. The tests can be demonstrated and given to the entire class and then students can repeat tests before and during class as time permits.

2. The tests can be self-administered with all instructions on the card. Students can take the tests before or during class when time permits as, for example, during a bye in a tournament.
    b. The value of "repeatable" skills tests lies in the fact that students repeat them until the skill is learned, thereby profiting from skills tests as a learning activity and not just as a means of evaluation.

Programmed learning

Definition

A method of organizing instruction into small steps that can be readily learned by a student (a process, not a product).

1. Linear—Everyone reads the same frames at different speeds.

2. Branched—Multiple-choice questions have alternatives that lead to different frames.

3. Characteristics
    a. The subject matter is carefully organized into a logical sequence with each step building on the one preceding it.
    b. The subject matter is divided into small steps.
    c. The student is presented with and actively responds to one question or skill movement at a time.
    d. The student is provided with immediate knowledge of results.
    e. Each student can progress at his or her own rate.
    f. Programs are written or created to insure a minimum of error.

Examples

1. Method I—Archery Terms. (See figure 14.11.)

2. Method II—Split Recognition. (See figure 14.12.)

3. Method III—Archery Scoring. (See figures 14.13 and 14.14.) Also, Programmed Instruction for Archery. (See figure 14.15.)

Uses

1. To individualize learning by allowing students to work at their own pace.

2. To encourage student responsibility for learning.

Advantages

1. It frees the teacher for individual help and to help students apply the learning gained.

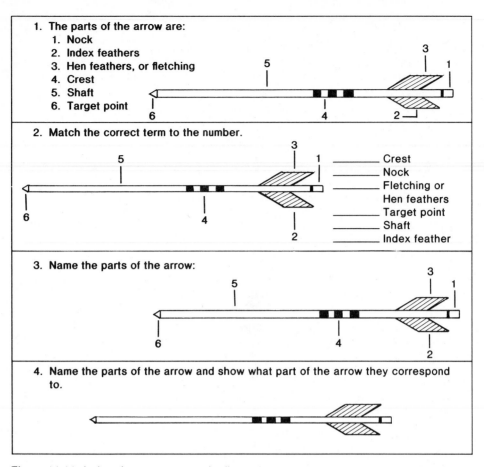

Figure 14.11 Archery terms programmed unit.

2. Individuals can learn at their own pace.
   a. Branched programs can speed up by skipping material or slow down with remedial detours.
   b. Students with low IQ can learn well.

3. Immediate knowledge of results yields higher motivation and learner confidence.

4. Some well-constructed programs compensate for weaknesses on the part of instructors.

5. It results in greater efficiency in learning per unit of time.

6. It yields higher retention.

7. It insists that each point is thoroughly understood before proceeding on.

Limitations

1. One can't program attitudes, opinions, values, concepts.
   a. One can teach opinions, comparisons, and understandings to some extent with branched programs.
   b. It can leave the teacher free to teach values.

2. It is impersonal.

3. It is expensive or time-consuming.

4. Students can cheat or lose interest, especially with linear programs.

Procedures

1. Orient the students to the method if it is new.

2. Develop class management procedures and make certain students know what is happening.

3. Integrate the learning from the unit with other class instruction.

Programmed learning—method I

Examples

1. Place the words of a song on the chalkboard. Sing the song several times. Erase one or more words. Continue to sing the song, erasing several words at the conclusion of each trial, until all of the words are erased and the song is learned.

2. Archery Terms—Frames 1–4 (figure 14.11).

Uses

1. Terminology, facts.

Procedures

1. Identify the objective and state it.

2. Compose a test question based upon the objective. This will be the last frame.

3. Answer the test question. This will be the first frame.

4. Write several practice frames in between, each time providing less information and requiring the student to supply the necessary information.

5. Place the frames one behind the other on separate pages. Read through all of the top frames, then begin again with page one. Continue until all frames have been read.

Split Recognition: A Programmed Unit

Objective

   You will be able to pass a ten-item quiz on split recognition with 90 percent accuracy.

Preassessment

   Read item 1. Then, take the quiz in 2. If you have all items correct, go to 6 for practice, if desired; then proceed to 7. If you missed any items, continue with frame 3.

Instructions

   Cover the answers on the left with your hand or a card, uncovering them in turn as you proceed through the frames.

Evaluation

   See Objective.

---

1. A split is a leave of two or more pins when the headpin (#1) is down and one or more spaces remain between or in front of standing pins. Examples:

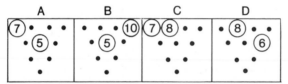

2. Identify the splits below. (Cover the frame above.)

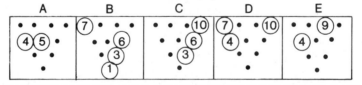

A, D, E If you have all 3 correct you may go to #6

3. Remember, to be a split, the headpin must be down. Which of the following are *not* splits?

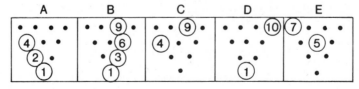

Figure 14.12 Split Recognition: A programmed unit.

Figure 14.12—*Continued*

A, B, D are *not* splits	4. A split may have at least one pin down between standing pins, *as you look from the front.* Which of the following are *not* splits?

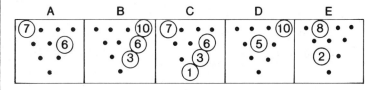

B, C, E are *not* splits	5. Instead of having spaces between pins, a split may have no intermediate pins left standing in front of the pins. Example:

Which of the following are *not* splits?

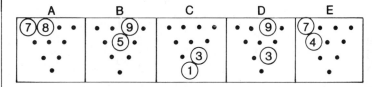

B, C, D, E are *not* splits	6. (Cover the frame above.) Identify the splits below by circling the letters for leaves that are splits.

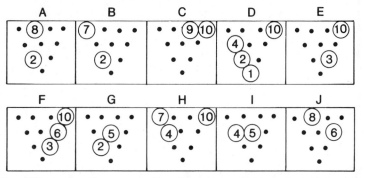

A-No B-Yes C-Yes D-No E-Yes F-No G-No H-Yes I-Yes J-Yes	7. If your answers were correct, you are ready to take the quiz on recognition of splits. Ask your instructor for the quiz. If your answers were incorrect, go back to 3 and review the frames again. Then, if needed, ask your instructor for assistance.

6. Arrows are always scored in order from the *highest to the lowest*.

   10, 9, 8, 7, 6, 5, 4, 3, 2, 1

   Place the following arrows in the correct order by numerical value: inner white, inner black, outer red, inner blue, outer red, outer gold.

   ____ ____ ____ ____ ____ ____

9, 7, 7, 6, 4, 2

7. Mary shot the following arrows: outer gold, outer red, outer white, outer black, outer blue, outer red, outer red. Her scores are recorded as follows:

   __7__ __7__ __7__ __5__ __3__ __1__

   The rule to follow when shooting seven arrows instead of six is:
   ____ Subtract the lowest scoring arrow.
   ____ Subtract the highest scoring arrow.
   ____ Subtract the last arrow shot.

Subtract the highest scoring arrow.

8.

9, 9, 8, 6, 4, 2

Which rule best describes how to score an arrow on a line?

____ An arrow on a line scores the higher value.
____ An arrow on a line scores the lower value.

An arrow on a line scores the higher value.

9. Score the following arrows.

Figure 14.13 Archery scoring—a linear program.

6. Add a title sheet, instructions, and answers to frames.

7. Try out on a few students. Revise.

Programmed learning—method II

Examples

    1. Split Recognition (figure 14.12).

Uses

    1. Concepts.

Procedures

    1. Define the concept (i.e., A split is . . .).

    2. Create as many examples of the concepts as possible (all kinds of splits).

    3. Create as many nonexamples of the concept as possible (all pin set-ups that are not splits). Be sure to include all necessary nonexamples.

    4. Create a test question that indicates understanding of the concept. (For example, "Identify all of the splits below.") This is the last frame.

    5. Define the characteristics of the concept for the students. (The head pin is down, one or more spaces between or in front of standing pins.)

    6. Identify characteristics that may be confusing. (The space must be viewable from the front, not the side) or problem examples (the 9–10 split).

    7. Using one characteristic at a time, build one upon another to arrive at the test question.

    8. After presenting the material in each frame, ask the learner to identify examples and nonexamples of the concept, being careful not to include examples and nonexamples that do not meet the characteristics already presented.

    9. Add instructions, answers to frames, and a concluding frame. Try out and revise.

Programmed learning—method III

Examples

    1. Archery Scoring—Linear (figure 14.13).

    2. Archery Scoring—Branched (figure 14.14).

Archery Scoring—Branched

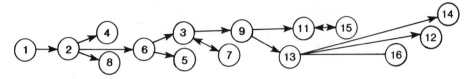

1. **Layout of a target archery face:**

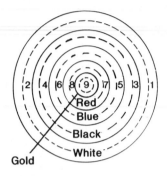

Give the color and value for each of the arrows shown.

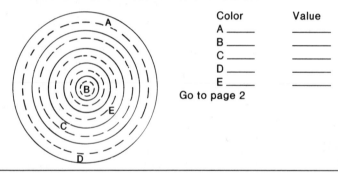

	Color	Value
A	_____	_____
B	_____	_____
C	_____	_____
D	_____	_____
E	_____	_____

Go to page 2

3. If an archer shot a perfect end of six arrows, the resulting score would be

_____ .

   a. 60. Turn to item 7.
   b. 54. Turn to item 5.
   c. Any other score. Turn to item 9.

4. **That's right!**
   Mary shot the following arrows: gold, red, white, black, blue, red, red. Her scores are recorded as follows:

   7, 7, 6, 5, 3, 2

   The rule to follow when shooting seven arrows instead of six is:
   a. Subtract the lowest scoring arrow. Turn to item 8.
   b. Subtract the highest scoring arrow. Turn to item 10.
   c. Subtract the last arrow shot. Turn to item 8.

Figure 14.14 Archery scoring—a branched program.

Figure 14.14—*Continued*

5. That would be correct if you were shooting on a target face divided into five scoring rings. This target face, however, had ten scoring rings. Recalculate your answer from the information given you on page 1. Return to page 2 and choose again.

6. Oops! Go back and look at the numerical order shown in the examples. Then, choose again.

7. That's right, 6 × 10 = 60.
   Some examples of scores recorded by Barbara Bowslinger follow:
   7, 7, 2, 1, 1, 0
   10, 9, 6, 5, 3, 2
   10, 4, 3, 2, 1, 1
   The rule to follow when recording scores is:
   a. Record scores in order from highest to lowest. Turn to page 4.
   b. Record scores in order from lowest to highest. Turn to page 6.
   c. Record scores in the order shot. Turn to page 6.

8. You should have converted each color to a score, then looked to see which arrow was eliminated when the scores were recorded. Go back to item 4 and try again. Then, select another answer.

9. Perhaps you don't know how to figure the score for a perfect end. Six arrows multiplied by ten points (All arrows were in the bullseye or inner gold ring) equals _____ . Turn to item 6.

Uses

   1. Rules, principles.

Procedures

   1. Define the objective (i.e., to score the six arrows in one end of archery competition).

   2. Define all of the rules pertaining to the objective (i.e., arrows are scored numerically from high to low).

   3. Place the rules in some logical order for treatment.

   4. Write the frames, using one of the following formulas in each frame.
      a. Give the rule and an example. Ask for a second example. The first frame is usually of this type.
      b. Give one or more examples. Ask for a rule.
      c. Give an example. State the rule. Ask for a second example.
      d. Give the rule and ask for an example.
      e. Give the rule and ask for a restatement of the rule.
      f. Give an example. Ask for a second example.

To brace the bow, hold the bow in the right hand with the bow tips pointing to the right. Step through with the right foot. Place the lower tip of the bow around the shoelaces of the left foot and the center behind your left rear pocket. Press on the upper limb with the palm of the right hand and slide the string into the notches. If you have difficulty, spread your feet farther apart in a forward-backward stride position.

Figure 14.15 Programmed instruction for archery.

5. Insert test frames at intervals to review knowledges already learned.

6. Add instructions, answers to frames, and a concluding frame.

7. Try out on a few students. Revise.

Programmed learning—method IV

Examples

1. Programmed Instruction for Archery (figure 14.15).

Uses

1. Skills.

Procedures

1. Use task analysis as explained in chapter 13.

2. Divide the material into small tasks or steps.

3. Build in an evaluation technique.

4. Try out and revise.

Individualized learning packets

Definition

Packets of materials prepared in such a way that they can be used with little or no direct teacher supervision.

Examples

1. Elementary Rescues. (See figure 14.16.)

2. Bowling—How to Pick Up Spares. (See figure 14.17.)

Elementary Rescues

Objective

The student will demonstrate self-rescue skills to a partner, as follows (in seven feet of water):

    a. Treading water—five minutes
    b. Floating on back—minimum of movement of hands—remain in five-foot circle—one minute
    c. Survival floating—ten minutes fully clothed
    d. Disrobing and shirt and trouser inflation—without touching the side
    e. Staying afloat with inflated clothing—five minutes
    f. Jumping in and swimming in clothing, fully dressed—one length
    g. Releasing a cramp
    h. Removing self from weeds

Preassessment

1. Skills you already should know:
    a. Back float
    b. Treading water—two minutes
    c. Survival floating—two minutes
    d. Jellyfish float
2. Completion by having partner initial passed requirements on Skills Check-off Card.

Note: Clothes must be brought from home for skills requiring them.

Skill Statements (Example from total unit)

1. You will tread water for five minutes using any one of the following kicks and a sculling motion with the arms. (Floating is not permitted.)
    a. Whip or frog kick.
    b. Scissors kick
    c. Bicycle kick
2. You will survival float for ten minutes fully clothed.
    a. Assume a prone float or jellyfish float position in the water.
    b. Breathe by lifting the head while pushing gently down with the hands.
    c. *Sink* into the prone or jellyfish position and let the water buoy you to the surface. Exhale.
    d. Repeat b and c alternately with less than five breaths per minute.

Learning Activities

1. Read pages 120–27 in *Swimming and Water Safety*.
2. Read pages 20–29 in *Life Saving and Water Safety*.
3. Study and try to do the skill statements as they are outlined for you.
4. Have a partner check you off on each skill as you pass it.
5. If you have difficulty inflating clothing, ask for a demonstration by your instructor.

Evaluation

Have a partner initial passed skills on Unit IV Skills Check-Off Card.

Figure 14.16 Elementary Resources: An individualized unit.

How to Pick up Spares

Objectives

Upon completion of this unit, you will be able to:
1. Identify the proper stance position, arrows, and target for picking up leaves with a straight ball and do so with 90 percent accuracy on an objective test.
2. Use spot bowling to pick up spares, thereby improving your game score.
3. Identify the difference between pin and ball deflection.

Preassessment

1. Before beginning this unit you should be able to roll the ball fairly consistently over the desired arrow into the 1-3 pocket. (or 1-2 pocket, if left-handed)
2. You should be aware of the difference between pin and spot bowling and know how to read the rangefinder.
3. If you are already converting all of your leaves into spares, this unit is not for you.
4. See Evaluation for information on scoresheets to be turned in before beginning the learning activities.

Ideas to Be Learned

1. Use the same delivery on the second ball as you did on the first ball. (i.e., hook, straight, etc.)
2. Equipment
   Ball—8.59 inches in diameter
   Pins—4.76 inches in diameter
   Hitting area—Almost 22 inches

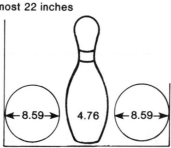 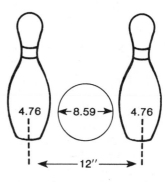

3. Face the target pin with the body and walk in a straight line toward the target.
4. Cross-alley bowling
   a. Left and right side spares are where the pins are, not where the stance is.
   b. For a leave on the left, start the ball from the right.
   c. For a leave on the right, start the ball from the left.
   d. Leaves in the center are picked up with the strike ball.
   e. Head pin and leaves to left (1-2 pocket), to right (1-3 pocket).
5. Ball deflection
   a. Contact with a pin or pins deflects the ball from its path.
   b. The amount of deflection is dependent upon:
      1. the angle of contact with the pins
      2. the speed of the ball
      3. the type of ball (straight, hook, etc.)
      4. the weight of the pins (a heavier pin yields greater deflection).
   c. When given a choice between pin and ball deflection, ball deflection should be selected as there is less chance of error.

Figure 14.17 How to Pick up Spares.

Figure 14.17—*Continued*

6. Pin deflection
   a. A ball hitting a pin deflects it from its position into other pins or positions.
   b. The amount of deflection is dependent upon:
      1. the angle at which the pin (or pins) is contacted
      2. the speed of the ball
      3. the weight of the pins

Evaluation

1. Take the quiz on spare conversion. It can be obtained from your instructor. Ninety percent is a passing score.
2. Turn in three game scores before beginning and after completing the unit. Indicate the number of pins knocked down by each ball in each frame and the resulting game score.

Example:

5 4	9 1	9 -	3 7	3 1	
9	10	9	10	3	145

Learning Activity Options

1. Read the section "Ideas to Be Learned."
2. Check out some bowling pins and a ball from the desk. Place them in the appropriate formation on the carpet (away from interference with others). Then roll the ball and attempt to determine how the ball and pins deflect differently when hit at different angles. Write a paragraph on what you learned.
3. Based on your experiences with 3 or from other sources, determine what ball and pin action makes a strike occur. Draw a diagram of the action, indicating which pins are knocked down by the ball and which are downed by pin deflection.
4. Study the programmed section of this unit on how to convert specific leaves into spares. In a brief paragraph comment on how the unit helped you, how it could be improved, etc.
5. Study the summary sheet on How To Pick Up Spares. Try to determine the principles governing pick-ups or the combinations of pins that are converted by aiming over each different arrow. Then, summarize them in a brief paragraph or outline.

Uses

1. To individualize instruction.

2. To increase student responsibility for learning.

Advantages

1. It is self-paced.

2. It provides for various levels of development, i.e., different goals for different learners.

3. It reduces discipline problems.

4. It provides variety in learning modes.

5. It allows in-depth study of an area.

6. Students learn to provide their own individual feedback.

Limitations

1. Class management can be more difficult.

2. Time is required for writing, evaluating, and updating programs.

3. It can assume the classification of busy work.

Procedures

1. Choose a project that will be a meaningful learning experience within the ability level of the student.

2. Write units that include the following:
   a. Performance objectives—cognitive, psychomotor, and affective.
   b. Preassessment procedures.
   c. Ideas to be learned or skill statements.
   d. Learning activities designed to provide for individual differences in:
      1) Rate of learning.
      2) Amount of practice needed to perfect skills.
      3) Mode of instruction preferred.
      4) Optional enrichment activities.
   e. Evaluation of achievement of the objectives.
   f. Instructions on how to use the unit—how, where, when, with whom, what, why, and how to get help.

3. Provide a wide variety of learning activities that require the student to read, view, discuss, listen to, analyze, do, identify, describe, construct, use media, survey, demonstrate, visit, participate in, videotape, etc.

4. Models of skills in individualized units can be provided in advance by the teacher or by photos, loop films, videotapes, drawings, or highly skilled students.

5. Evaluate in terms of the goals.

Contract learning

Definition

An individual-learning packet in which a student contracts (or agrees) with the teacher to complete specified objectives in order to receive a specified grade. Types of contracts include:

1. Teacher-controlled contracts in which the tasks and reinforcers are determined by the teacher.

2. Transitional contracting in which control is shared by the student and the teacher.

3. Student-controlled contracts in which the tasks and reinforcers are determined by the student. (These are not self-check activities.)[6]

Examples

1. Gymnastics grade contract. (See figure 14.18.)

Uses

1. To individualize learning.

2. To encourage student responsibility for learning and self-assessment.

GYMNASTICS GRADE CONTRACT

Please read the following contract carefully and ask any questions you may have. Remember: teachers *do not give* students grades: students *earn* the grades they receive.

* * * * * * * * * *

To earn a grade of C you must complete the following

1. Attend class regularly, be dressed, and participate each day.
2. Actively participate in all activities taught by your instructor.
3. Earn a minimum score of ten out of twenty on the written examination. A study guide is available for your use.
4. Learn and perform for the instructor ten stunts from any or all of the events at your level.
5. Select and complete ten Learning Experience points.

To earn a grade of B you must complete the following

1. Apply items 1 and 2 from contract C.
2. Earn a minimum score of twelve out of twenty on the written examination.
3. Learn and perform for the instructor twelve stunts from any or all of the events at your level.
4. Select and complete twelve Learning Experience points.

To earn a grade of A you must complete the following

1. Apply items 1 and 2 from contract C.
2. Earn a minimum score of fourteen out of twenty on the written examination.
3. Learn and perform for the instructor fourteen stunts from any or all of the events at your level.
4. Select and complete fourteen Learning Experience points.

Figure 14.18 Gymnastics contract.
Source: Linda Fleming and Joyce M. Harrison,
Brigham Young University.

Figure 14.18—*Continued*

Name _____

GYMNASTICS LEARNING EXPERIENCES

Number	Level	Points	Description
1	B	1	Demonstrates knowledge of beat, rhythm, etc. for music
2	B/I	2	Create and perform a pyramid with five or more people
3	B/I/A	2	Paint or draw a picture of a gymnast
4	B/I/A	2	Make a set of judging cards
5	B/I	2	Write four warm-up exercises applicable to each piece of apparatus
6	B/I/A	2	Write a report on the US Olympic Gymnastics team
7	I/A	3	Teach a beginner a skill
8	B/I/A	3	Write a biographical sketch of a famous gymnast
9	B/I	3	Discover six different ways to jump from the floor or on the beam (change of arms, legs, etc.)
10	B	3	Create five unique stationary positions for the beam
11	B/I/A	3	Learn which primary muscle groups are used predominantly on the uneven parallel bars
12	B/I/A	3	Design and put up a gymnastics bulletin board
13	B/I/A	3	Write a twenty-five-point gymnastics test
14	B/I	3	Put together four moves on the unevens
15	B/I/A	4	Put together three moves on the beam
16	B/I/A	4	Take pictures of gymnastics skills
17	B/I/A	4	Play (piano or other instrument) a song to accompany a free exercise routine
18	B/I/A	4	Describe in a written paper the mechanics of judging an event; then judge an event
19	B/I/A	4	Enter a competitive event
20	B/I/A	5	Demonstrate to instructor and write down directions for spotting each stunt on a piece of apparatus
21	I/A	5	Perform a vault followed by a tumbling series
22	B/I/A	6	Choreograph, write down, and perform a tumbling series of five or more moves
23	B/I/A	6	Choreograph, write down, and perform a balance beam routine, (mount, five stunts, dismount)
24	B/I/A	6	Choreograph, write down, and perform a bar routine (mount, three moves, dismount)
25	B/I/A	7	Choreograph, write down, and perform your own free exercise routine
26	B/I/A	7	Teach a routine to another person
27	B/I/A	8	Talk three performers from your level into entering an event. Get three judges from any level to judge. Make an entry form, write rules of the event, calculate winners, present awards.

Make up your own learning experience and present
it to the instructor for approval and
point value ....!!!!

Figure 14.18—*Continued*

STUNTS

BEGINNING	INTERMEDIATE	ADVANCED
Uneven Parallel Bars	**Uneven Parallel Bars**	**Uneven Parallel Bars**
1. front support mount	1. Hip circle mount	1. Single leg through
2. single leg over the high bar	2. Single leg over the high bar	2. Mill circle
3. leg swing over the low bar	3. Cast off wrap hip circle (low bar)	3. Double leg bounce
4. straddle dismount	4. Front hip circle	4. Kip to high bar
5. skin-the-cat Russian Pivot	5. Skin-the-cat Russian pivot	5. Handstand dismount
		6. Front hip circle

Vaulting	**Vaulting**	**Vaulting**
1. Squat mount	1. Wolf vault	1. Head-spring vault
2. Squat vault	2. Straddle vault	2. Handspring vault
3. Flank vault	3. Headspring	3. Layout squat
4. Squat vault one-half twist	4. Handspring	4. Layout hand-spring
5. Wolf mount	5. Straddle one-half twist	5. Straddle twist
6. Straddle mount		

Balance Beam	**Balance Beam**	*Balance Beam*
1. Squat mount	1. Straddle mount	1. Step-up mount
2. Front support mount	2. Wolf mount	2. Step-up mount without support
3. Walking-forward and backward	3. Jumps	3. Arabesque
4. dips	4. Leaps	4. Forward roll
5. hop or skip	5. Arabesque	5. Back roll
6. V-sit	6. One-half kick turn	6. Full kick turn
7. knee scale	7. Round-off dismount	7. Round-off dismount
8. swan pose	8. Straddle dismount	8. Single leg squat
9. pivot standing/squatting		
10. dismount		

Tumbling	**Tumbling**	**Tumbling**
1. Forward roll	1. Cartwheel	1. Right and left cartwheels
2. Back roll	2. Tip-up	2. Pike head stand
3. back straddle roll	3. Pike headstand	3. 1-hand cartwheel
4. tripod	4. Forearm headstand	4. Pike back roll
5. cartwheel	5. Mule kick	5. Tiger stand
6. headstand	6. Backbend	6. Backroll extension
	7. Front or back walkover	7. Front and back walkover
	8. Handstand	8. Front handspring
	9. Round off	9. Kip-up

Figure 14.18—*Continued*

GYMNASTICS CONTRACT

Name _____   Class Hour _____

Contracted Grade _____   Level _____
                                         (Beg./Int./Adv.)

1. Attendance (Abs.) _____

2. Written test _____ (Score)
3. Skills
   Tumbling 1 2 3 4 5 6 7 8 9   _____
                                     (Elective skills)

   Beam 1 2 3 4 5 6 7 8 9 10   _____
                                     (Elective skills)

   Vaulting 1 2 3 4 5 6   _____
                                     (Elective skills)

   Unevens 1 2 3 4 5 6   _____
                                     (Elective skills)

   Total skills _____ Total learning experience _____

4. Learning Experiences
   1   1 point   10   3 points   19   4 points
   2   2 points   11   3 points   20   5 points
   3   2 points   12   3 points   21   5 points
   4   2 points   13   3 points   22   6 points
   5   2 points   14   3 points   23   6 points
   6   2 points   15   4 points   24   6 points
   7   3 points   16   4 points   25   7 points
   8   3 points   17   4 points   26   7 points
   9   3 points   18   4 points   27   8 points

5. Read and sign
   "I accept responsibility for completing this contract and
   understand that if it is lost, it must be started over."

                          _____   / /
                             (Name)   (Date)

Instructors Comments:

Approved by _____ _____
                                          (Date)

Grade earned _____

Advantages

1. It allows diversity among students in terms of tasks or learning activities.

2. It permits students to work at their own pace.

3. It increases learning due to student's assumed responsibility for items personally selected.

4. Tasks are clearly defined.

Limitations

1. Preparation may be time consuming.

2. Contracts may require the use of additional media and outside facilities.

3. Some students are not ready to work on their own without constant teacher direction.

Procedures

1. Specify the performance and/or process objectives for a given unit of study.

2. Develop evaluation methods and materials, including progress checks that tell students when they are correct. (They also serve as reinforcers.)

3. Develop preassessment techniques.

4. Break down the subject area into short tasks, equivalent in time to about two per period.

5. Specify possible learning activities and learning materials.

6. Specify reinforcers.

7. Student and teacher meet together to discuss the conditions of the contract and specify proposed dates for the completion of various phases of the contract.

8. The teacher serves as a resource person when needed.

9. Students should be allowed to recontract with the approval of the teacher.

10. The student and teacher evaluate the achievement of the stated objectives in terms of the stated criteria. Inferior work should be redone.

11. A grade is awarded based on the specified criteria.

The inclusion style

The major difference between the inclusion style and the other styles we have discussed is that in this style the learner selects the level of performance for each task and alters it according to each self-assessment of the performance. The teacher selects the task and defines the various levels of the task according to the degrees of difficulty. Some factors that contribute to differences in difficulty include distance, height of basket or net, size of ball or implement, weight of ball or implement, size of the target or hoop, angle of shot or kick, quantity of tasks to be done, and body positions. It is important that the task to be done remains the same in this style (i.e., all push-ups or all striking skills).

The inclusion style permits all students to be
successful in the task to be performed.

The purpose of the inclusion style is to permit all students to be successful in the task to be performed, thereby increasing each student's self-esteem and enjoyment of physical activity. For this reason, the inclusion style is especially important when teaching classes that are coed and also have handicapped students mainstreamed within them. The inclusion style can be combined with other styles.

Inclusion skill checklist

Definition

A list of skills in which multiple levels of performance are available, from which students choose.

Examples

1. Archery—Shoot 200 points in five consecutive ends at:
   a. twenty yards.
   b. twenty-five yards.
   c. thirty yards.
   d. thirty-five yards.

2. Badminton—Do ten consecutive underhand drop shots with a partner under a rope:
   a. twenty inches above the net.
   b. sixteen inches above the net.
   c. twelve inches above the net.

3. Volleyball—Volley the ball consecutively against the wall above a line eight feet high:
   a. five times.
   b. ten times.
   c. fifteen times.

4. Swimming—Tread water:
   a. fifteen seconds.
   b. one minute.
   c. two minutes.

Uses

1. To ensure participation and success by all students.

Advantages

1. It accommodates individual differences.

2. It challenges highly skilled or fit, as well as low-skilled or fit, and handicapped students.

3. It increases students' awareness of own abilities.

4. It increases students' ability to set realistic goals.

5. It reduces learner anxiety.

Limitations

1. It is time-consuming for the teacher.

2. New or different equipment may be necessary.

Procedures

1. Determine the tasks.

2. For each task, determine one or more factors that change the level of difficulty of the skill.

3. Make up a checklist of the tasks, quantity to be done, multiple performance levels, and criteria for successful performance.

4. Have students circle or put an x through the starting level and the level completed.

5. Games can also be adapted by giving students choices, such as the choice of hitting implement and ball in softball.

Reaction and opinion papers

Definition

Papers submitted by students expressing their feelings, opinions, or reactions to something.

Examples

1. I Urge Telegrams: Send a "telegram," urging someone to do something, change something, or stop doing something. For example: To Mother, "I urge you to stop smoking. Your loving daughter."[7]

2. "I Learned" Statements: Write a brief statement of what you learned by doing a specific activity—such as going on a field trip or participating in a challenging activity, such as rapelling.[8]

3. Questions: Answer questions such as "What was the high point of the week?" "Whom did you get to know better this week?" "What did you learn about yourself this week?"[9]

4. Write reactions to a statement or quote such as "It's not whether you win or lose, but how you play the game," or "Winning is not the most important thing; it is the only thing," or "When the going gets tough, the tough get going."

Uses

1. To increase student awareness of their own feelings.

2. To increase teacher awareness of student feelings.

Advantages

1. It helps students think through their own feelings.

2. It accommodates individual differences.

Limitations

1. Students may not feel free to express their true feelings.

2. It could take up time used to learn psychomotor skills.

Procedures

1. Establish a nonthreatening, supportive environment in which students feel free to express their feelings.

2. Have students write their feelings about some specific topic.

3. Avoid grading reaction papers.

Goal Setting

Definition

Each person sets goals for himself or herself.

Examples

1. The Goalpost
   a. Decorate the bulletin board in the form of a goalpost.
   b. Have students record goals on footballs (3 × 5 cards) and post them below the crossbar.
   c. Each day students achieve their goals, they can move the football above the goalpost.
   d. Allow students time to share their successes with the class.[10]

2. The Envelope
   a. Have students record long-term goals.
   b. Place them in a sealed envelope for each class.
   c. Open the envelope at the end of the semester and redistribute them so students can see their progress.
   d. Allow students to share their successes.

Uses

1. To increase student skill in goalsetting.

2. To accommodate individual differences.

Advantages

1. It helps students to overcome laziness by setting goals.

2. It helps students learn to set realistic goals.

3. It helps students think through what is most important in a course.

Limitations

1. Students might set goals that are lower than their true expectations so they won't be penalized by failure to reach their goals.

2. It takes time.

Procedure

1. Help students get ideas for goals using some of the following techniques (or make up some of your own).
   a. Questions.
      1) If you had three wishes, what would they be?
      2) List three things about yourself that you would like to change.
      3) What do you wish you had time for? Money for?
      4) What talent do you wish you had?
   b. Twenty things you love to do. (See Figure 14.19.)
      1) List twenty things you like to do.
      2) Code the list as follows:
         a) Put a dollar ($) sign next to each item that costs over five dollars every time you do it.
         b) Place a *P* next to each item that you enjoy more when you are doing it with somebody and an *A* next to those things you enjoy more when you are doing it alone.
         c) Put a *PI* next to each activity that requires planning.
         d) Beside each activity, place the date when you did it last, if you can remember.
         e) Place an *F* or *M* next to each item you think your father or mother would have listed when they were your age.
         f) Place an * next to each item you would want your future wife or husband to have on their list. See the example in figure 14.19.[11]

	$	P/A	P1	F/M	•	Date	You can invent other codes			
1 Go surfing		P	P1			8/5/70				
2 Play basketball		P	P1	F		9/27/70				
3 Dance		P		M		3/28/71				
4 Read poetry						3/25/71				
5 Go to the movies	$	P	P1	F		2/31/71				
6										
7										
8										
9										
10										
11										
12										
13										
14										
15										
16										
17										
18										
19										
20										

I learned that I _____

Figure 14.19 Twenty things you love to do.
Source: Canfield, Jack and Harold C. Wells. *100 Ways to Enhance Self-Concept in the Classroom,* Englewood Cliffs, New Jersey: Prentice-Hall, 1976, pp. 133–4. For information about current Values Realization materials and a schedule of nationwide training workshops, contact Sidney B. Simon, Old Mountain Rd., Hadley, MA 01035.

c. Suppose a doctor just told you that you have only one year to live. What would you do differently? How would you change your life? What is stopping you from doing these things now? Let's set a goal to achieve some of them.[12]

2. Help students clarify goals. Goals should be:
   a. Clearly defined.
   b. Desirable, worthwhile, challenging.
   c. Achievable.
   d. Measurable in terms of time and quantity.
   e. Controllable. (Goals involving someone else should have their permission.)
   f. Achievement should result in a better self.[13]

The guided-discovery style

The main purpose of the guided-discovery style is to increase learning in the cognitive area. The role of the teacher is to determine the concepts and principles to be taught and the best sequence for guiding the students to the desired response. Strategies that can be used to achieve this include questioning; experiments, projects, and simulation activities; inquiry learning; discussion; and role playing.

As the students are involved in these strategies, the teacher varies the size and interrelationship of the steps and the speed of the learning sequence so that students are constantly moving toward the desired objective.

The guided-discovery style requires a warm, accepting environment in which students are allowed time to think through their questions or responses and helped to experience success in the discovery process. This style also requires a certain amount of risk on the part of the teacher. The teacher must be able to trace backward from the desired objective to get the first question and the sequence from which to proceed. Whenever a student response deviates from the desired response, the teacher must be able to ask a question that brings the students back into the desired sequence.

The advantage of the discovery style is its ability to help students understand the basic concepts of physical activity.

Questioning strategies

Definition

Question asking by the instructor and response by the students.

Examples (Cognitive):

1. Knowledge or fact questions: who, what, where, when. Involves recognition or recall of facts, events, places, person's names, etc.

2. Comprehension: Compare the belief in . . . of . . . and. . . . Explain in your own words. Involves understanding of what was expressed.

3. Application: If you were   . . . , what might you do? How does this apply in our lives? Involves using knowledge in new ways.

4. Analysis: Give evidence. . . . Explain. . . . What caused. . . . What effect was caused by. . . . Tell why. . . . Involves breaking information into parts.

5. Synthesis: Write a journal of your reactions to your fitness program. Describe how physical education makes a difference in your life. Involves combining parts to make a whole.

6. Evaluation: Should people. . . . Judge whether behavior was right or wrong. Defend the. . . . Involves making judgments based on standards. Affective: How do you feel about . . . ?

Uses

1. To help the learner perceive the referent of the concept.

2. To lead the student to a step-by-step evaluation of experience.

3. To sample understanding.

4. To stimulate thought.

5. To develop understanding.

6. To apply information.

7. To develop appreciations and attitudes.

8. To review information.

9. To spark or direct discussion.

10. To arouse interest and hold attention.

11. To provide emphasis.

12. To build student values.

13. To learn decision making.

Advantages

1. It increases individual student participation.

2. It stimulates learning.

3. It provides for evaluation of student learning.

4. It clarifies misconceptions.

Limitations

1. It requires considerable skill on the part of the teacher.

2. It embarrasses some students.

3. It is sometimes limited to "yes" and "no" recall questions.

4. It is sometimes answered by only a few students.

Procedures

1. Preparation. Prepare questions that:
   a. Relate to the purpose of the lesson.
   b. Are clear, definite, easily understood.
   c. Engage the attention of the whole class.
   d. Relate to the students' world and interests.
   e. Cause students to stretch their minds.
   f. Take into account individual differences in intelligence, background experiences, etc.
   g. Avoid manipulation of student responses.
   h. Build upon knowledge students now have.
   i. Can be answered in the time available.
   j. Are phrased in such a way as to obtain a discussion answer.

2. Introduce the discussion session with a story, diagram, chart, filmstrip, film, record, tape, object, case study, a well-planned question written on the chalkboard, etc.

3. Ask questions by:
   a. Directing the question to the entire class, pausing, and then calling on volunteers.
   b. Directing the question to the class, pausing, and then calling on a specific student.
   c. Directing a question from one student to another student or the entire class.

4. Encourage student involvement by:
   a. Pausing after each question to encourage more thoughtful and meaningful responses (at least three seconds). Say, "Think carefully before you answer," wait, then call on someone.
   b. Using nonvolunteers. Inform students that you would like everyone to contribute and that you will call on anyone whether or not their hands are raised. Avoid embarrassing a student. Try to adjust questions to student abilities. If a student hesitates, say, "Think about it for a minute and we'll come back to you."

c. Redirecting questions. Ask one question, then ask "Jane, can you add anything else?" or just nod at another student. Encourage students to direct questions to other students.

d. Rephrasing. Listen to the students' answer and then attempt to restate what you heard. For example, "Barry, do you mean . . . ?" Avoid inserting your own ideas into the answer.

e. Probing. Accept the students' initial response and then ask the student to extend, justify, or clarify it by asking, "Can you tell me more, Nathan?" Probing helps the student think more carefully and express a more complete answer.

5. When answers are off the subject, only partially complete or correct, or wrong, treat responses with courtesy and tact.

a. Acknowledge each answer with a smile, nod, or brief "Thank you," or "That's interesting, Brent."

b. Say something like, "That's not quite right. Let's think it through together."

c. Avoid rejecting good ideas that were not the answer you wanted. Instead, rephrase the question.

d. Avoid negative responses that might lower the student's self-esteem or discourage future responses. Always attempt to make the student feel good about responding.

e. Avoid praising answers excessively. Other students may assume their answers were no good.

6. Keep the discussion organized by relating questions to the previous answers or to questions students raise about the topic under discussion.

7. Summarize often to show students the progress they are making toward a solution, to focus the class on the solution, and to emphasize truths students are learning. Give credit to students who made important contributions. Use students to summarize when appropriate, and list the main points on the chalkboard.

8. Show how the solution can be applied to real life. Challenge the students to apply it.

9. Evaluate your questions against the following criteria:

a. Did the sequence of questions display a logical development of ideas leading students directly to the heart of the problem and to its solution?

b. Was each question related in some useful way to the problem statement?

c. Was the question accurately stated, specific, and to the point?

d. Was the question within the ability of the student to whom it was addressed?

e. Was the question relevant to students?

f. Did the question stimulate students to think and investigate?[14]

Experiments, projects, and simulation activities

Definition

A selective simplification or representation of a real-life situation, sometimes in a game or laboratory experiment.

Examples

1. Simulated track, gymnastics, or diving meet. (See figure 14.20.)

2. A golf course in the gym. By contacting local carpet stores for pieces of carpet and utilizing discarded or broken pieces of sports equipment, a nine-hole golf course can be designed for the locker room areas in the physical education building. A floor plan of the course should first be designed, then transferred to the carpet. The carpet is then cut to fit the appropriate area. Score cards can be duplicated similar to those used on a regulation golf course. Golf course courtesy is utilized. The course design is limited only by the imagination of the individual.[15]

3. Sensitivity modules, such as staying in a wheelchair for a day to see what it is like to be handicapped.

Uses

1. To learn knowledges, attitudes, skills, strategy.

2. To promote awareness of the consequences of one's actions.

3. To promote student initiative in solving problems.

4. To involve students in learning through the use of real-life and laboratory experiences.

Advantages

1. It results in high motivation and involvement.

2. It can assist in the development of social skills.

3. It promotes self-judging and introspection through rapid feedback on the consequences of one's actions.

Simulation—Diving Meet

There are three students at each station. The rotation from station to station is illustrated here. Students change stations after three divers have each performed two dives. The teacher roves back and forth between the two scoring tables to offer needed assistance. Eighteen people can participate at one time, and more can be added.

Equipment Needed
1. Extra diving forms
2. Ten sharp pencils with erasers
3. Two diving calculators
4. Six judges scoring cards
5. Two tables and twelve chairs
6. Extra towels
7. Instructions taped to the announcer's and scorer's tables. (In case they have trouble remembering their duties.)

Scorers XXX Announcer
XXX Judges
XXX Divers
XXX
XXX Judges
Announcer XXX Scorers

There are six teams (assigned by the instructor to assure the teams are evenly divided as far as diving ability). Each team (consisting of three members) should select a captain and a name. Each team captain has the responsibility to write each team member's two (2) dives on the diving sheet with their names in the left margin.

Figure 14.20 A simulated diving meet.
Source: Jack Romine and Joyce M. Harrison, Brigham Young University.

4. It provides more rapid and more meaningful learning.

5. It can be used with a wide range of student abilities.

6. It can provide experiences students might not get otherwise.

7. It increases retention.

8. It can be used to turn values into action.

Limitations

1. It is more time-consuming than just "telling."

2. It is heavily dependent on teacher competence.

3. It demands considerable time.

4. It can result in oversimplification of life situations.

5. It can be expensive in terms of equipment.

Procedures for laboratory experiments and projects

1. Assign laboratory or real-life experience or help students develop their own.

2. Counsel students on how to accomplish the goals of the assignment.

3. Supervise student activities.

4. Evaluate the results and provide feedback.

5. Tell what the results have to do with real life.

Procedures for simulation activities

1. Progress from simple to complex.

2. Emphasize the meaning of the simulation activity through preassessment and follow-up.

3. Assign heterogeneous teams.

4. Allow teams to select their own positions in the group.

5. Place faculty in legitimate roles, not as advisors to teams.

6. Define rules.

7. Play game.

8. Discuss principles involved.

9. Allow students to create their own games.

Materials needed

1. Laboratory, resource center, or community.

2. Scientific instruments, charts, models, etc.

Inquiry learning

Definition

A process through which students learn how to seek out answers scientifically by asking thought-provoking questions.

Examples

1. Twenty questions.

Uses

1. To promote student initiative for learning.

2. To help students learn how to learn.

3. To help students understand that all knowledge is tentative.

Advantages

1. It puts the responsibility for learning on the students.

2. It provides more meaningful learning.

Limitations

1. It is more time-consuming than conventional learning.

2. It places more emphasis on the learning strategy than on the subject matter.

Procedures

1. Provide and introduce the focus of the lesson—a puzzling or unfamiliar object, event, situation, etc.

2. Define rules of questioning.
   a. All questions must be answered by "yes" or "no."
   b. Ask only one question at a time.
   c. One student may ask a series of questions until a train of thought has been completed.
   d. Students may confer or call for a summary at any time.

3. Answer questions to help students gather data and verify information, reminding students of the rules when necessary.

4. Help students organize the information they have obtained, identify relationships among the variables, and create hypotheses to explain the situation. For example, if x is true, then would y be so.

5. Summarize the questioning procedure and identify how it can be improved.

Discussion

Definition

The group consideration of a question or real-life problem situation in order to arrive at truth, clear up difficulties, or generalize learning. (This is not a recitation session.)

Examples

1. Continuum
   a. Draw a continuum on the chalkboard.
   b. Label 0 in the center, degrees toward the ends, and name the ends:
      Cooperative _____ Competitive
         Clark   40 30 20 10 0 10 20 30 40   Connie
   c. Have students place themselves on the continuum. (Do not let them position themselves in the center.)
   d. Discuss where the most popular, happiest (etc.) student would be and why.

2. Priority or ranking
   a. Rank order a list of three to five situations from best to worst.
   b. Think of an idea that is better than and one that is worse than the situations given.
   c. Discuss the rankings.
   d. Example:
      Rank the actions you might take when you see another student cheating off your paper on a test.
      1) Do nothing.
      2) Hide your paper.
      3) Tell the teacher.[16]

3. Value Voting
   a. Read questions and have the class vote for or against each one.
   b. Sample questions:
      1) Would you try rapelling?
      2) Would you turn in a friend who cheated on a test?[17]

4. Case studies—Situations that need a decision and a plan of action.

5. Devil's advocate—Teacher takes a nonpopular view of an issue and encourages reactions from students.

6. Incomplete sentences—Have students complete sentences such as the following and discuss them: Competition is . . . . Winning is. . . .

Uses

1. To clarify concepts by discussing their implications, similarities, differences, etc.

2. To make concepts more relevant to group members through individual participation.

3. To provide opportunities for students to organize and communicate their thoughts.

4. To clarify values.

Advantages

1. It allows everyone to participate.

2. It encourages individual contributions.

3. It teaches respect for the viewpoints of others.

4. It increases class cooperation and interaction.

Limitations

1. It is time-consuming.

2. It is easily side-tracked.

3. It can be monopolized by a few talkative students or by the teacher.

4. It is often demoted to a question-answer session.

Procedures

1. Make sure students have the learning on which the discussion will be based.

2. Define the topic.

3. Work from an idea—visual aid, demonstration, quote, provocative question, film, etc.

4. Keep to the topic.

5. Involve everyone who wants to participate; avoid criticism or required participation.

6. Summarize periodically.

7. Draw conclusions.

Role Playing

Definition

An exploration of interpersonal relations problems by re-creating or acting out real-life situations and then discussing them.

Examples

1. A coach kicks a player off the team for not conforming to the rules regarding length of hair. The student threatens the coach's life.

2. A football player fails a test in English and is ineligible for the championship game this weekend. You are the player's best friend and the English teacher is your aunt.

Uses

1. To explore the feelings, attitudes, and values of groups or individuals.

2. To analyze social situations.

3. To develop problem-solving skills and attitudes.

Advantages

1. It helps individuals to understand the feelings or behavior of others through playing another role.

2. It increases student awareness of personal views and the consequences of behavior.

3. It increases student awareness that there are alternative ways to solve problems.

4. It increases student awareness of the values of society.

5. Students can act out real feelings without risk of reprisal.

Limitations

1. It is time-consuming.

2. It can't really reproduce real-life situations.

3. Some students have difficulty portraying feelings.

Procedures

1. Introduce students to a problem through a real-life situation far enough away from the students to remove threat or stress yet close enough to draw out the relationship between the behavior in the problem and parallel behavior within the class, school, etc. Ask students to think about what they would do under the same circumstances.

2. Select participants from volunteers. Avoid assigning roles based on peer pressure or the natural role of the student. Assign minor roles to the shy individuals.

3. Clarify the setting—place, time, situation, roles, etc.

4. Assign observers specific things to look for—feelings of certain players, alternative endings, etc.

5. Role play, several times if needed, to bring out possible alternative behaviors and their consequences.

6. Discuss behaviors, feelings, etc. Relate the role-playing situation to students' actual behavior in a nonthreatening way.

7. Discuss the role-playing situation, successes and failures, and how it could be improved.

Materials needed

1. Problem situation:
   a. Types—social problems, personal concerns, values, problem behaviors, social skills.
   b. Complexity—Choose easy ones first.

2. Role sheets that describe the feelings or values of the character to be played (optional).

The divergent style

In the divergent style, the student is encouraged to come up with multiple solutions to a given problem. The teacher selects the subject and designs the problem. The student discovers alternative solutions to the problem and evaluates them in terms of their ability to solve the problem. In some situations, where the quality of the movement is part of the solution, verification must be done by the teacher.

Individual problems can be offered to students, or problems can be clustered in groups. Finally, students can be allowed to select from a list of problems those that are relevant to their own interests.

The divergent style requires an environment in which the teacher feels secure enough to accept a wide variety of alternative solutions to problems. Students must have time and a supportive environment in which to work out solutions.

The major advantage of the divergent style is its ability to help the student develop creativity and the higher levels of cognitive development. In fact, in the divergent style, the process is as or more important than the solution. Social development is dependent upon whether the student is working in a group or individually.

Brainstorming and buzz sessions

Definition

The generation of solutions to a defined problem by stating any idea that comes to mind.

Examples

1. Brainstorming—A small group of students generates ideas for a new game or dance.

2. Buzz sessions—A large group is divided into small groups that generate ways to solve a case-study situation. Group members can be rotated to increase the diversity of ideas.

Uses

1. To solve a specific problem.

2. To define creative approaches to problem-solving.

Advantages

1. It provides for maximum group participation in small groups.

2. It results in unique, creative solutions to problems.

3. It develops individual creativity.

Limitations

1. It is more effective with homogeneous groups.

2. It is more difficult to use with very large groups.

Procedures

1. State the problem clearly.

2. Establish a time limit of five to ten minutes.

3. List ideas about the subject as they come to mind with no attempt to evaluate them. Try to get as many as possible.

4. At the end of the time specified, restate the problem and evaluate the ideas.

5. Narrow the ideas to one or more final solutions.

Materials needed

1. Chalkboard or scratch paper.

Problem-solving strategies

Definition

Solving a problem.

Examples

1. Strategy Talks—Divide the class into teams. Have each team think up five new plays. After a specified amount of time, each team shares its plays with the class. Discuss the strong and weak points of various plays. Then, try them out.

2. Choreograph a dance, gymnastics routine, etc.

3. Develop a new game.

Uses

1. To develop creativity.

2. To encourage application of concepts already learned.

3. To develop teamwork through student interaction.

4. To develop the ability to solve problems and verify solutions to problems.

Advantages

1. It encourages student interaction.

2. It encourages higher-level cognitive thinking.

3. It can increase retention.

Limitations

1. It takes time away from practicing the "real" game.

2. It is more time-consuming than teacher-dominated instruction.

3. It is difficult to involve some students meaningfully (i.e., slow learners, culturally disadvantaged, and students who lack the knowledge necessary to solve the problem).

Procedures

1. Define the problem in a few words.

2. State conditions necessary for the problem to be considered solved.

3. List possible solutions.

4. Find the best solution.

5. Evaluate success in solving the problem.

Going beyond

The purpose of this style is to increase the creativity of the student by allowing the learner to choose the problem and design the learning activities. Because of this, the style can be used only with individual students who are ready to take the initiative for their own behavior.

The teacher's role is to facilitate the student's formulation of the problem, the learning activities, and the final presentation and evaluation. During learning, the student checks in periodically to keep the teacher up-to-date on the learning process.

Quests

Definition

An individualized learning activity in which the student writes the objectives and learning activities (subject to teacher approval). In other ways it is similar to contract learning.

Examples

1. A Quest Contract (figure 14.21).

Uses

1. To allow students to set and pursue their own goals at their own pace.

2. To encourage student responsibility for learning.

Advantages

1. It decreases unhealthy competition between students, since students can have different goals.

2. It encourages individual initiative and creativity.

Limitations

1. It is difficult to state and/or measure the quality of different types of projects.

2. Some teachers are not accustomed to students doing their own things.

Procedures

1. The student selects the topic to be pursued and writes a performance objective (with the teacher's help) describing what is to be done.

2. Evaluation criteria are agreed upon.

3. The student selects the learning tasks and the materials or resources to be used.

```
┌─────────────────────────────────────────────────────────────────────┐
│                        A Quest Contract                             │
│  1. My objectives                                                   │
│                                                                     │
│                                                                     │
│  2. My plans for evaluation                                         │
│     _____ videotape recording                                     │
│     _____ expert or professional                                  │
│     _____ other:                                                  │
│                                                                     │
│  3. My learning activities                                          │
│                                                                     │
│                                                                     │
│  4. I plan to present evidence of my achievement of each objective by│
│                                                                     │
│     _____                                        │
│           (Date)                                                    │
│                                                                     │
│  5. My contract is for an _____ grade.                        │
│                                                                     │
│                                    _____    _____   │
│                                    Signature of student   Date      │
│                                    _____    _____   │
│                                    Signature of instructors  Date   │
└─────────────────────────────────────────────────────────────────────┘
```

Figure 14.21 A Quest Contract.

4. A schedule of progress checks and completion dates is created.

5. The student records what is done and evaluates progress in terms of the criteria agreed upon.

6. The final presentation is made in a written or verbal format or as a physical performance.

Questions and suggested activities

1. Do you think teachers should provide different teaching strategies to fit the needs of individual students or that students should develop a wide range of learning strategies?

2. Prepare a lesson plan for each of the seven styles of teaching.

3. Identify different teaching styles and strategies you have experienced. Which ones did you learn the most from? Ask other students which ones they learned best from. Did they agree with you?

4. Teach a lesson using each of the seven styles of teaching.

Suggested readings

American Alliance for Health, Physical Education, and Recreation. *Ideas for Secondary School Physical Education: Innovative Programs from Project Idea,* Washington, D.C.; AAHPER, 1976.

Dowell, Linus J. *Strategies for Teaching Physical Education.* Englewood Cliffs, N.J.: Prentice-Hall, 1975.

Geiger, William, and Kizer, David. "Developing A Teaching Awareness." *The Physical Educator* 36 (March 1979): 25–26.

Hellison, Don. *Beyond Balls and Bats,* Washington, D.C.: AAHPER, 1978.

Hill, Charles E. "Computer-Based Resource Units in Health & Physical Education." *Journal of Physical Education and Recreation* 46 (June 1975): 26–27.

Kraft, Robert E. "An Analysis of Student Learning Styles." *The Physical Educator* 33 (October 1976): 140–42.

The command style

Saylor, J. Galen, and Alexander, William M. *Planning Curriculum for Schools.* San Francisco: Holt, Rinehart and Winston, Inc., 1974, p. 252.

Shively, Michael Jay. "Lecture and Lecturer." *Phi Kappa Phi Journal* (Spring, 1976), pp. 40–42.

The practice style

Chafin, M. B.; Moore, C. A.; and Thomas, J. R. "An Experiment in Tennis Methodology." *The Physical Educator* 35 (March 1978): 7–10.

Del Rey, Patricia. "The Task Method of Teaching Tennis Skills Using Video-taped Replays." *The Physical Educator* 33 (December 1976): 194–97.

The reciprocal style

Mosston, Muska. *Teaching Physical Education,* 2d ed. Columbus, Ohio: Charles E. Merrill Publishing Company, 1981.

The self-check style

Anderson, Eugene W. "New Role Expectations for Contract Teaching." *Journal of Health Physical Education Recreation* 45 (October 1974): 37.

Annarino, Anthony A. "Another Way to Teach." *Journal of Health Physical Education Recreation* 45 (October 1974): 43–46.

———. "High School Mini-Activity Physical Education Programs Based on a Multi-Media Individualized Approach." *The Physical Educator* 32 (December 1975): 190–99.

Burkett, Lee N., and Darst, Paul W. "How Effective is Contract Teaching in Theory Class?" *Journal of Physical Education and Recreation* 50 (April 1979): 86–87.

"Contract Learning—One Approach to Developing and Maintaining Physical Fitness." *Physical Education Newsletter* (April 1981).

Dunn, Rita, and Dunn, Kenneth. *Practical Approaches to Individualizing Instruction.* Nyack, N.Y.: Parker Publishing Co., 1972.

Mather, Jim. "Contracts Can Motivate Physical Underachievers." *Journal of Physical Education and Recreation* 49 (June 1978): 23–24.

Netcher, Jack R. "A Learning System: What Is It, Why Is It, How Does It Work?" *Journal of Physical Education and Recreation* 47 (June 1976): 29–30.

O'Donnell, Leo E. "Experience Based Contracting in Elementary Physical Education." *The Physical Educator* 33 (October 1976): 135–39.

Youngberg, Linda, and Jones, Dee Dee. "Performance Contracts Help Teach Tumbling." *Journal of Physical Education and Recreation* 51 (November–December 1980): 63.

The inclusion style

Canfield, Jack, and Wells, Harold C. *100 Ways to Enhance Self-concept in the Classroom—A Handbook for Teachers and Parents.* Englewood Cliffs, N.J.: Prentice-Hall, 1976.

The guided-discovery style

Canfield and Wells, *100 Ways.*

Gagne, Robert M., and Briggs, Leslie J. *Principles of Instructional Design.* Chicago: Holt, Rinehart and Winston, 1974.

Harmin, Merrill, and Simons, Sidney B. "How to Help Students Learn to Think . . . About Themselves." *The High School Journal* (March 1972), 256–64.

Hunkins, Francis P. *Involving Students in Questioning.* Boston: Allyn and Bacon, 1976.

Joyce, Bruce, and Weil, Marsha. *Models of Teaching,* 2d ed. Englewood Cliffs, N.J.: Prentice-Hall, 1980.

Kirschenbaum, Howard. "Sensitivity Modules." *Media & Methods* (February 1970): 34–38.

The divergent style

Harmin and Simons, "How to Help Students."

Hawley, *Human Values in the Classroom.*

Hellison, Don, ed. *Personalized Instruction in Physical Education.* Washington, D.C.: AAHPER, 1977.

Hudgins, Bryce B. *Problem Solving in the Classroom.* New York: The Macmillan Company, 1966.

Schueler, Annemarie. "The Inquiry Model in Physical Education." *The Physical Educator* (May 1979): 89–92.

Selecting, Producing, and Utilizing Instructional Materials

Study stimulators

1. What factors should be considered in the selection of instructional materials?
2. How should the class be prepared when using media in the classroom?
3. When are instructional materials harmful? What factors should be considered in evaluating the effectiveness of your media presentation?
4. How can a learning resource center or instructional materials center be of help in physical education?
5. What is a resource file? Why is it important to teachers?

The purpose of instructional materials is to help achieve instructional objectives more effectively and more economically. Instructional aids can increase motivation on the part of the student and create heightened interest and enjoyment in learning by reducing the amount of teacher talk and increasing visual involvement. It has been said that approximately 83 percent of all learning occurs through sight, only 11 percent results from hearing, and less than 6 percent through the other senses. Retention of learning is increased fourfold over hearing only by the use of visual involvement and nearly sevenfold by combining the use of visual and auditory senses. Instructional materials accomplish these tasks by activating the students in the learning process. An old Chinese proverb points this out very well. It says:

> I hear, I forget.
> I see, I remember.
> I do, I understand.

Instructional materials can be used to introduce a lesson, present new material, clarify a subject of discussion, or summarize a lesson. But, most of all, instructional media can be used to bring learning experiences closer to real-life situations and to provide feedback to the learners on how their performance approximates the performance required by the objective.

Although instructional materials can be used effectively to enhance motivation and learning, research seems to indicate that in many cases no increase in learning has taken place. Students are media-saturated. Teachers compete with the multimillion dollar budgets of television and movies. Therefore, media has to be exceptional for students to respond positively toward it. Instructional media have proven to be of the most value when they have been closely correlated with the instructional objectives, so that they can supplement and increase the effectiveness of the teacher. In no way should media be used just to take up the time on a rainy day or when the teacher is unprepared. Teachers should remember that no medium can substitute for a concerned, well-prepared teacher.

A live demonstration is much more effective than a visual aid. Motion pictures or loop films can be advantageous when no competent performer exists. They can also give the entire class the view obtained by the observer in the most advantageous position. Close-ups afford all members of a large class the opportunity to see the motion clearly. Another benefit of the motion picture is that it can reproduce action which the observer rarely sees, such as an underwater view of a swimming stroke or a slow-motion view of a complex skill.

Motion pictures, loop films, and videotapes can contrast good with bad positions by showing the person in the act of changing from one position to the other. Through the use of slow motion, it is possible to analyze sports skills in terms of body position, timing, and the relationship of skills to game play. The instant replay feature of the videorecorder makes it a terrific teaching aid because the players can see themselves in action. Videotaping helps the learners see their own mistakes or successes. By helping students compare their own performance with the performance of a model, videotape feedback can be even more valuable.

When videotape machines are unavailable, Polaroid pictures can be used to provide feedback in activities, such as archery, and in posture classes. A Polaroid-type "graphic sequence camera" can take a series of timed snapshots with a single shot, which can then be analyzed for feedback purposes. A summary of various types of instructional materials with their advantages and disadvantages is shown in table 15.1.

Selection of instructional materials

When selecting instructional materials, teachers should always attempt to choose materials that are as close to the real-life experiences as possible. Several years ago, Dale developed the "cone of learning experiences," which became a classic in describing the hierarchy of media use.[1] A simplified version is presented in figure 15.1. Experiences closest to the bottom of the cone of experience are closest to real-life situations. For example, a demonstration with a live model would be better than a film. Other considerations—such as student safety, money, and practicality—will, of course, restrict the teacher in making a selection. The selection of costly materials is a process that should be shared by teachers, students, parents, and administrators so that the needs of all are considered.

The use of a systematic evaluation guide will facilitate the selection of materials. The guide will consider the potential of the materials for relevant learning by asking the following questions about them:

1. Do they make a meaningful contribution to the topic under study?

2. Do they develop concepts that are difficult to convey through another medium?

Table 15.1 A summary of the various types of instructional materials

Medium	Uses	Advantages	Disadvantages
Videotapes.	Evaluation of student performance. Self-evaluation of student or teacher. Magnification of small objects.	Instant replay. Can save for future use. Can prerecord. Inexpensive. Portable.	Need skilled production staff.
8-mm films and loops. Videodiscs.	Individual study. Homework. Students make own films. Stimulates verbal communication and creativity.	Highly portable—compact. Inexpensive: more accessible. Ease of operation. Versatility. Replay without rewinding.	Silent.
16-mm films	Present meanings involving motion. Compel attention. Heighten reality. Speed up or slow down time. Enlarge or reduce size. Bring past or present into class. Build common denominator of experience. Influence and change attitudes. Promote understanding of abstract concepts.		Sound film is costly. Production time is long. Requires darkened room. Internally controlled pacing. Fixed sequence.
Models. Mock-ups. Exhibits. Displays. Objects, specimens.	Examples of real-life situations. Comparisons.	Enlargement or reduction High reality—3-D	
Computers.	Programmed instruction. Tournament recordkeeping.	High interest. Fast.	Relatively expensive unless terminals can be hooked up to a main computer. Software is currently limited.

Material	Uses	Advantages	Limitations
Tape recorders. Audio tapes. Records.	Authority resource. Create a mood. Grading comments. Student interview. Exams.	High reality. Inexpensive software. Available equipment and tapes. Ease of production.	Low cost, accessible equipment.
Slides or filmstrips.	History, geography. Concepts.	Magnification or reduction. Inexpensive software. Availability. Inexpensive hardware. High reality. Flexible sequence and pacing (slides). Can be combined with audio.	Requires darkened room. Fixed sequence (filmstrips).
Overhead transparencies.	Graphic presentations.	Inexpensive software. Availability. Project in light room. Flexible sequence. Base of operation at front of room. All advantages of chalkboard plus.	
Duplicated materials.	For important information: as a quiz; as a guide; as a reminder. To emphasize a point. For a complete explanation.	Can be prepared in advance. Can be retained for future reference and review.	
Opaque projections.	Still pictures.	High reality. Flexible sequence.	
Magnetic boards.	Sequence material. Tell stories with simple illustrations. Illustrate hard-to-understand concepts. Display materials. Strategy talks.	Inexpensive. Easy. Creative. Attention-getting.	

Table 15.1—_Continued_

Medium	Uses	Advantages	Disadvantages
Chalkboards.	Clarify sequence of events. Focus attention. Stimulate discussion.	Flexibility and versatility. Availability. Size.	

Still pictures
  Charts
  Posters
  Bulletin boards
  Flip charts
  Graphs
  Maps
  Diagrams
  Cartoons
	Attract attention.
	Arouse interest.
	Reinforce and add dimension.
	Provide concrete meaning to
	   abstract ideas.
		Very inexpensive.
		No equipment needed.
		Easy to use and store.
		Readily available.
			Too small.
			Limited to two dimensions.
			No motion.

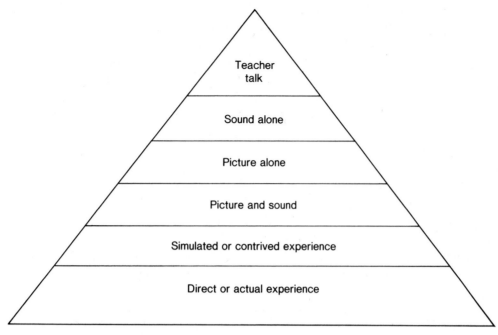

Figure 15.1 The cone of learning experiences.

3. Are they true to fact and life, accurate and authentic?

4. Are they up-to-date?

5. Are they worth the time, cost, and effort involved?

6. Do they develop critical thinking skills?

7. Are they appropriate for the age, intelligence, and experience level of the students?

A second consideration of the systematic evaluation guide is the technical quality of the materials. The picture and sound should be examined for quality. The mode of communication should be adequate for the intended purpose and the media should be unbiased and free from objectionable propaganda or distractions.

The ease of presentation of media is the third consideration. Often, the management problems associated with the use of instructional materials renders them useless when, in fact, it is the management system that is ineffective. When purchasing media equipment, an evaluation should be made before buying of ease of operation, ease of maintenance, quality of picture and sound, durability, and portability.

Sources of instructional materials include commercial sources such as catalogs of instructional aids, and printed materials such as tests, journals, newspapers, and learning packets. Professional persons, parents, and friends are excellent sources, as are many students. A college or university media center or a district or school instructional materials center often have access to many of these sources. The American Alliance for Health, Physical Education, Recreation and Dance also publishes catalogs of instructional materials.

Production of instructional materials

When producing instructional materials, care should be taken to plan and prepare materials systematically. The teacher should utilize the evaluation questions to determine appropriate media for the instructional process. Care should then be taken to insure quality of production within the limits of cost, materials, and available help and equipment. Poor-quality materials detract from the teaching effort. Space will not permit the inclusion here of specific production techniques. Classes are offered in most colleges and universities in the production of instructional materials and many books have been written to convey the information necessary.

Utilization of instructional materials

The use of instructional materials is dependent upon proper planning, preparation, and follow-up. The first step, of course, is to define the objective of the lesson. The media are then analyzed in terms of the contributions they can make to the objective, and their weaknesses or deviations from achievement of the objective.

After the equipment has been tried out under classroom conditions, the class is oriented to the media through use of a discussion or handout. The orientation should include (1) the objective for viewing or listening, (2) an overall view of the material to be presented, (3) points to look or listen for, (4) new vocabulary or concepts, (5) motivating statements, and (6) a quiz or outline to fill in.

After using the instructional materials, the teacher should answer questions raised, correct misunderstandings, bridge gaps in the material, summarize the concepts taught, and evaluate student learning through a written or oral test or discussion. The teacher should relate the presentation directly to the objectives of the lesson and direct the discussion to include the pertinent points brought out by the instructional medium. Students should be allowed to express their own reactions to the experience. The teacher should also evaluate the usefulness of the medium of instruction in terms of student progress toward the lesson objectives and the students' application of learning in the classroom experience.

Some things to watch for in the use of media include proper time allotment, effective physical arrangement of the class, and the appropriateness of the medium to the lesson objectives. Avoid media saturation by using the same type of media too often.

Evaluation of the use of instructional materials

Instructional materials have been used so frequently in education that we often tend to ignore the fact that media can teach incorrect information. Media can be harmful when:

1. They are not true-to-fact or true-to-life.

2. They are misleading.

3. They are not appropriate to or have no bearing on the lesson.

4. They are wasteful of time and effort that could be better spent.

5. They are confusing or too complicated.

6. They are of poor quality.

7. They are used without adequate preparation and follow-up.

8. They are used just to be using media ("media for media's sake").

In evaluating the use of an instructional medium, ask yourself the following questions:

1. Was it selected only after the objectives of the lesson had been determined?

2. Was it used only if it improved the setting for learning?

3. Was it pertinent to the purpose of the lesson?

4. Was it used at the point in the learning sequence when it made the greatest contribution to learning? Was its use timely?

5. Was it accurate? (up-to-date rules, form, strategy, court size, scoring, etc.)

6. Was it technically excellent? Large enough so that all could see? Contrasting colors to emphasize important points? To scale so as not to confuse students? Sturdy enough for outdoor use?

7. Were you skillful in using it? Did your manner of presentation contribute to or detract from its effectiveness? Did you fumble? Bring necessary parts? Introduce it adequately? Explain effectively? Stand out of students' line of vision? Ask for and answer questions? Summarize its presentation? Speak facing the class so that you could be heard?

8. Was your use of the medium effective? Why or why not?

9. Would you use it again? Why or why not?

10. Would you change the manner in which you used it? Why or why not?

11. Was it administratively feasible in cost and time?

Students use the computer in the Learning
Resource Center to individualize their fitness
programs.

Use of the learning resource or instructional materials center

The learning resource center or instructional materials center can contribute significantly
to the instructional program by providing experiences to supplement class instruction. Instructional materials can be utilized to develop the knowledges and skills necessary to profit
from instruction (prerequisite or enabling skills), to introduce new skills and knowledges, or
to review those already presented. Both remedial and enrichment experiences can be made
available to individuals, small groups, or entire classes. Self-paced instructional units can
also be made available through an instructional materials center.

A learning resource center should include the following hardware (equipment): 8-mm
and 16-mm film projectors; slide projectors; videotape camera, recorder and monitor; audio
cassette tape recorders; record players; cameras; and even computers. Software should include 8-mm loop films, 16-mm films, slides, audio tapes, videotapes, charts, and reading
materials of various kinds.

Facilities should include areas for film viewing, audio listening, and reading as shown
in figure 15.2. Private earphones can be helpful when facilities are limited in size. The best
arrangement is to have the learning resource center close to practice areas. When this is not

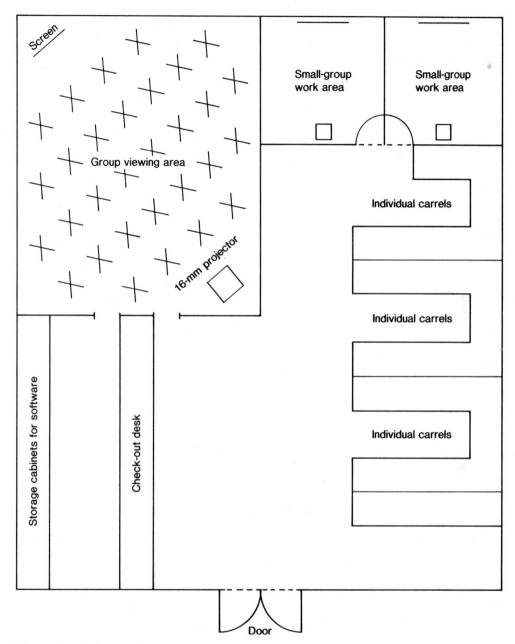

Figure 15.2 A diagram of a learning resource center for physical education.

possible, many resource materials can be housed in the school instructional materials center for use by students during their individual study time. Materials can be checked out by faculty and brought to the classroom for use with individuals or groups of students during class time.

Use of a personal resource file

A personal resource file is a file in which instructional materials are located and where they can be easily obtained for use and replaced for future reference and use. Every teacher should devise a system of filing that is practical in the situation in which he or she is working. Materials should include pictures, items for lesson and unit planning, skill analyses, evaluation materials, handouts, study sheets, instructional media lists, books, pamphlets, etc. Each item should be labeled as to its location so it can be returned when not in use. Files should include community resources and lists of people who might be willing to assist you in developing or conducting learning activities, or for special reports or projects.

One of the simplest methods of filing is to have a file folder for each sport or topic you might teach. This might be expanded later as in the following examples of file titles:

Archery—Unit Plans

Archery—Equipment

Archery—Skill Evaluation

Archery—Knowledge Evaluation

Of course, the filing system must follow a plan that agrees with your personal style and with which you can most easily locate materials.

Questions and suggested activities

1. Demonstrate your proficiency with educational media equipment by operating the following (getting assistance if necessary):

   16-mm projector   slide projector
   overhead projector   opaque projector
   8-mm projector   8-mm loop film projector
   cassette tape recorder   reel-to-reel tape recorder
   record player   spirit process duplicator (ditto)
   thermofax copier

2. Create typewritten and hand-drawn dittoed handouts to show that you know how to create masters and how to make corrections on masters.

3. Begin a professional resource file.

4. Evaluate an instructional medium using the questions provided in the chapter.

Suggested readings

Batesky, James. "Improving Instruction Through a Videotape Library." *Journal of Physical Education and Recreation* 50 (February 1979): 83.

Biles, Fay. "The Physical Education Public Information Center." *Journal of Health Physical Education Recreation* 42 (May 1971): 53–55.

Brown, Wayne. "Using the Media Center in Physical Education." *Journal of Physical Education and Recreation* 50 (June 1979): 75.

Publications by the NASPE Media Resource Center, College of Health and Physical Education, University of South Carolina, Columbia, South Carolina 29208.

Putting It All Together—Unit and Lesson Planning

Study stimulators

1. Write a lesson plan for a specific lesson in your unit.
2. Write a unit plan as outlined in the chapter.

The yearly curriculum is usually divided into two kinds of instructional plans—unit plans and daily lesson plans. Basically, these plans include the answers to three questions expressed by Mager as follows: (1) where am I going?, (2) how will I get there?, and (3) how will I know I've arrived?[1]

Where am I going? The plan should specify the performance objectives of the lesson or unit in the cognitive, psychomotor, and affective domains.

How will I get there? The plan should delineate the learning experiences that will be used to help students meet the objectives specified.

How will I know I've arrived? Evaluation techniques that will help the teacher determine whether or not the students have achieved the objectives must be included.

How to write a lesson plan

I. Principles

The process of teaching psychomotor skills involves the following:
A. Determination of the desired level of achievement.
B. Preassessing readiness or ability to perform the skill.
C. Providing a model of the skill for the learner.
D. Providing guided practice until the learner can perform the skill correctly.
E. Providing practice to facilitate retention of the newly learned skill.
F. Provision of a maximum of student activity through proper facilities, equipment, and time.
G. Evaluation of skill performance.
H. Teaching of concomitant cognitive and affective behaviors.

II. Experiences
A. Review the completed lesson plan form in figure 16.1
B. Choose a topic for your lesson and write it under "Activity" on your plan. Then, study the following areas of the plan, constructing your plan as you go.

1. *Behavioral Objective*
   a. Write down what you expect the students to be able *to do* after you instruct them.

      Examples:
      1) Hit correctly three out of five balls.
      2) Use correct rules during tournament play.
      3) Perform one lay-up with correct form as specified.
      4) Refrain from arguing with the official.
   b. You may have as many objectives as you need to cover the material you are teaching in each of the three domains.

2. *Preassessment*
   a. Write down how you *already* know if students have achieved the objective.

      Examples:
      1) *Pretest*—The students completed a pretest the previous day, week, etc.
      2) *Observation*—The students have been observed performing the desired behavior.
   b. Write down how you *will* know if students can already achieve the objective. If this type of preassessment is used, write in "included in plan."
      1) *Questioning*—How many students can serve overhand?
      2) *Pretest*—A written or skills test is given before instruction.
      3) *Teacher observation*—Send students you see performing the skill well to do another objective with a team teacher or to practice for retention or accuracy.

3. *Evaluation of Objectives:*
   a. Write how you will know when the behavior specified in the objective has been achieved.

      Examples:
      1) *Skills test*—The student will hit eight out of ten serves into the back court as scored by a partner.
      2) *Teacher observation*—The teacher will evaluate each student on lay-up form.
      3) *Game scores*—The game scores will indicate a knowledge of how to pick up leaves in bowling.
      4) *Written test*—A written test will indicate knowledge gained by the student.
      5) *Check-off chart*—A check-off chart will be used to record negative comments to officials.
   b. If you have more than one objective, then you will also need more than one evaluation technique.

Name:
Date:

Activity: Softball-batting

Preassessment: In plan
Objectives: (1) Students will use correct batting form and hit three out of five balls; (2) Students will develop cooperative group atmosphere.
How can objectives be evaluated: Teacher observation of form and group atmosphere; self-evaluation—number of balls hit.
Sources of information: "Team Sports for Girls and Women", Handout—"Rules for One-Swing Softball"

Equipment needed: All softballs, gloves, eight tees, eight bases, eight to sixteen bats
Play space needed: Field—two diamonds
Markings: Bases
Media to be used: None

Time Allotment	Teaching and Learning Experiences	Skill Analysis	Teaching Cues	Class Organization	Safety Ind. Differences	Motivation Techniques
Five minutes	I. Warm-ups before class. Throwing and catching.			I. X ------ X X ------ X X ------ X X ------ X X ------ X	All throwing north and south.	Not having to do exercises.
No time.	II. Roll call. Student assistant marks each girl as she enters the field.					

Two to three minutes	III. Demonstration of batting with cues.	III. Batting
		A. *Grip*
		  a. Right hand above and close to left, 2-3 inches from end of bat.
		  b. Trademark—mark up—even with "v's."
		B. *Stance*
		  a. Body and knees easy, feet apart comfortably, left shoulder to pitcher.
		  b. Right foot opposite the back corner of the plate.
			a. Firm but not tense grip.
			b. Check trademark.
			
			a. Assume a natural position.
			b. Elbows away from body.
				III. Whistle. Sit in squad order.
				
				Sitting—squad order
				X X X X X X
				X X X X X X
				X X X X X X T
				First three from each group go to tees 1-4 second three to 5-8.
					Facing away from sun or other disturbance.	Batting will be needed in game. *Short* demonstration.

Time	Content	Cues	Organization	Safety/Comments
Ten minutes	c. *Contact* a. Elbows away from body, wrist cocked. b. Bat is back as far as left arm can reach easily across chest. c. Step simultaneously with left foot. IV. Pepper (drill). A. With tee. B. Without tee as students show proficiency. C. Preassessment: Self-scoring—when objective is met, can play work-up on nearby field.	a. Keep eye on ball. b. Swing level. c. Follow through. d. Step and swing. *Meet* the ball. *Guide* it to a teammate.	Tee ⟨ X X X Tee ⟨ X X X Tee ⟨ X X X etc. for 8 groups. Rotate: pitcher, batter, pitcher.	Spaced far enough to avoid collisions. Bat in same direction. Gloves for retrievers. Keep eye on ball. Meet ball, not hit away. Success. Individual help. Get to play when successful.

Figure 16.1 A lesson plan.

Figure 16.1—Continued

Lesson Plan—continued

Time Allotment	Teaching and Learning Experiences	Skill Analysis	Teaching Cues	Class Organization	Safety Ind. Differences	Motivation Techniques
Fifteen minutes	V. Play "One Swing Softball."	V. Rules on handout (attached)	Use "Team-work" game strategy. Choose best pitcher to pitch to you.	Teams 1 and 2 play on Diamond 1. Teams 3 and 4 play on Diamond 2.	No bat throwing. Don't block baseline. Call for fly balls. No sliding.	Competition. Fun. Different—more movement and turns.
One minute	Conclusion—gather equipment.					

4. *Sources of Information*
    a. Write where you acquired the material for this lesson.
       Examples:
       1) Handout— "Marking" (P. E. 233)
       2) Colleague or teacher—Ms. Jones.
       3) Resource file—pictures from magazine
       4) Book—Allsen and Harrison, pp. 36–37.
    b. If you need no sources for your plan, write "previous experience."
5. *Teaching and Learning Activities*
    a. Write *how* you will teach the lesson.
       Examples:
       1) Demonstration with cues
       2) Brief explanation of traveling
       3) Skit on proper etiquette
       4) Inquiry (questioning by students)
       5) Questions by teacher to review rules or for evaluation
       6) Nonoral presentation
       7) Roll call
    b. Write *learning activities* to be used by students.
       Examples:
       1) Drills
       2) Games
       3) Mimetic drills (pantomime)
       4) Guided practice
       5) Skills test
       6) Written test
       7) Check-off chart
       8) Warm-ups
6. *Skill Analysis*
    a. Write down the components of the skill to be taught (the *what's*).
       Examples:
       1) Forehand drive
          a) Starting position
             i
             ii
          b) Backswing
             i
             ii

        c) Contact

           i

           ii

        d) Follow-through

    2) Front Crawl

        a) Arms

           i

           ii

        b) Legs

           i

           ii

        c) Breathing

           i

           ii

        d) Coordination

           i

           ii

7. *Teaching Cues*

    a. For each skill, choose three components that are essential to proper execution of the skill. For each component, write a brief (one to four words) cue that expresses what the performer should do. Limit yourself to three or four cues per skill.

    Examples:

      1) Overhead pass—volleyball

        a) Look through the triangle.

        b) Get under the ball.

        c) Extend.

      2) Badminton—overhead clear

        a) Scratch your back.

        b) Reach for the birdie.

        c) Make it whistle.

      3) Swimming—breast stroke

        a) Pull.

        b) Kick.

        c) Glide.

    b. Cues may be visual, verbal, or kinesthetic.

    Examples:

      1) Moving a student's arms in front crawl motion.

      2) Placing a hand on the string hand to prevent jerking to the side in archery.

3) Visual diagram of how to change lanes when league bowling.

4) Visual cues for footwork drill in badminton.

8. *Class Organization*

   a. Diagram each separate pattern of organization you will use during the period. Use *x*'s for students, *T* for teacher, etc.
   Examples:

   1)
   ```
       x x
     x     x
   x    T    x
   ```

   2)
   ```
   x   x   x   x

   x   x   x   x

   x   x   x   x

   x   x   x   x

           T
   ```

   3)

x x x	x x x	x x x
x x x	x x x	x x x
x x x	x x x	x x x
x x x	x x x	x x x

   b. Tell how you will move the class from each formation shown into the one following (transitions).
   Examples:

   1)
   ```
   x   x   x   x    Squad 1 go to
   x   x   x   x        court 1,
   x   x   x   x    Squad 2 go to
   x   x   x   x        court 2,
   1   2   3   4        etc.
   ```

   2)
   ```
   xxxxxxxxxxxxxxx      one's stay
   123412341234 1234    two's take five steps

   x    x    x    x     three's take ten steps

   x    x    x    x     four's take fifteen steps

     x    x    x    x

       x    x    x    x
   ```

9. *Safety and Individual Differences*
   a. Write in appropriate safety provisions.
      Examples:
      1) Safe spacing.
      2) Rules enforced.
      3) Surfaces free from obstacles:
         a. around walls, that might be run into.
         b. balls, pinnies, etc. on floor that might be stepped on.
      4) Glasses guards.
      5) Jewelry, long nails, etc.
      6) Shoelaces tied, shoes on.
      7) Equipment in good repair and used properly.
   b. Write in how you will be aware of and deal with individual differences.
      Examples:
      1) Handedness—Help left-handers with converting bowling leaves because the switch is not exactly opposite to that of right-handers.
      2) Handicaps—In jump rope unit, the one-armed girl can tie one end of rope to door knob, etc.
      3) Skill level—Students who can already do the underhand serve will move to court 3 and practice overhead serves.
      4) Social abilities—Try to promote group acceptance of Robbie.
      5) Mental abilities—Assign partners so that Mary can help Dwayne with drills.
10. *Motivation Techniques*
    a. Write down appropriate motivation techniques.
       Examples:
       1) *Fun!!*
       2) Competition.
       3) Grades—sometimes.
       4) Written or skills tests—sometimes.
       5) *Success!*
       6) Extrinsic rewards—treats, ribbons.
       7) Desire for activity.
       8) Playing the game (not drills, but the real thing).
    b. It may be helpful to think of yourself as one of the students and write those items that would make you want to participate in the learning activities if you *were not* required to do so.

11. *Time Allotment*
    a. Write down the approximate amount of time to be spent on each teaching or learning activity.
       Examples:
       1) 8:05–8:07—Roll Call.
       2) 8:07–8:15—Warm-ups   or
       3) Two minutes—Roll Call.
       4) Eight minutes—Warm-ups.
       5) Three minutes—Demonstration.
    b. Remember to plan your time for a *maximum amount of activity*. Students learn by *doing* not by being told.
12. *Facilities and Equipment*
    a. Write in the equipment needed. Be sure to plan for maximum activity for each student.
       Examples:
       1) Balls.
       2) Bats.
       3) Pinnies.
       4) Score sheets.
    b. Write in the playing area and any marks that will be needed.
       Examples:
       1) Three volleyball courts, tape line fifteen feet from net on north side.
       2) Two basketball courts, no markings.
       3) Four badminton courts, tape lines at six-inch intervals from short service line back.
    c. Write in any media to be used.
       Examples:
       1) 8-mm loop film projector, screen, film.
       2) Magnetic chalkboard, chalk, magnets.
C. If you still fail to understand any area of the plan, ask your instructor for assistance.

How to write a unit plan

A unit plan should consider the same three basic components as the lesson plan—objectives, learning activities, and evaluation techniques. The amount of time spent on the unit and on various aspects of the unit should be based on the previous experience and expertise of the students. Teachers should take advantage of the possibilities of transfer from previous units by pointing out when the transfer can be expected. Sufficient time should be provided so that students can overlearn a few skills to achieve high levels of performance and retention. This is more desirable than to attain low levels of proficiency in many skills.

The teacher who fails to plan, plans to fail.

I. Principles
   A. Unit plans for physical education revolve around the following considerations:
      1. An identification of student characteristics.
      2. An identification of subject matter.
      3. An identification of instructional methods.
      4. A determination of administrative organization.
   B. A daily progression of activities must be planned that provides for the following:
      1. Progression from simple to complex.
      2. Maximum student participation.
      3. Successful learning.
      4. Safety.
      5. Motivation.
      6. Pacing of instruction commensurate with individual skill levels.
II. Experiences
   A. Review the unit plan shown in figure 16.2.
   B. Choose a topic for your unit.
   C. Identify student characteristics, including:
      1. Maturation—physical, social, emotional, and intellectual characteristics.

2. Ability levels—equal opportunity for all students: left-handed, low-skilled, high-skilled, male, female.
3. Needs—challenging activities with possibility for success: help students achieve self-esteem; special needs of:
   a. Foreign or socially unadapted students.
   b. Urban, suburban, or rural students.
4. Interests—surveys or informal assessment.
5. Learning styles and capacities—consistent with intellectual capacity and attention span.
6. Grouping pattern—how students are assigned to physical education classes.

D. Identify Subject Matter
   1. *Objectives (Performance)*
      a. Write down what you expect the student *to do* at the completion of the unit.
      b. *Skills:* These are psychomotor skills that the student will be able *to do.*
         1) *Shoot* three types of shots.
         2) *Bat* and *bunt* successfully.
         3) *Serve.*
         4) *Bowl* a score of 120.
         5) *Play* safely.
         6) *Officiate* a game.
      c. *Ideas:* These are cognitive skills or knowledge that the student will be able *to use* in some way. Examples:
         1) *Select* the proper golf club for each distance.
         2) *Demonstrate* a knowledge of the rules by. . . .
         3) *Use correct strategy* in game play.
         4) *Describe* a fitness program for a given situation.
      d. *Physical fitness:*
         1) Achieve or maintain "good or excellent" on the 1.5-mile run.
         2) Keep a log of his or her strength training program.
      e. *Attitudes and appreciations:*
         1) Demonstrate sportsmanship in game play.
         2) Act as a squad or other leader when requested.
   2. *Preassessment Techniques*
      a. Write down how you will know if all or some of the students have achieved some of the objectives.
      b. Examples:
         1) Teacher observation.
         2) Pretest (written or skills).

Unit Plan

Activity: Tennis
Class size: 25
Number of class days necessary: 22

Facilities needed: 6 tennis courts
Equipment needed: 25 tennis racquets, 50 balls
Media needed: Charts to record scores, loop films

Performance Objectives	Preassessment	Learning Activities	Evaluation
Cognitive:			
1. Pass a multiple-choice test on the rules and scoring of tennis with 70 percent correct.	1. Give multiple-choice test on rules of game. If student gets 70 percent on preassessment test, no final test will be taken.	1. Handouts on rules. 2. Study guides. 3. Informal tests. 4. Bulletin boards with the rules and scoring. 5. When presenting the skill, present the rules at that time. 6. Correct rule infractions during game play.	1. Give final test. Students can retake test to improve grade. A = 90%–100% B = 80%–89% C = 70%–79% D = 60%–69% F = 59% and lower
Psychomotor:			
1. Demonstrate and use proper grip. 2. Be able to use the following skills in game play: forehand stroke backhand stroke serve	1. Ask who has played tennis before. 2. Teacher observation.	1. Demonstrate the skills with cues. 2. Apply these skills in gamelike situations. 3. Partner checklist. 4. Teacher checklist.	1. Teacher observation of use of skills in game play. 2. Skills tests of strokes. 3. Tournament results.
Affective:			
1. Demonstrate good sportsmanship during the activity by not bending rules to gain advantage, using proper language, and congratulating opponents' good shots.	1. Teacher observation.	1. Have an open discussion on etiquette with student input. Teacher will stress that foul language will not be tolerated. 2. Play games. Correct affective problems as they occur.	* Checklist will be used daily to check on all affective behaviors.
Motivational techniques: 1. Fun. 2. Success. 3. Getting to play the game.			

Example of Daily Progression

Day	Cognitive	Psychomotor	Affective	Learning Activities	Evaluation
1	Terms—racquet parts, grip, etc.	Grip. Forehand stroke.	Stress supportive environment of partners.	1. Demonstrate grips and forehand stroke with cues. 2. Practice drills with feedback.	1. Preassess skills and knowledges by teacher observation. 2. Observe grip for accuracy. 3. Observe stroke.
2	Review terms.	Grip and forehand stroke.	Stress supportive environment of partners.	1. Redemonstrate skills. 2. Practice drills with feedback. 3. Distribute handout on terms. 4. Review terms.	Observe skill development.
3	Terms—backhand and backhand grip.	Backhand grip and stroke.	Stress proper language.	1. Demonstration with cues. 2. Practice drills with feedback.	Observe skill development.
4	Review terms.	Backhand grip and stroke.	Stress proper language.	1. Redemonstrate skills. 2. Practice drills. 3. Partner check using skill checklist.	Observe skill development.
5	Game rules.	Forehand and backhand strokes.	Stress game etiquette.	1. Review rules. 2. Distribute handout on rules and scoring. 3. Play simplified game.	Observe skill development and game play.

Figure 16.2 A unit plan.

3) Previous experience—last year, out-of-school, etc.
4) Questionnaire.
5) Questioning the students.
3. *Evaluation Techniques*
   a. Write how you will know when the behavior specified in the unit objective has been achieved. Is it:
      1) Norm-referenced.
      2) Criterion-referenced.
   b. Examples:
      1) Skills tests: on baserunning, batting, throwing, and fielding.
      2) Teacher observation: of form, use of strategy, officiating, playing ability.
      3) Game scores: in individual sports, such as bowling, archery, badminton.
      4) Times: in track, fitness tests.
      5) Written test: on rules.
      6) Checklist or rating sheet: in swimming or gymnastics.
      7) Incidence chart.
      8) Tournament results.
      9) Accumulative tournaments—swim and stay fit.
      10) Attitude or effort inventory, questionnaire, interview, etc.
E. *Learning Activities* (Translates subject matter into meaningful learning experiences for students.)
   1. Write down the activities you and the students will use that will help them to achieve the objectives.
      Examples:
      a. *Psychomotor*
         1) Demonstration with cues.
         2) Skills check-off chart.
         3) Drills.
         4) Games.
         5) Guided practice.
      b. *Cognitive*
         1) Brief explanation.
         2) Visual aid.
         3) Question-answer session.
         4) Study sheet.
         5) Programmed unit.
         6) Quiz.

      c. *Affective*

        1) Role-play.

        2) Brainstorming.

        3) Case study.

2. Select learning activities in terms of:

    a. Student needs and learning characteristics.

    b. Subject matter to be taught.

    c. Teacher—personality, etc.

    d. Learning environment—facilities, equipment, weather, etc.

    e. Principles of learning.

    f. Teaching styles.

    g. Variety of learning activities.

3. Checklist for appropriate learning activities. See chapters 6, 7, and 8.

F. Determine the organization necessary to achieve learning.

1. Identify the appropriate class size for:

    a. Group of students.

    b. Learning task.

    c. Instructional method.

    d. Safety.

2. Identify the appropriate length of time for the unit in terms of:

    a. Age and ability of learners.

    b. Instructional methods.

    c. Intricacy of the learning task.

    d. Achievement of the stated objectives.

3. Identify teacher(s) on the basis of:

    a. Competency.

    b. Preferences.

4. Identify teaching stations.

    a. Gym.

    b. Fields.

    c. Classroom.

    d. Community facility.

5. Identify equipment needed or equipment that can be modified to meet the need. Make sure that adequate equipment is provided to insure maximum participation.

G. *Motivation Techniques*

1. Write down appropriate motivation techniques.

  Examples:

    a. Intrinsic:

      1) Success.

      2) Challenge.

3) Self-confidence.
4) Self-fulfillment.
b. Extrinsic:
1) Competition.
2) Ribbons for winners.
3) Unique drills.
4) Unusual warm-ups.
2. See chapter 9 for more ideas.
H. Write down a daily progression of teaching as in the example provided.

The resource unit

Resource units are master units to which teachers refer when developing units for their specific classes. They are often formulated by state departments of education or district committees. Resource units generally contain the following:

1. Title page and introduction.

2. Table of contents.

3. Specific performance objectives.

4. Details to consider before teaching.

5. Preassessment techniques.

6. Introductory activities.

7. Subject matter content.

8. Teaching and learning activities.

9. Culminating activities.

10. Evaluation techniques and grading.

11. Resources.

12. Index (if needed).

Title page and introduction

The title page should include the name of the activity or content area included in the unit, the appropriate grade levels, and the publication date.

The introduction should include an overview of the unit, its educational purpose, its intended audience, and the persons who served on the committee.

Table of contents

The table of contents should include the major divisions of the unit with appropriate page numbers.

Specific performance objectives

Performance objectives should be specified in cognitive, psychomotor, and affective domains.

Details to consider before teaching

Several factors that must be considered before teaching a unit include an appropriate facility, adequate equipment, and qualified faculty. All of these affect the class size. Weather may affect the facility and the dress requirements. The length of the unit must be planned to produce the desired learning.

Preassessment techniques

Preassessment techniques should be specified for each of the objectives—cognitive, psychomotor, and affective. Pretests for skills and written tests and interest inventories or goal-setting activities are also valuable.

Introductory activities

A variety of experiences for initiating the unit provide the teacher with some options from which to choose. These might include a film, a demonstration by several advanced players, or playing the game the way it was when it was created.

Subject-matter content

This section includes a description or outline of the subject matter to be taught with an analysis and appropriate teaching progressions.

Teaching and learning activities

A variety of teaching and learning activities should be included, such as ways to adapt the subject matter to meet individual needs, study guides, motivational techniques, activities for inclement weather, and other special needs.

Culminating activities

Tournaments, field trips, interclass games, faculty-student activities, etc. can be included in this section.

Evaluation techniques and grading

A variety of evaluation techniques should be included for each objective specified—cognitive, psychomotor, or affective. Grading and reporting procedures for the specific unit in question should include what to grade, the emphasis on each area, and the process to be used. Provision should also be made for evaluating the unit and the teacher.

Resources

Lists of student and teacher reference materials, instructional media, community resources, and special instructional aids (equipment, etc.) should be accompanied by information on how and where to obtain them.

Questions and suggested activities

1. Write a unit plan for a selected activity.

2. Prepare lesson plans for your unit.

Suggested readings

Ritson, Robert J. "A Lesson Plan Is Like a Menu." *The Physical Educator* 35 (December 1978): 208.

Establishing an Environment for Learning

An appropriate environment for learning is essential to the achievement of the goals of physical education. Three factors are essential in achieving such an environment.

Chapter 17 discusses adjusting the components of the environment for effective learning. Some of these components are department policies and procedures, class management techniques, and record keeping.

Chapter 18 deals with one of the major problems of public school teachers—class control or discipline. The chapter reviews unacceptable and acceptable discipline techniques and tells how to select an appropriate technique for a given situation.

Chapter 19 delineates a number of ways in which teachers can evaluate their effectiveness in providing instruction. The effective use of these techniques will result in an environment which will help students achieve all of the objectives of instruction.

Adjusting Environmental Components for Effective Learning

Study stimulators

1. What school and departmental policies and procedures are essential to a smooth operation of the department of physical education? How can these policies be communicated to students and parents?
2. What is classroom management? Why is it essential to good instruction in physical education? What governs the choice of a management technique?
3. Why is record keeping important? What types of records should you keep?

Effective physical educators stand out because of their ability to manage the dozens of components that make up an effective learning environment. Many of these components must be taken care of long before any instruction can begin. Some of them can be handled most effectively by establishing and implementing a number of department policies and procedures. Others are dependent upon the preferences of the individual teacher and the subject to be taught. Good record keeping can facilitate both of the preceding management tasks. The balance of this chapter will examine techniques for dealing with each of these areas.

Departmental policies and procedures

Departmental policies and procedures should be developed to regulate those components that must be consistent for all students taking physical education. These policies and procedures govern such components as: (1) uniforms, (2) excuses from activity, (3) locker room policies, (4) locks and lockers, (5) towels, and (6) showers.

A departmental handout or handbook can be developed to include each of these items, thereby reducing misunderstandings between home and school. A creative example of a departmental handout is the work contract shown in figure 17.1. Items that might be included in such a handout are:

1. The department's philosophy.

2. Physical education objectives.

3. Registration procedures and course offerings.

4. Policies concerning uniforms, dressing, showers, locker room, and laundering uniforms.

Work Contract

Wanted—Students
Ninety days of work available

Type of Work
Preparation for lifetime physical fitness, team sports skill development, and individual sport skill development

Wage
One-half unit of P.E. credit

Payroll Issued
After forty-five days and after ninety days

Daily Wage
Five credit points if dressed in proper uniform
Five credit points for being on time
Ten credit points for participation and completing the day's required work satisfactorily.
(You must be dressed in proper clothes in order to participate.)

Qualifications
Must be willing to work, be cooperative, possess the ability to get along with fellow workers, and be punctual

Hours
One hour per day at the scheduled time

Special Requirements
A uniform will be needed each day consisting of:
Shorts—White, yellow, or black
Shirts—T-shirt, either white, yellow, fifty-miler, or seventy-five-miler
Gym Shoes—preferably in good condition
White Stockings
Long hair must be tied back from the face to prevent injuries
Long pants and sweatshirt for cold weather outside.
No cutoffs, bare midriff tops, or tank tops

Sick Leave and Vacation Time
The State of Utah requires a minimum of seventy-five class hours before credit can be issued (this would allow a maximum of fifteen days absent time). No credit will be given if exceeded.

Make-up Time
All make-up work will be due *one week* from the day you return after an illness or excused absence. No make-up will be allowed if you cut (sluff) class without being properly excused.

Figure 17.1 A work contract.

Figure 17.1—*Continued*

Types of Overtime Accepted

Equal to one hour's work for the hour missed in terms of—(1) a poster, (2) written report, (3) teach a new game, (4) organize and direct a ten-minute exercise routine for class, or (5) anything else with *prior* approval of the instructor.

(Running miles, swimming, hiking, bowling are things you do for fun, *not* for make-up after you've been ill. You need recuperation time.)

Extended absence for illness is covered by a doctor's excuse, which is honored, and no make-up is required. Your grade will be based on work completed up to that time.

Failure to complete this employment will result in termination of contract.

If interested in applying for this work, please sign after carefully reading the terms of the contract. Parent or guardian should be aware of your commitment. Have them sign one copy and return it to your new employer.

_____   _____
Parent/Guardian   Employee

5. Policies for medical excuses, safety, accidents, and first aid.

6. Grading standards and policies.

7. Policies for making up absences.

8. Physical fitness appraisals.

9. Policies concerning student leaders.

10. Extraclass activities.

Uniforms

The use of a uniform for physical education can be justified on the basis of good hygiene, safety, and the reduction of distractions in the instructional setting. The uniform should be made from a durable material that "gives" with activity, absorbs sweat to reduce body odor, and has minimal skin irritation. Safety prohibits the use of buckles and other metal adornments. Seams should be strong to prevent the potential embarrassment of tears.

Popular attitude dictates that uniforms should be similar for both boys and girls, usually consisting of shirt, shorts, tennis shoes, and socks. It is a good idea to have students and parents participate in the selection process through surveys, voting, or committee action. Various manufacturers' samples can be acquired for the selection process. Students can also be asked to provide warm clothing for outdoor use if needed. Usually a specific outfit is not required.

Although controversy exists on what can legally be required, if common sense is used to permit reasonable deviations from policy, there is no reason why a school cannot have a policy for a given style and color of uniform. The use of the school emblem on uniforms encourages students to purchase them and increases school spirit and student cooperation, thus reducing discipline problems.

Identical uniforms facilitate dividing students into teams and identifying them with a colored pinnie or mesh jersey, without competition from innumerable student-selected colors. They also reduce discrimination between rich and poor students because of differences in the activity clothes they can afford.

Uniforms are generally less expensive when bought in quantity and sold in a school bookstore. However, they can be made available for purchase by local department and discount stores. Students should be allowed to provide uniforms that differ from the school-selected uniform in such cases as when the student (1) is obese or has another problem that causes the uniform not to fit properly or not to hide embarrassing deformity: (2) is a transferee from a school that used a different uniform, or (3) has religious reasons for noncompliance. Some provisions must be made for students who cannot afford a uniform. The parent-teacher organization can often help in these cases or uniforms left behind by former students could be issued to these students.

Whatever uniform is provided should be marked with the student's name in permanent ink to facilitate recovery in case of loss. Uniforms should be laundered regularly to promote good hygiene. Students usually are asked to launder uniforms each weekend and return them on Mondays.

When a uniform is included because of departmental policy, teachers should explain to students and parents what type of uniform is requested, why it is necessary, and possible purchase locations. An example of the uniform should be available in class for students to see. A handout could be prepared to explain the uniform and laundry policies to parents.

Teachers should also dress in appropriate activity clothes as an example for students to follow. Clothing should be such that the teacher can immediately be located within the activity area.

Excuses from activity

A sound policy should be established regarding excuses from activity; and the policy should be communicated to students and parents at the beginning of the school year. Excuses from activity generally consist of two types (1) medical excuses and (2) nonmedical excuses.

Medical excuses

All medical excuses should be cleared through the school nurse if possible, using a form such as the one shown in figure 17.2. In this way, a record of the frequency of illness can be kept for each student. Notes from the parent or physician should be kept for future reference. After two or three days of excuses in a row, the student should be asked to obtain a note from his or her physician.

```
┌─────────────────────────────────────────────────────────────┐
│                                                               │
│         Temporary physical education excuse form              │
│                                                               │
│   To physical education instructor:                           │
│                                                               │
│   Please excuse _____ Section _____      │
│                                                               │
│   from:                                                       │
│   ☐  participation ____                                       │
│                                                               │
│   ☐  showers ____                                             │
│                                                               │
│   ☐  dressing for class ____                                  │
│                                                               │
│   From _____     To _____       │
│                                                               │
│   Reason _____        │
│                                                               │
│   Recommended by:                                             │
│                                                               │
│   Physician's note _____ Parent's note _____          │
│                                                               │
│   School nurse _____                                     │
│                                                               │
│                  _____                  │
│                                  School nurse                 │
│                                                               │
└─────────────────────────────────────────────────────────────┘
```

Figure 17.2 A temporary physical education excuse form.
Source: Walker, June. *Modern Methods in Secondary School Physical Education,* 3rd ed.; Boston: Allyn and Bacon, Inc. 1973.

When a student brings a note from a parent or doctor asking that he or she be excused from activity, some alternate way of meeting the physical education objectives must be considered. A good short-term activity is to have the student complete a project related to the unit being taught. The project might include a written report, or a bulletin board or poster. An area in the physical education facility can be set aside for this purpose. When no supervised area is available, the student can be sent to the library for this assignment. When this is done, make sure the librarian knows that the student is there and what is to be expected of the student.

When a long-term but temporary or a permanent disability exists, the physician should be contacted for further input about the activities in which the student can engage. A letter such as the one shown in figure 17.3 should be sent to the physician. Activities can then be modified within the regular class setting or in an adapted class to meet the needs of the student.

Physician's Request for Modified Physical Education

To The Family Physician:

     We would appreciate your help in designing a program to meet the individual needs of the student whose name appears below.

     The physical education program includes a wide variety of activities indicated below. Please check the activities in which this student may participate.

Name of student _____ Age _____

Parent or guardian _____

Address _____ Phone _____

Nature of illness / injury _____

_____ 1. No restrictions.

_____ 2. Participation in all activities except interschool athletics.

_____ 3. Adaptations in physical education to fit individual needs:

          _____ a. Little running or jumping
          _____ b. No running or jumping
          _____ c. No activities involving body contact
          _____ d. Exercises designed for rehabilitation
          _____ e. Strenuous conditioning activities or prolonged endurance activities

_____ 4. Other adaptations: (specify) _____

Date of return to normal activities _____

Name of physician _____ Phone _____

Signed: _____, M.D.   Date_____

Please send this form to _____
                    School   Address

Figure 17.3 Physician's request for modified physical education.

Nonmedical excuses

When students consistently fail to dress for activity, teachers should look for the cause behind the behavior. Hardy identified three underlying causes for failure to dress for activity. They are (1) physical, (2) moral or religious, and (3) defiance of authority.[1]

    Physical excuses include stomach ache, headache, menstrual cramps, etc. They may also include personal embarrassment such as obesity, a disfigured or deformed body, or peer ridicule. These latter excuses can often be remedied by allowing these students to dress before or after the other students or in a private area, or by allowing them to wear a different uniform, such as longer pants or a long-sleeved shirt.

A second reason students fail to dress can be moral or religious. In *Mitchell* v. *McCall*,[2] the court ruled in favor of a school policy requiring a girl to attend physical education classes dressed in a uniform of her choice and to participate in activities that she considered appropriate. Undoubtedly, the fact that the school allowed her freedom to choose her uniform and activities helped it to win the case.

A third reason for failure to dress is defiance of authority. Although very little can be done with some of these students, others will respond positively to activities that they have had a part in choosing and to a teacher whom they know cares.

Hardy also suggested some remedies to the problem, including: (1) making our classes so exciting that students will look forward to participating in them, (2) setting an example of appropriate dress, (3) exhibiting a genuine desire to understand and help students resolve self-consciousness about their bodies or their performance skills, and (4) refusing to punish students who fail to dress for activity.[3]

Teachers need to explain to students why dressing for activity is important and refuse participation to those students who are not dressed for activity. If students have forgotten their own uniforms, those left by former students can be loaned or rented to them or the parents can be called and asked to deliver the uniform. The latter procedure works very well for students who have the uniform stored in their hall locker and are just looking for an excuse. Loaned uniforms can be washed and returned by the students or washed in the home economics room.

Students with minor excuses can be encouraged to dress and do what they can. Students who are not dressed should not be allowed to participate. Athletes should be required to dress and participate in less strenuous activities on the day of a game.

Dressing for activity should not be used as our chief tool of evaluation. If students fail to dress, they will usually fail to do well on written, fitness, and skills tests and in other evaluative measures. There is really no need to use dressing as a part of the evaluation system.

Locker room policies

Locker room policies should be clearly defined to students at the beginning of each term. Policies should include (1) traffic patterns to ensure safety; (2) use of long lockers to secure clothing and books during class and small lockers to secure gym clothing at other times; (3) lost and found for locks, uniforms, clothing, and other items; (4) procedures for showering; (5) guidelines for cleaning out lockers each week and laundering uniforms; (6) information about the responsibility to keep lockers closed and locked at all times and to leave valuables at home or in the office; and (7) guidelines as to the responsibility to keep the locker room clean and organized. In some situations, teachers will wish to have students assist in making these policies.

The locker room should be checked each period for clothing and towels left out and locks left open. One teacher can be assigned to supervise the locker room each period or a paraprofessional aide can be used for this responsibility. Student leaders should not be given the responsibility of supervising students in the locker room. Some teachers prefer to lock the locker room during class to prevent thefts.

Locks and lockers

Lockers

Two types of lockers are generally used for securing students' clothing and possessions. The first is the wire basket. The basket is the least expensive and has the advantage of good air circulation for drying clothes. However, it has the disadvantage of being too small to include all of the students' possessions such as coats, boots, and books. It is also possible to remove small items between the wires.

Metal lockers are often supplied in banks of six small lockers to one large locker to solve the storage problem as shown in figure 17.4. Gym uniforms can be stored in the small lockers and street clothing can be placed in the long lockers during class time. By locating them together in this manner, traffic in the locker room is minimized.

Locks

Locks can be built into metal lockers or combination locks can be used. Although built-in locks reduce the problem of distribution, collection, and loss of locks, they can often be opened with a knife. Because they are built-in, they can not be transferred to the large locker to secure valuables during class time. They are also difficult to repair.

Locks are available with changeable combinations that can be changed from year to year to prevent theft. Combination locks are preferred over key locks because students tend to lose keys while participating in activity.

Locks can be provided by the school or the student. When students purchase locks, teacher access is more difficult unless locks are purchased that have a master keyhole built in for emergency use. Students' names can be marked on purchased locks with a metal engraver or on school-supplied locks with masking tape. When locks are provided by the school, a lock deposit is often required to ensure that the locks are returned in good condition.

Assigning locks and lockers

Lockers should be assigned to students in horizontal rows by class period. The lowest rows should be assigned to the lower grades and the higher rows to the higher grades. This spreads students throughout the locker room and prevents overcrowding with its resulting safety hazards. It also facilitates dressing quickly.

A master list of lockers such as that shown in figure 17.4 can be kept, showing each bank of lockers, with students names and period written in pencil. Using pencil makes erasing easy when students move out.

Locker cards can be used to record the student's name, lock number, combination, and assigned locker. A sample locker card is shown in figure 17.5. A second card, which is shown in figure 17.6, can be used to record the combination of each lock when locks are collected for redistribution at the end of each semester or year.

A master lock book can be acquired from the manufacturer. This lists the lock serial numbers and their combinations.

1		2		3		4		5		6	
1A Kristi Anderson	2A Sheila Ballard	3A Sue Boucher	4A Lida Crowder	5A Shauna Foster	6A Gloria Jensen
1B Nancy Alexander	2B Sandy Andres	3B Dana Bergstrom	4B Chris Bindrup	5B Audree Dixon	6B Georgina Edwards
1C Karin Cardon	2C Barbara Durrant	3C Kristin Goodwin	4C Sharane Hepworth	5C Terrie Jarvis	6C Cindy Jemmett
1D Renee Baker	2D Debbie Bemis	3D Janis Brock	4D Kay Brown	5D Laura Cameron	6D Paula Campbell
1E Carole Brisbin	2E Cheri Clark	3E Janiece Dee	4E Donna Dupaix	5E Kelly Fredericks	6E Jennifer Kee
1F Elsie Bishop	2F Rosa De la Cruz	3F Debra Evans	4F Shelley Huber	5F Maria Vasquez	6F Alana Walker

Figure 17.4 A master locker list and example of physical education lockers.

STUDENTS ONLY

Women's Locker Card

Locker Rental Card
$3.00 each time period: Fall, Winter Spring, Summer

Name: ....

S.S. #: ....

Cashier #: ....

NO REFUNDS   NO RENEWALS

Locker Name Card

Print Name: ....

Locker #: ....

Phone #: ....

PLEASE LEAVE AT ISSUE ROOM WINDOW

Name ....
(Print)   (Last)   (First)   (Middle)

School
Address .... Apt. #...............
              (Street)

....
(City)   (State)   (Zip)

Phone .... S.S. #..............................

Parents'
Address ....
              (Street)   (Apt. #)

....
(City)   (State)   (Zip)

I understand and agree that I will not share or loan the locker nor the BYU clothing assigned to me with anyone else.

Signed: ....

For Locker #..................... Date ....

Locker # ....

Padlock # ....

Comb. # ....

Shorts .... ☐
T-Shirt .... ☐
Socks .... ☐
Towels # .... ☐
Swim Suit .... ☐
Leotard .... ☐
GIA .... J or K .... ☐
Other .... ☐
Other .... ☐
Other .... ☐
Other .... ☐

Figure 17.5 A locker card.
Source: Brigham Young University Women's Issue
Room.

This three-way system allows teachers to locate locks and lockers by student name, locker number or location, or lock serial number. Lost locks can be locked on to a towel bar placed in or near the teacher's office or on the wire screen of an issue room cage. Some teachers charge students a small fee of five to twenty-five cents for retrieving their locks or telling them their combinations.

Towels

Three decisions need to be made with regard to towels. They are (1) the method of acquisition of towels, (2) the laundering of towels, and (3) the distribution and collection of towels.

```
┌─────────────────────────────────────────────────┐
│                                                 │
│        LOCKER COMBINATION CARD                  │
│    DATE ISSUED:                                 │
│                                                 │
│    ----------------------------                 │
│                    LOCKER NO. ................. │
│                    LOCK NO. ................... │
│                              R. ..............  │
│      CAUTION:      COMBINATION: L. ...........  │
│      READ BACK                                  │
│       OF THIS                                   │
│        CARD                  R. ..............  │
│                                                 │
└─────────────────────────────────────────────────┘
```

Figure 17.6 A locker combination card.

Acquisition of towels

Towels can be purchased by the school or district, leased from a towel service, or students can be asked to bring one or two towels each year for the school supply.

Laundering of towels

Towels purchased by the school are often laundered at a school or district facility. This requires purchasing laundry equipment and hiring someone to launder towels. Leased or purchased towels may be laundered by the towel service. This requires a bid by local laundries for pick-up, laundry, and delivery. Students are often charged a towel fee for this service. Fees for indigent students are often paid by welfare or other community services or absorbed by the school.

In some cases, students are required to bring a towel each week and launder it at home. This generally results in mildew and odor problems as towels are left in lockers throughout the week. It also results in students missing showers because of failure to bring a towel. Some districts, however, prohibit charging towel fees to students and, therefore, the cost must be absorbed into the regular budget or a system such as this one must be used.

Distribution and collection of towels

Towels can be distributed to students by their roll call numbers and checked in after showers as in this example:

Distributed	1 2̸ 3 4̸ 5	Collected	1 X̸ 3 X̸ 5
	6 7̸ 8 9 1̸0		6 7̸ 8 9 1̸0̸

Note that towels were distributed to numbers 2, 4, 7, and 10, but that number 7's towel has not yet been returned. This system helps to keep stray towels off the locker room floor and can also be used to check on which students took showers. Other more informal procedures can be used in some schools.

Showers

Required showers have often resulted in negative attitudes toward physical education. This is because some teachers require showers unnecessarily and do not consider the students' feelings when developing policies for showers.

Students should be taught the health-related concepts about exercise and showering and helped to understand when a shower should be taken and when one is not necessary. Showers should never be required when students have been relatively inactive during the period, such as in archery or golf.

When showering is necessary, make certain students have enough time to do it right. The amount of time will depend on the number of students in the locker room and the number of showers available, but ten to fifteen minutes is usually adequate. More time is needed after swimming for drying hair. Private showers should be provided for girls who are menstruating and for boys and girls who have physical deformities or emotional concerns about displaying their bodies.

Safety should be emphasized and students should dry off in a specified area to prevent students from slipping on water near the lockers. Glass bottles should never be allowed in the locker room.

If showers are used as a part of grading, one solution might be to have students give themselves a grade on showering.

Effective classroom management

Effective classroom management is the ability to organize the components of the classroom so that effective instruction occurs. Good classroom management is essential to quality instruction in physical education. In fact, it is even more vital than in the more traditional academic classroom. This is partly due to the variety of activities provided, often in different facilities and with different equipment. The need for safety is an essential consideration in most of these activities. A third factor is the restricted amount of time often allotted to physical education and the additional limits imposed by dressing and showering. Because of this, it is essential that the time be carefully planned to provide the maximum instructional benefit.

Classroom management in physical education involves (1) preparing the environment, (2) distributing and collecting equipment, (3) planning preclass activities, (4) calling roll, (5) leading warm-up and fitness activities, (6) getting students' attention and giving directions, (7) teaching and utilizing various class formations, (8) organizing groups or teams, (9) supervising class activities, (10) using student leaders, (11) adapting to interruptions, and (12) summarizing and reviewing lessons. Techniques for managing each of these activities will be discussed in this section of the chapter.

Teachers should teach students self-management skills and provide practice in using them just as other skills are practiced. On the first day of class, teach the procedures for assembly, dismissal, roll call, excuses, tardies, collecting and distributing equipment, organizing teams and getting into formations, etc. Also teach why each of these procedures is used. Then, during instruction, whenever a difficulty occurs with a management skill, stop and take time to teach or review the skill before proceeding. It will save instructional time in the long run and will reduce the incidence of serious discipline problems.

As you consider each of these techniques, remember that there is no one best way to manage a class. Each teacher needs to develop a wide variety of management techniques from which to choose as the situation changes. The choice of a management technique depends to a large extent upon the experience and personality of the teacher and the maturity and self-management capabilities of the students.

As the style of teaching changes from the more teacher-directed styles to the more student-directed styles, the management style will also proceed from the use of formal to more informal techniques. Other factors that influence the selection of a management technique include the subject matter to be taught, the facilities and equipment available, the size of the class, and the school or department policies under which the teacher must work.

A good teacher will select the best technique for a given situation, carry it out effectively, and modify it as the need arises. When choosing any technique, a balance must be achieved between concern for the student and efficiency of instruction.

The true test of a successful management technique is whether or not the objectives of the lesson or unit in question have been realized. Whenever the objectives are not being accomplished, the teacher should select a new plan of action.

Preparing the environment

Prior to teaching each day, facilities and equipment should be inspected for safety, proper lighting, adequate towels, and comfortable room temperature. Nets can be set up, baskets raised or lowered, apparatus arranged, and special markings put in place by paraprofessional or student aides before class begins or by students who come in before school or prior to class time. Try not to use instructional time to accomplish these tasks unless it is absolutely necessary.

Always check the equipment the day preceding the class to ensure that there is enough equipment and that balls are pumped up, arrows are repaired, pinnies are washed, and other essentials are attended to.

Storage facilities for loose equipment should include movable bins or racks, such as shopping carts (donated or purchased), plastic trash cans attached to plywood with wheels attached, or ball racks or bags that can be moved to and from the classroom for ease of distribution. To avoid loss, equipment must often be moved to and from the classroom each hour. Student assistants or squad leaders can be assigned to assist with the movement of equipment.

Distributing and collecting equipment

A number of techniques can be used for distributing and collecting equipment.

The teacher

The teacher or an aide distributes and collects equipment as students enter and leave the gymnasium. Students can sign the roll as they pick up equipment. This technique can "tie up" a teacher who could be helping students with other needs.

Squad leaders

Squad leaders acquire the equipment needed for their individual squads and return it at the end of the practice period.

Numbers

Students are assigned equipment numbers corresponding to their roll call numbers. Student #1 picks up bow #1, arrows #1, armguard #1, etc. Equipment can be picked up in the locker room, as students enter the gymnasium, or as they complete warm-up and fitness activities. One advantage to this technique is that students feel more responsible for returning the equipment in good condition each day. A second advantage is that students can become accustomed to a particular racquet, bow, or glove.

Grab bag

Students can be asked to get a piece of equipment and return to their space. This often results in students converging upon a given box of equipment and grabbing out the best they can find. Chaos and a loss of instructional time usually result and the less aggressive students always feel cheated by getting the worst equipment. This can be avoided by sending one squad or student at a time (changing squads each day) and by insuring that all equipment is in good condition. When sending a few students at a time, it is best to have students pick up or return equipment as they enter the gym or as they complete an activity in which students finish at different times, such as after jogging or completing self-check activities.

Handing in assignments

Assignments can be collected very efficiently by placing a basket or box for each class in a convenient location. Students can place their assignments in the box as they enter or leave the gymnasium. Handouts for students who have been absent can be placed in a different colored or labeled box.

When choosing an equipment distribution and collection technique, always consider the relationship of the technique to the safety of the students and to effective learning.

Planning preclass activities

A good deal of time is wasted by students between the time they enter the gymnasium and the time for roll call or instruction. In fact, students who come in last are rewarded by not having to sit around doing nothing. When students are allowed to begin activity the minute they enter the area, they also begin to dress faster and come to class earlier. A preclass

A fast, effective roll call gets things started on
the right track.

activity chart, listing skills that students can practice, can be posted. The accumulative tournament described in chapter 11 is an effective preclass activity as are many other self-testing activities.

When equipment loss or damage or student safety are problems, teachers can take turns supervising the locker room and the gymnasium or a teacher aide can be used to supervise one of the two areas.

At a given time or signal, students can report to roll call or a posted or preannounced area for instruction or practice.

Calling roll

A fast, effective roll call gets things started on the right track. Generally, roll call can be taken in only one or two minutes at the most. A number of different roll call techniques can be used, depending on the class size, maturity of the students, and the learning situation. The major criteria for selection of a roll call technique are time and accuracy. Since most schools receive some funding based on the average daily attendance (ADA) of students, schools insist on accuracy in attendance taking.

Time spent in roll call reduces the learning time for students, so efficient use of time is essential. When too much time is taken for roll call, students become bored and discipline problems can arise.

Five general techniques are commonly used. They include (1) numbers or spots, (2) squads, (3) student check-in, (4) silent roll, and (5) oral roll call.

Numbers or spots

Each student is assigned a number. Students sit or stand in a specific spot, either in a line or in squad order. When numbers are painted on the floor, on a bench or bleacher, or on the wall, a blank number indicates a student who is absent. When no numbers are available, students can be asked to call out the numbers in sequence. Although this method is rather impersonal, it is very fast.

Squads

Each student is assigned to a squad and a leader is chosen for each squad. Each day, the squad leader records the attendance of the squad members on a squad card. This could be done while students are participating in a squad activity.

Student check-in

In this technique, students check in as they enter the gymnasium by signing their name and time of entry, by checking in with the teacher, by handing in an assignment, or by removing their name tags from a board or box and placing them in a specified location or wearing them. When using name tags, those remaining indicate absent students.

Silent roll

In this technique, the teacher or a teacher's aide takes roll silently while students are participating in activity. This permits students to remain active.

Oral roll call

In this technique, the teacher calls out the students' names and listens for a response. This technique is only effective when used with very small classes or when employed to get acquainted with students during the first few days of instruction before rolls have been finalized. Another use is as an accuracy check by calling out only the names of those students who have been marked absent by one of the other methods.

Leading warm-up and fitness activities

A variety of warm-up techniques and fitness activities should be employed to increase student motivation. Some ideas include:

1. Squad leaders direct warm-up activities for their squads.

2. Students warm up on their own.

3. Students rotate through a number of fitness stations.

4. Selected student leaders direct warm-up activities for the entire class.

5. Students alternate jogging and weight-training at two-minute intervals.

6. Students run three days a week and weight-train two days.

A variety of warm-up techniques and fitness activities can increase student motivation.

7. Students run daily with a timed run once a week.

8. Students participate in an obstacle course.

9. Relays or games are used to emphasize certain fitness activities.

10. Students exercise to popular music, using prechoreographed routines or "follow the leader."

Innumerable other techniques can be invented by the creative teacher for warm-up and fitness activities.

Getting students' attention and giving directions

Teacher directions and attention signals are used to get students' attention, assemble students, give directions, dismiss students, and handle emergencies. Either verbal signals such as "roll call" or "ready, go!" or nonverbal signals can be used to gain attention or give directions.

Verbal signals

A teacher who speaks softly yet loudly enough to be heard encourages students to listen carefully when he or she talks and also leaves room for a future increase in volume for the purpose of gaining attention. In contrast, when a teacher consistently shouts at students with a loud voice, they tend to increase their noise level to a level that prohibits the use of verbal signals. A general rule is to gather the students around you and talk so that the student farthest from you can hear you clearly.

In addition to volume, effective teachers vary the speed, inflection, and vocabulary to either calm students or incite them to action. Such terms or phrases as "hustle," "quickly," and "Let's go!" are built-in motivators when used with appropriate inflection and enthusiasm.

The voice can be saved by using a number of nonverbal attention-getters. In fact, a lesson taught completely by gestures and written instructions can be highly effective on occasion in getting students to pay attention.

Nonverbal attention signals

A whistle, horn, hand clap, drum beat, or raised hand can be used effectively to gain attention once students have become accustomed to its use. Flicking the lights off and on quickly is effective when teaching activities such as racquetball where students are dispersed in a wide indoor area.

Students should be taught what behavior is expected when the attention signal is given. For example, students can be taught to sit or kneel where they are and wait for instructions or to gather to an appointed place for direction. Once the students learn the signal and the expected response, time can be saved by praising those who respond quickly or by rewarding them with extra time for activity. Feedback can also be provided on the amount of time spent, such as "You were ready five seconds faster than yesterday." The use of a large time clock, such as those used for swim meets, provides effective visual feedback on the use of time.

Giving directions

When giving directions, gather the students close enough so all of them can see and hear and face them away from the sun and other distractions. When students may not be able to stand quietly, ask them to sit.

Directions should be given in a clear, concise manner. They should tell students the location to move to, the signal for moving, and what to do when they get there. For example, the teacher might be as specific as "On the signal, 'Ready, go!' move quickly to the black line and line up facing the net." A less teacher-oriented example might be, "On my signal, find a partner, get one ball between you, and locate a space on the floor where you can safely practice the volley."

Occasionally, directions can be written on the chalkboard, posted on a bulletin board, or written on a skill checklist or individual contract.

Following complex directions, the teacher might ask students if there are any questions or ask questions to see if the students understand the directions. Avoid repeating the directions to students. They will learn not to listen the first time.

La Mancusa listed some pitfalls in giving directions.[4] They are (1) using words that students do not understand, (2) saying the same thing over and over in hopes the students will "catch on" instead of thinking it through and using a few brief statements, (3) using extraneous words like "well" and "okay," and (4) failing to wait until everyone is listening before talking. She stated:

> It is the wise teacher who will **not speak** until **everyone** is listening. If it means that the teacher will be forced to stop what he is saying and wait, then by all means WAIT. If it means that the teacher will have to stop a second time, or a third time, then stop and WAIT. Silent teacher disapproval and exasperated peer disapproval is too strong a factor to override. Soon enough the offenders will understand that when **their** teacher talks, **everyone listens** because **their** teacher **means it** when he says, "I will not repeat this a second time."
> There is nothing more to it than that. If a teacher allows himself to overlook rudeness, he will receive rudeness in return. Children will respond either to the **highest** or to the **lowest** of teacher-expectations.[5]

The key to avoiding these pitfalls is proper planning before speaking and careful evaluation of one's own ability to give directions. One of the best methods for evaluating the effectiveness of giving directions is to record a class session on a tape recorder. After recording a class session, play it back to yourself. Would you like to be a student in your own classroom?

Teaching and utilizing class formations

Innumerable class formations can be created to assist students and teachers in the instructional setting. It is important to remember that the choice of a formation is determined by the needs of the instructional situation. A number of types of formations follow.

Circles and semicircles

Circles can be formed by asking students to form a circle on a painted line on the floor, such as a free throw circle, and then taking three giant steps backward. With younger students, students can follow the teacher into a circle as the teacher purposely catches up with the last person in line. In folk dancing, students can be asked to join hands to form a circle. (Avoid holding hands in other activities. It usually leads to giggling and tugging.)

Circles can be used for practice drills or lead-up games and for relays. Be careful to stay on the edge of the circle when giving directions, so that students are never behind you.

The semicircle can be formed by asking students to gather around you. It is often used for giving directions to small classes or for demonstrating to a group of students.

Lines and columns

Lines are formed by asking students to line up facing the net or wall on a particular line on the floor, or between several cones or chalk marks. Lines are often used for roll call formations and for some lead-up games, such as line soccer.

Columns are formed by selecting four to eight students as leaders and having other students line up behind one of the leaders in designated areas of the floor. Cones can be used instead of leaders. Columns are used to create relay teams or squads.

Extended formation

The extended formation is formed from a line. For example, students number off in four's. The one's stay where they are. The two's move forward five steps, three's move ten steps, and four's move fifteen steps. The extended formation is often used for warm-up and fitness activities, for demonstrations that students can't see when grouped close together, and for mimetic drills (pantomime).

A variation of the extended formation is "waves," in which all the one's swim across the pool, then the two's, etc. This technique permits the teacher to observe and give feedback to a small group of students at one time.

Partners or small groups

Partners and groups can be assigned, or students can be asked to simply find a partner or get in groups of three or four. Ask students to raise their hands if they need a partner or to sit down with their partner as soon as one is found. When an extra person exists, be specific on how that person is to be included. If you must have a student partner, select the best student so that that individual will not suffer as you help the rest of the class. Partners and small groups are often used for warm-up and fitness activities and for practice drills or peer tutoring.

Variations

The formations above can be combined into any number of formations for use in various drills. Some examples include:

1. Double lines for use in passing or volleying drills

2. Teacher-class formation for passing and volleying drills. Rotate teacher each time through. Use two balls for agility.

3. Shuttle for relays or practice drills.

In the command style of teaching, formal formations are used. As instruction moves toward the less teacher-dominated styles, teachers are more apt to ask students to spread out, find a partner, or find a space on the floor.

Whatever formations are used, students should be taught how to assume them quickly on a brief, consistent signal. Always be specific in terms of exactly where you want the students to be, such as on the red line; what formation they are to assume; and the direction they are to face. Use painted lines and circles when they are available. If there are none, use chalk marks, traffic cones, or masking tape.

Keep transitions between formations to a minimum. Try to avoid transitions such as from a line to a circle to a line by thinking through how you will get students from one formation to another. Use x's and o's to plot out your formations and to help you visualize the movement of the class from formation to formation. An example is shown in figure 17.7.

Organizing groups or teams

There are as many ways to choose teams as there are teachers to choose them. However, many teachers resort to only one or two techniques. A little variety here could be more motivating. Some common techniques and ideas follow.

Counting off

Students line up, count off by five's and are asked to remember their number. Then, all the one's become one team, the two's another team, and so on. This method takes too much time to be recommended. Also, students tend to change their numbers or position themselves to be on the same team as their friends.

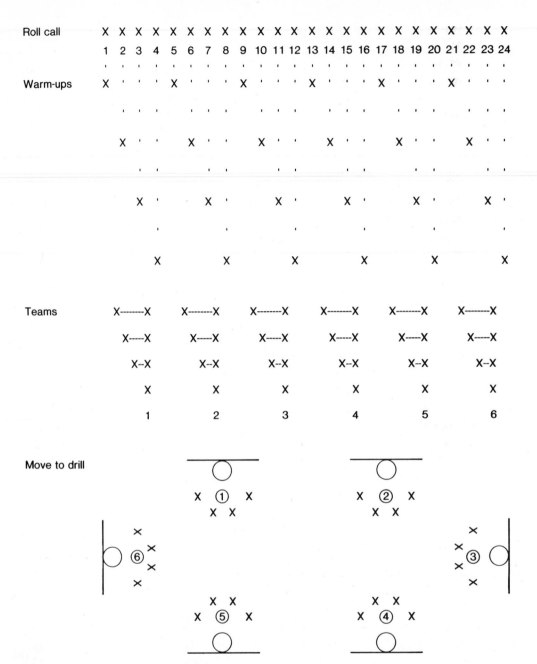

Figure 17.7 A class transition map.

Choosing teams

Team captains are chosen and each one in turn picks a member of the class until all are chosen. This results in some students always being chosen last. This ruins self-esteem. It also wastes valuable class time. If this method is selected, captains should pick the teams in private from the roll. Another method is to have captains pick teams for each other or draw a team at random from those chosen. Teachers can then alphabetize the list for posting.

Assigned teams

Teams can be assigned by the teacher and posted or read to the class. Squads can be used as assigned teams.

At random

Students are told to "get in groups of four" or to "stand behind the captain you prefer," or behind a number of markers. A second method is to say, "You five go to court one, you five to court two, etc., while indicating certain students as they happen to be grouped around you.

Variations

Give each student a card with a color, shape, and number on it, such as:

Triangle	Circle	Square
Orange	Red	Blue
2	3	1

By varying the number of colors, shapes, and numbers, groups of different sizes can be formed. For example, if only three groups are desired, limit shapes to triangle, circle, and square. If five groups are desired, use orange, red, blue, yellow, and green. If ten groups are necessary, use the numbers one to ten. Groups can then be formed by calling out "shapes," "colors," or "numbers" and students move to join others who have the same shape, color, or number in a designated spot.

Other variations might include birthday, height, eye or hair color, right-handed, or left-handed, depending on the size of teams wanted or the purpose for grouping students. Use your creativity to think of other variations for special occasions.

Identifying teams

When teams are used for game play, pinnies can be used to distinguish one team from another. Whatever technique is used for selecting teams, change the teams often for variety and to encourage positive social interaction among students.

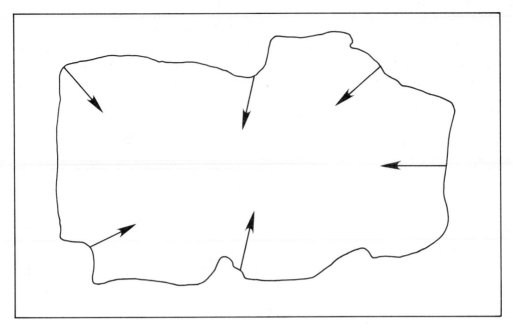

Figure 17.8 A supervision plan.

Supervising class activities

Two teacher activities are essential in supervising class activities—vision and movement. The teacher should employ a wide range of vision by scanning the class with one eye even when talking directly to a specific student. Never get so involved in the subject matter that you forget about the students.

Keep moving along the edges of the class as shown in figure 17.8. This permits you to keep all of the students in constant view and allows you to avoid favoring students in one part of the playing area. Never stand in the center of the class because some students will then be behind you. When a discipline problem exists, move toward the offenders and stand beside them, and if necessary, quietly speak to them.

Provide as much freedom as possible, considering the nature of the task and the maturity of the students. As the teaching style moves toward the student-directed styles of the spectrum, more and more freedom should occur, with increased student responsibility for their own learning. Allow students to work together as long as they work cooperatively. When disturbances occur, separate them. Locate attention getters away from students who reinforce them, but continue to keep an eye on them.

Using student leaders

The physical education program should provide numerous opportunities for students to develop leadership skills. Within individual classes, students can serve as squad leaders, team captains, officials, equipment monitors, and in many other capacities. Student leaders should be rotated often to allow every student a chance for developing leadership skills.

In addition to these in-class leaders, student assistants can be assigned to assist the teacher with various nonteaching activities. Student assistants have proven to be an inexpensive method for improving teacher effectiveness and morale in large classes. In addition to helping teachers, student assistants can improve themselves in the following ways:

1. Develop and improve physical activity skills.

2. Develop social skills, such as leadership, followership, responsibility, and cooperation.

3. Develop improved skills in written and oral communication.

4. Learn more about the teaching profession and about physical education as a profession.

5. Grasp the significance of serving others and of working with others to accomplish stated objectives.

6. Develop a better understanding of students who are less able.

7. Learn how to plan and lead activities.

Student assistants should be selected by a committee of teachers on the basis of their interest, scholarship, physical ability, character, ability to get along well with others, and a willingness to do what is required.

Student leaders should be assigned to a specific class section other than their own physical education classes and should have uniforms distinct from the other students—perhaps, a different shirt—to set them apart.

Because student assistants are students and, therefore, lack professional training and experience, they must be prepared for their new role. Much of this preparation can precede the actual experience, while some of it must continue throughout the term in which the duties are performed. A leader's club or class can be used to instruct student assistants in their duties. Students should thoroughly understand the policies and procedures of the department and the duties that they will be expected to perform.

The major duty of the student assistants is to assist the instructor in any way possible, consistent with their own capabilities and potential. Some other possible duties include:

1. Preparing the play area.

2. Distributing, collecting, and caring for equipment.

3. Taking roll.

4. Making out squad cards.

5. Checking uniforms.

6. Recording tardy and absence slips.

7. Checking showers.

8. Leading exercises and drills.

9. Demonstrating skills.

10. Officiating.

11. Assisting with media hardware.

12. Turning showers on and off.

13. Assisting with test administration and scoring.

14. Providing individual assistance to students.

15. Assisting with any other duties, according to interests and abilities.

During their period of service, student assistants should be brought together periodically to discuss experiences, solve problems, and determine new and better ways for approaching their assignments.

Some problems have been associated with the use of student leaders. These problems include students not being adequately prepared for their assignments, students doing teachers "dirty work," students placed in situations where they "know too much," students assisting during their own physical education period losing out on practice needed to improve their own skills, and students losing friends by attempting to cope with grading or discipline problems. Each of these problems can be prevented by adequate preparation and by recalling that the duties of the student assistant are to assist with the class work and not to be responsible for grading or disciplining students.

Periodic evaluation of student assistants and the program should be made and a follow-up made of the results. An evaluation form that could be used for this purpose is shown in figure 17.9.

Adapting to interruptions

A number of interruptions that reduce instructional time occur during school hours. They include such things as assemblies, school dances, field trips, testing, fire drills, injuries, etc. Some of these activities reduce the length of the instructional period, sometimes making it impractical to dress for activity. Others take students away from physical education classes, thereby leaving the teacher with only a few students in class. Another deviation is caused by inclement weather.

Dealing with emergency interruptions

Preplanning for emergencies is essential so that when emergencies occur you can act in the most efficient manner. For example, what will you do when the fire alarm sounds and students are in the shower or how will you handle a serious injury that occurs in your class? An accident plan might include sending one student for first aid supplies, another to the office for the principal or school nurse, and a third to call the paramedics. Of course, first

EVALUATION OF THE TEACHING ASSISTANT

Name: _____
(Last)   (First)

Instructions: Rate the student on each of the items listed below. If there is no basis for determining a rating on an item, write "no basis."

		Strong	Average	Weak
I.	*Personal Qualities*			
	Adaptability, flexibility	_____	_____	_____
	Initiative, originality	_____	_____	_____
	Responsibility	_____	_____	_____
	Well-mannnered, well-groomed	_____	_____	_____
	Punctual, dependable	_____	_____	_____
II.	*Teacher--Teaching Assistant*			
	Friendly	_____	_____	_____
	Asks for and accepts suggestions	_____	_____	_____
	Acts upon suggestions	_____	_____	_____
	Cooperates well	_____	_____	_____
III.	*Teaching Assistant--Students*			
	Likes students	_____	_____	_____
	Understands students	_____	_____	_____
	Students respond well to her or him	_____	_____	_____
	Fair and impartial	_____	_____	_____
IV.	*Teaching Skills*			
	Knowledge of subject	_____	_____	_____
	Demonstrates well	_____	_____	_____
	Officiates well	_____	_____	_____
	Communicates knowledge to students	_____	_____	_____
	Keeps accurate records	_____	_____	_____
V.	*Class Management*			
	Effective organization of groups	_____	_____	_____
	Good control	_____	_____	_____
VI.	*Professional Growth*			
	Interest in the profession	_____	_____	_____
	Growing knowledge of the profession	_____	_____	_____

The teaching assistant was:
Valuable--a great deal of help _____
Some help _____
A burden--little or no help _____

Comments: _____

Signature: _____

Figure 17.9 A student assistant evaluation form.

```
                    AN ACCIDENT REPORT
  Name _____ Date of report _____

  Address _____ Age _____ Sex _____

  Date of accident _____ Time of day _____

  Location of accident _____

  Supervisor _____

  What was the class or group doing?


  What was the injured person doing that caused the accident? Describe
  the sequence of activity that led to the accident.


  What was the nature of the injury?


  What procedure followed? By whom?


  What could the victim have done to prevent the accident?


  Witnesses: _____    _____

  Addresses: _____    _____

  Report prepared by _____

  Title or status _____
```

Figure 17.10 An accident report form.

aid supplies, phone numbers, and so forth must be prepared in advance so they are readily available when emergency strikes. Give first aid if needed, wait for the paramedics, and then make sure the parents are called.

When the emergency is over, complete an accident report as soon as possible while the incident is fresh on your mind. A sample accident report is shown in figure 17.10. Accident reports should be kept for many years in case of lawsuits. They should be reviewed each year to analyze problem areas that could be resolved.

Dealing with shortened periods or inclement weather

Three types of activities can be used when the planned lesson must be changed. One type is an adaptation of the activity currently being taught to an indoor facility; a lesson on terms, rules, strategy, or other cognitive concepts related to the activity; or an evaluation activity such as a skill or written test.

If the use of an activity-related lesson is not feasible, a fitness-oriented lesson could be taught. This might include teaching fitness concepts, teaching a fitness activity such as an aerobic dance or circuit training, giving physical fitness tests, or evaluating posture.

A third activity is the use of a values-oriented activity from the affective domain. Chapter 14 includes a number of activities from which you might choose.

Dealing with a small class

Practice time can be provided for skill development. This gives students an opportunity for individual help from the teacher. An alternative is to play a recreational or lead-up game using the skills you have been teaching.

Summarizing and reviewing lessons

A carefully prepared summary at the end of a lesson ties together the loose ends and highlights the important points. It also gives the students an opportunity to ask questions and provides the teacher with an opportunity to correct any inaccuracies acquired by the students. Some ideas for summarizing a lesson include:

1. Summarize the main idea of the lesson with a short statement and tell what you hope the students will realize as an outcome.

2. Assign one or two students to listen carefully and tell the class afterwards what the lesson was about.

3. Have students write or tell in their own words what they think the main idea is.

4. Use a worksheet to help students summarize the main idea of the lesson.

5. Have several students in turn tell one thing learned from the lesson.

6. Divide the class into small groups. Each group in turn acts out a part of the lesson while the other groups try to guess what is being depicted (charades).

7. Present a real-life situation that could be resolved by using lesson ideas.

8. Give an oral or written quiz.

9. Use instructional games to test the information taught.

Some ways to review a lesson include:

1. Have students keep records of their progress with lesson objectives.

2. Have students write briefly on a previous lesson topic.

3. Have students perform any specific skill previously taught.

Record keeping

The main purposes of record keeping are to provide information to administrators, parents, and guidance counselors; and to help teachers evaluate students, themselves, and the curriculum. Only pertinent, up-to-date records should be kept.

Types of records include: (1) attendance records; (2) records of achievement, including grades; (3) health and medical records; and (4) equipment and locker records.

Attendance records

Teachers are required to keep an accurate record of the daily attendance of all students assigned to them. The record should be kept up-to-date each day. Because pencil tends to blur, the records should generally be kept in ink.

Attendance register

Figure 17.11 shows a sample page from an attendance register. The top section identifies the class as Mrs. Jackson's second period physical education class at Younowhere Junior High School during the Fall semester. No text is required. In the left-hand column, the students are listed in alphabetical order. Next to their names are their sex, grade, entry code, and exit code. The entry codes are as follows:

E1—Enrolled from within the state

E2—Entered from another state this school year

The exit codes are as follows:

T1—Transferred to another class

T2—Transferred to another school

D —Dropped out of school

Attendance markings may differ from state to state or district to district. Two common sets of markings follow. The first set has been used in this sample:

Absence	—	/
Excused absence	(—)	⊘ or x
Tardy	∸	⼊
Excused tardy	(∸)	⼊ or Ⓐ
Excused for another school event	Ex	Ex

Days enrolled includes the total number of days each student was enrolled in the class. Absences and tardies are also summarized for the term.

Period	Instructor(s)	Course Title	Text(s)
2	Mrs. L. Jackson	Physical Education	None
Fall (Term)	Younowhere Jr. High (School)		9/8 (Date Class Began) to 1/12 (Date Class Ended); 80 (Total Days Held)

Ref.	Pupil	Sex	Grade	Entry Code	Exit Code	Mo. Day M	Sept. Wk. 1 8 T	9 W	10 T	11 F	Wk. 2 14 M	15 T	16 W	17 T	18 F	Wk. 3 21 M	22 T	23 W	24 T	25 F	Oct. Wk. 4 28 M	29 T	30 W	1 T	2 F	Wk. 5 5 M	6 T	7 W	8 T	9 F	TERM SUMMARY Days Enrolled	Days Absent		Times Tardy		YEAR-END SUMMARY Days Enrolled	Days Absent	Final Mark	Credit
1	Alexander, Claudia	F	8	E1				—																		(–)					44	2		0					
2	Bishop, April	F	8	E1																											44	0		0					
3	Carter, Susan	F	8	E1											(–)												(–)				44	2		0					
4	Dixon, Lonnie	M	8	E1	T1			(–)																				[T1]			21	1		0					
5	Dove, Jim	M	8	E1																	•										44	0		1					
6	Eden, Sherron	F	8	E1																											44	0		0					
7	Giles, David	M	8	E1								(–)			(–)									(–	–	–	–	–	–)		44	8		0					
8	Herton, Giles	M	8	E1																											44	0		0					
9	Johnson, Kyle	M	8	E1											Ex																44	0		0					
10	Killian, Teresa	F	8	E1																											44	0		0					
11	Lance, Cathy	F	8	E1																											44	0		0					
12	Limb, Susan	M	8	E1	D				(–	–)					(–)		(–	–	–	–)		(–	–	–	–	–	–	–	–)		44	16		0					
13	Peery, Phyllis	F	8	E1																											44	0		0					
14	Rasmus, Jody	F	8	E1	T2										Ex												T2				19	0		0					
15	Skinner, David	M	8	E1													•														44	0		1					
16	Sousa, Pepe	M	8	E2																	[E2]						(–)				28	1		0					
17	Stevens, Jim	M	8	E1							(•)																				44	0		1					
18	Walden, Heather	F	8	E1											Ex																44	0		0					
19	Wardell, Mark	M	8	E1														(–)													44	1		0					
20	Wilson, Rosalie	F	8	E1																											44	0		0					
21	York, Ryan	M	8	E1						(–	–	–	–)		—	—				—			—	—							44	9		0					

Figure 17.11 An attendance register.
Source: Marilyn Harding, Springville Junior High School, Springville, Utah.

Period _____		ATTENDANCE																							
Squad _____		1st Week					2nd Week					3rd Week					4th Week					5th Week				
Members	Roll No.																									
		M	T	W	T	F	M	T	W	T	F	M	T	W	T	F	M	T	W	T	F	M	T	W	T	F
1.																											
2.																											
3.																											
4.																											
5.																											
6.																											
7.																											
8.																											
9.																											
10.																											

Figure 17.12 A squad card.

Squad cards

Squad cards are often used to take roll and the attendance record transferred to the attendance register after class. A sample squad card is shown in figure 17.12.

Records of achievement

Records of student achievement are usually kept on class record cards and on individual permanent record cards. A discussion of each of these types of records follows.

Class record cards

A class record card is a record of the achievements of all students in a particular class. It provides information to the teacher and to the student on each student's progress in the class. A sample class record card is shown in figure 17.13.

Individual permanent record cards

A permanent record card for each student provides a valuable source of information about student progress in the physical education program. It provides a record of the parents' names and phone number for emergencies, the students fitness test results, all of the activity or content units completed by the student, and awards and honors in the extraclass programs. Individual record cards should be filed alphabetically in the department office. A sample individual permanent record card is shown in figure 17.14. A sample of a yearly record card for a selective program is shown in figure 22.1.

BADMINTON PERIOD 4	Serves	Clears	Drops	Smashes	Strategy + Positioning	FORM	Skills Test Clears	Skills test Smashes	Skills test Drops	Skills test Serves	SKILL TEST	TOURNAMENT	QUIZ - RULES	FINAL TEST	SKILL	KNOWLEDGE	GRADE
Babbett, Mark R.	3	2	2	3	3	A	35	35	36	25	A-	A	B	A	A	A	A
Bagat, Devendra	2	3	1	1	2	C	13	26	20	25	C	B	C+	A	C+	B+	B-
Bushman, Virnell	3	3	3	3	3	A	36	30	17	14	C	A	B	A	B+	A-	B+
Crow, Craig J.	3	3	2	2	3	A	27	39	41	23	A-	B	A	A	B+	A	A-
Davis, Karen A.	3	2	3	3	2	A	34	38	10	43	B	B	B	B	B+	B	B+
Erickson, Craig A.	2	3	2	3	2	B	34	44	40	21	A	C	B	A-	B+	B+	B+
Gold, Lu Anne	3	3	2	2	2	B	31	40	29	38	A	B	C	B	B+	B-	B
Hansen, Marilyn A.	3	2	3	2	1	B	22	38	36	32	B	B	A	A-	B	A-	B
Hendrickson, Jan	3	3	1	1	1	C	4	30	25	36	C	C	C	B	C	B-	C+
Jackson, Linda A.	1	3	1	2	2	C	36	33	34	15	B	B	B-	A	B-	B+	B
Kramer, Terry May	3	3	2	3	2	A	20	43	24	31	C	A	B	B	B+	B	B+
Liscom, Leslie J.	3	2	2	2	1	C	24	31	15	34	B	C	C-	B	C+	C+	C+
Melner, Eric C.	3	3	2	3	2	A	27	33	29	29	B	B	A-	B	B+	B+	B+
Nielson, Lucy A.	2	3	3	1	2	B	32	29	32	14	B	A	C	C	B+	C	B-
Payne, Pamela M.																	
Pyper, Dana L.																	
Rodgers, Rebecca A.																	
Samson, Jill																	
Wells, Farina																	

Figure 17.13 A class record card.

The computer provides an alternative method of keeping information about student progress. A print-out can be used to obtain information about individual or class achievement in any area of physical education.

Health and medical records

In the first part of this chapter, we discussed medical excuses for temporary or long-term illness or injury and forms were presented for each of these situations. Each of these forms should be kept on file in the physical education department office.

Another type of record that should be kept on hand is a record of health status for each student. The school nurse can be helpful in collating this information from permanent school records. Such conditions as asthma, allergies, diabetes, heart conditions, muscular or orthopedic disorders, and many other conditions can affect student participation in the physical education program.

AN INDIVIDUAL RECORD CARD

Name _____ Date of Birth _____

Address _____

Parents' Names _____ Phone _____

PHYSICAL FITNESS TESTING

Grade	1.5 mile run R.S.	%	% Fat R.S.	%	Flexibility R.S.	%	Strength R.S.	%
9 Pre								
9 Post								
10 Pre								
10 Post								
11 Pre								
11 Post								
12 Pre								
12 Post								

AN INDIVIDUAL RECORD CARD

Activity	Skills	Knowledge	Citizenship	Grade	Year Taken
Archery					
Badminton					
Basketball					
Flag Football					
Folk Dance					
Golf					
Gymnastics					
Modern Dance					
Soccer					
Social Dance					
Softball					
Swimming					
Tennis					
Volleyball					

Intramural participation--Activities and awards:

Extramural participation--Activities and awards:

Figure 17.14 An individual record card (front).

Equipment and locker records

Locker records were discussed earlier in the chapter under school policies and procedures. Equipment records include a yearly equipment inventory, copies of purchase orders, and check-out forms for athletic equipment. For further information regarding these subjects, refer to a textbook on administration.

Questions and suggested activities

1. Read the faculty handbook, student handouts, etc. from a secondary school and become familiar with school and department policies and procedures. Do you agree with them? What policies would you change and why?

2. Talk to a principal regarding the policies and procedures in a secondary school.

3. Survey one or more schools to determine policies for uniforms, excuses, towels, showers, locker room procedures, selection of student leaders, and record keeping. Do you agree with their policies? What would you change and why?

4. Read cases from a book on school law about uniforms and what can or can not be required.

5. From the techniques for classroom management, choose several you need to work on and try them out in a practicum class or with a group of children or youth outside of school.

6. While teaching a practicum class, have a student or another practicum student evaluate your classroom management techniques by using a stopwatch to record the amount of time students in your class are *actively* engaged in learning. (See chapter 19.)

7. Tape record or videotape yourself while teaching a class or working with a group of children or youth. Analyze your management skills, using the suggestions in chapter 19.

8. Observe several teachers and analyze their management skills. Are they effective? Why or why not?

9. Talk to several physical education teachers to obtain ideas for (1) adapting activities for large groups, (2) learning students' names, and (3) adapting for interruptions.

10. Help a physical educator take an inventory of equipment. Study how it is stored and note the care techniques that are used.

11. Get sample record keeping forms from a nearby public school physical education program.

12. You are a junior high school physical education teacher. In the middle of the semester, you get a new student who is the only minority member in the class. It is a rule in your class that each boy must take a shower, but the new boy refuses to do so. You are receiving much static from other students over this situation. When talking to the new student, you sense that he seems very concerned about showering with the other boys. You want to be fair to all. What will you do?

Suggested readings

Clumpner, Roy A. "Maximizing Participation and Enjoyment in the PE Classrooms." *Journal of Physical Education and Recreation* 50 (January 1979): 60–62.

Fuller, Link. "Required Uniforms." *The Physical Educator* 33 (May 1976): 85–86.

Haering, Franklin C. "Safety Is Big Business." *Journal of Physical Education and Recreation* 50 (June 1979): 41–43.

Hellison, Don. *Beyond Balls & Bats*. Washington, D.C.: American Alliance for Health, Physical Education and Recreation, 1978.

Herman, William. "Have a Junk Day." *Journal of Physical Education and Recreation* 46 (October 1975): 35.

"Physical Education for the Temporarily Disabled." *Physical Education Newsletter* (September 1981).

Siedentop, Daryl. *Developing Teaching Skills in Physical Education*. Boston: Houghton Mifflin Company, 1976.

Wolven, Barry. "1 to 1." *Journal of Health, Physical Education and Recreation* 44 (October 1973): 29.

Establishing Effective Class Control

Study stimulators

1. Why is a study of discipline so important?
2. What is discipline?
3. What disciplinary techniques are generally considered to be unacceptable?
4. What disciplinary techniques are generally considered to be acceptable? Which ones would you use and when?

Of the major problems facing the public schools, discipline has been ranked number one by the annual Gallup Poll for the past ten years.[1] Most teachers leaving the field of education do so because of disciplinary problems, and the percentages are much higher for beginning teachers who are worried about questions like the following: "Can I handle the class?," "Will the students respect me?," "What will I do if a crisis occurs?" A large majority of experienced teachers believe that there is a greater problem of maintaining discipline now than when they began teaching. Therefore, classroom control is very important to the teacher.

Students are critical of teachers who do not keep adequate control of classroom behavior. They indicate that few teachers can teach well without establishing good class discipline. They are aware of the fact that beginning teachers have less control than experienced teachers.

The most important concern of discipline, of course, is in the establishment of a good learning environment—one in which students can grow both in knowledge and self-control. Each student has a basic right to an educational experience free from the unnecessary distractions caused by a few unruly students. Good order, based on a cooperative effort of all of those involved, contributes both to the teacher's goal of optimum learning and to the student's growth as a responsible member of society.

Discipline is difficult to define because its meaning has evolved over the years to include many aspects of behavior. In fact, some authors have equated the word *discipline* with behavior itself. However, because each individual reacts differently to his or her environment, many variations in behavior must be accepted as normal; whereas we often think of discipline as a cut-and-dried situation of good versus bad.

Historically, classroom discipline could have been defined primarily as an unquestioning, immediate, and strict obedience imposed by a teacher to create a teaching-learning environment through the maintenance of good order. This order was probably maintained by fear. Although the intelligent application of psychological principles to the maintenance of order has increased the chances of success with this type of discipline, it is best used only for restraint of the immature learner.

Children go through various stages as they mature and come to understand control. Preschool children are trained to follow established rules and procedures. Children learn to relate to nonpersonal objects, becoming familiar with natural laws and governing themselves so as to use those laws for their own purposes. As children enter school, they are helped to develop a certain amount of conformity to group patterns, which we might call social control. They learn to relate to the culture and its institutions—the sociological, political, and economic laws of force. They develop the capacity for some reciprocal adjustment with their environment. Finally, children learn to interact with others through a process of self-control. They interact on a psychological level and need no extrinsic reward or punishment.

Thus, *discipline becomes a process of assisting youngsters to adjust to their environment and to develop acceptable inner controls.* The process involves a slow progression from the direct, authoritative control of behavior needed by some learners to the level of desirable self-control experienced by only a few. In education today, the emphasis is on the student's natural ability to interpret the situation and react accordingly, reaping the natural consequences of any undesired act, rather than on a strict code of behavior for all students.

Discipline involves knowing when to be authoritative, when to be permissive, and when to straddle the middle ground. Classes can change dramatically from one hour to the next or one week to another. Pep rallies, assemblies, lunchtime activities, weather, or the activities of the previous classes can cause normally quiet students to stampede into the room. Success or failure with homework or previous assignments can affect the attitude of students before the lesson has even begun.

As students and teacher embark upon a day's activities, many results can occur. The ideal situation is one in which both teacher and students are successfully engaged in teaching and learning activities, neither interfering with the activities of the other. However, since teachers and students often have different personalities and values, conflict often occurs, resulting in behavior unacceptable to either the teacher or the student.[2] If the problem is on the part of the student, the teacher must listen to the student's problem and attempt to understand and resolve it if possible. If the problem is a hindrance to the teacher's activities, the teacher must communicate to the student how he or she feels in an attempt to resolve the conflict. For example, the teacher might say, "I'm trying to help everyone learn the . . ., but I can't when I'm constantly interrupted." Sometimes the student will understand and alter the behavior. If not, the teacher will be forced to (1) take a stand and authoritatively decide what to do to solve the problem, (2) allow the student to continue the behavior at the expense of the teacher and often of the other students, or (3) attempt to work out a solution that is acceptable to both parties.

Unacceptable practices

Some disciplinary practices used in the past generally are considered to be unacceptable because they generate resentment on the part of the student or cause the student to withdraw into an apathetical state. These practices include (1) coercion; (2) ridicule; (3) forced apologies; (4) detention without a specified purpose; (5) imposition of schoolwork or homework for punitive purposes; (6) punishment, including grades; (7) group punishment for misbehavior by one or a few; and (8) corporal punishment. Methods such as appealing to the student's sympathy; the use of vague, unfulfilled threats; and exclusion of the student from the room without supervision result in a lack of control on the part of the teacher.

Acceptable practices

Acceptable practices are many, but their effectiveness depends upon how well they work for each teacher. Several practices will be discussed in the next few pages.

Waiting aggressively

Waiting aggressively is letting students know you intend to wait for their attention. Make your waiting obvious. Waiting signals can include a frown, a shake of the head, a disapproving look at an offender, a mild reproof, or movement toward the trouble spot. Often these techniques will resolve problems before they become difficult.

Individual conference

The individual conference with a student outside of class time is one of the most effective techniques that can be utilized. A serious and frank talk would appear to be the logical first step in the understanding of behavior problems. Conferences help the teacher understand the causes of misbehavior and problems the student faces. They can also be useful in interpreting school or class regulations to the student.

Cooperation between home and school

Genuine cooperation between home and school through conferences, home visits, and social contacts can achieve remarkable results, provided both parties are willing to understand the student's behavior and are sincere about wanting to help the student. Home-school cooperation can produce fruitful information and lead to correction of misbehavior. A positive, cooperative effort is usually most successful.

Restitution and reparation

Restitution of things taken and *reparation* for things damaged or destroyed willfully are generally conceded to be fair forms of punishment. To be effective, this form of punishment must educate the student to realize that when something is destroyed it affects the welfare of the entire group. This technique also teaches the student to make amends. The teacher's responsibility lies in explaining the reasons for the punishment and in following through to see that restoration is made. If the student is financially unable to pay expenses for reparation, the school should find a way in which the student can work off the debt. Where parents are too free with money, the school should solicit their cooperation to make the punishment effective by permitting the student to work out the debt to society.

An individual conference is one of the most
effective disciplinary techniques.

Loss of privileges and time out

The loss of privileges, particularly those of a social nature, is generally a well-accepted method of discipline. When this method is applied, it should follow as a natural, logical form of correction with no sort of retributory attitude on the part of the teacher. Ways must be made available so that, after the student has had time to examine the misbehavior, the student can be restored to full privileges. Often students will plead to be allowed to work after being excluded.

Time out consists of cutting off all reinforcement for a period of time.[3] Usually, the student is required to sit out away from other students until the decision is made to engage in appropriate behavior.

Isolation

Isolation removes the offender from the class and facilitates instruction to the other students. However, it also bars the student from necessary instruction. Occasionally it creates a scene in which the offender may be humiliated or, on the contrary, become a hero to classmates. It appears that this method is justified only in severe cases. Isolation from the activity while watching the enjoyment of the other students can be effective.

Judicious use of administrative assistance

Use the expertise of the administration only after you have been unsuccessful while trying everything you can to correct a disturbing situation or after there have been repeated incidents of misbehavior. A principal once told a teacher, "After you've done everything you can and the student doesn't improve, don't let it bother you out of proportion. Let it give the principal an ulcer." The administration has the duty to do everything possible to help the teacher deal with discipline problems for the sake of the student, the teacher, and the school as a whole. However, the teacher should seldom refer a student to the administration until all the resources at hand have been exhausted.

Procedures for utilizing administrative assistance include the following:

1. When it becomes necessary to send a student to the office of the administrator, *send along a note* (with another student) *that states the difficulty and the depth of treatment you expect.*

2. See the administrator as soon as possible to discuss the situation.

3. Do not send more than one student to the office at a time.

4. If the student is sent back to class, calmly readmit the student and ignore any face-saving behavior the student displays.

5. Know the student. A trip to the office may be just what the individual wants at that moment in order to get out of a difficult assignment.

Behavior modification and contingency contracting

Behavior modification is an inclusive term for a number of techniques designed to reinforce the desired behavior of individuals or groups and to eliminate undesired behavior. It is based on the premise that people will repeat behaviors that are reinforced or rewarded and will not repeat behaviors that are consistently ignored.

Some techniques used to modify behavior include conditioning, shaping, reinforcement, and extinction. **Conditioning** is getting students to respond in a specific way to a specific stimulus. An example is "roll call," to which students respond by standing on their numbers. **Shaping** involves rewarding behavior that is closer and closer to the desired goal. It is used to teach sports skills by rewarding first a gross motor skill and then increasingly refined movements until accuracy and efficiency are obtained. **Reinforcement** uses a thing or event following a behavior to increase the likelihood that a person will repeat the behavior for which it is given. **Extinction** occurs when a response or behavior is no longer reinforced.

Most of us have practiced behavior modification on ourselves. You are probably saying to yourself right now, "As soon as I finish reading this chapter, I'm going to eat a cookie." That is an example of contingency contracting.

Contingency contracting is reinforcement that is contingent upon the performance of the desired behavior. Homme summed up the principle of contingency contracting in "Grandma's Law," which states, "First clean up your plate, then you may have your dessert."[4] A more sophisticated explanation was developed by Premack and is called the Premack principle. It suggests that any behavior that occurs frequently can be used to reinforce a behavior that occurs less frequently. For example, "getting to play the game" (a highly desired activity) becomes a reinforcer for practicing one's skills (a less desired activity).

Since preferred activities can serve as reinforcers, all instructors have to do is observe students to determine what activities they like to do best. In fact, teachers can even ask students what activities are worth working for.

Contingency contracting places the responsibility on students for decisions regarding their behavior. It can be used along with extinction to reduce undesirable behavior, to develop new behavior, or to strengthen and maintain existing behavior. Joyce and Weil describe contingency contracting as "the heart of effective classroom management."[5]

The major advantage of contingency contracting is a feeling of accomplishment on the part of students and teachers.[6]

Some teachers worry about the use of behavior modification techniques in the classroom. You should remember that reinforcement is a part of life. As adults we are rewarded with pay checks, recognition by society, praise from friends or bosses, and many other types of reinforcement. In fact, we are constantly making modifications in our behavior as we interact with others in our environment. It is the same with school. We must take students where they are and assist them in trying out new kinds of behavior until they learn the satisfaction that comes from success in the activity itself. As La Mancusa stated, "The teacher does neither himself nor his students a favor by perpetuating the climate of failure."[7] Giving students attention for good behavior is far more desirable than giving them attention for misbehavior. Reprimands tend only to increase the behaviors they are intended to eliminate. Consistently ignored behaviors tend to increase in frequency initially and then weaken and disappear.

According to Homme,[8] contingency contracts should be:

1. Clear—The directions should be stated in explicit terms that are easily understood by the student, such as:
   If you do . . . , then you will get. . . .
   If you do . . . , then I will do. . . .
   If you do . . . , then you may do. . . .
   (Note: *You* is a student or a group.)

2. Fair—The two sides of the contract must be of relatively equal importance.

3. Honest—The reward should be given immediately *after* the performance but *only* for the performance specified in the contract.

4. Positive—The contract *should not* say, "If you do . . . , then I will *not* do. . . .

5. Systematic—The instructor should be consistent in reinforcing only the desired behavior.

When establishing a contract, the following procedures should be employed:

1. Clearly specify a few rules that tell exactly what is expected. Limit rules to five or less.[9] Establish the target behavior in terms of performance and criteria for achievement. Establish what the reward will be for correct performance. Stress academic achievement rather than obedience.[10] Academic achievement is usually incompatible with disruptive behavior.

2. Initiate a contract with students. The contract may be a short statement by the teacher that states the consequences to be gained by certain behaviors.

3. Ignore disruptive, *nondestructive* behavior.

4. Reward the student immediately after completion of the desired behavior. Initial rewards should be given for behavior that approximates the goal (i.e., small, simple tasks). Later, behaviors should be increasingly close to the final objective.

5. Use a variety of reinforcers to reward appropriate behaviors. Work toward the use of higher-order reinforcers and an intermittent reinforcement schedule (random or unpredictable reinforcement) to increase resistance to extinction. This reduces teacher approval to only a few times a day. The needs of each individual will determine what things or events will serve as reinforcers. Therefore, teachers need to plan in advance to see what is reinforcing and what is not for their particular students. In order to be worthwhile, rewards must be highly desirable and not obtainable outside the conditions of the contract.[11]

6. Be consistent in following the plan.

7. Progress from teacher-directed contracts to mutually directed contracts to student-initiated contracts.

Becker identified three ways in which reinforcers lose their effectiveness.[12] One is **competing reinforcers.** These are reinforcers available from a source other than the teacher, such as those from the peer group. Second is **satiation,** in which the reinforcer has been used so often that it loses its effectiveness. Third, is the **lack of transfer** of reinforcers to new situations. When learning a new task, the learner may fail to understand that the rules for achieving reinforcement are the same. Several solutions to these problems include withholding reinforcement for a short time to make it worthwhile again, changing the reinforcer, or strengthening the reinforcer. It should be noted that reinforcement is not effective with all students. Different personalities of teacher and student, different student learning styles, and different environmental conditions can affect the success or failure of contingency contracting.

Examples of reinforcers

Some suggestions for reinforcers are listed below, from highest to lowest. Higher-order reinforcers are found more frequently in the normal environment.

1. Competence (skill acquisition).
2. Being correct (feedback).
3. Social approval (praise).
4. Contingent activity (for example, "Do . . . and then you can have 5 minutes of free time").
5. Tokens or check marks (exchanged for other reinforcers).
6. Tangibles (toys, trinkets).
7. Edibles (food, candies).[13]

Punishment

Punishment is negative contingency contracting—"if you do x, you will get y," y being undesirable. Punishment usually implies mental or physical pain or discomfort.

Although a behavior may be temporarily suppressed when punishment or the threat of punishment follows behavior, it will often reappear later. One possible reason for this is that punishment tells the student what not to do, but gives no direction as to the appropriate behavior. Therefore, the student will probably experiment with a whole range of inappropriate behaviors while searching for the appropriate behavior. Reward, on the contrary, immediately tells the student what the appropriate behavior is. In addition, undesirable side effects, such as a negative self-concept or a dislike of school, the subject, or the teacher can develop. These negative feelings may predispose the student to retaliate or withdraw. A third reason for avoiding the use of punishment is that it reduces the behavior only in the presence of the punishing agent. Students may learn how to avoid getting caught by more sophisticated cheating, lying, etc. A fourth reason why punishment should be avoided is that it teaches students to be aggressive through imitation of the aggressive behavior of adults.

Punishment should only be used in a planned, careful way to deal with problems that cannot be resolved in a better way. Becker suggests two circumstances in which punishment may be needed: (1) when direct reinforcement procedures are likely to fail because the negative behavior is so frequent that there is no positive behavior to reinforce and (2) when someone might get hurt.[14]

Punishment, when it is used, should result primarily as a natural consequence of the choices made by students. Students should be counseled as to the consequences of alternatives when they make their choices. Negative reinforcement should never be used to punish one student in front of a group of students. The following procedures are suggested when using punishment.

1. Allow an undesirable act to continue (or insist that it continue) until the student is clearly bored with it. For example, a teacher could insist that a student throwing spit wads continue to make spit wads until the student has clearly learned how unattractive the behavior is and can make a decision to follow a desired behavior.

2. Always accompany punishment by a suggestion of something positive to do (i.e., the desired behavior).

3. End the punishment with the student's decision to perform the desired behavior.

4. Reward the positive behavior or the student will revert to the bad behavior in order to get recognition, even if it takes the form of punishment.

Reality therapy

Reality therapy was developed by Glasser to help students assume the accountability for their own behavior.[15] Persons who can fulfill their needs through responsible behavior will have no need to act irresponsibly. These needs, according to Glasser, are the need to know that one is of worth to oneself and to others and the need to love and be loved. A person who is unable to fulfill these needs through responsible behavior is forced to fulfill them in irresponsible ways. Glasser's technique is dependent upon three factors: (1) acceptance as a person but rejection of irresponsible behavior; (2) a meaningful relationship between teacher and student; and (3) education of the student into better ways of behaving by fulfilling the student's needs in responsible ways.

Reality therapy requires the teacher to become involved and care about students. The teacher must work in the present and toward the future, ignoring the student's excuses. The teacher helps the student (1) identify the inappropriate behavior, (2) identify the consequences of the behavior, (3) make a value judgement about the behavior, (4) make a plan, and (5) follow the plan. The procedure is for the teacher to ask the following questions.

1. What is your goal? What do you want to happen?

2. What are you doing? *or* What did you do?

3. Is that what you should be doing? *or* How will that help you?

4. What is your plan? *or* What will you do that will help you?

5. What will be the consequences?

6. What can I do to help you?

If the student fails to apply the plan, the student should be allowed to suffer the consequences of the irresponsible behavior, but within a framework of love and understanding. The student should then be helped to reconsider the commitment that has been made. An example of reality therapy follows.

This reality therapy session takes place in a tenth-grade gymnastics class. The students have been assigned to develop an individual routine on a chosen piece of apparatus. The routine is to be completed by the end of the hour. A substantial portion of the student's grade will be based on the routine. Louise sits over in the corner. She has not even attempted to create a routine. Instead, she is staring into space. The teacher approaches Louise and confronts her with the situation.

TEACHER: "Louise, what are you doing?"
LOUISE: "I'm just sitting here." ⓐ
TEACHER: "What are you supposed to be doing?"
LOUISE: "I don't know."
TEACHER: "What is the rest of the class doing?"
LOUISE: "I guess they're working on the routine."
TEACHER: "What are *you* supposed to be doing?"
LOUISE: "I guess I'm supposed to be working on the routine." ⓑ
TEACHER: "How far will sitting around get you?"
LOUISE: "Probably no where."
TEACHER: "What will happen if you don't do the routine?"
LOUISE: "I'll probably flunk the class." ⓒ
TEACHER: "Do you want to fail?"
LOUISE: "I don't know."
TEACHER: "What will happen if you do fail?"
LOUISE: "I'll probably have to take the class over."
TEACHER: "Is that what you want?"
LOUISE: "No."
TEACHER: "What can you do to keep from failing?"
LOUISE: "I guess I better work on the routine." ⓓ
TEACHER: "What can I do to help you?"
LOUISE: "Tell me what skills to do."
TEACHER: "That's not acceptable. What else can I do?" ⓔ
LOUISE: "Explain what things I'm supposed to have in my routine." ⓕ
TEACHER: "Okay. Will that help you?"
LOUISE: "I think so."
TEACHER: "Will you be ready to perform tomorrow?"
LOUISE: "I guess so."
TEACHER: "Okay."

Notes: a. Student identifies behavior.

b. Student makes a value judgement.

c. Student identifies the consequences of behavior.

d. Student makes a plan.

e. Teacher guides development of the plan.

f. Teacher helps the student with the plan.

Norm setting

When reality therapy is used with a group of students, it is known as **norm setting.** Norm setting is based on the principle that students are more responsible for implementing behavior expectations or goals that they have participated in selecting. Teachers and students work together to formalize and publicize essential rules and regulations. Rules should be clear, brief, reasonable, easily applied to all, and enforceable by teacher observation. For norm-setting to work, the teacher must recognize the worth and intelligence of students.

Norm setting can be used with groups of all ages and in many different settings. The procedures include the following.

1. Help students share their goals or expectations regarding either learning or behavior. Focus on what students *need* to learn or do, not what they *want* to do.

2. State goals you feel students need to achieve.

3. Refine goals into one set of mutually acceptable goals by eliminating undesirable goals (those that can't be achieved within the course) and adding any desirable goals that were omitted.

4. State goals in such a way that students and teacher will know what each goal is and when it has been achieved.

5. State what you are willing to do to help students achieve the class goals (such as availability, being prepared, willingness to admit mistakes, caring for students, listening to students, etc.) Do not promise to do anything you will not do. Teachers who really care are willing to risk asking students to share additional expectations they may have for the teacher.

6. Help students describe what they need to do and are willing to do to insure attainment of class goals.

7. Identify consequences for nonattainment of goals.

8. Commit yourself and your students to the class goals. Agreements may be written down and signed in the form of a contract.

9. Use various motivational techniques to reward behavior that is consistent with the norms or standards previously agreed upon.

10. Use reality therapy techniques to help the misbehaving student judge behavior in terms of the commitments made by the class.

11. Review goals and commitments from time to time and make changes when necessary.

Handling explosive situations

An **explosive situation** is a situation requiring immediate action to prevent personal injury or property damage. It is best to prevent an explosive situation from occurring whenever possible by using the following suggestions.

1. Don't let misbehavior go too far before you attempt to handle the problem.

2. Don't lose your cool. Explosive situations become volcanic when the teacher and student are not in control of themselves.

3. Be decisive, act quickly, and disarm the situation. The teacher might use a "time out" period or, if possible, remove the student or students from the classroom situation.

4. Don't use too harsh a punishment as that action can result in later aggressive behaviors being manifest.

5. Avoid confrontations with students. Don't accept a challenge as a personal matter.

When an explosive situation occurs, however, the following procedures may be helpful.

1. Decide whether you need help or can handle it alone.

2. If you need help, get it! Send a student for another teacher, principal, etc.

3. Move toward the problem.

4. Insist calmly but firmly that the behavior be stopped immediately.

5. Suggest an alternative behavior—an "out" by which the student can save face.

6. Act to stop the problem if you can do so safely. Don't touch the student if you can avoid it.

7. Remove the student from the area, if appropriate.

8. Calm the class by restructuring the incident or using it as a topic for discussion. Introduce humor.

Selecting the appropriate disciplinary technique

Whatever the problem might be that arises, proper action depends upon (1) the teacher, (2) the students, and (3) the incident.

The teacher

An understanding of a variety of suitable techniques and success in carrying out different methods allows the teacher to shift positions as conditions change. Teachers should experiment to see what works best for them, because what works for one teacher may not work for another. Administrative policy may limit the choices from which a teacher is allowed to select.

The students

It is easy to assume that all students are alike, but no method of control is usually effective with all students. One must consider the age, sex, personality, and social values held by the student or group. Teachers should be alert to individual needs of students. Occasionally, deafness, poor vision, or other handicapping conditions create supposed discipline problems.

The incident

An attempt to determine the cause of the behavior and what actually happened should be made without relying too heavily on statements made by students. Often the cause of the incident results from the environment within the classroom itself. Poor, haphazard, and unproductive instruction or a curriculum that is too easy, too hard, or not relevant to the needs of students may cause many discipline problems.

With all of these items in mind, the teacher will first need to stop the ineffective behavior and then help to overcome individual problems, thus preventing a recurrence of the problem. The action must be clear, definite, and one in which the teacher truly believes. By continually being alert to the early signs of trouble and dealing with them firmly and calmly before they become serious, major discipline problems can be avoided.

Preventive discipline

Preventive discipline involves more than just the establishment of sound methods of control. It involves (1) the personality, self-confidence, and attitudes of the teacher; (2) the development of proper interpersonal relations; (3) a psychological insight into the background and characteristics of students and the causes of behavioral problems; (4) proper planning and preparation, both long-range and short-range; (5) a wholesome, attractive, and well-managed environment; (6) the use of routine for recurring situations; (7) the establishment of a relevant, challenging curriculum; and (8) proper instructional techniques. Each of these items is discussed in another section of this book.

The key to classroom control comes from understanding the worth of each individual student. Whatever method is used, students need the guidance and security provided by well-defined rules of expected behavior and the knowledge that adults care enough about them to enforce those rules.

Discipline begins in a serious, no-nonsense vein with adult rule and pupil obedience. The teacher then attempts to work toward student self-control by planning with the individuals in the class. Teacher-directed group planning, in which the scope and area of planning are predetermined, is the next step toward self-direction. Self-management through group planning is achieved only after all of the other skills and understandings needed have been achieved.

It must be noted, however, that even after self-direction in known areas has been achieved, some students will fail to be self-directing when a new situation presents itself. For this reason, patterns of control must be applied according to the appropriateness of the situation. At times, the teacher needs to provide the students with a choice between self-direction and teacher direction and let them decide which will be more valuable to them in the specific learning environment.

Hints for new teachers

1. Learn school policies and procedures thoroughly.

2. Be an example you want your students to emulate.

3. Be a teacher—not a pal—to your students.

4. Plan and organize.

5. Be flexible but consistent in carrying out your plan.

6. Respect and appreciate your students as individuals.

7. Let your students know from the start what the payoff will be for working hard in your class.[16]

Questions and suggested activities

1. Role-play each of the discipline techniques with a partner.

2. Given a classroom situation, role-play how you would handle the situation. Then, discuss with the group the principles of class control that you used in solving the case.

3. Analyze the discipline techniques used in a public school classroom. How might you improve them?

4. Try to create a plan defining which discipline technique you would use in given situations.

Suggested readings

Barr, Norman J. "The Responsible World of Reality Therapy." *Psychology Today* (February 1974): pp. 64–67.

"Disruptive Behavior." *Today's Education* 70 (November-December 1981): 61.

Evans, Jane. "Implications of Behavior Modification Techniques for the Physical Education Teacher." *The Physical Educator* 31 (March 1974): 28–32.

Gallahue, David L. "Punishment and Control, Part I. Negative Results." *The Physical Educator* 35 (May 1978): 58–59.

Gallahue, David L. "Punishment and Control, Part II. Alternatives to Punishment." *The Physical Educator* 35 (October 1978): 114.

Glasser, William. *Schools Without Failure.* New York: Harper and Row, Publishers, 1969.

Johnson, Les. "Looking for a Fence." *Scout Magazine* (December 1964): 14–15, 27.

Martin, Robert J. "Avoiding Help That Hinders." *Today's Education* 70 (September-October 1981): 58–61.

Singer, Robert N. "Achievement Motivation." *Journal of Physical Education and Recreation* 50 (February 1979): 37–38.

Taylor, John L. "Curbing Discipline Problems Through Physical Education." *Journal of Physical Education and Recreation* 49 (February 1978): 38.

Evaluating the Teacher

Study stimulators

1. Why is teacher evaluation important?
2. List the steps in teacher evaluation.
3. What are the advantages and limitations of evaluation that is based on student achievement or improvement, informal analysis, informal analysis by students, descriptive analysis, and interaction analysis?

Effective teachers have the ability to adapt their teaching behaviors to meet the needs of their students. Studies demonstrate that evaluating teachers increases their awareness of these different instructional behaviors and helps them to improve both student achievement and teacher morale. This is true because teachers often perceive their teaching behavior quite differently from that which actually occurs. By evaluating your own teaching, you will be able to retain effective teaching behaviors and eliminate ineffective behaviors, thereby making your actual behavior more congruent with what you wish to achieve.

Teacher evaluation involves the following steps.

Step 1. Determine what to evaluate.

Step 2. Become familiar with specific evaluation techniques.

Step 3. Use the appropriate techniques to record information.

Step 4. Evaluate or interpret the data.

Step 5. Make changes and reevaluate.

Step 1. Determine what to evaluate

The first step in any evaluation plan is to specify your goals. This can be done by examining what you believe to be the most important goals of teaching and the behaviors teachers should assume in order to achieve those goals.[1] Some examples of goals and related behaviors, which are based on the characteristics of effective teachers discussed in chapter 5, are shown in table 19.1.

Step 2. Choose or construct specific evaluation techniques.

Evaluation techniques generally assess either the performance of the students or the performance of the teacher. Since learning is what education is all about, teachers should be accountable for student achievement of the objectives of instruction. If students are learning

Table 19.1 Goals and behaviors for teachers

Goals	Teacher behavior
Teacher warmth	Calls student by name. Provides more positive than negative feedback. Interacts with students.
Teacher expectancy	Facilitates achievement of instructional objectives. Facilitates improvement in student learning. Selects tasks in terms of student abilities.
Task-oriented climate	Helps students spend a large amount of time in productive behavior. Provide feedback on behavior. Decrease time spent on class management.
Effective instruction	Provides appropriate model and explanation. Provides appropriate feedback for skills. Provides opportunity for student practice.

and have positive feelings toward activity, then the teacher is effective, no matter how unorthodox the instruction appears to be. However, if students are not learning or do not have positive attitudes toward activity, then an analysis of the teacher's performance can help to pinpoint possible problem areas for remediation.

Teacher analysis generally begins with an observation of the teacher's classroom behavior. This can be done by an administrator or peer or by videotaping the class and evaluating your own behavior. The observation is recorded for follow-up evaluation and decisions are made as to changes needed to improve future teaching performance.

Because teaching is so complex, a variety of observation and recording techniques must be employed to describe the total teaching process. The techniques discussed in this chapter include: (1) student achievement or improvement, (2) informal analysis, (3) informal analysis by students, (4) descriptive analysis, and (5) interaction analysis.

Student achievement or improvement

The principal duty of teachers is to help students learn. Therefore, the key to evaluating teaching is to determine the extent to which learning has taken place. The use of performance objectives facilitates this process by providing an observable student behavior for each skill or content area to be learned.

Common techniques for evaluating student achievement include knowledge tests, skills tests, and various affective measurements. Each of these techniques was discussed in chapter 11.

One method for evaluating student learning is to record student performance each day and compare it with the objectives of the daily lesson plan. This can be as simple as having students check off skills as they accomplish them (such as in gymnastics or swimming), count the number of successful attempts (such as basketball free throws or tennis serves), or turn in a score (such as in archery or bowling). See chapter 11 for examples. If the lesson has been well-planned, most of the students should be able to achieve the lesson objectives.

An accountability log can be kept each day. This log shows student achievement not only toward the objective for that day but also the achievement of previous unit objectives. An accountability log can be a tremendous eye opener into how much review and practice students need in order to achieve course objectives. The log might include a list of objectives and the number of students who have completed each one or a class record sheet like the one shown in figure 17.13.

A second method is to preassess students, teach, and then evaluate the improvement. Again, a knowledge or skills test or an affective measurement can be employed. Examples include:

1. Sprint—Check for improvement in time.

2. Knowledge—Check the number of students improving scores on a quiz or the class average on a quiz.

3. Attitude—Check the number of students changing from a negative to a positive attitude toward an activity. Review chapter 8 for specific suggestions on evaluating affective behavior.

4. Basketball strategy—Count the increases in successful passes per team.

There are limitations when evaluating teachers based on student performance. One of the major limitations is the difficulty of accurately evaluating student performance. Weather, time of day, illness, fatigue, and innumerable other factors can influence student performance scores. Subjective evaluation techniques and teacher-constructed tests may be unreliable. Measurements may not be sensitive enough to determine improvement during short units of instruction. A second limitation is that it is difficult to establish a cause and effect relationship between a specific teaching behavior and learning. Students may have learned from a parent, friend, or from private lessons. If you did not preassess skills, students may have begun with the skill level you are now evaluating. Students may learn because of you or in spite of you. When they do learn, it is difficult to prove which of your teaching behaviors may have caused the improvement.

These limitations, however, should not keep you from making some educated guesses about your own teaching based on student achievement. By checking for achievement or improvement each day, you will get a better idea of which teaching behaviors helped to create the changes in student behavior.

Informal analysis

The most common method of teacher evaluation is informal analysis by oneself, a supervisor or administrator, another teacher, or by students. Some informal analysis techniques that can be utilized include a written or verbal description of a lesson, a checklist, or a rating scale.

```
                    EVALUATION OF TEACHING
    Name _____        Activity _____

    School _____        Date _____

    Time _____


    Instruction:
         Objective clear
         Demonstration
         Practice
         Correction
    Selection of Activity:
         Success potential
         Challenging-motivational
         Progression
    Maximum Participation:
         Time
         Transitions
         Organization-space-equip-
         ment
         Opportunity for all
    Safety:
         Progressions
         Safety rules
         Equipment
    Teacher Relating to Class:
         Aware of class
         Aware of individuals
         Rapport
         Personal appearance
         Voice
```

Figure 19.1 A recording form for informal analysis.

A written or verbal description of a lesson is generally influenced, either consciously or unconsciously, by the biases of the observer. The description may focus on only one portion of the teaching-learning situation, such as on discipline or on teacher-student interaction. Furthermore, the definition of the behavior may be vague and mean different things to the teacher and the observer. Sometimes a recording form is used to direct the observer's attention to various aspects of the teaching situation. An example of a recording form is shown in figure 19.1. This particular form refers to many of the suggestions for teaching psychomotor skills discussed in chapter 7.

Informal analysis serves a useful purpose because it focuses on aspects of performance that are important to you in making day-to-day decisions. Although it is limited by its subjectivity and narrow focus (i.e., you see what you want to see), it is convenient for a quick

Informal analysis can be used for day-to-day
evaluation of one's own teaching.

look at your teaching each day. Informal analysis is most useful when comments are highly specific, such as "The light drained from Paul's face when you started the next relay before he was finished," or when a record is kept over a period of time. Written records, tape recordings, or videotape recordings can provide a valuable journal of progress when kept for periodic review.

Because of its lack of validity and reliability, informal analysis should not be used to evaluate a teacher for retention or tenure.

A checklist can be used to direct the observer's attention to specific parts of the lesson. The observer simply "checks" each item that was included in the teacher's behavior during the lesson. An example of a checklist is shown in figure 19.2.

The checklist provides the appearance of scientific accuracy; but, vague, undefined statements or characteristics result in a very low level of reliability for most checklists. A checklist like this provides no information concerning the frequency with which a given behavior occurs.

Rating scales can be valuable as a tool for self-evaluation and goal-setting by teachers. They can also be completed by both teachers and supervisors and the results compared to encourage discussion of different points of view concerning the teacher's performance. Goals should then be set to evaluate and correct specific areas needing attention.

An advantage of rating scales is that they take a minimum of time to complete and can provide information sufficient to get you started on a personal improvement plan. However, as an evaluative device, the rating scale is generally less valid and reliable than many of the other techniques that will be presented in this chapter.

When constructing a rating scale, remember that the less choices you have, the more reliable the scale will be. However, enough points must be included to make the scale useful for the purpose for which it is intended. By having two observers complete the scale independently and then talking over discrepancies, you can change the items so that differences in understanding of the characteristics in question can be corrected. Then, you can be more sure that the differences reflect differences in teacher performance rather than differences in understanding the scale.

Any of the types of rating scales presented in chapter 11 can be used to assess teaching performance. The choice is dependent on how you feel about a specific tool.

Many schools, districts, and universities provide rating scales of various standards of performance that can be used for self-evaluation or by peers or supervisors. The rating scale in figure 19.3 is one part of such an evaluation tool and can be used for self-evaluation or evaluation by your peers or supervisor. The results can be compared to determine areas that might need improvement.

Other rating scales can be developed to evaluate such items as demonstrations, questioning skills,[2] and interpersonal relations.[3]

```
                    TEACHER EVALUATION FORM

Name _____ Date _____ Evaluator _____

Personal Qualifications

_____ Displays knowledge of the subject
_____ Projects enthusiasm and interest
_____ Maintains confidence and respect of the students
_____ Is easily heard and understood
_____ Displays self-confidence

Organization

_____ Lesson flows smoothly into activity, from activity to activ-
       ity, (1) equipment available and ready (2) teacher doesn't
       talk too much
_____ Students know where to go and what to do
_____ Students understand the objective of the activity or lesson
_____ Available equipment and space is used effectively
_____ Time allotment is appropriate

Instruction

_____ Adequate safety precautions are taken
_____ Individual and group help is given
_____ The activity is challenging, enjoyable, and has success poten-
       tial
_____ Students are motivated, interested, and involved (not standing
       too long)
_____ Teacher uses appropriate disciplinary techniques so students
       are controlled

Comments (Includes strengths, suggestions for improvement, clari-
fication of above)



Lesson Plan

_____ Instructional objectives stated in behavioral terms
_____ Performance cues sufficient for skill execution
_____ Estimate of instructional time is appropriate
_____ Practice situations specified in detail (with diagrams)
_____ Sufficient equipment provided to maximize participation
```

Figure 19.2 A checklist of teacher functions.

Informal analysis by students

Because informal analysis relies on each person's individual perceptions, it can be used to help you see things as others see them. Thus, informal analysis can be especially helpful in determining how students feel about what they have learned and their perceptions about the learning situation. To be most effective, informal analysis by students should be written, not oral, and should be kept anonymous to allow for free and honest responses. Caution should be used in asking young students to analyze teacher behavior. Questionnaires should not be

TEACHER EVALUATION RECORD

Name _____ Date _____ Evaluator _____

Instructions: Rate yourself (or have someone else rate you) on each of the major items by placing an "X" on the liens provided.

	Outstanding	Good	Fair	Poor	Doesn't Apply	Comments
Works Well with Associates						
Is friendly and cordial	____	____	____	____	____	
Possesses tact and courtesy	____	____	____	____	____	
Gains the respect of associates	____	____	____	____	____	
Promotes cooperative action among individuals and groups	____	____	____	____	____	
Listens attentively when associating with others	____	____	____	____	____	
Has a genuine desire to help others without concern for personal benefit or credit for achievement	____	____	____	____	____	
Is sensitive to own effect on others	____	____	____	____	____	
Accepts and utilizes suggestions from others	____	____	____	____	____	
Keeps informed on policies and procedures and follows them	____	____	____	____	____	
Asks questions to clarify assignments and responsibilities	____	____	____	____	____	
Carries own share of school responsibilities willingly and cheerfully	____	____	____	____	____	
Keeps commitments reliably	____	____	____	____	____	
Serves on committees and participates in other group projects	____	____	____	____	____	
Is prompt and accurate with reports	____	____	____	____	____	
Goes through regular "channels" on matters affecting the welfare of associates or of the institution	____	____	____	____	____	
Is loyal to associates, school, and district	____	____	____	____	____	

Figure 19.3 A portion of a teacher evaluation record.

used with students who do not have the ability to understand the intent of the questions and to provide valid answers. Some examples of questions that might be asked on a student questionnaire include the following.

1. What are the two most important things you have learned in this class?

2. What factors helped you learn them? (Be specific. Who did what to help you?)

3. How could this class be improved to make it better?

4. List the strengths of your teacher.

5. Tell how your teacher could help you learn better.

To score the analyses, simply tally the number of times a similar response was given to each question. Then, look seriously at the ones listed most often. Also, take note of perceptions that may not have occurred to you previously.

Checklists can also be used to obtain an overall estimate of student feelings toward specific aspects of teacher performance. Items might include some of the following.

1. Place a check beside *each* characteristic that describes your teacher:

_____ Interesting	_____ Organized	_____ Strict
_____ Smart	_____ Pushover	_____ Disorganized
_____ Uninformed	_____ Dull	

2. Place a check beside the answer that best describes your feelings toward the teacher:

a. The teacher helps me learn or improve my skills.

_____ Yes   _____ No   _____ I don't know.

b. The teacher has good discipline.

_____ Yes   _____ No   _____ I don't know.

Each of the different categories of rating scales discussed in chapter 11 can be used for student evaluation of teachers. Questions using the semantic differential scale to score student attitudes toward the teacher might appear as follows.

Friendly ___/___/___/___/___/___/___ Unfriendly

Dull   ___/___/___/___/___/___/___ Interesting

Items are scored from 1 to 7, with 7 being the most positive. An average of the scores for the entire class on each item would undoubtedly provide the most information.

The Likert scale can be used to determine student attitudes toward the teacher or to compare how the students feel versus how the teacher feels about each characteristic. For example, in the following questions, *x* marks how the student feels, and *o* marks how the teacher feels on each item.

	Mostly true	Usually true	Neutral	Usually false	Mostly false
1. The teacher is concerned about student learning.	o			x	
2. The teacher likes teaching.		x	o		

When a serious discrepancy exists between the teacher's and the student's feelings, as in item 1, the teacher becomes aware of the need to communicate feelings differently.

Students' perceptions about the instructional system can also be acquired via a rating scale. A rating scale used at Kent State University is shown in figure 19.4.[4] This scale could be used as a report card for students to grade you at the end of a unit of instruction or grading period. The scale could be written at a lower level of reading ability for use by younger students.

Descriptive analysis

One way to avoid the subjectivity inherent in informal analysis is to use descriptive analysis. Descriptive analysis is used to collect data that describe various components of the teaching performance. The data are then analyzed to determine the extent to which the intended teaching behavior actually occurred during teaching.

The primary purpose of descriptive analysis is to collect objective data that accurately describe events occurring in the classroom. The data must be recorded in such a way that they can be used to analyze one or more components of the teaching/learning process.

Literally hundreds of analytic systems have been developed to encode student and teacher behaviors. Some are relatively easy to learn and use; others are so complex that only trained researchers can utilize them. In this chapter, we will take a look at the simpler kinds of descriptive analysis that can be used for self-improvement. These systems require only an observer, a paper and pencil, and a stopwatch. A tape recorder or videorecorder can be valuable if you wish to analyze your own teaching behavior rather than have an outside observer evaluate you.

Descriptive analysis is generally limited to a description of what the teacher and students were doing. It tells very little about the quality of the performance. Other limitations are the limited sample size (sometimes only one student), the limited time sample, and the limited set of categories used for describing behavior. For this reason, descriptive analysis should be accompanied by other forms of evaluation.[5]

STUDENT OPINIONNAIRE—
BASIC INSTRUCTION PHYSICAL EDUCATION PROGRAM
KNOWLEDGE—CLARITY—ENTHUSIASM

1. The instructor effectively explained or demonstrated the skills of the activity.
   INEFFECTIVE A_____ B _____ C _____ D _____ E VERY EFFECTIVE

2. The instructor was perceptive in diagnosing and skillful in correcting individual errors in performance.
   OBLIVIOUS/NOT HELPFUL A_____ B _____ C _____ D _____ E PERCEPTIVE/HELPFUL

3. The instructor clearly explained the rules, scoring and strategies involved in the activity. (May not apply to dance, gymnastics, skating, etc.)
   VAGUELY A_____ B _____ C _____ D _____ E CLEARLY

4. The instructor was enthusiastic and interested in teaching the subject matter.
   APATHETIC A_____ B _____ C _____ D _____ E ENTHUSIASTIC

5. The instructor demonstrated a comprehensive knowledge of the activity.
   UNINFORMED A_____ B _____ C _____ D _____ E VERY KNOWLEDGEABLE

6. The instructor encouraged and motivated you to attain a higher skill level.
   UNCONCERNED A_____ B _____ C _____ D _____ E VERY PERSUASIVE

7. The instructor seemed capable of teaching the more highly skilled performers.
   INCAPABLE A_____ B _____ C _____ D _____ E VERY CAPABLE

ORGANIZATION AND PREPARATION

8. The instructor provided, verbally or via a course outline, the course objectives, expectations, assignments, examination information, and grading procedures.
   UNDEFINED A_____ B _____ C _____ D _____ E CLEARLY DEFINED

9. The instructor's lessons reflected planned learning sessions and efficient utilization of class time.
   DISORGANIZED A_____ B _____ C _____ D _____ E WELL PLANNED

10. Within the limitations of the facilities, the instructor provided maximal active participation time for all students.
    INACTIVE A_____ B _____ C _____ D _____ E VERY ACTIVE

11. The textbook and other instructional materials were of value in the course.
    NO BENEFIT A_____ B _____ C _____ D _____ E VERY VALUABLE

12. A safe learning environment was provided for the class.
    HARMFUL A_____ B _____ C _____ D _____ E VERY SAFE

INSTRUCTOR-STUDENT INTERACTION & RAPPORT

13. The instructor provided evaluative feedback concerning your skill development.
    UNINFORMATIVE A_____ B _____ C _____ D _____ E INFORMATIVE

14. The instructor was impartial and fair in dealing with students.
    UNFAIR A_____ B _____ C _____ D _____ E VERY FAIR

15. The instructor was interested in you and your skill development.
    DISINTERESTED A_____ B _____ C _____ D _____ E VERY INTERESTED

16. The instructor was understanding of and helpful to students who experienced difficulty acquiring the activity skills.
    NO HELP A_____ B _____ C _____ D _____ E VERY HELPFUL

GENERAL EVALUATION

17. Fun and enjoyment were experienced throughout the course.
    BORING A_____ B _____ C _____ D _____ E VERY ENJOYABLE

18. Based on your experience in this course, would you enroll in another physical education course and/or recommend activity courses to others?
    ABSOLUTELY NOT A_____ B _____ C _____ D _____ E DEFINITELY

19. Considering all aspects of the course, how would you rate this course?
    POOR A_____ B _____ C _____ D _____ E EXCELLENT

20. Considering all of the instructional aspects of this course, how would you rate the instructor?
    POOR A_____ B _____ C _____ D _____ E EXCELLENT

Figure 19.4 A student rating scale.
Source: Zakrajsek, Dorothy B. and Ronald R. Bos.
"Student Evaluations of Teaching Performance,"
Journal of Physical Education and Recreation, 49
(May 1978): 64–65.

Descriptive analysis uses the techniques of time analysis, time sampling, spot-checking, and event recording. A discussion of each technique follows.

Time analysis

Time analysis is useful for determining the amount of time spent on the various functions that teachers perform. Such functions include instructing students (demonstrating, explaining, questioning, etc.); class management (roll call, organizing students, distributing equipment, discipline, etc.); active student practice with feedback from the instructor; and student practice with no feedback from the instructor. A stopwatch is used to record the amount of time spent in each category. Simply record the time on the stopwatch under the appropriate category on the time analysis form in figure 19.5 and restart the stopwatch each time the teacher changes functions.

At the conclusion of the lesson, total the time in each category and divide by the total class time to obtain the percentage of time spent in each category. Then, analyze the results to see if your time has been spent in the best way. Individual functions such as roll call, explanations, etc. can also be analyzed by time analysis to determine where the time is going and changes can be made to eliminate the nonproductive use of time.

Another variation of time analysis is to record the amount of time spent in actual practice by an individual student. You may discover that while the class is engaged in what appears to be a large amount of practice time individual students spend a large amount of time waiting for a turn or "standing out in right field".

Time analysis can also be done for several brief periods of time spaced throughout a lesson. For example, three five-minute samples can provide a valid indication of the percentage of time spent in each type of behavior.[6] To obtain a percentage, merely divide by fifteen minutes instead of the total class time.

Time-sampling

In time-sampling, the observation session is divided into a number of equal intervals and a specified behavior is observed and recorded at the conclusion of each interval. For example, in a thirty-five-minute period there are thirty-five one-minute intervals or seventy thirty-second intervals. The number of intervals selected will depend upon the behavior to be sampled. Because time-sampling occurs only at the end of each interval, it saves considerable time. In fact, some time samples can even be done while teaching, such as checking on a student every five minutes to determine student involvement in activity.

The easiest kind of time-sampling involves only two categories—such as active or passive, productive or nonproductive. A student is selected and at the end of each interval, a check or tally indicates the behavior the student demonstrates. Several students can be observed by observing the first student during intervals 1, 4, 7, . . ., the second student during intervals 2, 5, 8 . . ., and the third student during intervals 3, 6, 9. . . . The intervals can be recorded on a tape recorder or a watch or stopwatch can be used to determine the end of each interval.

TIME ANALYSIS FORM

Class __Badminton__   Date __March 16__

Total class time __35 minutes__

Instruction	Management	Participation with feedback	Participation without feedback
4:30	3:06	6:18	2:06
1:10	1:24	3:50	6:00
1:10	2:50	9:08	8:06
2:00	1:50		
8:50	:46		
	9:56		
25.14%	25.43%	26.00%	22.89%

Suggestions for improvement

1. I should try to reduce the time spent organizing students during each management episode to less than 1 minute.
2. I should provide more feedback during student practice.

Figure 19.5 A time-analysis form.

To code a number of behaviors, select an average student and code what the student is doing at the end of each interval. To make it easier, you can code three minutes and rest three minutes, repeating the coding and resting throughout the period.

Figure 19.6 shows a time-sampling form designed by Anderson to determine how students are spending their time during a class session. It uses a five-second interval for coding. The categories include the following.

1. Performs motor activity—Plays game or sport, practices skill, does exercises or calisthenics, explores movement.

2. Receives information—Listens, watches demonstration, uses media, reads written material.

Sample Coding Form and Record

TIME SAMPLING OF A SINGLE STUDENT'S BEHAVIOR

RECORD A CHECK (✓) FOR EACH
5 SECONDS OF STUDENT ACTIVITY.

STUDENT'S NAME: Alice Smith
CLASS: Elementary Gymnastics

SEGMENT (3-MIN)	PERFORMS MOTOR ACTIVITY	RECEIVES INFORMATION	Gives INFORMATION OR ASSISTS	WAITS	RELOCATES	OTHER	NOTATIONS
I 9:00-9:03	✓✓✓ ③	✓✓✓✓✓ ✓✓✓✓ ✓✓✓✓✓ ✓✓✓✓ ⑳		✓✓✓✓✓ ✓✓✓✓ ⑩	✓✓ ②	✓ ①	Waited for teacher to begin Rec. info on class organization
II 9:06-9:09	✓✓✓✓✓ ✓✓✓ ⑧	✓✓✓✓✓ ✓✓✓✓✓ ✓✓✓✓✓ ✓✓✓✓✓ ✓✓ ㉓		✓✓ ②	✓✓✓ ③	✓ ①	End instruction / began tumbling and head stand
III 9:12-9:15	✓✓✓✓✓ ✓✓✓✓ ✓✓✓✓✓ ✓✓ ⑰	✓✓✓✓✓ ⑤	✓✓✓✓✓ ⑤	✓✓ ②	✓ ①	✓✓✓✓✓ ✓ ⑥	Cont'd. tumbling "Other" = replaced mats
IV 9:18-9:21	✓✓✓✓ ✓✓✓✓ ✓✓✓✓ ✓✓✓✓✓ ✓✓ ㉑	✓✓✓ ③	✓✓✓ ③	✓✓✓✓✓ ⑤		✓✓✓ ③	Performed on ropes
V 9:24-9:27	✓✓✓ ③	✓✓✓✓✓ ✓✓✓✓✓ ✓✓✓✓✓ ✓✓✓✓ ㉓		✓✓✓ ③	✓✓✓ ③	✓✓ ②	Recd. instruction on bars
VI 9:30-9:33	✓✓✓ ③	✓✓✓✓✓ ✓✓✓✓✓ ⑩		✓✓✓✓✓ ✓✓✓✓✓ ✓✓✓✓✓ ✓✓✓✓✓ ✓ ㉑		✓✓ ②	Waits turn on bars and performs
TOTALS	f = 56 %= 56/216 = 26%	f = 85 %= 85/216 = 39%	f = 8 %= 8/216 = 3%	f = 43 %= 43/216 = 19%	f = 9 %= 9/216 = 4%	f = 15 %= 15/216 = 7%	

<u>SUMMARY COMMENTS AND EVALUATION</u> (made by teacher of class)

Too much time spent waiting for teacher and getting organized.

Good activity levels on mats and ropes – too much waiting around on bars.

Overall, a greater proportion of time should be spent in performing activities.

Figure 19.6 A time-sampling form for student behavior.
Source: From Anderson, William G. *Analysis of Teaching Physical Education,* St. Louis, 1980, The C. V. Mosby Co.

3. Gives information or assists—Talks to teacher or student, demonstrates, spots.

4. Waits—Waits for turn, waits for game or drill to begin, etc.

5. Relocates—Moves from one place or activity area to another.

6. Other—Ties shoes, gets equipment, gets a drink, etc.

At the end of each three-minute period, notes can be recorded to help the teacher recall information explaining the recorded behaviors. At the end of the period, each column is totaled and a percentage calculated. The behavior is then analyzed and goals set for improving teaching.

Teacher behaviors can also be coded using time-sampling and the categories used for time analysis. An example of a time-sampling form for teacher behavior appears in figure 19.7.

Spot-checking

Spot-checking is time-sampling applied to a group.* It is useful when you want to know what most of the students in a group or class are doing. Spot-checking involves counting the number of students engaged in a particular behavior at the conclusion of a specified interval of time, such as every two or three minutes. Behaviors to be checked should be limited to two or three so that the spot-check takes only about ten seconds to do. The observer should scan from left to right each time and record the number of students who are engaged in the less-frequently occurring behavior. For example, in an actively involved class, count the inactive students. Then, subtract from the total number of students to get the number in the actively involved category. A sample spot-checking record is shown in figure 19.8.

Anderson suggests the use of the following categories for spot-checking: "active/inactive, on-task/off-task, safe/unsafe, attentive/unattentive, cooperative/disruptive, and interacting with others/isolated."[7] Siedentop indicates that 90 to 100 per cent of the students should be engaged in appropriate and productive behavior in order for teaching to be effective.[8]

At the conclusion of the class, calculate the percentage of students in each category by dividing each column total by the sum of the two or three columns. Analyze the data and plan changes for improving your teaching behavior.

Event recording

Event recording is merely tallying the frequency with which a given behavior occurs during a specified time period. It is done by identifying one person to observe (the teacher, an average student, etc.) and one or more behaviors to tally. The observer then proceeds to put

* Called Pla-chek by Siedentop.

TIME SAMPLING OF TEACHER BEHAVIOR

Class _____ Date _____

Total Class Time _____

Instructions: Record a check (✔) for each five seconds of teacher activity.

Segment (3 min.)	Instruction			Management Activities	Student Participation	
	Class	Group	Individual		With Feedback	Without Feedback
I						
II						
III						
IV						
V						
Totals						

Summary Comments and Evaluations:

Figure 19.7 A time-sampling form for teacher behavior.

down a mark each time the specified behavior occurs. For simple behaviors, a golf counter can be used to record frequency. Five three-minute intervals, spaced throughout the period, are usually adequate for event recording.

Event recording can be used to collect meaningful data on a wide variety of teacher or student behaviors. It produces a numerical value that can be converted into rate per minute. The rate per minute on different occasions can then be compared to determine whether improvement in the behavior has occurred. Event recording can be used to record items involving instruction, class management, student practice, use of first names, and feedback.

SPOT-CHECKING RECORD FORM

Class _Track and Field_   Date _May 10_

Time / Categories	Off-task	On-task active	On-task waiting	Comments
8:50	1	2	7	tieing shoes
8:56	0	3	7	
9:02	0	3	7	
9:08	3	2	5	talking
9:14	4	3	3	playing around
8:52	0	1	9	
8:58	0	1	9	
9:04	2	1	7	talking
9:10	5	1	4	talking
9:16	4	1	5	wandered off
8:54	0	4	6	
8:00	0	4	6	
9:06	0	4	6	
9:12	1	3	6	getting a drink
9:18	2	4	4	talking
Column Totals	22	37	91	
Total of All Columns		150		
Percent of Total	14.7%	24.7%	60.7%	

Rows labeled at left: High Jump (first 5 rows), Long Jump (next 5 rows), Hurdles (last 5 rows)

Summary Comments and Evaluation:

on-task, active = performing or helping
on-task, waiting = watching performance
off-task, = talking, wandering around,
            daydreaming

Students are spending a lot of time waiting
and seem bored, especially at end of period.

Figure 19.8 A sample spot-checking record.

Instruction

The extent to which the intended concepts are conveyed to the students can be determined by listing each concept and recording a check beside the concept each time it is mentioned by the teacher. An example of content evaluation is shown in figure 19.9.

Class management

Event recording can be used to tally the number of times the students have to be told how to assume a formation for roll call, drill, or game play. For each transition from one activity to another, only one teacher behavior should be emitted. A possible form for tallying management behavior is shown in figure 19.10. Time analysis for each management transition has also been included on this form.

Student practice

The number of practice trials a student attempts or the number of times a student touches the ball or uses a piece of equipment can be easily tallied as shown in figure 19.11. This can be done during practice drills, in lead-up games, or during actual game play. A list of skills or tasks to be accomplished with a check by each one attempted provides an overall view of the distribution of practice over the entire range of tasks inherent in the activity. Figure 19.12 shows how this can be done. Study the record to determine the adequacy and distribution of practice trials.

Feedback

Feedback has been defined as one of the key elements in the acquisition of psychomotor skills. Feedback also occurs regarding appropriate and inappropriate student behavior. Event recording can be used to record the extent to which both kinds of feedback occur. Both skill feedback and behavior feedback can be analyzed in the following ways by using the form in figure 19.13.

1. Rate of feedback per minute.

2. Ratio of positive to negative feedback.

3. Percent of specific feedback.

4. Percent of value feedback.

5. Percent of group-directed feedback.

6. Percent of nonverbal feedback.

7. Ratio of reinforcement of appropriate behavior to punishment of off-task behavior.

Sample Coding Form and Record

CONTENT OF TEACHER'S INSTRUCTIONS

A check (✓) is recorded each time the teacher refers to a listed item of content

TENNIS LESSON ON BACKHAND DRIVE	BASIC MOVEMENT LESSON ON THROWING
1. Entire stroke (general) ✓✓	1. Performance elements
2. Grip (general) ✓	— Eyes on target ✓
— ⅛ th turn ✓	— Feet apart ✓✓
— 45 % angle	— Rotate trunk
— other (list) too loose ✓	— Weight to back foot
3. Back swing (general)	— Elbow bent
— Short ✓	— Transfer weight to front foot
— Help with left hand ✓	— Point of release ✓✓
— Body pivot ✓✓✓✓✓✓✓✓	— Follow through ✓✓
— Elbow position ✓	2. Major concepts
— Other (list)	— Point of release affects direction ✓✓✓✓
4. Forward swing (general) ✓	— Transfer of weight gives power
— Arc of racket ✓	3. Common errors
— Point of contact ✓✓✓✓✓✓✓✓✓	— Facing front ✓✓✓✓✓✓✓✓✓
— Angle of contact	— No rotation ✓✓✓
— Other (list) eye on ball ✓✓✓✓✓	— Pushing
5. Follow through (general) ✓	4. Other (list)
— Racket head rises	forgot to snap wrist ✓✓
— Topspin	"stride" toward target ✓
— Other (list) smoothness ✓	angle of projection ✓
6. Common errors	
— Excessive body action	
— Chopping	
— Other (list) backswing too long ✓✓	
elbow push ✓	
7. Other (list)	
getting into position ✓✓✓✓✓✓✓	
anticipating flight of ball ✓✓✓✓ ✓✓✓✓	

SUMMARY COMMENTS AND EVALUATION	SUMMARY COMMENTS AND EVALUATION
I neglected the "follow through". I forgot to include "eye on ball" in initial plan, but covered it with individual students. "Positioning" and "anticipation" came up frequently, include in future presentations. Emphasized "point of contact" and forgot about "angle of contact".	Tried to cover too much with these third graders so purposely left out some things. Forgot to cover weight transfer = greater power. Too many students had to be corrected for facing front, emphasize sideward stance next time. Performance elements were covered at beginning, but not during later practice.

Figure 19.9 A sample content evaluation record.

Source: From Anderson, William G. *Analysis of Teaching Physical Education,* St. Louis, 1980, The C. V. Mosby Co.

RECORD OF TEACHER MANAGEMENT BEHAVIORS

Length of Each Episode	Number of Teacher Management Behaviors	Types of Management Behaviors
3:06	⊤⊦⊦ II	Organizing drills
1:24	III	Changing drills
2:50	IIII	Starting games
1:50	III	Rotating teams
:46	II	Ending class

Total Management Time = 9:56
Average Time Per Episode = abt 2 min
Average Number of Teacher Behaviors Per Episode = 3.8

Summary Comments and Evaluation:

I need to clarify my expectations so that I don't need to repeat instructions more than once.

Figure 19.10 A sample record of management behaviors.

STUDENT PRACTICE RECORD

Class *Soccer*   Date *Oct. 15*

Skills	Student #1 Period *I*	Student #2 Period *I*	Student #3 Period *I*	Student #4 Period ___
Number of times each student touches the ball	⊥⊥⊥ ⊥⊥⊥ ⊥⊥⊥ III	II	⊥⊥⊥ IIII	

Summary Comments and Evaluation:

Apparently student #2 rarely touches the ball. Perhaps I need to use smaller teams or rotate players so each student has an equal opportunity for skill development.

Figure 19.11 A sample record of student practice.

Each column of the form can be used separately or several columns can be recorded at once. Categories can be defined as follows:

1. Positive—A tone that conveys acceptance of a student's performance or behavior.

2. Negative—A tone that conveys rejection of a student's performance or behavior.

STUDENT PRACTICE RECORD

Class _Badminton_   Date _March 17_

Skills	Student #1 Period _1_	Student #2 Period _2_	Student #3 Period _2_	Student #4 Period ___
Short serve	①①①11①1	①①①11①①	①①①①①①① ①①①	
Overhead clear	1①11①1①①	①①①①①	①①①①①①①1 ①1①①	
Underhand clear	111①111①	①①①11①① 1①①1①1	①①①11①①①①	
Smash				
Drop				

Summary Comments and Evaluation:

I circled the successful attempts in a five-minute game. Student #1 needs to review basic skills. No student attempted drops or smashes. Perhaps I need to reteach the drop and smash.

Figure 19.12 A record of student trials on key skills.

3. General—Feedback with no specific information given about the skill or behavior.

4. Specific—Feedback with specific information given about how to perform the behavior or skill.

5. Value—Feedback that tells why a specific behavior or skill should be done in a certain way.

EVENT RECORDING OF BEHAVIOR OR SKILL FEEDBACK

____ Skill Feedback
✓ Behavior Feedback

Five-minute Event Recording	Tone Pos./Neg.		Kind General/Specific Value	To Whom Individual/Group		Skill-Feedback Type Verbal	Visual and Verbal	Kinesthetic and Verbal	Behavior-Feedback Type Reinforces Appropriate Behavior	Punishes Off-Task Behaviors
I	II	卌 I		卌	II			I	卌
II	I	卌 卌		II					II
III		III		卌 III II	I			II	卌 III
IV	II	卌		II	I			I	II
V	III	II		卌 卌	I				卌 卌
Totals	8	26		29	5			4	27

Summary:

Feedback per minute =
Ratio of positive to negative feedback = 8/26
Percent of specific feedback =
Percent of feedback that explains why =
Percent of group-directed feedback = 14.7%
Percent of nonverbal feedback =
Ratio of reinforcement to punishment = 4/27

Comments and Evaluation:

Feedback is generally negative in tone and directed toward individuals. I need to look for what students do well and reinforce them, especially in group situations.

Figure 19.13 Event recording of behavior or skill feedback.

6. Individual—Feedback to one student.

7. Group—Feedback to more than one student.

8. Verbal—Feedback that is only verbal.

9. Visual and verbal—Feedback that demonstrates how the skill or behavior should be performed.

10. Kinesthetic and verbal—Feedback that uses touch or manipulation of body parts to correct the movement (such as spotting in gymnastics).

11. Reinforces appropriate behavior—Feedback that rewards appropriate behavior.

12. Punishes off-task behavior—Feedback that is nonreinforcing or punishing for inappropriate behavior.

Creating your own descriptive system

A descriptive system generally involves the following: (1) a single behavior focus, (2) a definition of categories, (3) an observation and coding system, and (4) reliability.

The behavior focus

Select a single teaching component for analysis. *Trying to analyze too much can defeat your system.* Define the component so you will know what is and what is not included in the behavior focus.

Definition of categories

Categories within the behavioral focus must be defined so that any observable behavior can be assigned to only one category. Examples of behaviors falling into each category should be provided.

An observation and coding system

Decide whether to use time analysis, time-sampling, spot-checking, or event recording. Develop a form for recording the data.

Reliability

Reliability results when two observers obtain similar results after independently rating the same lesson or when one observer obtains the same results on two separate occasions from a videotaped recording. When this occurs, it tells us that the definitions of the behavior categories are sufficiently clear to ensure that behaviors are recorded accurately by the observer and reflect the actual behavior that occurred during the lesson.

Interaction analysis

Interaction analysis provides objective feedback about the type and quality of teacher-student interaction. Most of the interaction analysis systems have been based on verbal interaction and nearly all of them are based on teacher dominance of instruction. The best-known tool for interaction analysis is the Flanders system.[9] A number of adaptations of the Flanders system have been produced. However, they made the system even more cumbersome to use for teacher improvement.

Anderson identified a simpler method for recording the interaction of teachers and students.[10] It is based on Morgenegg's findings that interaction in physical education classes focuses on the three behaviors of teacher solicitation of movement, student movement responses, and teacher reactions to the movement responses.[11] A sample coding form is shown in figure 19.14. Each entry shows who solicited the response (the teacher or the student), who reacted and how (motor activity, verbal activity, or other behavior), and the reaction caused by the behavior. For example, the teacher asks students to get ready to shoot and the students respond; or the teacher asks a student to shoot an arrow, the student responds by shooting, and the teacher replies, "Good!"

Coding should include four or more five-minute coding periods. At the conclusion of the lesson, evaluate the amount and direction of the interactions. Are all solicitations initiated by the teacher or are students encouraged to seek out solutions to their problems? Is there a balance between teacher-directed instruction and student-directed instruction? Does the teacher react enough? Or too much?

Step 3. Use the appropriate techniques to record information

The best evaluation technique is the one that provides precise feedback related to your specific teaching goal. Table 19.2 shows possible evaluation techniques for the teaching goals and behaviors we specified in step 1.

Since only a few events can be recorded during each lesson, a plan should be formulated to utilize the most effective techniques for the objectives of the specific lesson. A sample evaluation plan for a lesson is shown in figure 19.15. Keep the plan simple. Don't try to do the impossible. Two or three evaluation techniques at a time is probably as many as can be checked accurately.

Step 4. Evaluate or interpret the data

So far, research has been unable to find one best way to teach. Therefore, you may need to experiment to determine the best combination of teaching skills to create the results you want with your particular students and situation.

The major purpose of the evaluation is to determine how close the actual teaching behavior matches up with the intended behavior. This can be done by referring back to the plan established in step 3. Some questions to ask yourself are:

1. What teaching behaviors are satisfactory?

2. What changes in teaching behaviors might improve student learning?

Sample Coding Form and Record

TEACHER - STUDENT INTERACTION

CLASS: Jr. H.S. Archery   TEACHER: Dick Martin

CODES: (T) Teacher, (S) Student
(M) Motor activity
(V) Verbal activity or response
(O) Other behavior

SOLICIT	RESPOND	REACT
T	S o	
T	S o	
T	S o	T
S	T v	
T	S m	
T	S m	
T	S m	T
T	S m	T
		T m
		T m
		T
T	S o	
T	S m	
T	S m	
T	S m	
T	S v	T
T	S m	T m
S	T v	
T	S m	
T	S m	T
T	S m	T m
		T m
		T m
T	S o	
T	S o	
T	S v	
T	S m	T
T	S m	T
T	S m	
T	S m	
T	S m	T m
		T m
S	T o	
T	S m	
T	S m	
T	S m	
T	S o	
T	S o	

TOTALS:

SOLICITATIONS: 32					
By teacher: 29			By students: 3		
of verb.	mot.	oth.	of verb.	mot.	oth.
2	19	8	2	1	0

RESPONSES: 32					
By teacher: 3			By students: 29		
to verb.	mot.	oth.	to verb.	mot.	oth.
2	0	1	2	19	8

REACTIONS: 16					
By teacher: 16			By students: 0		
to verb.	mot.	oth.	to verb.	mot.	oth.
0	15	1	0	0	0

MOST COMMON PATTERNS: $T \rightarrow S_M = 13$
$T \rightarrow S_M \rightarrow T = 6$
$T \rightarrow S_O = 8$
$T_M = 8$

SUMMARY COMMENTS AND EVALUATION (by observed teacher)
I do virtually all the soliciting and reacting; the students do almost all the responding.
I focus on eliciting student motor responses - which is OK - but I virtually never elicit verbal responses from students - which is not OK.
I seem to be reasonably conscientious about reacting to what students do.
Overall, I'm concerned that I seem to start (solicit) and end (react) all the interactions.

Figure 19.14 A sample coding form for teacher-student interaction.
Source: From Anderson, William G. *Analysis of Teaching Physical Education,* St. Louis, 1980, The C. V. Mosby Co.

Table 19.2 Goals, behaviors, and suggested evaluation techniques

Goals	Teacher behavior	Suggested evaluation techniques
Teacher warmth	Calls student by name.	Event recording
	Provides more positive than negative feedback.	Event recording
	Interacts with students.	Student evaluation of instructor Interaction analysis
Teacher expectancy	Facilitates achievement of instructional objectives.	Student performance
	Facilitates improvement in student learning.	Student improvement
	Selects tasks in terms of student abilities.	Student evaluation of teacher Informal analysis
Task-oriented climate	Helps students spend a large amount of time in productive behavior.	Time-analysis Spot-check Time-sampling
	Provides feedback on behavior.	Event recording
	Decreases time spent on class management.	Time-analysis Time-sampling
Effective instruction	Provides appropriate model and explanation.	Informal analysis Event recording
	Provides appropriate feedback for skills.	Event recording
	Provides opportunity for student practice.	Time-analysis Time-sampling Number of practice trials/person

3. Which changes are practical?

4. Which one or two changes in teacher behavior would result in the most important changes in student performance?

5. What will you have to do to implement these changes?

6. What target goal for the change would be indicative of a successful change effort? (i.e., call ten students by name each period)

Anderson explains some problems with attempting to interpret the match between your actual and your intended behaviors:

> There will be a natural tendency to be pleased when reality matches your plans and to be disheartened when there is a mismatch. . . . That's as it should be, most of the time—but not always. There are times when unfolding events in class signify the need for a change of plan in midstream. A teacher who is tuned in to such signals is likely to digress from his or her original plan. In such cases the record will show a mismatch. Is that bad? There are times when unfolding events in class signify the need for a change of plan but the

AN EVALUATION PLAN

Lesson Plan	Evaluation Plan	Data
Objectives		
1. Students will hit three out of five balls pitched to them during drill.	Students record number of successful hits during a specified time period.	
2. Students will hit 100 percent of the times at bat in one-swing game.	Tally number of students at bat and number of successful hits.	
Teaching and Learning Activities		
1. Demonstrate and explain batting.	Event recording of content of teacher's instruction.	
2. Pepper drill for maximum participation with teacher feedback.	Event recording of student trials during drill and skill feedback of teacher.	
3. One-swing softball game for application to game situation.	Event recording of student trials and successes during game.	
Specific Teacher Goals		
1. Reduce management time.	Time analysis of management time.	
Summary Comments and Evaluation		

Figure 19.15 A sample evaluation plan.

teacher is *not* tuned in to such signals, and so he or she plows ahead as originally planned. (Some teachers who *are* tuned in plow ahead anyway.) Such behavior will produce a record that shows a close match with the original plan. Is that good?

Sometimes, in the midst of a lesson you come up with a brilliant idea that you hadn't thought of before. You try it out and it works. So you continue to pursue it and in the process abandon your original intentions. The lesson turns out to be a smashing success. The record shows an enormous mismatch. So? . . .

Interpreting matches and mismatches can be tricky business. Be careful.[12]

Step 5. Make changes and reevaluate

An attempt should be made to incorporate the selected changes into your teaching repertoire. Make sure you do not try to make more than one or two changes at a time. Reteach the same or a similar lesson, concentrating on the intended changes. Reevaluate the lesson to determine whether or not the changes produced the desired results. If not, select a new procedure and try again.

An example of teacher evaluation

Step 1

During a softball unit, the goals selected for evaluation included: (1) to increase student skill achievement and (2) to reduce class management time.

Step 2

The specific evaluation techniques selected were (1) student achievement, (2) time-analysis and event recording of management time, (3) event recording of student practice, and (4) event recording of skill feedback.

Step 3

Student assistants were used to record student achievement and practice. Several lessons were videotaped for evaluation of management time and skill feedback. A sample evaluation plan for one of the lessons is shown in figure 19.15.

Step 4

The results of the data showed that students were spending too much time practicing without the help of teacher feedback and the feedback when given was primarily verbal. With regard to class management, the analysis showed that the teacher had to tell students several times before they proceeded to do what they had been told.

Step 5

The teacher decided to use a golf counter to keep a tally of the number of feedback attempts during one period each day in order to increase the frequency of feedback. Later, an event recording of skill feedback also showed an increase in the number of nonverbal feedback attempts.

The second result of the evaluation occurred in class management. The teacher told the students what they were to do, asked several questions to determine whether or not they understood, and then refrained from repeating instructions. Students were timed to determine how long it took to get into the next formation, drill, or game, and feedback provided on the length of time it took. The result was a rapid decrease in management time.

Questions and suggested activities

1. Utilize two different evaluation techniques to evaluate yourself as a teacher. Report on what you did and what you learned about your teaching. Tell what you will do to become a more effective teacher.

2. This is the first year that you have been the department chairperson of physical education in your school. It has been your observation that teachers have become lax in their duties and decide that it might be because of a lack of evaluation. What methods of evaluation might you consider implementing to improve the situation?

3. Develop an evaluation plan for a lesson using appropriate evaluation techniques.

4. Role-play the following situation: The school board wants to implement an accountability plan in which teachers are evaluated strictly on student performance.

Suggested readings

Allard, Ray and Frank Rife. "A Teacher-Directed Model of Peer Supervision in Physical Education." *The Physical Educator* 37 (May 1980):89–94.

Ebel, H. C. and Howard Berg. "Student Evaluations in Physical Education: Role of Course Type and Grade Expectation." *The Physical Educator* 33 (March 1976): 13–17.

Hall, W. Dianne. "Improving Instruction Through Positive Performance Evaluation." *The Physical Educator* 37 (March 1980): 7–10.

Martin, Thomas P. "A Case and Procedures for Student Evaluation." *The Physical Educator* 30 (May 1973):79–82.

Quarterman, Jerome. "An Observational System for Observing the Verbal and Nonverbal Behaviors Emitted by Physical Educators and Coaches." *The Physical Educator* 37 (March 1980):15–20.

Siedentop, Daryl. "O.S.U. Teacher Behavior Rating Scale." *Journal of Physical Education and Recreation* 46 (February 1975): 45.

Soper, Barlow. "Can Students Evaluate Teaching Effectiveness?" *National Forum: The Phi Kappa Phi Journal* (Spring 1980): 20.

Templin, Thomas J. "Taking the Blinders Off." *The Physical Educator* 36 (October 1979): 123–26.

Thomas, Nelson. "Thoughts on Teacher Evaluation." *The Physical Educator* 37 (December 1980): 176–78.

The Process of Curriculum Design

What is a curriculum?

Bain describes the physical education curriculum as follows:

The physical education curriculum is an overall plan for the total physical education program, which is intended to guide teachers in conducting educational activities for a specific group of students. The curriculum specifies the program content in terms of objectives and activities.[1]

What is the relationship between the curriculum and instruction?

The curriculum should be a reflection of the society within which it operates. It should take into account the philosophy of that society, as well as knowledges handed down by that society that have an influence on students and how they learn.

The teacher becomes the intermediary whereby the curriculum is translated into the instructional methods and strategies that influence student learning. The personality and abilities of the teacher will, of necessity, influence his or her ability to translate curricular content into student learning.

The students' interests and abilities will, in turn, influence their input into the instructional system. Unit figure 5.1 demonstrates graphically how this interaction occurs.

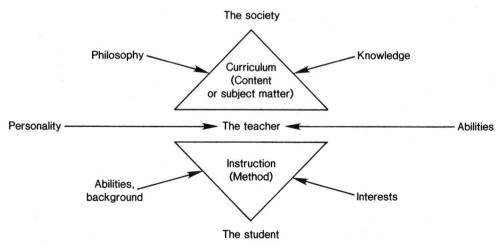

Unit Figure 5.1 The relationship of curriculum and instruction.

What is curriculum design?

Curriculum design is the creation of a plan of action that eliminates guesswork and translates educational knowledge and philosophy into teaching methodology by establishing principles for guiding the faculty in all phases of the program.

Why is curriculum design important?

Of the problems confronting the public schools, the 1981 Gallup Poll listed poor curriculum as third.[2] The National Commission on the Reform of Secondary Education stated: "Our large city school systems are on the verge of complete collapse. Two decades ago the cities operated the best school systems in the United States. Today these schools are at the bottom in academic accomplishment."[3]

Parents and students are becoming increasingly dissatisfied with curricular offerings because many programs lack an orderly plan for achieving the objectives of physical education. One reason for this is that the basic needs of students and, therefore, the purposes of education are changing as the culture undergoes serious modifications.

Throughout history, social patterns and values have changed almost imperceptibly, from generation to generation. Preparing youth for the responsibilities of adulthood was a relatively simple matter. With the acceleration of social change in the twentieth century, schools are preparing youth for adulthood in a society not yet envisioned by its members. As Hawley stated

> It's not a question of whether or not to change, but whether or not we can control the way we are changing. We are living in an *Alice in Wonderland* world where you have to run just to stay where you are. To get anywhere you have to run even faster than that. The pieces on the chess board keep changing and the rules are never the same.[4]

As educators, then, we must accept fundamental differences in the role of the curriculum we have considered to be appropriate in recent years. In a society that is characterized by change, it is imperative that the curriculum change to meet the needs of the learner in a constantly changing environment.

Other factors that force curriculum change are cuts in financial resources, outdated and inadequate facilities and equipment, changes in student populations, reduction in and lack of turnover of faculty with the resulting need to retrain those available, changes in student needs and interests, and other environmental and technological changes.

Progress is not possible without change. However, all change does not result in progress or improvement. In fact, some changes may be worse than no change at all. It is essential, then, that change efforts be carefully considered and evaluated before implementing them on a full-scale basis. At the same time, schools that continue to lag behind in curriculum development may be forced to implement changes not of their own choosing.

Curriculum change should be based on a careful, well-informed evaluation of past, present, and future, with consideration of the best thinking of professionals who have researched and tested each proposal. That which has proven effective should be retained. That which has proven ineffective should be discarded. New ideas should be tried on a small scale (perhaps with only one or two classes) before being adopted.

Planning and preparation are the keys to a successful and meaningful program. Traditionally, physical educators have made two mistakes with regard to curriculum design. They have either just let things happen in the "curriculum," or have looked around for a good curriculum and adopted it, whether or not it fit their particular needs. Lawton described the problems of curriculum design as follows:

> If we wish to be completely frank we would probably say that the typical curriculum is a mess—an uneasy compromise between traditions (of doubtful pedigree) and various pressures for change; a mixture of high-sounding aims and classroom practice which could not possibly attain the aims and sometimes flatly contradicts them. . . .
>
> One of the problems of curriculum, as with many other aspects of education, is the enormous gap between theory and practice. . . . The difference between what teachers suggest should happen and what can be observed in the classroom, the gap between educational theory as taught in colleges and universities and the "commonsense" practical approach of teachers in schools.[5]

The task of the curriculum designer, then, is to carefully merge cultural elements, both old and new, into a curriculum that fits the existing students, school, and community. Since the society in which we live is in a state of perpetual change, a continuous, systematic process of evaluating and designing the curriculum is essential so that the objectives of the program can be realized.

Steps in curriculum design

Unit 5 assists the curriculum designer through the steps of the curriculum process. The steps are presented here as an overview of the entire process.

1. Establish a curriculum committee.
2. Study the bases of curriculum planning and determine the philosophy, aims, and objectives of physical education.
3. Decide on an appropriate curriculum model.
4. Determine the scope of the program.
5. Determine sequencing.

6. Schedule.
7. Implement the program.
8. Evaluate and revise.

In order to make the learning meaningful, it is suggested that you actually form a curriculum committee, choose a school with which to work, and study these chapters as a basis for designing a curriculum.

In chapter 20, the role of the administration in stimulating curricular improvement is discussed. The makeup of various curriculum committees is then identified. A number of resources for the curriculum committee are also included.

Chapter 21 reviews the bases or foundations on which the curriculum is built. Many of them were discussed in detail in units 1 and 2. Their implications for the curriculum are presented here.

Chapter 22 describes commonly used curriculum patterns in physical education. It also points out the importance of reviewing the research and current trends and innovations as a basis for making curriculum decisions.

Chapter 23 identifies the process for selecting activities for inclusion in the curriculum. A well-balanced program that meets the objectives established for the program is essential.

Chapter 24 discusses the criteria for determining the sequence of instruction for the activities selected in chapter 23. Two kinds of sequencing are discussed— the sequencing of activities by grade level and the sequencing of skills and knowledges within each unit of instruction.

A number of scheduling considerations are presented for review in chapter 25. The chapter also outlines the procedures for scheduling.

The processes for evaluating a curriculum are presented in chapter 26, along with a variety of techniques that can be used for that purpose. A program evaluation of the existing curriculum could be done by making a visit to the school selected for the curriculum project.

It is suggested that the curriculum committee present their curriculum to the Board of Education in a simulated board meeting in which other students assume the roles of board members, superintendent, principals, other faculty members and local citizens.

As indicated in units 3 and 5, the next step after evaluation is to follow the feedback loops back to the beginning of the cycle and examine our objectives and instructional programs to determine how we can improve them through the new information gained.

Suggested readings for unit 5

Burnstine, Deidre. "On Considering Curriculum Design." *Curriculum Improvement in Secondary School Physical Education* (Washington, D.C.: American Association for Health Physical Education Recreation, 1973), p. 67–74.
Carmichael, Larry. "Research Into Practice." *Journal of Physical Education and Recreation* 49 (March 1978): 29–30.

The Administration and the Curriculum Committee

Study stimulators

1. What is the role of administrators in curriculum design? Of teachers? Of other resource persons? Why are all of these important?
2. Should students be involved in curriculum design? Why or why not?
3. Who should be included on a curriculum committee?
4. What resources will be of most value to you in designing a curriculum for your particular school?

The role of administrators in curriculum design

The instructional program, or curriculum, is the most important responsibility of school administrators. All other tasks are subservient to it. The National Association of Secondary School Principals has listed five challenges that administrators should consider in attempting to upgrade the curriculum in physical education.

Challenge I: To use all of the resources of this burgeoning discipline to create instructional programs that will contribute to the growth and well-being—intellectual, physical, emotional—of *ALL* young people.

Challenge II: To assemble a teaching corps whose professional competences range over the entire discipline in its modern form, and then to arrange assignments that will permit the full use of the special knowledge and scholarship of each individual teacher.

Challenge III: To equalize opportunities and services available to girls with those provided for boys—and, in other respects, to produce a better balance in the amount of time and other resources devoted to the various significant groups (in PE terms) in the student body.

Challenge IV: To apply—directly or by adaptation—the many innovative instructional practices that have come into use in other curriculum areas.

Challenge V: To encourage school authorities to break out of traditional systems and adopt new curricular methodologies and substance.[1]

Administrators provide the leadership required for curriculum initiation, planning, implementation, evaluation, and revision. This leadership may occur directly or indirectly. Direct leadership occurs when administrators help teachers assess program needs, define goals and objectives, and evaluate the quality of the curriculum.

Once a decision has been made to study or revise the curriculum, administrators select a curriculum committee and present them with goals and guidelines for action. Released time should be arranged for committee meetings and provision should be made for adequate resources, including equipment and supplies, secretarial help, and the assistance of experts and consultants if needed. Administrators should continue to work closely with the committee by providing input based on experience and knowledge and by reviewing proposals for new programs.

An administrator should preside at faculty meetings when the changes are presented, present proposals to the appropriate school officials, and interpret the program to the public. Administrators are responsible for facilitating the implementation of the program after it has been approved and directing the development of curriculum materials.

Indirectly, administrators have the responsibility to provide a climate in which personal and group growth can occur. This requires the establishment of (1) effective communication, (2) time and resources for personal and group study, and (3) freedom to experiment with new ideas.

Effective communication

Communication is facilitated by grouping teachers who have similar concerns in the same area of the building where they can interact in small, supportive groups. Communications between teachers and administrators are increased when administrators work with teachers and not over them.

Time and resources for personal and group study

Teachers who have the time and resources available for studying and experimenting with new ideas and practices generally are more innovative than teachers who perceive little support for innovation. A teachers' study area with books and journals, opportunities to attend conferences or visit innovative schools, regular discussions about innovations during faculty meetings, and the provision for clerical help motivate teachers to continue their personal study of new ideas.

Freedom to experiment with new ideas

Freedom evolves from the confidence of administrators in the ability of teachers to resolve their own problems. When administrators are willing to listen to the viewpoints and ideas of others, teachers have the freedom to experiment with new ideas and programs.

The role of teachers in curriculum design

Teachers have a responsibility to study and keep abreast of changes in the field of physical education and in how it can be learned most effectively. They should take the opportunity to attend conventions and in-service meetings, visit other schools, read professional journals, and discuss ideas with other teachers in the school and in other schools. Whenever possible, teachers should serve on committees to develop instructional materials, write curriculum guides, and evaluate and revise curricular offerings. Released time should be provided for these types of professional development.

The curriculum committee

Although program development has often been a product of individual teachers, administrators, or supervisors, experience shows that a curriculum cooperatively planned by all of those involved in its implementation will yield the best results. The committee should include the following individuals.

1. Administrators, who can provide insights into time schedules, budgets, facilities, resources, and other administrative details.

2. Teachers, both men and women, who represent the grass roots level, work daily with students, and know what will or will not work.

3. Students, who can provide information regarding their own interests, obstacles to desired learning, relevance of learning experiences, and recommended extraclass programs.

4. Parents and community leaders, who can provide varied, fresh ideas. These people may feel more qualified to serve on subcommittees.

5. Curriculum specialists, who can provide expertise in the process of curriculum design as well as ideas that have worked well in other schools.

6. Clerical help, who can record, type, copy, collate, and distribute information should also be made available to the committee.

Persons chosen to serve on curriculum committees should be representative of and have the respect and support of their peers and of the administration. Care should be taken to keep committees small enough so that a consensus can be achieved and the work can get done. Members should be rotated periodically to avoid fatigue and to promote a fresh attack

A curriculum committee should include
administrators, teachers, parents, and students,
as well as a curriculum consultant.

on the problems at hand. The secret of group action is that when several people of various backgrounds join together in a group effort, synergy occurs; that is, the result is greater than the sum of its members.

Several kinds of curriculum committees might exist depending upon the grade level or extent of the curriculum project. A coordinating committee should be selected to act as a clearing house of ideas and suggestions. In smaller school systems, each member of the physical education staff might take part on this committee. In larger school systems, volunteers or representatives from the various schools make up the committee. The functions of the coordinating committee are as follows.

1. Establishes the overall philosophy of physical education for the school district or school.

2. Explores satisfactions and dissatisfactions with the present program (survey, interviews, etc.)

3. Schedules meetings, establishes sequence of work, and coordinates activities of all committees.

4. Selects members for subcommittee assignments.

5. Serves as a clearing house for proposals from subcommittees.

6. Provides for evaluation of the curriculum.

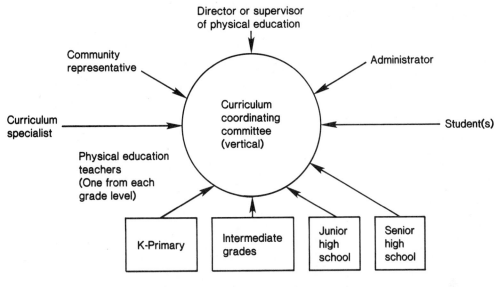

Director or supervisor
of physical education

Community
representative

Administrator

Curriculum
specialist

Curriculum
coordinating
committee
(vertical)

Student(s)

Physical education
teachers
(One from each
grade level)

| K-Primary | Intermediate grades | Junior high school | Senior high school |

Grade-level subcommittees (Horizontal)

Figure 20.1 A possible organization for a
district curriculum development program.

Subcommittees can be organized to give input at specific grade levels or for input into intramural, extramural, and athletic program needs. Such committees should be temporary and might consist of the following personnel.

1. Elementary—A principal, nonphysical education teacher(s), parent, elementary physical education specialists.

2. Secondary—Physical education teachers, coaches, principal, community representative, parents, students.

The functions of the subcommittees might be to:

1. Establish specific grade-level objectives.

2. Establish scope and sequence of programs for each grade level.

3. Make teaching suggestions, including specific lesson and/or unit plans.

A possible organization for a district curriculum development program is shown in figure 20.1

Since curriculum development is a time-consuming process, care should be taken to not place an unreasonable demand on any person's time and effort. Released time or pay for extra work should be considered for committee members.

Resources for the curriculum committee

Persons responsible for curriculum design should become aware of the many resources available, such as people, organizations, commercial publications, model programs and facilities, and media.

People

Curriculum and instruction specialists at colleges and universities are often more than willing to be of service as consultants. If none are available, try writing to authors of curriculum articles in professional journals.

Organizations

Two national organizations that can provide tremendous resources are The American Alliance of Health, Physical Education, Recreation and Dance (AAHPERD), and the President's Council on Physical Fitness and Sports. The AAHPERD has three excellent position papers outlining guidelines for physical education. They are:

Essentials of a Quality Elementary School Physical Education Program

Guidelines for Secondary School Physical Education

Guide to Excellence for Physical Education in Colleges and Universities

They also publish *The Research Quarterly for Exercise and Sport*; the *Journal of Physical Education, Recreation and Dance*; *Completed Research in Health, Physical Education, and Recreation*; and a number of other pertinent publications.

The President's Council provides speakers, public relations help, and bulletins on various areas of interest to physical educators.

A large number of national agencies also have materials or journals of value to physical education. Check your university or local library for addresses and publications. A few of them include:

Amateur Athletic Union

Association for Supervision and Curriculum Development

Athletic Institute

American Medical Association

American Heart Association

American Red Cross

American College of Sports Medicine

National Association of Secondary School Principals

National Education Association

National Federation of State High School Athletic Associations

Society of State Directors of Health, Physical Education and Recreation

At the state level, the state department of education will often provide consultants, in-service activities, conferences, clinics, and workshops. Many states also have a state course of study or curriculum guide. State education associations and state Associations of Health, Physical Education, Recreation and Dance can be of inestimable service.

Commercial publications

Textbooks and physical education equipment and media are available through various commercial companies. University libraries, salespeople, and school catalogs can be useful in helping you locate these sources.

Model programs and facilities

Professional journals and associations and state departments of education can provide a lead on programs or facilities you can visit or write to for ideas.

Media

Hardware catalogs are usually available at district offices. For software, write to AAHPERD, the NASPE Media Resource Center,[2] or check commercial catalogs.

Questions and suggested activities

1. Talk to a number of girls and boys from a junior or senior high school that is considered to have a good program of physical education. Ask them what they like or dislike about the program and whether or not they have any input into curriculum considerations.

2. Review several articles in the *Journal of Physical Education, Recreation and Dance*; *The Physical Educator*; *Quest*; or *The Research Quarterly for Exercise and Sport*. Tell how these articles can help you in curriculum design.

3. Visit a curriculum committee meeting in your college or university or in a local school district. Who was on the committee? What kind of input did each one give to the committee?

4. You have taught physical education in the local high school for one year and have been asked to chair a curriculum committee for upgrading the physical education program, K–12, in your local district. You are located in a small rural community district that includes one senior high school, one junior high school, and two small elementary schools. How will you go about selecting your curriculum committee? What characteristics will you look for in each member of your team? What goals would you want your group to reach?

5. You are the department chairperson at Lakeview Junior High School. You receive students from four different elementary schools, causing a varied background among incoming seventh graders. Each elementary school program has its own emphasis. Some stress skill development, some movement experiences, some fitness, some social skills. It seems that the first year in junior high school is somewhat wasted in that it is used to prepare the students for the eighth- and ninth-grade programs. How will you attempt to solve this problem?

6. You have been a physical education teacher in Jefferson County School District for eighteen years. There are four high schools and eight junior high schools in the district. The superintendent has just hired you as a specialist in physical education to help improve the present curriculum and teaching techniques. The first assignment you are given is to upgrade the curriculum for the district. How will you proceed?

Suggested readings

Luxmore, James. "An Administrator Looks at Physical Education." *Journal of Physical Education and Recreation* 52 (February 1981): 31.

The Bases of Curriculum Design

Study stimulators

1. What factors should be considered before designing a curriculum?
2. Describe the influence of each of the bases of curriculum design.

In order to be effective, a curriculum must be built on a foundation that considers the context within which the curriculum will be implemented. This consideration should include the following: (1) a sound philosophy and objectives of education and physical education, (2) social forces, (3) students' needs and interests, and (4) the subject matter and how it is learned. An in-depth study of each of these areas was presented in units 1 and 2.

Philosophy and objectives

The greatest variable influencing the curriculum is the philosophy of the physical education faculty. If the faculty is comfortable with a traditional activity-based curriculum, then that is what the curriculum will be. Geiger and Kizer recommend that teachers gain an awareness of their philosophy in order to form a philosophical base on which to build a meaningful program. To accomplish this, they suggest that teachers grapple with the following issues:

> What is the purpose of education?; what is physical education and how does it relate to education in general?; what is the role of a teacher?, should the learning situation be teacher centered or student centered?; is the purpose of physical education to teach sport skills or is there another purpose?; what is the humanistic physical education?; is conceptual teaching possible in physical education.[1]

The board of education is generally responsible for establishing the overall philosophy and goals of the schools within their jurisdiction. This may be accomplished through a written statement or through their actions over a period of time. These general goals should be broken down into subgoals and performance objectives that are consistent with the general educational goals. Physical education goals and objectives should be formulated in the same manner. Unless the goals are explicit, they will have no value in the curriculum.

Hass listed some guidelines for evaluating goals and objectives as follows:

1. Have the goals of the curriculum or teaching plan been clearly stated, and are they used by the teachers and students in choosing content, materials, and activities for learning?

2. Have the teachers and students engaged in student-teacher planning in defining the goals and in determining how they will be implemented?

3. Do some of the planned goals relate to the society or the community in which the curriculum will be implemented or the teaching will be done?

4. Do some of the planned goals relate to the needs, purposes, interests, and abilities of the individual learner?

5. Are the planned goals used as criteria in selecting and developing learning activities and materials of instruction?

6. Are the planned goals used as criteria in evaluating learning achievement and in the further planning of learning subgoals and activities?[2]

Social forces

A large number of social forces affect the lives of students and the school curriculum. These include: (1) governmental activity; (2) cultural forces; (3) research; (4) educational leadership; and (5) community needs, interests, and resources.

Governmental activity

Legislation at both state and federal levels, judicial decisions, and government regulations and supervisory powers, including the power to allot or withdraw funds, play a major role in the change process. Legislation can be one of the quickest forms of change. For example, by reducing the state per pupil expenditure, schools can be forced to cut back on their programs. On the other hand, when legislation is enacted without public support, the schools or the public may resist government attempts to enforce compliance. Such was the case in some schools with P.L. 94–142 and Title IX.

Judicial decisions, such as those on legal liability, integration, and busing, have also forced changes upon the schools as indicated in chapter 4.

State boards of education or departments of education sometimes provide leadership for promoting educational change. However, many departments are too small to promote all of the changes needed.

Cultural forces

A great number and variety of cultural forces affect the schools. Among these are war, with its demand for increased physical fitness; television, with its sedentary life-style; racial inequality, integration, and forced busing; and many others.

Students demand to make educational decisions on courses and teachers. Teachers strike for shorter days, no extracurricular assignments, and regulations on class size and student loads. Parents demand the addition or removal of certain courses, instructional materials, and extracurricular activities.

Two other groups have a direct influence on curriculum change. The first is private philanthropic foundations. Their major contribution is in providing teachers with released time from school to develop and promote innovative instructional programs. The second group includes commercial enterprises such as textbook publishers and instructional materials producers. These organizations have a powerful effect on the curriculum in that changes are quickly adopted with each new product. However, once adopted, they can be a deterrent for change because of the loss of revenue from continual revision of the product.

Research

Researchers, often housed in universities and commercial institutions, conduct basic research that is often rejected by teachers because of a failure by researchers to make their findings adaptable to the school setting. Teachers, who could do applied research that is directly applicable to the schools, often lack the time, training, or money to do so. A solution might be a joint arrangement in which researchers and teachers work together to identify and investigate problems and alternatives for resolving them.

Educational leadership

Most of the major innovations in the public schools are introduced by administrators and teachers within the schools. Teachers' strikes, accrediting agencies, and local education associations also play a direct role. In their role as teacher-trainer institutions, colleges and universities assume an indirect form of educational leadership.

Community needs, interests, and resources

A survey of the community can provide information concerning the following:

1. The historical background of the community.

2. The philosophy of community members and their willingness to support education and physical education programs.

3. The economic and tax base factors of the community that affect school finances and, therefore, facilities, class sizes, and instructional supplies, as well as the needs and interests of students.

4. The social, cultural, and political factors—such as population and prospective changes in population, ethnic populations, social and cultural attitudes, religious orientation, and political pressures and form of government.

5. Geographical and locational factors, including regional factors such as climate, altitude, etc., that affect the activity interests of students and the time that can be spent out-of-doors, and the environment (urban, suburban, or rural), which affects personal and family income and, therefore, the activity choices of students and the choice of physical education uniforms.

6. The resources of the community, including centers of higher education, private and parochial schools, public libraries, parks and playgrounds, swimming pools, cultural programs, government agencies, citizens' groups, and commercial ski resorts, bowling lanes, equestrian clubs, etc.

As you learn more about the community, you will begin to understand not only its organization but also the climate of life that takes place there. You will become more sensitive to the destructive feelings of the people and to the fear and insecurity, poverty, hunger, and disease that exist. You will also become aware of individuals and groups who are trying to bring about constructive changes. From community to community, and even within the same community, conditions may range from poverty to riches.

Hass provided us with a list of curriculum criteria to consider when dealing with social forces.

1. What social or cultural factors contribute to the individual differences of the learners?

2. How can the curriculum and/or teaching provide for these differences?

3. What values are we teaching?

4. What values do we wish to teach?

5. What can the curriculum do to assist learners in their goals of social self-understanding and self-realization?

6. How can the curriculum and teaching be planned and organized so that learners are assisted in confronting personal and social problems?

7. How can learners be helped to develop the problem-solving skills needed to cope with problems?[3]

Student needs and interests

Educational goals and objectives arise from the basic needs of students. It is easy to generalize that all seventh graders need instruction in team sports and all twelfth graders need to develop skills in individual and dual sports for use in their leisure time. It is not that simple, however, since students vary considerably within a single grade level in both age and intellectual, physical, social, and emotional development.

Student needs and interests play an important
part in the selection of curriculum content.

Data concerning both the student population as a whole and the individual students
within that population is essential. Curriculum designers need to consider the nature of the
student body—the number of students, their ages, sex, grade levels, personal and family
characteristics, interests, talents, and goals. Data from physical fitness, knowledge, skill, and
attitude tests can be helpful in describing students' past achievements. Health assessments
can also provide essential information about students.

Students who differ dramatically from group norms, including potential dropouts, bilingual students, the mentally and physically handicapped, and the gifted also need to be
considered. In fact, the courts have ruled that schools must begin to meet the needs of all
learners, whatever their differences might be.

Again, Hass provided us with several questions to ask ourselves about how well we
have planned to meet the needs of our students:

1. Does the planned curriculum provide for the developmental
   differences of the learners being taught?

2. Does the planned curriculum include provisions so that learning
   may start for each learner where he or she is?[4]

The subject matter and how it is learned

When dealing with the subject matter of physical education, curriculum designers must consider all of the domains of learning, including the cognitive, psychomotor, and affective, and the various levels of learning within each domain. They must also remember that each student selects from the subject matter those areas of perceived importance and organizes them in a way that is most meaningful to him or her. Students should be helped to discover how physical education relates to them and how they can use the information gained to solve problems that have personal meaning for them. The new *Basic Stuff Series* can be a helpful resource in identifying content and teaching strategies to accomplish this.[5] Curriculum designers need to plan for a variety of learning modes to accommodate the individual learning styles of students.

Some questions to consider when planning the subject matter and instructional methodology include the following:

1. What subject matter is of most worth?

2. Does the curriculum allow students to develop at all levels in each of the domains of learning?

3. Does the curriculum help the learner to identify and organize the key concepts and principles of physical education?

4. Does the curriculum prepare the student to utilize the content of physical education to solve personal problems, now and in the future?

5. Does the curriculum provide alternative approaches to learning to accommodate individual learning styles?

These four bases of the curriculum can be used as a foundation upon which to plan and select curriculum content and structure and teaching strategies.

Questions and suggested activities

1. Discuss the relationship of the physical education curriculum as it relates to the total school curriculum.

2. What are some influences on education that must be considered when designing a curriculum for physical education?

3. Examine several older and more recent curriculum guides to determine what if any changes have been made to meet the changing social forces of our time. What changes would you suggest?

4. Identify how student needs affect curriculum design.

5. Identify the growth and development patterns of children and adolescents. How do these patterns affect the curriculum? How do individual variations from these patterns influence the curriculum? (Review chapter 3.)

6. Visit a school (or study a curriculum guide) and try to determine what kinds of learning are occurring in the cognitive, psychomotor, and affective domains. What kinds are omitted? Suggest ways in which all three domains could be included in the curriculum.

7. You are a physical education specialist in a large metropolitan school district. A first-year junior high school physical educator from an outlying rural school district comes to you for advice. They are in the process of developing a physical education curriculum for the upcoming year. Currently such a curriculum is nonexistent. What advice can you give them that will help them plan their program for the coming year?

8. You have just been hired to teach physical education at a brand new school in Dhahran, Saudi Arabia. The school is for grades seven to nine and has approximately 250 students. There is no school district, just a superintendent and board of directors. What factors will you consider before designing the new curriculum?

9. Would a national curriculum model in physical education fulfill the purposes of education in the United States?

10. Conduct a survey of your community in terms of the factors listed in the chapter. What does the data suggest about an appropriate curriculum for a school in your community?

11. Visit a school board meeting and discuss what occurs there.

12. Watch the film "Fable for School People," (available for purchase from BYU Media Marketing or for rental from BYU Audio Visual Services, Brigham Young University, Provo, Utah 84602). Discuss the implications of the "animal school" on the present-day curriculum.

Suggested readings

American Association of Health, Physical Education, and Recreation. *Knowledge and Understanding in Physical Education,* Rev. ed. Washington, D.C.: AAHPER, 1973.

Haywood, Kathleen M. and Thomas J. Loughrey. "Growth and Development Implications for Teaching." *Journal of Physical Education and Recreation* 52 (March 1981): 57–58.

Jewett, Ann E. and Marie R. Mullan. *Curriculum Design: Purposes and Processes in Physical Education Teaching-Learning.* Washington, D. C.: American Association of Health Physical Education and Recreation, 1977.

Lawson, Hal A. and Judith H. Placek. *Physical Education in the Secondary Schools: Curricular Alternatives.* Boston: Allyn and Bacon, Inc., 1981.

Melograno, Vincent. "Status of Curriculum Practice: Are You a Consumer or Designer?" *Journal of Physical Education and Recreation* 49 (March 1978): 27–28.

Meredith, Marilu. "Expand Your Program—Step Off Campus." *Journal of Physical Education and Recreation* 50 (January 1979): 21–22.

Peddiwell, J. Abner. *The Sabertooth Curriculum.* New York: McGraw-Hill, Co., 1939.

Reavis, G. H. "The Animal School." *Missouri Schools* 13 (January 1948): 16.

Siedentop, Daryl. "Physical Education Curriculum: An Analysis of the Past." *Journal of Physical Education and Recreation* 51 (September 1980): 50.

Curriculum Patterns, Research, Trends, and Innovations

Study stimulators

1. Explain why a knowledge of curriculum theory and patterns are important.
2. Name the common curriculum patterns of physical education. Give an example of each.
3. What criteria are used to determine the specific curriculum pattern to be used?
4. Why should curriculum trends, innovations, and research findings be studied before designing or changing a curriculum?

Curriculum developers should study curriculum patterns, research, trends, and innovations in order to develop a basis for intelligent action. Bain describes the value of studying curriculum theory as follows:

> Curriculum theory describes potential criteria for selection and structuring of content and predicts the impact of such criteria upon the instructional process.[1]

Curriculum patterns in physical education

In physical education, subject-centered and student-centered curriculum patterns predominate. Subject-centered patterns include the traditional activity-based curriculum and the more recent movement-based and concepts-based curricula. Student-centered patterns include the developmental needs curriculum and the student-centered pattern.

The activity-based curriculum

The activity-based curriculum is the most common curriculum pattern. The curriculum is organized around activity units, including dance, fitness, and sports. Meaningful participation in activities is the goal of this curriculum pattern. It is not a means toward other goals, such as physical fitness or social development. Since not all possible activities can be included, a percentage of the total time is usually established for each activity category. Local considerations and the school situation influence specific selections within each category. Progression is from basic skills in the elementary grades to a specialization in a few activities at the high school level.

The advantage of this pattern appears to be the ease of administration. Disadvantages include boredom, caused by repetition, and the failure to develop skills beyond the basic level of instruction when programs are inadequately planned and implemented. Students also fail to develop the concepts necessary for a total understanding of the purpose of physical education throughout one's life.

The movement-based curriculum

The movement-based curriculum is based on the work of Rudolf Laban and is used primarily in elementary school programs.[2] The curriculum is organized around themes involving the body and its interrelationship with space, time, effort, and flow. Both movement skills and movement concepts are included in the instructional process. Emphasis is on the exploration of a large variety of movement skills in the areas of dance, gymnastics, and sports. Students use problem solving or discovery learning to create new ways of using their bodies to achieve specified goals with various pieces of equipment or with each other.

The concepts-based curriculum

The concepts-based curriculum is based on the body of knowledge about human movement, including such areas as exercise physiology, biomechanics, motor learning, and the sociology and psychology of sport. The concepts approach is organized around key ideas or principles. Concepts must be broad enough to permit instruction in a wide variety of activities and meaningful enough to justify the time and effort expended. The goal is to help the students understand the why, what, and how of physical education through problem solving in laboratory and activity settings. Any or all appropriate sport and movement skills can be used to teach concepts. Progression is from simple to more complex knowledge.

The concepts approach is based on two assumptions: (1) that transfer of concepts to new skills and situations occurs and (2) that students learn concepts better by emphasizing the concept (i.e., force production) rather than by teaching the concept within each activity unit.

The concepts-based curriculum is more easily justified in an academic sense and helps physical education achieve a more respected place in the school curriculum and even in the community. It is readily adapted to individual differences in students and to different locales. Students who do not excel in physical education activities like the concepts approach. Another advantage is the carry-over of basic concepts about health and fitness into real life.

The main disadvantage of the concepts approach is that students never experience a complete unit of instruction in a given sport or activity and therefore never learn the skills needed to participate in the activity. Another disadvantage is that the concepts approach is based on the assumption that concepts will transfer to new skills and situations, while research shows that transfer usually occurs only when the application is made clear in the new situation.

Several variations of a concepts-based curriculum have been tried. They include: (1) integrating concepts with the traditional activity-based curriculum; (2) teaching a separate unit on concepts; and (3) teaching concepts on special occasions such as rainy days, shortened periods, etc.

The developmental needs curriculum

The student needs curriculum is based on the developmental stages and growth patterns of children and youth. Thus, basic skills are taught in elementary school programs, team sports are emphasized in middle and junior high school programs, and lifetime activities in senior high school and college curricula. The curriculum is often divided into activity units chosen by the faculty to meet student needs. This curriculum pattern is based on the assumption that students go through the same stages of development at the same rate. The developmental needs curriculum is widely accepted and often combined with the activity-based curriculum.

The student-centered curriculum

The student-centered curriculum is based on the student's own purposes for enrolling in physical education activities such as for social interaction, adventure, emotional release, physical fitness, self-discipline, or personal expression.[3]

The student-centered curriculum is based on the assumption that students are capable of assessing their own purposes and making appropriate choices. Of course, values clarification and counseling can be used to assist students in making choices appropriate to their values and interests. It also assumes that a wide variety of activities will be provided and that beginning, intermediate, and advanced levels of instruction are available to meet student needs.

The advantages are that students have better attendance, are more cooperative, and learn more when they are allowed to concentrate on activities in which they have real interest and develop competence in activities in which they will participate outside of school hours.

The main disadvantage lies in teachers being forced to teach activities that are of interest to students, but for which they were never prepared. A second disadvantage is that teachers do not get to know students as they continually shift from one teacher to another. Some students can get lost in such a system. Therefore, it is generally implemented only at the high school level, although some selection of activities should be encouraged on a limited basis at lower levels.

Selecting appropriate curriculum patterns

No one curriculum pattern is adequate to serve the varied populations of our schools. Curriculum designers must select elements from several patterns and combine them to form a curriculum pattern that suits the needs of the particular school or system within which they are working. This requires a knowledge of the elements of each of the curriculum patterns and the creativity to adapt them to the needs of the situation.

The selective curriculum allows students to
participate in activities of their own choosing.

The selective curriculum

A popular combination of the subject-centered and student-centered curriculum patterns is
the selective curriculum. This curriculum consists of a variety of concept or activity units
from which students are allowed to choose the courses or activities they take. Options are
changed at periodic intervals, usually six to nine weeks, although some students are allowed
to choose only a specified group of activities and must remain with the same teacher throughout an entire semester.

The major advantage of this type of system is that students can develop expertise in
activities in which they will participate throughout their adult lives. A second advantage is
the ability to meet student needs and interests more adequately, even within a traditional
school system.

Disadvantages of this system are that it takes more time for organization and record
keeping and for counseling students toward the appropriate selection of activities.

These disadvantages can be minimized by proper planning. Students can be assigned
to a specific teacher who can diagnose strengths and weaknesses and provide assistance in
making choices tailored to their individual needs. Students who have had an introduction to
a wide variety of activities in earlier grades will find it much easier to make appropriate
choices. Students can be required to select a specified number of sports in each category
during each school year, as shown in this example:

Class	Team sports	Individual	Fitness	Aquatics
Sophomore	3	1	1	1
Junior	2	3	1	
Senior	1	4	1	

Another way to balance the program would be to require a certain number of specified activities to be taken anytime prior to graduation. This is easier to schedule and works out much like the above pattern if seniors are allowed to select activities first.

Organization and record keeping duties can be distributed among teachers by assigning a different teacher each period as the *master teacher*. The master teacher is responsible for all of the students for that period. This includes distributing class rolls, accumulating grades, distributing and collecting lockers and towels, etc.

On the first day of each unit, students all meet to select the next activity. Students should be told the activities and the teacher who is teaching each activity. Seniors choose first, then juniors, followed by sophomores. When the class enrollment for an activity is reached, the class is closed for that block. A card may be issued to each student on which the activity is marked for that block. The cards are collected and processed by hand or by computer. Roll sheets for each teacher are made from the cards. A sample record card is shown in figure 22.1.

Name _____ Sex: M/F Period _____

First Block
Tennis
Soccer
Flag football
Social dance
Archery
Fencing

Second Block
Swimming
Fitness
Aerobic dance
Soccer
Basketball
Volleyball

Third Block
Wrestling
Volleyball
Badminton
Jazz dance
Basketball
Aerobic dance
Swimming

Fourth Block
Basketball
Swimming
Fencing
Modern dance
Volleyball
Gymnastics
Wrestling
Outdoor pursuits

Fifth Block
Fencing
Fitness
Swimming
Ballet
Outdoor pursuits
Basketball
Track and field
Social dance

Sixth Block
Aerobic dance
Softball
Tennis
Track and field
Social dance
Modern dance
Cycling
Golf
Fitness

Figure 22.1 A sample record card.

Coeducational programs increase the number of faculty members and teaching stations in the program and, therefore, the range of activities that can be provided to both boys and girls. Use of a selective program can also facilitate the adaptation of class sizes in terms of the facilities available for instruction. Thus, instruction can be effective in areas such as tennis or racquetball where facilities are often limited.

A major problem of the selective program is the tendency to conduct recreational rather than instructional programs. This is a result of teacher laziness. The selective program provides an excellent environment in which to conduct instructional programs of the highest level possible in physical education.

A student-centered curriculum does not require modular or flexible scheduling. It can be easily implemented within the traditional school system.

Curriculum trends, innovations, and research

The curriculum designer has an obligation to study the trends, innovations, and research that have implications for physical education and to utilize the ideas learned without being dominated by them. Care should be taken to take the best of the old and the new, and to avoid change for change sake, without proving the worth of the new idea. Alvin Toffler makes a strong case when he says:

> The adaptive individual appears to be able to project himself forward just the 'right' distance in time, to examine and evaluate alternative courses of action open to him before the need for final decision, and to make tentative decisions beforehand.[4]

A number of trends that affect the curriculum were reviewed in chapter 1. Other trends and innovations can be found in recent issues of professional journals.

Research in the psychology of learning and motor learning, in exercise physiology, and in other areas of education have implications for curriculum development. It is up to the curriculum designer to determine the effects of research on the curriculum. Chapters 6, 7, and 8 reviewed the research in the cognitive, psychomotor, and affective domains.

Questions and suggested activities

1. Describe the curriculum patterns that best reflect your philosophies of education and of physical education.

2. Visit a school or study the program described in a curriculum guide. Try to determine the dominant curriculum pattern of the program. What changes would you suggest to make the program most effective?

3. Interview several teachers of physical education or peruse physical education literature to determine current trends and innovations in public education and physical education.

4. Two new physical education teachers were hired at Box Elder Middle School. One believes the curriculum should be activity-based because "students learn better when they learn specific activity skills." The second believes in a concept-centered approach, feeling that "this approach reaches a greater percentage of the children, especially those who are not highly skilled and fail to be active in an activity-based curriculum." You are the only other teacher in the department. As department chairperson, what will you do?

5. You have been asked to meet with a curriculum committee for your senior high school. For the past two years you have been an instructor at this school and during this time you have constructively offered some legitimate criticisms regarding the current program. The current program is strictly a subject-centered, activity-based curriculum. What might you suggest as a viable alternative?

6. You are a director of physical education for an entire school system. Some faculty members have suggested that a change of philosophy be adopted for the physical education program, that is, that the emphasis from K-8 be on movement exploration rather than on the traditional philosophy that presently characterizes the program. What will you do?

7. You have been invited to serve on a committee to investigate the possibilities of developing a strong interdisciplinary approach to education in your school. List five specific ideas on how your programs could enhance this philosophy.

Suggested readings

Corbin, Charles B. "Changing Consumers Mean New Concepts. *Journal of Physical Education and Recreation* 49 (January 1978):43.

Graham, G. M. "Bridge Between What Is and What Could Be." *The Physical Educator* 32 (March 1976): 14–16.

Grebner, Florence. "Voluntary Participation in Physical Activities." *The Physical Educator* 32 (March 1975): 24–25.

———. "Interdisciplinary Approaches to Physical Education." *Journal of Physical Education and Recreation* 46 (June 1975): 34.

Heitmann, Helen M. "Integrating Concepts Into Curricular Models." *Journal of Physical Education and Recreation* 52 (February 1981): 42–45.

Hick, Sandra. "Basic Movement: Building a Foundation for Educational Gymnastics." *Journal of Physical Education and Recreation* 50 (June 1979): 26–27.

"In Defense of Movement Education." *Journal of Physical Education and Recreation* 48 (February 1977): 46–47.

Kruger, Hayes. "A Focus on Body Management." *Journal of Physical Education and Recreation* 49 (September 1978): 39–41.

Loughrey, Tom. "Secondary School Curriculum Process." *Journal of Physical Education and Recreation* 49 (March 1978): 34–37.

Louvins, Harold. "Physical Education—Making Changes to Fit the Times." *National Association of Secondary School Principals Bulletin* 62 (May 1978): 10–14.

Riley, Marie, ed. "Games Teaching." *Journal of Physical Education and Recreation* 48 (September 1977): 17–35.

Sanborn, Marion Alice and Cynthia L. Meyer. "Curricular Constructs and Parameters for Today's Elementary Physical Education." *Journal of Physical Education and Recreation* 51 (September 1980): 42–43.

Standeven, Joy. "More Than Simply Movement Experience." *Journal of Physical Education and Recreation* 49 (September 1978): 35–38.

Taylor, John L. "Styles of Secondary School Physical Education Curriculum." *Journal of Physical Education and Recreation* 51 (September 1980): 44–45.

Establishing the Scope
of the Physical Education Program

Study stimulators

1. Explain what is included in a balanced curriculum.
2. Identify the methods that should be used in selecting content or activities for a specific curriculum.
3. What criteria should be used in evaluating whether or not credit should be awarded for nonphysical education activities?

Scope refers to the horizontal component or content of the curriculum at all grade levels. It includes *what* should be taught to meet the needs of the students and the objectives of physical education.

The curriculum must be broad in scope and encompass a wide variety of rich and guided experiences in order to meet the wide diversity of physical, intellectual, emotional, and social needs of children and youth.

Program balance

A balanced program ensures that the goals and objectives will be achieved. This balance should be achieved in the following three ways.

First, the time allotted to class instruction, intramurals, and extramurals must be balanced. Commitment should be first to class instruction, second to an intramural program, and last to an extramural program. Second, a balance among the goals or objectives of physical education in the psychomotor, cognitive, and affective domains should be maintained. Through the careful selection of activities and teaching techniques, all of these goals are attainable. Third, a balanced program of physical education should include a variety of physical activities.

Of course, the amount of time spent on each area of the curriculum will depend on the context for which the curriculum is developed.

Methods for selection of activities

In the past, the selection of activities has usually been based on the teachers' interests and abilities or the coaches' desire to develop the skills involved in the athletic program. This kind of program usually results in an unbalanced program based primarily on team sports.

A study done in 1974 by the Opinion Research Corporation of Princeton for the President's Council on Physical Fitness and Sports surveyed Americans over the age of twenty-one years in 360 communities. Most respondents participated in team sports during school years to the exclusion of lifetime sports.[1] Other studies have consistently revealed that very little curriculum time is allotted to lifetime sports. Parents and participants suggest the need for adding to the curriculum such activities as golf, swimming, tennis, bowling, dance, boating, camping, and fitness.

These results suggest that activities should be selected by a curriculum committee composed of educators, parents, and students, using a system of analyzing and selecting those activities that meet the needs of students and the objectives of the program.

Process for selection of activities

In selecting the activities for the curriculum, the following steps are suggested.

Step 1. Determine broad activity categories.

Step 2. List possible activities.

Step 3. Establish a systematic method for selecting curricular experiences.

Step 4. Assign weight values to criteria.

Step 5. Evaluate activities by awarding points for each criterion.

Step 6. Arrange activities by rank.

Step 7. Evaluate activities by relative value.

Step 1. Determine broad activity categories

Activity areas such as the following may be included:

Aquatics	Team sports
Gymnastics	Individual sports
Physical fitness	

A scope chart should be prepared that shows the percentage of the total program to be spent in each broad activity area. The percentages should reflect the philosophy of the curriculum committee and provide a balanced program of activities in terms of students' needs and developmental level. An example of a scope chart is shown in figure 23.1.

Step 2. List possible activities

Within each category, list all possible activities. Literally hundreds of activities *could* be included. A sample list of activities is shown in figure 23.2.

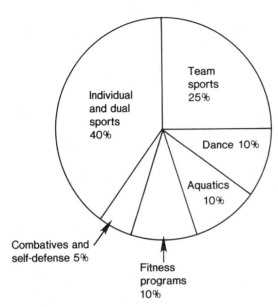

Figure 23.1 A scope chart.

Step 3. Establish a systematic method for selecting curricular experiences

Since school time is obviously limited and only the most appropriate experiences for a given situation can be considered, you will need to establish a systematic method for selecting relevant curricular experiences. List criteria which you consider to be essential for including an activity in your curriculum. Keep criteria few in number and stated as realistically as possible. The following criteria are generally considered to be essential:

1. Is the experience consistent with each of your stated objectives of physical education and education?

2. Is the experience consistent with the growth and developmental needs of students, present and future?

3. Is the activity relatively free of hazards?

4. Is the activity feasible in terms of local considerations?

Because of varying local conditions, specific criteria must be used to determine which activities are most suitable for use in a particular area. Some possible criteria might include:

1. Is the activity acceptable to the community? (For example, in some areas of the country, dancing may be prohibited by certain religious groups.)

2. Is the activity of interest to students? (Regional interests and inner-city factors, for example, may influence the interests of students and possible carryover values. For example, the cost of participating in golf would be prohibitive to most inner-city youth.)

| ACTIVITY | OBJECTIVES | | | | Total 100 | Rank | Safety High-Med.-Low | Student Needs and Interests | Rank | Locally Feasible Yes/No |
	Fitness 30	Skills 40	Knowledge 20	Social 10						
AQUATICS										
Lifesaving	16.5	28	17	6.5	68	1	Med.	15.2%	3	Yes
Swimming (Beg.)	19.5	28	12	5	64.5	3	Med.	25.4%	1	Yes
Swimming (Int.)	22.5	28	12	5	67.5	2	Med.	17.2%	2	Yes
DANCE										
Aerobic Dance	29	29	10.5	7.5	76	5	High	51.0%	1	Yes
Ballet	24	37	16	7.5	84.5	1	High	13.2%	6	Yes
Folk and Square Dance	22	30.5	16	8	76.5	4	High	24.9%	4	Yes
Jazz Dance	25	32	14.5	7.5	79	3	High	32.1%	2	Yes
Modern Dance	25	32	15	7.5	79.5	2	High	22.3%	5	Yes
Social Dance	18	30.5	13	8	69.5	6	High	31.5%	3	Yes
PHYSICAL FITNESS										
Jogging	30	20	10	5.5	65.5	1	High	59.0%	1	Yes
Weight Training	21	20	10	5	56	2	Low	45.3%	2	Yes
TEAM SPORTS										
Basketball	19	38.5	10	6	73.5	5	Med.	31.6%	3	Yes
Flag Football	19	37	12	6.5	74.5	4	Med.	26.0%	5	Yes
Field Hockey	23	35	13	6.5	77.5	2	Med.	18.4%	6	Yes
Soccer	27	36	14.5	8	85.5	1	Med.	29.9%	4	Yes
Softball	17	35	11	7	70	7	Med.	37.6%	1	Yes
Speedball	23	35	12	7	77	3	Med.	5.0%	7	Yes
Volleyball	17	34	13.5	7	71.5	6	Med.	33.0%	2	Yes
INDIVIDUAL SPORTS										
Archery	7	34	15	4.5	60.5	11	Low	11.0%	11	Yes
Badminton	18	34	12	5.5	69.5	9	Med.	25.3%	7	Yes
Bowling	6	30	11	5	52	12	High	42.1%	3	Yes

Cycling	24	27	14	5	70	8	Med.	45.0%	2	Yes
Fencing	16	34.5	16	5	71.5	7	Med.	10.8%	12	Yes
Golfing	8.5	33.5	14	6	62	10	Med.	28.8%	6	Yes
Gymnastics	25	38.5	16	6	85.5	1	Low	21.2%	9	No
Racketball/Hand-ball	22	33	13	5.5	73.5	5	Med.	42.0%	4	No
Skiing	22	34.5	12	5.5	74	4	Med.	41.0%	5	No
Tennis	22	35	11.5	6	74.5	3	Med.	59.0%	1	Yes
Track and Field	28	37	14	6.5	85.5	1	Med.	24.1%	8	Yes
Wrestling	24	32	12	5	73	6	Low	15.3%	10	Yes

Figure 23.2 A list of possible activities with assigned weights and ranks within categories.

Excellent programs take advantage of
community resources.

3. Are the necessary resources available in the school or community,
including facilities, equipment, finances, faculty members or resource
persons, time constraints, transportation, and climate?

Step 4. Assign weight values to criteria

Several possible ways exist for assigning weights to each criterion. One way is to weigh all
criteria equally with each one counting a set number of points. A more realistic way is to
weigh each criterion differently based on its importance to the selection process. This can
be done by assigning a different number of points to each criterion as shown in figure 23.2.
These weights should be based on the rank order of importance given to the objectives of
physical education. Individual factors such as safety and feasibility may be considered separately.

Step 5. Evaluate activities by awarding points for each criterion

Make up a chart with the criteria across the top and the activities down the side. Give a
copy to each member of your curriculum committee and have them evaluate each activity
by awarding points according to the plan you decided on in step 4. Then, average or total
the points from all members of the committee.

Step 6. Arrange activities by rank

Based on the total points for each activity, arrange the activities by rank within each category. Eliminate activities that do not meet the selected criteria. Activities that best meet the objectives for the program and the needs of the students should be given priority. Of course, some activities will satisfy the physical fitness objective but be of little value in terms of social skills. Others may contribute to the leisure-time interests of students and be of little value with regard to physical fitness. By ranking the activities within the broader categories selected in step 1, you will see which of the activities within each category best meet the criteria you have selected.

Step 7 Evaluate activities by relative value

When a number of desirable activities meet all of the criteria for inclusion in the curriculum, but because of time all can not be included, two possibilities exist. First, you can eliminate activities on the basis of local criteria. For example, of the field sports—football, soccer, speedball, and speed-a-way—soccer appears to command such an interest in your community as a leisure-time activity that you feel your students need specific instruction in it. Canoeing may be discarded due to inadequate facilities within reach of the school. Second, you could organize desirable activities into groups or categories and establish desirable time percentages for each area. Decide whether courses are essential or could be used for enrichment purposes. Heitmann suggested several patterns for broadening curricular scope to meet the needs of individual students while at the same time achieving curricular objectives. She stated:

> Explore the feasibility of the various *curricular patterns.* The basic pattern begins with the various objectives of the physical education program. Establish these global goals as areas into which the various activities will fall. Courses that can be accommodated can be placed into these areas.
>
> Once courses are organized according to the basic categories you can then decide if some courses are essential which you would require and if some could be enrichment.[2]

For example, area 1 might include health- and fitness-related courses; area 2 might be aquatics activities; area 3, rhythms; etc. Figure 23.3 shows examples of Heitmann's suggested organizational patterns.

Programs are often planned so that every student is required to experience a minimal exposure to (1) team sports, (2) individual and dual sports, (3) rhythms, (4) aquatics, and (5) fitness activities. Although a minimum exposure requirement exists, students are encouraged to explore activities beyond the minimum exposure in areas of their greatest interest.

Pattern I

Core Required

Area 1	Area 2	Area 3	Area 4
□	○	◇	△

Select one from each

□	○	◇	△
□	○	◇	△
□	○	◇	△

Pattern II

Core Required

Area 1	Area 2	Area 3	Area 4
□	○	◇	△

Select any four from any area or from three of the four areas

□	○	◇	△
□	○	◇	△
□	○	◇	△
□	○	◇	△

Pattern III

Core—Select one from each area

Area 1	Area 2	Area 3	Area 4
□	○	◇	△
□	○	◇	△
□	○	◇	△

Pattern IV

Select one track

Track 1	Track 2	Track 3
Area 1 □	Area 1 □	Area 1 □
Area 2 ○	Area 2 ○	Area 2 ○
Area 3 ◇	Area 3 ◇	Area 3 ◇
Area 4 △	Area 4 △	Area 4 △

Figure 23.3 Examples of suggested organizational patterns.
Source: From Heitmann, Helen M. "Curricular Organizational Patterns for Physical Education," presented to the NASPE Curriculum Academy Working Symposium, St. Louis, Missouri, Nov. 4–6, 1978.

Should substitute activities be allowed physical education credit?

In many schools and colleges, physical education credit is awarded for participation in marching band, ROTC, or varsity athletics. The question often arises as to whether or not this credit is justifiable. In order to answer this question, you should evaluate each experience in the same way you evaluated every other activity in the curriculum—by evaluating its ability to help students achieve the objectives of physical education.

Consideration should also be given to the many activities that might be missed through continued participation in one of these substitute activities. If the activity makes a contribution to the development of the student, it might be considered as a portion of the physical education requirement. If the activity does not meet these criteria, then physical education credit should be denied.

Questions and suggested activities

1. Obtain a list of activities included in the physical education programs at different schools. Evaluate their appropriateness for inclusion in the program based on the criteria discussed in this chapter.

2. You are hired to teach physical education and be the coach at a new high school in Alberta, Canada. The school has twelve seniors, thirty juniors, forty-seven sophomores, and thirty-eight freshmen. The nearest high school to yours is eighty-five miles. Due to the weather conditions, you are indoors for seven of the nine school months. The principal tells you to set up a program that will keep all the students active and interested during the school year. What will you do?

3. You have just been assigned as department chairperson of a school in your district. The school has been teaching the same sports year-in and year-out. The sports that have been taught are football and soccer in the fall, basketball and wrestling in the winter, and softball and track and field in the spring. What changes would you suggest to your faculty for broadening the scope of the curriculum?

4. Identify the procedures you would use to select the activities listed above that will meet the objectives or competencies you have identified.

5. Use the procedures identified in the above question to rank the activities you have listed in order of their contribution to the objectives you have identified for your program. Which activities did you eliminate? Why?

Suggested reading

Gaudiano, Michael G. "High Risk Activities: In Physical Education?" *The Physical Educator* 37 (October 1980): 128–30.

Lorenz, Floyd. "Mission Impossible." *Journal of Health Physical Education Recreation* 45 (September 1974): 98.

Naylor, Jay H. "Honey and Milk Toast." *Journal of Physical Education and Recreation* 46 (September 1975): 18–19.

Pate, Russell and Charles Corbin. "Implications for Curriculum." *Journal of Physical Education and Recreation* 52 (January 1981): 36–38.

Riley, Marie. "Title X: A Proposal for a Law to Guarantee Equal Opportunity for Nonathletes." *Journal of Physical Education and Recreation* 46 (June 1975): 31.

Robinson, Sarah M. "Anticipating the 1980s: Living and Being in Physical Education." *Journal of Physical Education and Recreation* 51 (September 1980): 46–47.

Seefeldt, Vern. "Middle Schools: Issues and Future Directions in Physical Education." *Journal of Health Physical Education Recreation* 45 (February 1974): 33.

Smith, Charles D. and Samuel Prather. "Group Problem Solving." *Journal of Physical Education and Recreation* 46 (September 1975): 20–21.

24

Determining the Sequence
of Physical Education Activities

Study stimulators

1. List the criteria that should be used in selecting appropriate activities for each grade level.
2. Describe appropriate objectives and activities for each grade level.
3. Describe how sequence relates to the teaching of activity skills or content.

Sequence refers to the vertical component of the curriculum. It tells *when* something is to be taught, either by grade level or by skill order, such as swimming before lifesaving. Failure to provide a graduated sequence of instruction in knowledge and skills has probably been the biggest stumbling block to quality programs in physical education. For example, the same basketball unit has often been taught to the same students year after year with no new learning occurring.

Grade-level sequence

The physical education program needs to be organized into a continuous flow of experiences through a carefully planned, graduated, sequence of ideas and skills from elementary school through junior and senior high schools to college. This sequence should be developed in the light of student needs and interests and built progressively toward the attainment of a single set of physical education objectives.

Elementary school students should acquire proficiency in fundamental motor patterns. Proficiency in motor skills used in active team games should be stressed in the junior high school, because of the physical and social needs of the students. Lifetime sports should be added during the high school years.

Planning must be coordinated at all grade levels to insure sufficient breadth to the activities, to provide for the development of skills that will be required for later activities, and to avoid unnecessary overlap or omissions or undue repetition of instruction. Students, therefore, will be able to progress toward an increasingly mature utilization of their knowledge and skills to solve complex problems related to themselves and to society. A sequence chart for grades K-12 is shown in figure 24.1.

SCOPE AND SEQUENCE CHART

Scope	Sequence												
Activity	K	1	2	3	4	5	6	7	8	9	10	11	12
Gymnastics: Educational	o	o	o	o	o	o	o						
Olympic								o	o	o	o	o	o
Rhythmic								o	o	o	o	o	o
Dance: Folk		o	o	o	o	o	o	o	o	o	o	o	o
Round		o	o	o	o	o	o	o	o	o	o	o	o
Square					o	o	o	o	o	o	o	o	o
Ballroom								o	o	o	o	o	o
Modern								o	o	o	o	o	o
Jazz								o	o	o	o	o	o
Creative	o	o	o	o	o	o	o	o	o	o	o	o	o
Aquatics: Swimming	o	o	o	o	o	o	o	o	o	o	o	o	o
Water Games					o	o	o	o	o	o	o	o	o
Diving								o	o	o	o	o	o
Sailing or Canoeing								o	o	o	o	o	o
Lifesaving											o	o	o
Synchronized								o	o	o	o	o	o
Water Safety	o	o	o	o	o	o	o	o	o	o	o	o	o
Track and Field: Sprint	o	o	o	o	o	o	o	o	o	o	o	o	o
Hurdles	o	o	o	o	o	o	o	o	o	o	o	o	o
Relays	o	o	o	o	o	o	o	o	o	o	o	o	o
Mid-distance					o	o	o	o	o	o	o	o	o
Cross-country								o	o	o	o	o	o
High Jump	o	o	o	o	o	o	o	o	o	o	o	o	o
Long Jump	o	o	o	o	o	o	o	o	o	o	o	o	o
Pole Vault											o	o	o
Discus								o	o	o	o	o	o
Shotput								o	o	o	o	o	o

Figure 24.1 A scope and sequence chart.

Figure 24.1—*Continued*

SCOPE AND SEQUENCE CHART

Scope						*Sequence*								
Activity	K	1	2	3	4	5	6	7	8	9	10	11	12
Outdoor Pursuits: Camping					o	o	o	o	o	o	o	o	o
Backpacking											o	o	o
Skating (Ice or Roller)								o	o	o	o	o	o
Skiing								o	o	o	o	o	o
Hiking	o	o	o	o	o	o	o	o	o	o	o	o	o
Orienteering					o	o	o	o	o	o	o	o	o
Cycling					o	o	o	o	o	o	o	o	o
Survival Skills					o	o	o	o	o	o	o	o	o
Manipulative Skills with Objects	o	o	o	o	o	o	o						
Tag Games	o	o	o	o	o	o	o						
Relay Games	o	o	o	o	o	o	o						
Low Organization Games		o	o	o	o	o	o	o	o	o	o	o	o
Hand, Paddle, Racquet Games: Handball			o	o	o	o	o	o	o	o	o	o	o
Two or Four Square	o	o	o	o	o	o	o						
Tetherball	o	o	o	o	o	o	o						
Paddle Tennis					o	o	o						
Table Tennis					o	o	o	o	o	o	o	o	o
Badminton								o	o	o	o	o	o
Racquetball										o	o	o	o
Tennis										o	o	o	o
Target Games: Shuffleboard	o	o	o	o	o	o	o						
Archery								o	o	o	o	o	o
Golf										o	o	o	o
Bowling										o	o	o	o

Figure 24.1—*Continued*

SCOPE AND SEQUENCE CHART

| Scope | | | | | | | | Sequence | | | | | |
Activity	K	1	2	3	4	5	6	7	8	9	10	11	12
Team Games: Basketball					x	x	x	o	o	o	o	o	o
European Handball								o	o	o	o	o	o
Field Hockey								o	o	o	o	o	o
Floor Hockey				x	x	x	x	o	o	o	o	o	o
Football-type				x	x	x	x	o	o	o	o	o	o
Soccer				x	x	x	x	o	o	o	o	o	o
Softball				x	x	x	o	o	o	o	o	o	o
Speedball								o	o	o	o		
Volleyball				x	x	x	o	o	o	o	o	o	o
Combatives: Combative Games				o	o	o	o	o	o	o	o	o	o
Wrestling							o	o	o	o	o	o	o
Fitness: Testing	o	o	o	o	o	o	o	o	o	o	o	o	o
Circuit Training						o	o	o	o	o	o	o	o
Calisthenics						o	o	o	o	o	o	o	o
Isometrics								o	o	o	o	o	o
Weight Training								o	o	o	o	o	o
Aerobics	o	o	o	o	o	o	o	o	o	o	o	o	o
Fitness Knowledge	o	o	o	o	o	o	o	o	o	o	o	o	o
Leadership: Instructional Assistants	o	o	o	o	o	o	o	o	o	o	o	o	o
Officiating						o	o	o	o	o	o	o	o
Athletic Training											o	o	o

Lead-up activities are indicated with x's.

Skill-order sequence

Obviously, students do not learn all there is to know or develop skill proficiency in an activity in a single encounter. Teachers are often frustrated by presenting a whole unit of instruction and having students absorb only the smallest part of it. Often we try to do too much and so none of it is learned well. Willgoose summed this up very well when he said:

> The chief problem facing most physical education teachers is not what to teach, but how far one should go at specific grade levels. One way to get around this dilemma is to think less in terms of stereotyped grade levels and more in terms of *skill levels*. For example, in a middle school or junior high school, it would be more efficient to build a sequence of skills and knowledge in an activity through at least three levels of expectation:
>
> Beginning level: Graduated presentation of fundamental skills and knowledge
>
> Intermediate level: Graduated presentation of more complicated and detailed skills and knowledge
>
> Advanced level: Graduated presentation leading to development of advanced skills, understanding, and appreciation.[1]

Table 24.1 shows an example of beginning, intermediate, and advanced levels of volleyball.

Table 24.1 An example of skill order sequence in volleyball

Beginning	Intermediate	Advanced
I. Skills: Overhead pass Dig Underhand serve Teamwork	I. Review: Overhead pass Dig Underhand serve Teach: Overhand serve Spike Block Team strategy	I. Review: All skills Teach: Rolls Emphasize: Advanced strategy and team play
II. Concepts: Basic rules Scoring Basic strategy	II. Official rules Offensive strategy Defensive strategy	II. Official rules Officiating Offensive strategy Defensive strategy
III. Lead-up games to learn skills, brief introduction to official game	III. Official game, including tournament play	III. Official game, with advanced strategy and tournament play

Determining sequence

Considerations for determining skill sequence or grade placement include student characteristics, the subject matter, and safety. The physical, mental, and social development of students, along with previous fitness, knowledge, and skill competencies, will be the primary considerations in placing activities into grade levels. Student interests should also be considered.

An attempt should be made to match the subject matter with the student characteristics. In doing this, consider the complexity and amount of information to be presented and the difficulty of skills to be learned.

Proper progressions will result in safe, effective learning and successful student participation.

Curricular scope and sequences for various school levels

Determining the scope and sequence of the curriculum from kindergarten through college is a complex and significant task requiring a careful consideration of the correct emphasis at the different stages of child and adolescent development. Following is an overview of recommended program emphases at the different school levels.

Preschool and kindergarten (ages three through five)

The orientation of the program is toward the child as a unique individual. The curriculum emphasis should be on: (1) the development of perceptual-motor skills, such as balance, eye-hand coordination, and laterality; (2) the development of gross motor skills, such as running, walking, crawling, climbing, and pushing; and (3) the development of self-awareness and expression through movement. Activities should emphasize spontaneous, vigorous, large-muscle movement in an environment that provides freedom and opportunity for the children to explore and create their own movement patterns.

Primary grades (ages six through eight)

The orientation of the program continues to be on the individual child as a unique person. The curricular emphasis should be on: (1) perceptual-motor development; (2) the development of fundamental or basic movement patterns, such as skipping, walking backwards, and rolling; (3) the development of self-awareness and an awareness of what the body can do within its environment, including force, space, and time relationships; (4) an improvement in muscular strength, endurance, flexibility, and agility; (5) basic safety; (6) the development of simple concepts about physical activity; and (7) the development of positive attitudes toward activity.

Activities should concentrate on large-muscle and creative movement. Rhythmic activities (singing games, creative movement and simple folk and aerobic dance movements), gymnastic skills (stunts, tumbling, self-testing activities, and apparatus), and basic sport

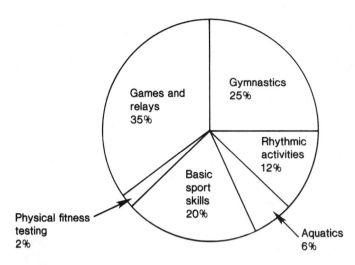

Figure 24.2 A possible scope chart for the primary grades.

skills (throwing, catching, dribbling, striking, etc.) are often combined into a movement exploration method of teaching which emphasizes the child's progress in relation to himself or herself rather than as compared to other students in the group. Aquatics should be included where facilities permit. Physical fitness should be maintained by participation in a variety of activities within the program. A possible scope chart for the primary grades is shown in figure 24.2.

Intermediate grades (ages nine through eleven)

The orientation at this level is to the individual child as a member of a group of peers. The curricular emphasis is on: (1) the development and refinement of specific motor skills, (2) the development of a high level of physical fitness, (3) the development of social skills through more highly organized activities, (4) the development of self-esteem through successful participation in peer groups, and (5) the development of basic activity-related concepts such as rules and strategies in games.

Activities should include rhythmic activities, gymnastics, basic sport skills, simple games and relays, sports lead-up games, and aquatics. Physical fitness should be an essential component of all activities within the program. A possible scope chart for this level is shown in figure 24.3.

Junior high school

The orientation at this level is on the individual student as an emerging adult with a need for a broad exposure to the challenges facing the individual in our society and strategies for coping with those challenges. The curricular emphasis is on: (1) the development and maintenance of physical fitness; (2) the development of a wide variety of specific activity skills;

Activities should be carefully planned to meet
the needs of the students at each age level.

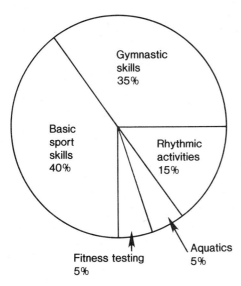

Figure 24.3 A possible scope chart for the intermediate grades.

(3) a basic understanding and appreciation of a broad variety of activities that will facilitate intelligent choices regarding out-of-school and future participation; and (4) the development of self-awareness and self-confidence—physically, emotionally, and socially.

Activities should include a variety of experiences so that students can make an intelligent selection of the activities they wish to pursue for future participation. In view of the physiological and emotional characteristics of these adolescents, care should be taken to select activities in which students can feel successful and that progress toward higher levels of skill proficiency. A minimum level of competence should be achieved in activities so that students will be able to use the skills for personal enjoyment. Team sports are important because of the social interaction they provide. In addition, the curriculum should include individual and dual sports, dance, gymnastics, aquatics, and fitness activities. Combatives should also be provided for boys and self-defense for girls. A possible scope chart for junior high school appears in figure 24.4.

Senior high school

The orientation is on the individual as a capable, intelligent pursuer of activities appropriate for one's own needs and interests when given guidelines and options for doing so. The curricular emphasis is on: (1) the development of competencies in and appreciation for participation in selected lifetime activities; (2) the development of knowledges and understandings essential to provide insight and motivation for a lifetime of vigorous physical activity; (3) the development and maintenance of personal physical fitness; and (4) the development of self-confidence, individual initiative, and responsibility to self and society.

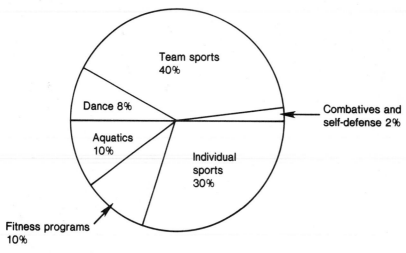

Figure 24.4 A possible scope chart for junior high school.

The activities should include a wide variety of activities from which to choose. The following should be provided: individual and dual sports, dance, aquatics, team sports, physical fitness, combatives and self-defense, outdoor pursuits, and opportunities for service and leadership development. A possible scope chart for senior high school appears in figure 24.5.

College

The orientation is on the individual student's adaptation to current and future life conditions. The curricular emphasis is on preparing the student for a lifetime of vigorous physical activity by developing: (1) skills and interests in selected activities; (2) a desire for maintaining physical fitness; and (3) a knowledge and understanding of physical education and its contribution to the *complete* life.

There should be a broad spectrum of activities that encourage lifetime participation, with several levels of entry for beginning, intermediate, and advanced students. Most of the activities will be the same as those found at the high school level, but with increased opportunities for developing advanced levels of skill. Physical fitness courses should emphasize the underlying concepts and develop the ability to design lifetime individualized fitness programs.

Questions and suggested activities

1. Review curriculum guides to determine what activities are normally taught at each grade level.

2. Visit several schools at the elementary and secondary levels. Discuss the curriculum at each level with teachers to determine what is being taught. Are students progressing in skill development?

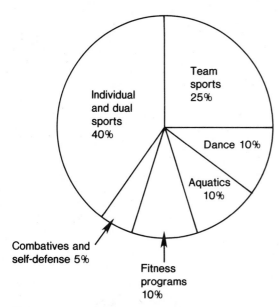

Figure 24.5 A possible scope chart for senior high school.

3. Select an activity for a particular school level. List the concepts and skills to be covered and arrange them in order of difficulty from easiest to most difficult.

Suggested readings

Bain, Linda L. "Socialization into the Role of Participant: Physical Education's Ultimate Goal." *Journal of Physical Education and Recreation* 51 (September 1980): 48–50.

Lewis, George T. "A Strategy for Reducing the Gap Between Theory and Practice in Physical Education." *The Physical Educator* 35 (October 1978): 132–33.

Stafford, Elba. "Middle Schools: Status of Physical Education Programs." *Journal of Health Physical Education Recreation* 45 (February 1974): 25–28.

25

Scheduling and Administrative Organization

Study stimulators

1. Describe each of the steps in the scheduling process.
2. Tell why scheduling is so difficult to do.

Scheduling is the process of adapting the physical education program to the individual school and its community, staff, students, facilities, and time restraints. It is a time-consuming but essential job.

Physical educators should work with local school administrators to achieve the best possible scheduling arrangement for physical education within the master schedule. In order to do this, physical educators need to be aware of the many trends in scheduling. The introduction of the computer into education vastly increases scheduling possibilities based on student need and subject matter requirements. Technology has provided loop films, videotape recording and playback, and programmed learning modules that can release the student from the teacher at certain times in the instructional program. Coeducational classes provide new possibilities for reorganizing staff and facilities creatively to meet student needs.

Scheduling innovations in education

Innovations in education are probably most obvious in the area of scheduling. They will be presented here briefly in order to help you become familiar with the various possibilities. For ease of discussion, they are broken into the following groups: (1) time utilization patterns, (2) student grouping patterns, and (3) staff utilization patterns.

Time utilization patterns

Time utilization patterns generally include traditional scheduling, modular scheduling, or flexible scheduling.

Traditional scheduling

Traditional scheduling involves the assignment of a specified number of students to an instructor for a given time period each school day. Each subject is allowed an equal amount of time each day. One teacher teaches a class for the entire semester. A student schedule in a traditional program might look like this:

Daily Classes

8:00 - 8:55	English
9:00 - 9:55	math
10:00 - 10:55	industrial arts
11:00 - 11:55	social studies
12:00 - 12:55	lunch
1:00 - 1:55	physical education
2:00 - 2:55	science

Some advantages attributed to the traditional schedule include ease of scheduling and time for the establishment of student-teacher rapport. Disadvantages include high teacher-student ratios; heterogeneous classification of students in classes; and time wasted repeating lectures, films, etc. that could be handled better only once with a large group.

It is important to remember that excellent programs of physical education have been and will continue to be conducted with traditional methods of organizing and scheduling.

Flexible and modular scheduling

Although modular and flexible scheduling are often used synonymously, there are some slight differences between the two. Both patterns involve variations in the number and length of class meetings for a given subject each week. Class sizes may also vary. In each case, the school day is divided into short periods of time called modules (or mods), usually ten to thirty minutes, although twenty minutes appears to be the most popular. Modules can be combined in almost any arrangement to provide appropriate lengths of time for different instructional purposes. Classes may vary in length from day to day and from subject to subject. An example of a schedule for one day is shown in figure 25.1.

In modular scheduling, students and teachers have a different schedule each day for a five- or six-day cycle. Once established, the cycle remains the same throughout the term. The modular schedule is much like many college schedules in which some classes are one and one-half hours twice a week, some one hour three times a week and others three hours once a week.

In flexible scheduling, instructors request class lengths and frequency of class meetings each week. A computer then revises the schedule, and at the beginning of each cycle, the teachers and students pick up their new schedules.

Advantages of modular or flexible scheduling are greater opportunites for individualized instruction, increased student responsibility for learning, and increased use of facilities. Disadvantages include the difficulties of scheduling, the need for increased supervision and discipline of students, and the insecurity of some teachers and students within the constantly changing environment.

Time	Day 1	Day 2	Day 3	Day 4	Day 5
8:00	Industrial arts	Industrial arts	Industrial arts	Industrial arts	Typing
8:30	Math		Math		
9:00					
9:30	Independent study				Math
10:00	Social studies	Social studies	Social studies	Social studies	
10:30		Physical education			Physical education
11:00	Physical education		Physical education	Independent study	
11:30				English	
12:00	L	U	N	C	H
12:30	English	English	English	English	English
1:00		Math		Math	
1:30	Chorus	Career education	Chorus	Independent study	Boys' chorus
2:00	Independent study	Independent study	English		Independent study
2:30			Independent study		

Figure 25.1 An example of a student modular or flexible schedule.

Mini-courses

Mini-courses are short-term, academic or nonacademic instructional units that allow students to develop their talents and increase their interests. Many are nongraded, with no tests and no homework. They can be scheduled during a student's free time, in a period set aside specifically for mini-courses, during lunch hours, or as a replacement for study halls. Some schools offer a whole week of mini-courses at a specified time during the year. The selective program in physical education is a variation of the mini-course system.

Class content for mini-courses might include counseling and guidance workshops, career education, instructional offerings not possible with large groups or not usually included in the regular program, and recreational offerings such as crafts and sports. A mini-course menu might include the following:

Course Title	Teacher	Room
Quiet study	Ames	12
Making movies	Teichert	Cafeteria
Math help	Hansen	13
Rap with principal	Petersen	20
Successful dating	Lungo	26
Football rules	Robison	4

Mini-courses provide a means of innovation that can be adapted to any school at low cost and with a minimum of disruption in the school schedule, yet they motivate both teachers and students to put more effort into the teaching-learning process. Teachers have the chance to teach a favorite subject or hobby. Students choose a topic of special interest to them. Students and teachers may share in the planning and teaching of courses or even switch roles, with students teaching their hobbies to teachers.

The only disadvantage of mini-courses is that they may be forced out of the curriculum by the budget crunch and the "back-to-basics" movement.

Student grouping patterns

Student grouping patterns are methods of grouping students into or within classes for instruction. They include homogeneous grouping and nongraded grouping.

Homogeneous grouping

The Committee on Exercise and Physical Fitness of the American Medical Association listed the reasons for classifying students for physical education as "1) to safeguard the health of the participant, 2) to group pupils for effective learning, 3) to equalize competitive conditions, and 4) to facilitate progress and achievement."[1]

Students should never be placed into classes merely on the basis of administrative expedience. Assignment of students to classes and learning groups should be made on the basis of individual needs. The ideal grouping arrangement would take into consideration all of the factors affecting learning—intelligence, capacity, maturity, knowledge, skill, interests, and so on. However, the inability to scientifically measure such factors has served as a deterrent to homogeneous grouping.

On the secondary level, the most feasible procedure appears to be the organization of subgroups within the physical education program. For example, where there are a number of teaching stations and teachers, ability grouping may be accomplished by sending a large number of students to physical education at one time. The physical education staff would then divide them into homogeneous groups. Groupings should vary as activities change, since students have different skill levels in different activities. Grouping persons with similar physical characteristics and skills enhances success and, therefore, the social and emotional development of students.

Instruction should be provided for students with physical limitations including those with inadequate skill development and the physically underdeveloped. Physical performance tests can be used to identify physically underdeveloped students and to appraise the motor aspects of physical fitness. Students should be placed in the least restrictive environment in which an appropriate learning situation can be provided.

Grouping can be accomplished by:

1. Grade level—The most common method, but maturity and skill level may still vary widely.

2. Height/weight or exponent systems—Useful in contact sports and in junior high school where physical maturity varies considerably.

3. Ability or skill level—By skills tests in specific sport skills. This provides for instruction on the students' level.

4. Physical fitness—By fitness test results. Students with low fitness levels can benefit from a different kind of program geared to their individual needs.

5. Interests (student choice)—Increases student motivation.

6. Competencies—By previous competencies passed in a given activity or sequence of activities.

7. Instructional method—Student choice of the teaching method preferred.

8. Sex—Preferred for some contact sports.

9. Period handy in schedule.

Nongraded schools

In the nongraded school, students are grouped homogeneously for each area of study. They may be in a low-ability group for one skill and a high-ability group for another. Team teachers facilitate this process. Students work at their own pace with no pressure on fast or slow learners to stay with the class. Students are evaluated by a criterion-referenced system. Reporting is often in narrative form or given orally in parent conferences.

Although increased teacher time is needed for student diagnosis, placement, evaluation, record keeping, reporting, and staff planning, some teachers prefer the system. They feel they can teach more effectively to homogeneous groups with common learning problems.

Year-round schools

Year-round schooling began as an economy move and has proved to be advantageous in other ways as well. Most students are under the 45–15 schedule, in which they attend classes for forty-five days and then have fifteen days off. Some advantages include savings in per pupil expenditures because of increased use of facilities, opportunities for individualized instruction and tutoring, decreased absenteeism and vandalism, and increased motivation. Both nongraded and year-round schooling are currently more prevalent at the elementary level.

Staff utilization patterns

Alternative staff utilization patterns include team teaching and differentiated staffing.

Students benefit from the additional help
provided by team teachers.

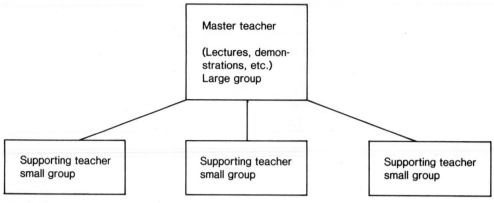

Figure 25.2 A possible team teaching arrangement.

Team teaching

Team teaching is an arrangement in which two or more teachers share the responsibility for planning, instructing, and evaluating one or more class groups for the purpose of improving instruction. It is a means of organizing personnel to provide a program more effective and efficient than each could provide separately. It capitalizes on the talents and interests of each team member.

One common type of team teaching is "turn teaching" in which teachers divide a large group of students into smaller groups, which rotate from teacher to teacher. Each teacher teaches a different topic, activity, skill level, or portion of the activity. An example of this is the American Red Cross progressive beginner course, where ten stations are set up and children are moved from one station to another as each skill is learned in the crawl stroke progression.

A second variation of team teaching occurs when a master teacher, who is chosen on the basis of expertise, directs the entire activity and supporting teachers assist with materials, equipment, discipline, and individual help as shown in figure 25.2. Master teachers often change from activity to activity on the basis of their competencies in the various activities.

Some advantages of team teaching are the utilization of individual interests and competencies of teachers and the ability to group and regroup students in varying teacher-pupil ratios in terms of facilities, student abilities, or type of activity.

Differentiated staffing

Differentiated staffing is a staffing pattern in which staff members play different roles in the educational process because of different skills, interests, and career goals. Although many different approaches have been developed, a team generally consists of a master teacher, two or more experienced or inexperienced teachers, student teachers, paraprofessional aides, and secretarial help as shown in table 25.1.

Table 25.1 An example of differentiated staffing

Degree	Title	Responsibilities
M.S. or Ed. D	Master teacher; twelve-month contract	Design programs Evaluate instruction Supervise other staff Provide in-service opportunities Plan and implement budget Teach Serve as liaison with other school personnel and with the community
B.S. or M.S.	Teacher; ten-to-twelve-month contract (tenured)	Teach and evaluate students Meet with parents
B.S.	Associate teacher or Intern; ten-month contract (nontenured)	Teach in areas of specialty Give individual tutorial assistance
Degree in progress	Student teachers	Supervised teaching Provide individual tutorial help Prepare teaching materials
None	Paraprofessional aides	Set up and care of equipment Call roll Keep records Supervise class or locker room Reproduce, administer, and grade tests Lead warm-up exercises Referee games Assist with practice drills Prepare learning materials Set up and operate media hardware Prepare bulletin board displays

Paraprofessional aides can be undergraduate or graduate students, community volunteers or paid part- or full-time staff. Each paraprofessional is assigned duties commensurate with his or her ability and training.

Since differentiated staffing provides for a variety of salaries dependent upon the differing responsibilities of staff, it rewards those who develop additional competencies in teaching, thereby allowing talented teachers to stay in teaching rather than move to the more lucrative areas of administration or business. At the same time, it discourages "endurance pay," which is based on years in teaching regardless of expertise or contribution.

Disadvantages are the modification of the entire school program needed to implement the system, the reduction of student contact hours by the most experienced teachers, and the threat of being replaced as a teacher by a paraprofessional.

Scheduling procedures

The following steps are suggested as a guide toward the achievement of a workable schedule:

Step 1.   Identify the most desirable grouping pattern for class assignments.

Step 2.   Determine class size.

Step 3.   Determine appropriate time allotments for daily, weekly, and unit instruction.

Step 4.   Assign teachers and teacher loads.

Step 5.   Identify teaching stations and equipment.

Step 6.   Develop a schedule.

Step 1. Identify the most desirable grouping pattern for class assignments

Students can be grouped for physical education classes on the basis of the factors already described in this chapter. The American Alliance for Health, Physical Education, Recreation and Dance recommends that "groupings for instruction in physical education should be appropriate to the objectives of the lessons being taught, and they [the classes] should be ordinarily consistent in size with those of other subject areas. . . ."[2]

Opportunities for individualizing instruction should be of primary concern in determining class groups. Class groupings must be flexible enough to provide for differences in interests, levels of maturity, size, abilities, and needs.

Step 2. Determine class size

Identify the appropriate class size for each learning group, task, and instructional method. Class size may range from very large to only one student, depending upon the aim of the instruction. For example, a film could be shown to a large group, skills need to be practiced in smaller groups, and individual help or contract learning may be on a one-to-one basis.

Ideally, class size should be consistent with the requirements of good instruction and safety in the activity to be taught. The class size should assure that the student can receive adequate teacher assistance and individual practice or study. For example, a tennis unit with four courts available would best be limited to sixteen students if the course objectives are to be met. Since it would be impossible to schedule sixteen students in a traditional class each period, a suitable alternative is to schedule a reasonable "average" class size (i.e., the same pupil/teacher ratio as for other subject areas in the school), and then to adjust class sizes among teachers in terms of the units to be taught. The average class size for physical education can be determined by the following formula:

Average class size =

$$\frac{\text{Total students in school}}{\text{Number of teachers} \times \text{Number of periods/day taught by each teacher}}$$

The average class size recommended is usually thirty-five. Adapted physical education classes should have no more than twenty. Physical education needs to demonstrate the sound instructional techniques that justify reasonable class sizes and avoid "throw out the ball" type programs.

Step 3. Determine appropriate time allotments for daily, weekly, and unit instruction

The individual states prescribe the minimum instructional time allotment per day or per week (either by law or by suggestion). The American Alliance for Health, Physical Education, Recreation and Dance publishes these in *State Requirements in Physical Education for Teachers and Students.*[3]

The American Alliance for Health, Physical Education, Recreation and Dance[4] and the Society of State Directors of Health, Physical Education, and Recreation[5] recommend a daily instructional period for elementary school pupils of 30 minutes, or a total of 150 minutes per week.

At the secondary-school level, the Society of State Directors of Health, Physical Education, and Recreation[6] and the President's Council on Youth Fitness[7] recommend a minimum of one standard class period daily.

One of the biggest areas of concern in curriculum planning is the failure to provide long enough periods of time in instructional units for students to develop the skill and knowledge needed for participation in a given activity. Units of two, three, and four weeks are inadequate for teaching skills. Research substantiates the fact that the beginning-level learner often experiences frustration in so short a period of time. Bain indicates that the curriculum should provide "in-depth instruction in those activities of particular interest to students. Units of instruction need to be of sufficient length to develop levels of skill in the activity required to enjoy participation in it (usually a minimum of 10–12 weeks)."[8] This is especially true when students participate in physical education classes for only two or three days per week.

Scope charts with percentages of times for each area can be translated into units by multiplying the percentage by the number of weeks (or periods) in the year to get the weekly (or period) allotment for each category. Time can be allotted to specific activities or to areas for student choice within the category time allotment. However, care should be taken to limit the number of activities so that each unit will have adequate time for learning to occur.

Yearly schedules should include (1) the sequence and length of time of physical education activity units within a school year, (2) the sequence of physical education activities over a span of several years, and (3) the relationship of curriculum parts to each other—class instruction, intramurals, and extramurals.

Two types of yearly plans have emerged. In the *cycle* plan, the course of study changes for the whole school each year as shown in figure 25.3. This means that all students are participating in the same activity at the same time. Activities are usually different each year. The advantages of this system are (1) that teachers have to prepare for only one class at a time and equipment can be left set up all day; (2) that motivation is increased by reducing the repetition of activities; and (3) that the length of time for each activity is increased, thus facilitating greater learning.

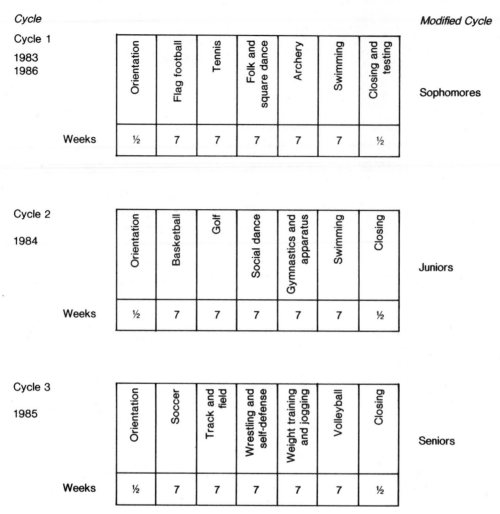

Figure 25.3 An example of cycle scheduling.

The disadvantages of the cycle plan are that students fail to progress from lower to higher levels of skill in each activity and that teachers become bored when they teach the same activity all day long. This system works well in small schools where teachers and facilities are limited.

The second type of yearly plan is a *modified cycle* in which all of the cycles are taught each year but to different classes. For example, the sophomores receive cycle 1; the juniors, cycle 2; and the seniors, cycle 3. Advantages are that progressions in specific activities can be built into the program and since teachers generally teach more than one grade level, boredom is reduced. A disadvantage may creep in, however, if too many activities are taught and the program is spread so thin that students fail to learn any activity well.

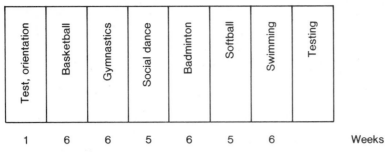

Test, orientation	Basketball	Gymnastics	Social dance	Badminton	Softball	Swimming	Testing
1	6	6	5	6	5	6	Weeks

Figure 25.4 An example of the block system.

Two methods of scheduling activities within the yearly plans are the block system and the alternating systems. The *block* system, which is shown in figure 25.4, involves instructional units in which the same activity is scheduled each class period for several consecutive weeks before another activity is scheduled. Blocks should usually be six or more weeks in length. Proponents argue that massed practice favors skill learning and retention and that facility scheduling is easier, especially in off-campus facilities. Opponents point to the fact that many schools teach the same sports year after year. The greatest danger is in trying to compress activities into very short units.

A modification of the block is teaching two activities (one week each) and then allowing students to choose which activity to devote their time to for the remainder of the block.

In the *alternating* system, students receive instruction in more than one activity each week. For example, on Mondays, Wednesdays, and Fridays, basketball is taught; on Tuesdays and Thursdays, instruction is in golf.

A modification of the alternating system is the finger system, usually used at the elementary-school level. In it a different activity is taught on each day of the week as shown in figure 25.5.

The major advantage of the alternating system is that variety increases motivation for some students. The disadvantage is the lack of continuity in each activity and the failure to provide long enough units for skill development.

When determining the length of time for lessons and units, consideration should be given to the age and ability of the students and the task to be learned. Younger students and beginners have shorter attention spans and fatigue sooner and so shorter lessons distributed daily are more appropriate. Older and more advanced students can benefit from longer periods of time occurring less often. Simple skills can be taught in a shorter length of time than more complex skills.

Units should be long enough so the objectives of the unit can be achieved, yet short enough to prevent boredom with the activity. Some units at the junior high school level may be devoted to learning basic skills so that students are introduced to activities from which they will be allowed to choose later on in the curriculum.

Days	M	T	W	T	F
	Speedball	Swimming	Tumbling	Paddle tennis	Square dance

Figure 25.5 An example of the finger system.

Step 4. Assign teachers and teacher loads

Analyze staffing requirements and existing staff strengths and assign qualified, competent teachers. One of the guidelines of the American Alliance for Health, Physical Education, Recreation and Dance states:

> Qualified and dynamic leadership is essential to the implementation of an effective and comprehensive program of physical education in the secondary school. The key to the teaching-learning environment is a competent, concerned teacher. The teacher must be knowledgeable about growth and maturation patterns and be sensitive to student needs, desires and concerns.[9]

Teachers should be assigned to classes on the basis of competencies (skills and knowledge) needed to teach the activity. The American Alliance for Health, Physical Education, Recreation and Dance recommends that:

> Teachers of potentially hazardous activity (aquatics, gymnastics, skiing) should have specialized training to the extent that they are recognized and certified by the national agencies associated with these sports.[10]

Special qualifications, including the ability to work with students at various skill levels, or with particular phases of the instructional program, and preferences about classes, times for planning, etc. should also be considered.

Elementary-school staffing pattern

Four methods of staffing physical education classes have emerged at the elementary-school level. In the first, a physical education specialist is employed to teach all physical education classes in a given school. The advantage of this method is that the specialist is prepared in physical education, with a knowledge of motor learning and teaching methods specific to physical education. The disadvantage, of course, is the cost of an additional salary for a specialist in each school.

In the second method, a rotating specialist assists classroom teachers by team teaching with them at least once a week and by providing leadership in program development. This system combines the specialist's knowledge of physical education with the classroom teacher's knowledge of the students. The specialist can present master lessons and in-service workshops and develop effective learning programs, but if the classroom teacher does not follow through, the program will be a once-a-week learning experience. Another problem is that specialists must often travel to several schools and may lack the time needed for effective planning as well as the rapport with teachers and students in each school.

The third method of staffing in elementary-school programs is for classroom teachers to trade assignments. One teacher teaches physical education for another, who in turn teaches art or music for the first teacher. In this way, teachers can teach in their areas of preference and expertise. The disadvantage is that they may not get to know the students as well in other than their own classes.

The fourth method is for classroom teachers to teach physical education to their own classes. Classroom teachers are generally more familiar with the children because they see them in a variety of subject areas. They can also integrate physical education with other classroom subjects. The disadvantage of this method is the teachers' lack of knowledge in physical education. It results in the least effective instruction in physical education.

Secondary-school staffing

Secondary schools may be staffed by "generalists" or "specialists" within the field of physical education. A specialist has an in-depth knowledge and skill in a few areas, such as aquatics or dance, and can usually assist learners to achieve higher levels of skill by anticipating and resolving potential learning problems with the subject matter. A generalist has a minimum level of skill in most curriculum offerings. The generalist sees the student in a variety of activities and can anticipate the learning needs of individual students.

Teacher loads

Consideration of the teaching load is essential to high-quality instruction. At the elementary-school level, the American Alliance for Health, Physical Education, Recreation and Dance recommends that consideration be given to the number of classes taught rather than to the length of time each class meets.[11] Time is needed between classes for preparation just as in secondary schools.

At the secondary-school level the recommendation is that class instruction per teacher not exceed five class periods or hours per day or more than 200 students per teacher. Teachers should have at least one free period daily for planning, preparation, and conferences.

Most physical education instructors are scheduled for after-school work such as coaching athletic teams, conducting intramural programs, coaching cheerleaders, and advising various clubs. Two prevalent methods used by school districts to compensate teachers for these extra duties include giving the teacher additional salary for the extra work (usually not commensurate with the responsibility and time involved) or to reduce the teacher's instructional load. Many physical education authorities prefer a reduced instructional load on the basis that no person, no matter how well paid, can work productively and efficiently for an excessive number of hours.

Step 5. Identify teaching stations and equipment

A teaching station is an area assigned to a teacher for a class, preferably with some physical or visual barrier between to cushion sound from one station to another. Distance may serve as a barrier between classes.

To calculate the number of teaching stations and teachers needed for an *elementary-school* physical education program:

1. Count the classes in the school (i.e., one class each of six grades + two kindergartens = eight classes)

2. Decide on the periods per week per pupil (five)

3. Decide on the number and length of each period (ten thirty-minute periods per day)

4. Teaching stations $= \dfrac{\text{Classes} \times \text{periods/week}}{\text{Number of periods/day} \times \text{days/week}} =$

   $\dfrac{8 \times 5}{10 \times 5} = .8$, rounded off to 1.

One teacher and one teaching station are needed.

To calculate the number of teaching stations and teachers needed for a *secondary-school* physical education program:

1. Number of sections to be offered $= \dfrac{\text{Total number of students}}{\text{class size}}$

2. Number of teaching stations (classes per period) $=$
   $\dfrac{\text{Total number of students}}{\text{Class size} \times \text{number of periods/day}}$

   Round off to the next higher whole number.

3. Number of teachers needed $= \dfrac{\text{Number of sections}}{\text{Number of periods taught/day/teacher}}$

An example is shown in the following chart.

Total number students	Class size	Periods per day	Periods per week	Sections offered	Teaching stations	Teachers needed
1,500	30	6	5	50	10	10.0
1,500	35	6	5	43	9	8.6
1,500	40	6	5	38	8	7.6

Note: Each teacher teaches five periods. Fractions = part-time teacher in physical education.

Program flexibility is increased when large numbers of students are assigned to a physical education program in which there are multiple teaching stations. Few schools possess all the facilities they need. Sometimes multipurpose rooms, hallways, auditorium stages, little theaters, and leftover classrooms can provide needed facilities for physical education.

Community resources should be used to supplement school facilities. For example, bowling alleys, skating rinks, swimming pools, ski resorts, and equestrian facilities can be rented, or students can be asked to pay a small fee. Transportation may cause legal problems. The use of community resources can help education bridge the gap between school and community. Discuss this situation with your principal for approval before adopting any off-campus program. Elective programs can help to resolve problems with fees and transportation, since the class is not required of those who can't afford the fees or transportation. Teachers should retain control of classes taught in off-campus facilities even when an outside professional is teaching.

Equipment

With regards to equipment, the American Alliance for Health, Physical Education, and Recreation recommends:

> Each area of the physical education program should be provided with appropriate equipment and supplies in sufficient quantity to provide each student with an opportunity to actively participate throughout the entire class period. A goal of one ball, one rope, etc., per child is realistic for a physical education class. If children are to be physically active and fully experiencing the learning situation, ample equipment and supplies for each child are as essential as pencils and books in the classroom.[12]

Good teaching also requires provision of appropriate books, periodicals, media, and other teaching aids. Equipment can be built by industrial arts classes, parents, or teachers, or purchased by parent-teacher associations.

	BLOCK 1		BLOCK 2		BLOCK 3	
Jones	Golf	g	Aerobic dance	b	Gymnastics	b
Garcia	Tennis	f	Volleyball	a	Basketball	a
Lungo	Flag football	g	Swimming (beg.)	e	Wrestling	h
Platero	Prep.		Prep.		Prep.	
Jones	Social dance	a	Cycling	i	Aerobic dance	b
Garcia	Prep.		Prep.		Prep.	
Platero	Flag football	g	Soccer	g	Swimming (beg.)	e
Lungo	Archery/		Fitness	b	Basketball	a
	Tennis	d,f				
Jones	Rec. dance	a	Bowling	i	Aerobic dance	c
Platero	Soccer	g	Swimming (beg.)	e	Volleyball	b
Lungo	Prep.		Prep.		Prep.	
Garcia	Archery/		Fitness	b	Basketball	a
	Tennis	d,f				
Jones	Prep.		Prep.		Prep.	
Platero	Flag football	g	Tennis	f	Aerobic dance	c
Lungo	Rec. dance	a	Swimming (beg.)	e	Volleyball	a
Garcia	Archery/		Fitness	b	Basketball	b
	Tennis	d,f				
Jones	Rec. dance	a	Bowling	i	Jazz dance	c
Garcia	Tennis	f	Aerobic dance	c	Outdoor	
Lungo	Soccer	g	Swimming (beg.)	e	pursuits	i
Platero	Badminton/		Fitness	b	Basketball	a
	Bowling	b			Volleyball	b
Jones	Golf/Softball	g	Fitness	b	Basketball	b
Lungo	Archery	d	Basketball	a	Volleyball	a
Platero	Tennis	f	Bowling	c	Swimming	e
Garcia	Cycling	i	Flag football	g	Aerobic dance	c

a--Gym A	d--Track	g--Field
b--Gym B	e--Pool	h--Wrestling room
c--Dance studio	f--Tennis	i--Community facility

Figure 25.6 A possible schedule.

Step 6. Develop a schedule

Work out a schedule that coordinates time, teachers, and facilities. A possible scheduling chart is shown in figure 25.6.

Although scheduling is essentially an administrative function, the success of the program is based on its implementation by the various faculty members involved. Care should be taken to avoid a curriculum which attempts to do a little bit of everything with nothing done well.

An example of scheduling

Given: 800 students, four teachers, six periods, five days per week

Figure 25.6—*Continued*

BLOCK 4		BLOCK 5		BLOCK 6	
Bowling	i	Cycling	i	Archery	d
Badminton	a	Soccer	q	Tennis	f
Swimming (int.)	e	Track and Field	d	Softball	q
Prep.		Prep.		Prep.	
Badminton	b	Gymnastics	b	Golf	q
Prep.		Prep.		Prep.	
Swimming (int.)	e	Basketball	a	Tennis	f
Volleyball	a	Golf/Softball	q	Badminton/	
				Bowling	a
Gymnastics	h	Badminton	b	Cycling	i
Basketball	a	Swimming (int.)	e	Archery	d
Prep.		Prep.		Prep.	
Volleyball	b	Golf/Softball	q	Badminton/	
				Bowling	a
Prep.		Prep.		Prep.	
Bowling	i	Softball	q	Badminton	a
Basketball	a	Swimming (int.)	e	Track and Field	d
Volleyball	b	Badminton/		Golf/Softball	q
		Bowling	a		
Modern dance	c	Ballet	c	Social dance	c
Volleyball	a	Badminton	b	Tennis	f
Swimming (int.)	e	Golf	q	Track and Field	d
Basketball	b	Archery/		Golf/Softball	q
		Tennis	d,f		
Volleyball	b	Tennis/		Badminton/	
Wrestling	h	Archery	d,f	Bowling	a
Swimming (int.)	e	Track and Field	d	Softball	m
Basketball	a	Badminton	b	Tennis	f
		Soccer	q	Golf	q

Ninth-grade activities are underlined.

Step 1

Our committee decides to implement a required program in grade nine and a selective program in grades ten through 12. Therefore, one ninth-grade class will be offered each hour and the remainder of the student body will be scheduled into the period best fitting their schedules. All classes will be coeducational.

Step 2

The average class size is forty.

$$\frac{800 \text{ students}}{4 \text{ teachers} \times 5 \text{ periods/teacher}} = 40$$

Since approximately one-fourth of the students are ninth graders (200), the number of sections of freshmen will be five: (200 ÷ 40 = 5). The remainder of the sections will have approximately 40 students per section, but all ten- through twelve-grade students will be placed on one roll. The schedule begins to look like this:

	Ninth graders	Tenth through twelfth graders
Period 1	0 classes = 0	3 classes = 120
Period 2	1 class = 40	2 classes = 80
Period 3	1 class = 40	2 classes = 80
Period 4	1 class = 40	2 classes = 80
Period 5	1 class = 40	3 classes = 120
Period 6	1 class = 40	3 classes = 120
	200 +	600 = 800

Once the students are scheduled by period, the tenth through twelfth graders will divide up into selected activities. Class enrollments may vary according to the activity.

Step 3

Our committee voted to have six six-week blocks per year. This fits in nicely with our thirty-six-week school year. This will give students enough time to learn the activities, but not so much time that they get bored. Ninth-grade units will vary according to subject matter. Team sport units will be longer, since students are expected to have basic skills before advancing to the selective program. Other units are introductory to give students a basis for choosing activities later on and are, therefore, shorter.

Step 4

Teachers will be assigned to classes on the basis of expertise, personal preference, and special qualification. All swimming instructors are certified Red Cross Water Safety instructors. The archery teacher is a certified National Archery Association instructor. All teachers can teach team sports and will rotate teaching those classes. Teachers will also teach at least one ninth-grade class each. Competencies are as follows:

Teacher	Expertise
Mrs. Platero	WSI, individual sports
Mr. Lungo	WSI, bowling, wrestling, track
Miss Jones	gymnastics, dance, individual sports
Mr. Garcia	tennis, golf, badminton

Step 5

Teaching stations include the following:

Gym A	Tennis courts
Gym B	Bowling lanes (community)
Dance studio	Golf course (community)
Pool	Field space, for three classes
Balcony	Wrestling/gymnastics room
Weight room	

Equipment is available for each student in the class sizes taught.

Step 6

Our schedule might look like the one in figure 25.6. Staff schedules are such that teachers with the competencies to teach activities scheduled for certain periods are available to teach them during the periods in question.

Questions and suggested activities

1. Locate and read articles or books on flexible or modular scheduling, team teaching, or differentiated staffing. Visit a school using one of these innovations. Do you favor or oppose the innovation?

2. Describe how differentiated staffing could be used advantageously in a physical education program.

3. Read several articles or books on alternative or nontraditional schools. Could physical education be taught in such settings?

4. Joe teaches physical education at Savannah High School. In the past ten years, the school has used a traditional time utilization method. The teachers have convinced the administration to try a modular approach on a trial basis. Outline a presentation to the parent-teacher association on the advantages and disadvantages of the modular program in physical education.

5. The school day at Younowhere Junior High is divided into six fifty-minute periods with five minutes between classes. The students complain that they never have enough time to finish activities that they start in class, and the teachers are frustrated by not having enough time to cover the materials in a class period. What creative scheduling methods could be used to help the teachers and students have more flexibility with their time?

6. Mr. Smith teaches cycling in the fall. His largest class is twenty with several classes having only twelve to fifteen students. Because of his small classes, you have ninety students in flag football. Should his class be dropped for lack of interest?

7. You have been hired to teach physical education and be the coach at a new high school in Alberta, Canada. The school has twelve seniors, thirty juniors, forty-seven sophomores, and thirty-eight freshmen. The nearest high school is eighty-five miles away. Due to the weather conditions, you are indoors for seven of the nine school months. The principal tells you to set up a program that will keep all the students active and interested during the school year. What will you do?

Suggested readings

American Association for Health, Physical Education and Recreation. *Organizational Patterns for Instruction in Physical Education,* Washington, D. C.: AAHPER, 1971.

Klappholz, Lowell A. ed. "Building and Maintaining Physical Fitness Through Selectives." *Physical Education Newsletter,* no. 124 (March 1981).

Cutler, Stan Jr. "The Nongraded Concept and Physical Education." *Journal of Health, Physical Education, Recreation* 45 (April 1974): 30–31.

Gross, Beatrice and Ronald Gross, eds. *Radical School Reform.* New York: Simon and Schuster, 1969.

Hausdorf, Walter F. and Julian R. Covell. "Expanding Programs with Limited Resources." *Journal of Physical Education and Recreation* 52 (February 1981): 50–51.

Johnson, Sandra. "Parents—An Untapped Resource." *Journal of Physical Education and Recreation* 47 (March 1976).

Moore, C. A. "Handy Gadget Simplifies Scheduling." *Journal of Physical Education and Recreation* 48 (June 1977): 18.

Munson, C. and E. Stafford. "Middle Schools: A Variety of Approaches to Physical Education." *Journal of Health, Physical Education, Recreation* 45 (February 1974): 29–31.

Spasoff, Thomas C. "Maintaining Student Interest in Elective Physical Education." *Journal of Physical Education and Recreation* 48 (June 1977):19.

Klappholz, Lowell A., ed. "Tips on Utilizing Teacher Aides in Physical Education." *Physical Education Newsletter,* no. 132 (December 1981).

Evaluating and Revising the Instructional Program

Study stimulators

1. Define formative and summative evaluation. What are the purposes of each?
2. Describe the process for evaluating a program in physical education.
3. Describe several kinds of data-gathering instruments and tell the advantages or disadvantages of each.

Several years ago, Cassidy proposed a curriculum merry-go-round on which you could climb at any point in the process of curriculum design and ride around until your purposes were accomplished. The advantage of this concept is that curriculum design is then perceived as the continuous process it ought to be.[1] One of the most important steps in this process is the evaluation of whether or not the objectives of the program have been achieved. The evaluation provides us with new information with which to begin the cycle all over again. Objectives must be reevaluated to see if they are desirable in our constantly changing environment. Curriculum patterns and teaching/learning strategies must be revised so that student achievement more nearly approximates the objectives that have been established.

An extensive review of the entire curriculum is often impractical on a continuous basis. In fact, the usual method is to select a specific portion of the curriculum to evaluate each year. Through constant appraisal and revision, the curriculum can be gradually improved to meet the purposes for which it was established. For the purposes of this discussion, let's evaluate a program called Fitness for Life, which was implemented as a part of the physical education curriculum.

Program evaluation involves both measurement (quantitative) and judgment (qualitative) appraisals. For example, fitness tests can be used to measure physical fitness. Knowledge tests measure concept acquisition. Questionnaires and inventories assess the extent to which students feel positively about physical fitness. The scores are then evaluated to determine whether or not the students achieved the objectives specified in the program.

With the increased concern for accountability in education, evaluation provides empirical data for reporting to students, parents, administrators, boards of education, state departments of education, public media, accrediting agencies, and sponsors of educational research regarding the successes or failures of our programs.

Since the curriculum is, in essence, a body of experiences that lie between the objectives and the teaching methods of a school, it is possible to develop an outstanding curriculum only to discover that students fail to achieve the desired learning outcomes because of failure to translate curriculum development into methods of teaching. Evaluation can help us determine whether the program works and how we can increase its effectiveness. The two major purposes of program evaluation are (1) to assess the validity and effectiveness (or success) of the curriculum—summative evaluation and (2) to provide information for program improvement—formative evaluation.

Summative evaluation

Summative evaluation is evaluation of the final product. It can tell us how well students have achieved specific objectives or whether a specific educational program is worth more than an alternative approach. It usually relys on more formal evaluation methods, such as standardized tests and inventories. Care should be taken to also analyze unexpected outcomes (such as negative attitudes produced or excessive costs).

Formative evaluation

Formative evaluation is feedback to teachers and program designers. It is used to evaluate whether or not students are achieving the instructional objectives and to revise portions of a program *while* it is being developed. Since most programs are only 60 percent effective the first time, they can only be improved if evaluation points out what is working or isn't working and where changes can be made to improve the program.

Formative evaluation generally uses informal evaluation techniques such as teacher observation, teacher-made tests, and student questionnaires to point out strengths and weaknesses of individual lessons or short units. Informal evaluation techniques vary in quality depending upon the skills of the person constructing the instruments. However, when carefully constructed, these instruments can be valid for evaluating local programs for which no valid standardized instrument can be found. They provide data that can help to determine the effectiveness of the instruction and the feasibility in terms of cost, teacher time, and student and teacher attitudes toward instruction. When teaching strategies are discovered to be impractical or ineffective, changes can be made at once to revise, add, or subtract lesson content or to change methods to achieve the desired results.

Procedures for program evaluation

The following steps are suggested to help you evaluate curricular programs:

Step 1.   Describe the program to be evaluated.

Step 2.   Identify the purposes of the evaluation.

Step 3.   Establish criteria for judging quality and making decisions.

Step 4.   Describe the information needed to make the decisions.

Step 5.   Obtain, record, and analyze information.

Step 6.   Interpret data in terms of standards.

Step 7.   Make decisions and formulate recommendations.

Step 1. Describe the program to be evaluated

A description of the program helps to avoid overlooking aspects that should be evaluated. The description should include:

1. A statement of the philosophy behind the program.

2. The people involved—students, their families, faculty, and administrators.

3. Performance objectives—cognitive, psychomotor, and affective—including entry behaviors, intended and unintended outcomes, arranged in a hierarchy from general to specific.

4. Subject matter content.

5. Instructional elements such as scheduling patterns, learning activities, student-student and student-teacher interactions, use of media, motivation, and evaluation and grading techniques.

6. Facilities and equipment.

7. Costs.

8. Administrative conditions.

The following is a brief description of the Fitness for Life program. Fitness for Life is an individualized program designed to help students write and apply their own fitness programs during school and throughout their lives. Students contract with an instructor to do the following:

1. Pass five mastery tests on (a) how to write programs for cardiovascular endurance, weight control, and strength and flexibility; (b) how to measure cardiovascular endurance, strength, and flexibility; and (c) fitness concepts.

2. Complete a nine-week contract for cardiovascular endurance according to the specifications on the course handout.

3. Take a fitness appraisal before and after completion of the contract and show progress.

Students complete the contract on their own time and check with the instructor for assistance as needed or to take mastery checks. A fourth outcome desired in the program is that students will have positive feelings about fitness activities and about the unit.

Step 2. Identify the purposes of the evaluation

Identify areas of concern about the program and anticipate decisions that will need to be made by asking questions, such as "Are goals and objectives appropriate?," "Are students achieving the objectives?," "What problems exist?," "What are the reactions of various audiences to the program?," and "What unanticipated outcomes are there?"

Decisions that might need to be made could include adopting a new program, discontinuing a program, changing student grouping patterns, increasing the budget, changing the staff, using community facilities, or implementing different instructional strategies. Possible alternatives should be identified in each instance.

Persons who will be responsible for making the decisions should be identified. These may include students, teachers, administrators, or the board of education.

A date should be specified for making the decisions, along with policies within which the evaluation must occur.

Some concerns about the Fitness for Life program included:

1. Did students actually increase physical fitness during the nine-week contract?

2. Did students have positive feelings about physical fitness and about the unit?

3. Were the instructors satisfied with the program?

4. Is the program better than the current program?

5. What administrative problems exist?

The faculty decided that a coordinator would be assigned to take responsibility for getting each portion of the data collected. The final evaluation would take place by the entire faculty one month prior to the end of the school year.

Step 3. Establish criteria for judging quality and making decisions

Two types of standards can be used for judging the quality of programs—absolute standards and relative standards. Absolute standards are those established by personal or professional judgment. These criteria are established in the same way that performance objectives are created. For example, 80 percent of the students will:

1. Achieve good or excellent on the 1.5 mile run.

2. Achieve a percent body fat of 20 percent or below for girls and 15 percent or below for boys.

3. Obtain a score of 80 percent or better on all five tests of fitness concepts.

4. Complete a fitness contract for nine weeks at the contracted level of exercise.

5. Have positive attitudes toward participation in physical fitness activities.

The problem with using absolute standards lies in selecting the level that is indicative of success in the program. Standards can be derived from criteria achieved in similar programs in other schools, in former programs in the same schools, or by guesstimates by administrators, teachers, parents, students, and community members working together. When

Periodic program evaluation helps
administrators, teachers, and students to reach
program goals.

students fail to achieve the standards, the program can be revised to produce the desired achievement, the objectives can be changed, or the program can be thrown out and a new one created.

Relative standards are those reflected by various alternative programs. In other words, the program is compared with other programs to determine which one has the best outcomes. National norms for fitness, skill, and knowledge are published by the American Alliance for Health, Physical Education, Recreation and Dance. These norms tell how students compare with other students nationally. Locally constructed norms can be used to evaluate how students compare with students previously completing your programs.

Standards which should be considered in all evaluation studies include (1) validity—the extent to which the evaluation provides the information it is supposed to provide; (2) reliability of the data—the degree to which the data would be the same on different trials of the test; (3) objectivity—the extent to which the data is the same for all persons administering the test; (4) cost effectiveness in terms of the time, energy and money invested; and (5) timeliness—in time to make a decision.

Step 4. Describe the information needed to make the decision

Prior to evaluating student achievement of program objectives, you should analyze the objectives to determine whether or not they are worthwhile and whether or not they will logically produce the intended outcomes. Empirical analysis should include the collection of information from other groups or specialists to determine the objectives most commonly considered to be essential. However, just because we find that we are in agreement with the objectives or methods used in other curricula does not mean that our objectives are worthwhile. Just because something exists does not mean that it *should* be so.

Information on achievement of the objectives can be gained from students, teachers, parents, and outside observers. Both summative and formative evaluation techniques can be used. Summative evaluation usually relys on controlled research, formal evaluation techniques, and structured external evaluation.

Controlled research involves the use of randomization to assign control and experimental groups. For example, students in Fitness for Life classes were tested and found to improve significantly more in physical fitness than students who were enrolled in regular physical education classes at the same time. In terms of the fitness objective, we can conclude that the Fitness for Life program was better than the regular program for achieving fitness.

Formal evaluation techniques include standardized tests and carefully constructed inventories and questionnaires. Standardized tests have been developed by the American Alliance for Health, Physical Education, Recreation and Dance to evaluate cognitive and psychomotor skills, and physical fitness. The Cooper 1.5 mile run and percent fat measured by calipers were used to evaluate the Fitness for Life program. An attitude inventory was constructed to assess attitudes toward fitness. A questionnaire measured continued participation in fitness programs several years after the program had begun.

Several problems exist when using standardized tests for program evaluation. One is the selection of inappropriate instruments for the type of program being evaluated. Tests must have content validity; that is, they must test the objectives specified in the program. Since most standardized tests are directed toward lower-level cognitive and psychomotor skills, other instruments may be needed in addition to standardized tests if the program is to be evaluated fairly. Face validity, reliability, and appropriate norms for the group to be tested must also be assessed if a test is to be adopted.

Teaching to the test is another common problem with standardized tests. This tends to demote the program to a lower level of objectives rather than to provide a wide variety of learning experiences. When evaluating a new program, it would be best if the teacher never sees the test before it is given. With regard to standardized tests, Worthen points out that "in all the history of evaluation in education it has proven exceedingly difficult to demonstrate the superiority of *any* procedure in terms of test performance."[2]

Structured external evaluation was one of the earliest methods used for evaluating the total physical education program. The first scorecard was developed by William Ralph LaPorte in the 1930s. Since that time a number of scorecards have been developed by various state departments of education. They are often used by evaluation teams from accrediting associations. The *Assessment Guide for Secondary School Physical Education Programs,* which was created by the American Alliance for Health, Physical Education, Recreation and Dance, provides a set of standards for evaluating the physical education program in the areas of (1) administration, (2) the instructional program, (3) the intramural program, and (4) the athletic program. A sample of the criteria in the areas of administration and the instructional program is shown in figures 26.1 and 26.2. An external evaluation team was invited to assess the effectiveness of the Fitness for Life program. They constructed their own evaluation instrument.

Criteria	Response (Circle)			Notes
	Instruc- tional Pro- gram	Intramural Program	Athletic Program	
16. Written department policies are available concerning standard operating procedures involving:				
A. Uniforms, lockers, towels, locks, lost and found.	Yes No	Yes No	Yes No	
B. Emergencies and location of first aid supplies.	Yes No	Yes No	Yes No	
C. Facility problems or hazardous conditions.	Yes No	Yes No	Yes No	
D. Teacher evaluation.	Yes No	Yes No	Yes No	
E. Absences, excuses and attendance.	Yes No	Yes No	Yes No	
F. Legal responsibilities of personnel.	Yes No	Yes No	Yes No	
G. Scheduling.	Yes No	Yes No	Yes No	
H. Facility supervision.	Yes No	Yes No	Yes No	
I. Purchase of equipment and supplies.	Yes No	Yes No	Yes No	
J. Maintenance and management of facilities, equipment, and supplies.	Yes No	Yes No	Yes No	
17. Secretarial and support personnel are available to meet program needs.	Yes No	Yes No	Yes No	
18. Allotment of time and facilities for all programs are equitable and meet program needs.	Yes	Yes No	Yes No	
19. Number of available indoor and outdoor teaching stations meet all programs needs. They:				
A. Are conducive to quality instruction.	Yes No	Yes No	Yes No	
B. Are adequate to handle peak hour loads.	Yes No	Yes No	Yes No	
C. Contain adequate office space.	Yes No	Yes No	Yes No	
20. Community facilities are utilized to avoid costly duplication, to expand program offerings, and to make use of superior facilities.	Yes No	Yes No	Yes No	

Figure 26.1 A sample of the evaluative criteria for administration.

Source: From the Assessment Guide for Secondary School Physical Education Programs, developed by the National Association for Sport and Physical Education of the American Alliance for Health, Physical Education, Recreation and Dance, 1977.

Criteria	Response (Circle)	Notes
6. Instructional program areas that are designed to meet objectives focusing on the organization, development, and refinement of skillful movement include the following units in *prescribed elective* courses: A. Sport, dance, and exercise activities offered at progressive skill levels.	Yes No	
B. Students grouped for instruction according to grade level or ability.	Yes No	
C. Formal instruction (coeducational whenever possible) provided in team sports, individual and dual sports, aquatics, dance, and lifetime/leisure time activities.	Yes No	
D. Adapted program that is an integral part of the regular program that provides instruction compatible with physical disabilities (goal to successfully integrate students into regular classes).	Yes No	
7. Instructional program areas that are designed to meet objectives focusing on knowledge of the basic theoretical concepts of human movement behavior as they relate to sport, dance, and exercise include the following areas in *required* theoretical course work and/or cognitive unit objectives within activity coursework:		

Figure 26.2 A sample of the evaluative criteria for instruction.

Source: From the Assessment Guide for Secondary School Physical Education Programs, developed by the National Association for Sport and Physical Education of the American Alliance for Health, Physical Education, Recreation and Dance, 1977.

Formative evaluation generally uses informal evaluation techniques such as teacher-constructed tests, inventories, and questionnaires; teacher-directed observation; frequency charts; subjective judgment; and informal analysis.

Teacher-constructed tests, inventories, and questionnaires and teacher-directed observation have been discussed in detail in chapter 11. In the Fitness for Life program, an inventory was constructed to measure attitudes toward participation. A questionnaire also requested feedback on preferred methods of instruction.

Frequency charts can be used to tally such items as student participation in extracurricular or leisure-time activities, attendance, tardiness, discipline, drop-outs, awards, assignments completed, library books checked out on a given subject, appointments kept, and

Criteria	Response (Circle)		Notes
A. Biomechanical and kinesiological concepts.	Yes	No	
B. Psychological concepts related to motor performance.	Yes	No	
C. Exercise physiology.	Yes	No	
D. Philosophy of human movement.	Yes	No	
E. Sports, medicine / athletic injury.	Yes	No	
F. Historical development of sport, dance, and exercise forms.	Yes	No	
G. Rules and strategies of sport forms.	Yes	No	
H. Motor learning principles.	Yes	No	
I. Motor development.	Yes	No	
J. Sport sociology.	Yes	No	
K. Humanities and sciences subject matter relationships to movement forms.	Yes	No	
8. Written course outlines are followed by instructors and available to students. These outlines include:	Yes	No	
A. Rationale for inclusion in instructional program	Yes	No	
B. Behavioral objectives.	Yes	No	
C. Prescribed evaluation procedures based upon stated behavioral objectives.	Yes	No	
D. Sequential skill progressions.	Yes	No	

choices made in selective activities. Parent and community involvement through attendance at parent-teacher association meetings, back-to-school nights, parent-teacher conferences, board of education meetings, and school visits can also be recorded. For example, students in the fitness program were required to log in each time they requested individual help. Dates on which tests were taken were recorded. A contract was required on which students recorded their weekly participation in selected activities.

Subjective judgment by teachers, administrators, parents, students, and community members can provide valuable information. Annual interviews or committee meetings to discuss goals and objectives, assess achievement of objectives, and predict needs and problems should deal with such questions as "Should we add anything to our program?," "Why or why not?," "Should we delete anything from our program?," "Why or why not?," "What is not going well?," "How could we make it better?" A continuous dialog between teacher and students in the Fitness for Life program helped to provide feedback on what was or was not working. Teachers met weekly to discuss the progress of the program.

Informal analysis by teachers and administrators should assess the effects of the program on faculty and staff. Adverse effects can result in physical and emotional deterioration resulting in a less effective program for teachers and students. Chapter 19 discussed a number of techniques for informal analysis. In the Fitness for Life program, teachers were frustrated by the procrastination of students in taking written tests. Students also complained about the need to log in each week.

In any evaluation program, care should be taken to utilize a variety of evaluation instruments. Failure to do so can result in a biased interpretation of program effectiveness. The selection of each technique should be based on the objective and the group to be evaluated.

A schedule or work plan should be formulated to keep the evaluation proceeding on time. The plan should include a description of who will do what, with what instruments, using what population sample, and by what date. A suggested format appears in figure 26.3.

Step 5. Obtain, record, and analyze information

Obtain and record the information specified in step 4, including such areas as student experiences, student gains and losses, unintended outcomes, and program costs in terms of time, money, and other resources. Determine a format for classifying and recording the information. Analyze the information by using appropriate statistical methods.

Figure 26.4 shows the results of the data collected during the evaluation of the Fitness for Life program. Note that only a sample of the total students participating in the program took the pretest on the mastery tests and completed the attitude inventory and instructional methods questionnaires. This was done by randomly assigning a few students in each class to each section of the inventory or questionnaire rather than by having all students complete all of the sections. This conserved student time and resulted in students being more attentive than they might have been to a long evaluation instrument. Since the fitness tests were used as a basis for the individual contracts, almost all of the students took them. The number of students achieving the 80 percent criterion on the mastery tests and the percentage achieving mastery are shown in the figure.

Step 6. Interpret data in terms of standards

The purpose of program evaluation is to determine the worth or value of the program. Thus, after all of the data has been collected, a judgment must be made as to whether or not the program has been successful.

As in the other phases of curriculum design, many people should be involved in making these judgments, including students, parents, faculty, administrators, the board of education, and community and professional leaders. Conclusions should be drawn concerning the effectiveness of the program and the progress of the students involved.

Two questions should be answered in the interpretation of the information collected: (1) were the objectives achieved? and (2) was there a logical connection between entry behaviors, learning activities, and desired outcomes? Achievement of the program objectives is determined by comparing the data with the standards specified in step 3.

OBJECTIVE	ACTION BY	METHOD	POPULATION	DEADLINE
1. Pass five mastery tests.	Mr. Ames	Mastery tests.	All students in the school.	January and June
2. Complete contract.	Miss Jones	Count of completed contracts, analyze uncompleted contracts for problem areas.	All students in the school.	January and June
3. Take fitness appraisal.	Mr. Sims	Fitness appraisals recorded on class record sheets.	All students in the school.	January and June
4. Increase fitness.	Mrs. Garcia	Computer analysis of fitness appraisals.	All students in the school.	January and June
5. Positive feelings of students toward the unit; toward fitness.	Mr. Platt	Inventory of student feelings.	Random samples of 100 students.	January and June
6. Comparison with current program.	Mrs. Garcia	Computer analysis of fitness appraisals.	Test random sample of students in regular program and statistics from Step 4.	January and June

Figure 26.3 An evaluation workplan for Fitness for Life.

OBJECTIVE	PRETEST DATA		
	Number of Students	Number Achieving Criterion	%
1. Pass five mastery tests.			
Test 1	20	2	10%
Test 2	20	1	5%
Test 3	20	0	0%
Test 4	20	1	5%
Test 5	20	3	15%
Total			
2. Complete contract.			
3. Take fitness appraisals.	200	200	100%

4. Increase fitness.	PRETEST MEAN Girls	PRETEST MEAN Boys
percent fat.	19.43	15.10
1.5--mile run.	14:38	13:24

5. Positive feelings of students.	FAVORABLE	UNFAVORABLE
Orientation session.	HHH HHH I	IIII
Mastery tests.	HHH HHH II	III
Contract.	HHH HHH	IIII
Fitness appraisals.	HHH HHH IIII	I
Grading system.	IIII	HHH HHH I
Instructor assistance.	HHH I	IIII
Toward fitness.	HHH HHH HHH	

6. Comparison with current program.	CURRENT PROGRAM		
	Number of Students	Number Achieving Criterion	%
Concept tests.	800	111	13.9
percent fat.	800	500	62.5
1.5--mile run.	800	436	54.5

Figure 26.4 A recording form for the Fitness for Life program data.

Figure 26.4—*Continued*

POSTTEST DATA Number of Students	Number Achieving Criterion	%	CRITERION MET Yes	No
200	180	90.0%	X	
200	185	92.5%	X	
200	150	75.0%		X
200	190	95.0%	X	
200	195	97.5%	X	
200	165	82.5%	X	
200	192	96.0%	X	

POSTTEST MEAN Girls	POSTTEST MEAN Boys	SIGNIFICANT Yes	No
16.7	12.28	X	
13:21	12:11	X	

COMMENTS

Great!

Too easy, except Test 3, which had confusing questions.

Want ABC system.

Too busy to talk, too many log-ins.

FITNESS FOR LIFE PROGRAM Number of Students	Number Achieving Criterion	%	CRITERION MET Yes	No
200	150	75	X	
200	152	76	X	
200	181	90.5	X	

An analysis of the data in figure 26.4 reveals that 80 percent of the students achieved the three unit objectives with one exception. In test 3, only 75 percent of the students achieved mastery. Data from the questionnaire reveal that the test questions were confusing to students. An analysis of the test shows that questions 6–10 were consistently missed. Perhaps the solution is better instruction in the area of planning the weight control program. Another solution might be to clarify the questions on the test.

The data show that students in the Fitness for Life program achieved significant increases in all four components of physical fitness. The differences in fitness between students in the regular program and the fitness program were also significant. Students appeared to be positive toward the instruction and toward physical fitness, with the exceptions noted. Some revisions in the program could resolve these problems.

In order to interpret the relationship between entry behaviors, learning activities, and desired outcomes, we must analyze the pretest and posttest data. If students score high on the pretest, we can *not* analyze whether the learning was or was not effective since students already could achieve the standard for proficiency. This indicates that the instruction was unnecessary and can be eliminated. When students score low on the pretest and low on the posttest, it shows that the instruction was inadequate. It needs to be revised or an alternative program adopted. Low pretest scores accompanied by high posttest scores demonstrate that sound instruction has occurred and students are learning as planned.

Step 7. Make decisions and formulate recommendations

Recommendations provide a basis for administrative action in the form of further implementation, a modification or revision of the objectives of the program, or a discarding of the program. The results of the evaluation with accompanying recommendations should be communicated to the faculty, administration, students, parents, and other interested community members.

In the Fitness for Life program, the following recommendations were made:

1. The program should be retained.

2. The grading system should be changed to an "A-pass-fail" system in which students can get an "A" grade or a "pass grade" (B or C equivalent) or a "fail" to provide more challenge to students to excell.

3. The test and the handout on weight-control should be rewritten.

4. Students in the "good" or above categories must log in only every other week. This will provide more time for students needing help.

5. Test deadlines for each test will be posted to reduce procrastination.

6. A meeting should be held in December to evaluate the changes.

Questions and suggested activities

1. Obtain copies of various scorecards and evaluate them. Choose the one best suited to your program level (elementary, junior high, senior high, or college) and evaluate a program of your choice. Discuss your findings with your class.

2. Using a curriculum for a junior or senior high school in your area, establish a plan for continuous and periodic evaluation of the curriculum in terms of the achievement of stated curricular objectives.

3. Evaluate the curriculum in several junior or senior high schools. Compare the program in terms of seasonal content, variety of activities, preparation for adult life, elective or required programs, etc.

4. Define accountability. Why is evaluation essential to achieve accountability in physical education?

5. Some parents of the community are concerned that their children are losing interest in the school's physical education program and are not acquiring any useful skills. They feel that the physical education classes are simply "glorified play times," that balls are merely handed out each period, and that students participate in the same activities from year to year. As head of the department, the principal asks you to evaluate the situation and make any needed changes to improve the program. How will you go about this?

6. Your program has been considered a reasonable curriculum for many years. However, you have not changed any of it since the late sixties. How and what will you evaluate to find out if it is still a good program?

7. You have been assigned to evaluate the physical education program at your school because the students scored below the fiftieth percentile on national fitness and knowledge test scores. What will you do?

Suggested readings

Aten, Rosemary. "Formative and Summative Evaluation in the Instructional Process." *Journal of Physical Education and Recreation* 51 (September 1980): 68–69.

Freedman, Mark S. and Ronald E. Perez. "Graphing Teacher Behavior Using the Computer in Physical Education." *Journal of Physical Education and Recreation* 51 (June 1980): 39.

Heitmann, Helen. "Curriculum Evaluation." *Journal of Physical Education and Recreation* 49 (March 1978): 36–37.

Lewis, George T. "A Practical System for Observing and Evaluating Student Behavior in Physical Education." *The Physical Educator* 34 (March 1977): 17–19.

Swanson, James R. "Developing and Implementing Objectives in Physical Education." *Journal of Physical Education and Recreation* 50 (March 1979): 68–69.

*B. R. C.

*A. R. C.

Fable of the Activity Curriculum
or
The Difference in Individual Differencies

**By Dr. G. H. Reavis,
Asst. Supt. Cincinnati Public Schools**

**Illustrations by W. A. Ownbey,
Supervisor, State College, Cape Girardeau**

Once upon a time, the animals decided they must do something heoric to meet the problems of "a new world," so they organized a school. They adopted an activity curriculum consisting of running, climbing, swimming, and flying and, to make it easier to administer, all the animals took all the subjects.

The duck was excellent in swimming, better in fact than his instructor, and made passing grades in flying, but he was very poor in running. Since he was slow in running, he had to stay after school and also drop swimming to practice running. This was kept up until his web feet were badly worn and he was only average in swimming. But average was acceptable in school, so nobody worried about that except the duck.

The rabbit started at the top of the class in running, but had a nervous breakdown because of so much makeup work in swimming.

The squirrel was excellent in climbing until he developed frustration in the flying class where his teacher made him start from the ground-up instead of from the tree-top-down. He also developed charlie horses from overexertion and then got C in climbing and D in running.

The eagle was a problem child and was disciplined severely. In the climbing class he beat all the others to the top of the tree, but insisted on using his own way to get there.

At the end of the year, an abnormal eel that could swim exceedingly well, and also run, climb, and fly a little had the highest average and was valedictorian.

The prairie dogs stayed out of school and fought the tax levy because the administration would not add digging and burrowing to the curriculum. They apprenticed their child to a badger and later joined the groundhogs and gophers to start a successful private school.

Does this fable have a moral?

---

*Before revised curriculum
*After revised curriculum

references

Chapter 1

1. By permission. From *Webster's New Collegiate Dictionary,* © 1981 by G. & C. Merriam Co., Publishers of the Merriam-Webster® Dictionaries.
2. James C. Enochs, *The Restoration of Standards: The Modesto Plan* (Bloomington, Ind.: Phi Delta Kappa Educational Foundation, 1979), p. 7.
3. Dennis A. Williams, et al., "Why Public Schools Fail," *Newsweek* (April 20, 1981): 62–65.
4. Charles E. Silberman, *Crisis in the Classroom: The Remaking of American Education* (New York: Random House, Inc., 1970), p. 28.
5. Williams, "Why Public Schools Fail."
6. Max Ways, "O Say Can You See? The Crisis in our National Perception," *Fortune* (October 1968): 121–23 and 198–204.
7. Williams, "Why Public Schools Fail."
8. "Schools Win Good Marks from The Public," *NEA Reporter* 20 (December 1981): 4–5.
9. Williams, "Why Public Schools Fail."
10. Silberman, *Crisis in the Classroom,* pp. 21, 29.
11. Williams, "Why Public Schools Fail."
12. Robert N. Singer and Walter Dick, *Teaching Physical Education: A Systems Approach* (Boston: Houghton Mifflin Company, 1974).
13. Frank R. Krajewski and Gary L. Pettier, ed., *Educational: Where It's Been, Where It's At, Where It's Going* (Columbus, Ohio, Charles E. Merrill, 1973), p. 134. Peddiwell, J. Abner, *The Saber Tooth Curriculum* (New York: McGraw-Hill Book Co., 1939).
14. Commission on Reorganization of Secondary Education, *Cardinal Principles of Secondary Education* (Washington, D.C.: U.S. Government Printing Office, 1918), pp. 7–15.
15. Educational Policies Commission, *The Purposes of Education in American Democracy* (Washington, D.C.: National Education Association, 1938), pp. 50–123.
16. Educational Policies Commission, *Education for ALL American Youth* (Washington, D.C.: National Education Association, 1944), pp. 225–26.
17. American Association of School Administrators, *Imperatives in Education* (Washington, D.C.: American Association of School Administrators, 1966).
18. As developed by the Institute for Educational Management for the Northwest Regional Educational Laboratory in preparation for the Employer Based Career Education program.
19. B. Frank Brown, *The Reform of Secondary Education* (New York: McGraw-Hill Book Co., 1973), pp. 32–35.
20. Richard E. Gross, "Seven New Cardinal Principles," *Phi Delta Kappan* 60 (December 1978): 291–93.
21. Glen Hass, *Curriculum Planning: A New Approach,* 2d ed. (Boston: Allyn & Bacon, Inc., 1977), p. 27.
22. Harold G. Shane, *The Educational Significance of the Future* (Bloomington, Ind.: Phi Delta Kappa, Inc., 1973), pp. 40–41.
23. Hass, *Curriculum Planning,* p. 27.
24. Shane, *The Educational Significance of the Future,* p. 47.
25. Ibid., p. 43.
26. Ibid., pp. 44–45.
27. Ibid., pp. 19–20.
28. Ronald C. Doll, *Curriculum Improvement: Decision Making and Process,* 4th ed. (Boston: Allyn & Bacon, Inc., 1978), p. 82.
29. George H. Gallup, "The 13th Annual Gallup Poll of the Public's Attitudes Toward the Public Schools," *Phi Delta Kappan* 63 (September 1981): 33–47.
30. Williams, "Why Public Schools Fail."
31. Ibid.
32. Shane, *The Educational Significance of the Future,* p. 19.
33. Ibid., p. 45.
34. Ibid., p. 46.
35. Ibid.

36. Ibid., pp. 48–49.
37. Ibid., pp. 22–23.
38. Ibid., p. 20.
39. Robert Benjamin, *Making Schools Work: A Reporter's Journey Through Some of America's Most Remarkable Classrooms* (New York: The Continuum Publishing Corporation, 1981), pp. 118 and 140.
40. Ibid., p. 113.
41. Silberman, *Crisis in the Classroom,* p. 97.
42. Ibid., p. 98.
43. Barak V. Rosenshine, "Academic Engaged Time, Content Covered and Direct Instruction," *Journal of Education* 160 (August 1978): 38–66.
44. Enochs, *The Restoration of Standards,* pp. 7–8.
45. Benjamin, *Making Schools Work,* p. 173.
46. Ibid., pp. 174–79.
47. Alvin Toffler, *The Schoolhouse in the City* (New York: Praeger, in cooperation with Educational Facilities Laboratories, 1968), pp. 367–69.
48. Silberman, *Crisis in the Classroom,* p. 114.
49. Ibid., p. 116.
50. Benjamin, *Making Schools Work,* p. 36.
51. Tom Evaul, "Organizing Centers for the 1980's," *Journal of Physical Education and Recreation* 51 (September 1980): 51–54.
52. Ronald C. Doll, "Alternative Forms of Schooling," *Educational Leadership* 29 (February 1972): 391–93.
53. Neil Postman and Charles Weingartner, *Teaching as a Subversive Activity* (New York: Dell Publishing Co., Inc.), 1969.
54. Shane, *The Educational Significance of the Future,* pp. 59–81.
55. Toffler, *The Schoolhouse in the City,* pp. 100–9.
56. Ibid., pp. 191–99.
57. Shane, *The Educational Significance of the Future,* p. 33.
58. Peter Everett, "Putting the 'Class' Back in the Classroom," *Alliance Update* (November 1981): 2.
59. Silberman, *Crisis in the Classroom,* p. 36.
60. American Association of School Administrators, *Imperatives in Education* (Washington, D.C.: American Association of School Administrators, 1966), p. 174.

Chapter 2

1. Delbert Oberteuffer and Celeste Ulrich, *Physical Education: A Textbook of Principles for Professional Students,* 4th ed. (New York: Harper & Row, Publishers, 1970), p. 6.
2. American Alliance for Health, Physical Education and Recreation, *Guide to Excellence for Physical Education in Colleges and Universities* (Washington, D.C.: AAHPER, 1970).
3. Leland Stanford, in *The Curriculum in Physical Education,* 2d ed. (Englewood Cliffs, New Jersey: Prentice-Hall, Inc., 1974), p. 174.
4. Charles H. McCloy, "How About Some Muscle?" *Journal of Health and Physical Education* 7 (May 1936): 302–3, 355.
5. Arthur Steinhaus, in *Physical Education: Introductory Analysis* (Dubuque, Iowa: Wm. C. Brown Company Publishers, 1972), p. 63.
6. Thomas D. Wood, "The Scientific Approach in Physical Education," in *The Making of American Physical Education,* ed. Arthur Weston (New York: Appleton-Century-Crofts, 1962), p. 151.
7. Luther Halsey Gulick, "Physical Training in the Modern City," in *The Making of American Physical Education,* ed. Arthur Weston (New York: Appleton-Century-Crofts, 1962), p. 169.
8. Clark W. Hetherington, "Fundamental Education," in *The Making of American Physical Education,* ed. Arthur Weston (New York: Appleton-Century-Crofts, 1962), p. 160.
9. Ibid.
10. Jesse Feiring Williams, "Education Through the Physical," in *The Making of American Physical Education,* ed. Arthur Weston (New York: Appleton-Century-Crofts, 1962), p. 219.
11. Jay B. Nash, "Character Education As an Objective," in *The Making of American Physical Education,* ed. Arthur Weston (New York: Appleton-Century-Crofts, 1962), p. 256.

12. Eleanor Metheny, "The Third Dimension in Physical Education," in *The Making of American Physical Education,* ed. Arthur Weston (New York: Appleton-Century-Crofts, 1962), p. 238.

13. Camille Brown and Rosalind Cassidy, *Theory in Physical Education,* Philadelphia: Lea and Febiger, 1963, p. 54.

14. American Association of Health, Physical Education and Recreation, *Guidelines for Secondary School Physical Education,* (Washington, D.C.: AAHPER, 1970).

15. Curriculum Action Project, Physical Education Department, Calgary Board of Education (Calgary, Canada: 1978).

16. Joel Rosentswieg, "A Ranking of the Objectives of Physical Education," *Research Quarterly* 40 (December 1969): 783–87.

17. Robberta Mesenbrink, et al. National Association of Secondary School Principals, *Curriculum Report,* vol. 4 (December 1974).

18. Greyson Daughtrey, *Effective Teaching in Physical Education For Secondary Schools,* 2d ed. (Philadelphia: W. B. Saunders, Co., 1973).

19. Carl W. Bookwalter and Harold J. VanderZwaag, *Foundations and Principles of Physical Education* (Philadelphia: W. B. Saunders Co., 1969), p. 1.

20. Richard L. Marsh, "Physically Educated—What It Will Mean for Tomorrow's High School Student," *Journal of Physical Education and Recreation* 49 (January 1978): 50.

21. Tom Evaul, "Organizing Centers for the 1980's," *Journal of Physical Education and Recreation* 51 (September 1980): 51–54.

Chapter 3

1. Daniel Fader, *The Naked Children.* Speech given at Brigham Young University.

2. Leslie J. Chamberlin and Ricardo Girona, "Our Children Are Changing," *Educational Leadership* 33 (January 1976): 301–5.

3. Ibid.

4. Margaret Mead, "Early Adolescence in the U.S." in *Readings in Human Development,* Harold W. Bernard and Wesley C. Huckins, eds. (Boston: Allyn & Bacon, Inc., 1967).

5. John Gustafson, "Teaching For Self-Esteem," *The Physical Educator* 35 (May 1978): 68.

6. Ronald C. Doll, *Curriculum Improvement: Decision Making and Process,* 4th ed. (Boston: Allyn & Bacon, Inc., 1978).

7. Educational Policies Commission. *Education for ALL American Youth* (Washington, D.C.: National Education Association, 1952), p. 29.

Chapter 4

1. Don E. Arnold, "Positive Outcomes of Recent Legislative and Case Law Developments Which Have Implications for HPER Programs," *The Physical Educator* 37 (March 1980): 24–25.

2. Larry Berryhill and Boyd Jarman, *A History of Law Suits in Physical Education, Intramurals and Interscholastic Athletics in the Western United States: Their Implications and Consequences* (Provo, Utah: Brigham Young University Publications, 1979), p. 2.

3. Arnold, *Positive Outcomes,* p. 25.

4. Herb Appenzeller, *From the Gym to the Jury* (Charlottesville, Va.: The Michie Co., 1970), pp. 83–84.

5. Charles Peter Yost, ed., *Sports Safety: Accident Prevention and Injury Control in Physical Education, Athletics, and Recreation* (Washington, D.C.: AAHPER), p. 9.

6. H. C. Hudgins, Jr., and Richard S. Vacca, *Law and Education: Contemporary Issues and Court Decisions* (Charlottesville, Va.: The Michie Co., 1979), p. 72.

7. *Molitor* v. *Kaneland,* 163 NE 2d 89 (Ill. 1959).

8. Arnold, *Positive Outcomes,* p. 25.

9. Berryhill and Jarman, *A History of Law Suits,* p. 2.

10. John N. Drowatzky, "Liability: You Could Be Sued!" *Journal of Physical Education and Recreation* 49 (May 1978): 17–18.

11. Berryhill and Jarman, *A History of Law Suits,* p. 3.

12. Appenzeller, *From the Gym to the Jury,* pp. 68–69.

13. Ibid., pp. 8–9.
14. Ibid., p. 171.
15. Hudgins and Vacca, *Law and Education,* p. 84.
16. J. N. Drowatzky, "On the Firing Line: Negligence in Physical Education, *Journal of Law and Education* 6 (1977): 481–90.
17. Appenzeller, *From the Gym to the Jury,* p. 174.
18. Ibid., p. 115.
19. Ibid., p. 146.
20. Ibid., p. 139.
21. Ibid., p. 137.
22. Arnold, *Positive Outcomes,* p. 25.
23. *Federal Register,* vol. 42., August 23, 1977 (part II), p. 42480.
24. Richard E. Orr, "Does the I.E.P. Really Deal With the Handicapped Individual's Special Need?" *The Physical Educator* 37 (March 1980): 4–6.
25. Janet Seaman, "Attitudes of Physically Handicapped Children Toward Physical Education," *Research Quarterly* 41 (October 1970): 439–45.
26. Bruce A. McClenaghan, "Normalization in Physical Education: A Reflective Review," *The Physical Educator* 38 (March 1981): 3–7.
27. Rita S. Dunn and Robert W. Cole, "Inviting Malpractice through Mainstreaming," *Educational Leadership* 36 (February 1979): 302–6.
28. Julian Stein, "Sense and Nonsense About Mainstreaming," *Journal of Physical Education and Recreation* 47 (January 1976): 43.
29. Joseph P. Winnick, "Techniques for Integration," *Journal of Physical Education and Recreation* 49 (June 1978): 22.
30. *Federal Register,* vol. 42 May 4, 1977, p. 22676.
31. *Federal Register,* vol. 40, June 4, 1975.
32. Rosemary Selby, "What's Wrong (and Right)! with Coed Physical Education Classes: Secondary School Physical Educators' Views on Title IX Implementation," *The Physical Educator* 34 (December 1977): 188–91.
33. Ibid., p. 191.
34. Ibid., p. 189.
35. Marian E. Kneer, "Sex Integrated Physical Education," *National Association of Secondary School Principals Bulletin* (April 1978): 79–84.
36. Selby, *What's Wrong,* p. 191.
37. Mary Domb Mikkelson, "Coed Gym—It's a Whole New Ballgame," *Journal of Physical Education and Recreation* 50 (October 1979): 63–64.
38. Kneer, *Sex Integrated Physical Education,* p. 82.
39. Ibid., p. 83.
40. Robert Benjamin, *Making Schools Work: A Reporter's Journey Through Some of America's Most Remarkable Classrooms* (New York: The Continuum Publishing Corporation, 1981), p. 119.
41. Ibid., p. 177.

Chapter 5

1. Eleanor Fisher, "What Is a Teacher," *Instructor* (May 1970): 23.
2. George Graham and Elsa Heimerer, "Research on Teacher Effectiveness: A Summary with Implications for Teaching," *Ouest* 33 (1981): 14–25.
3. Ibid., p. 18.
4. Neil Postman in an article that first appeared in *Sensorsheet,* a publication of the Earth Science Educational Program (Boulder, Colorado), and later in *Media Ecology Review,* published at the NYU School of Education.
5. Earl V. Pullias and James D. Young, *A Teacher Is Many Things* (Bloomington, Ind.: Indiana University Press, 1968).
6. Richard W. Calisch, "So You Want to Be a Real Teacher?" *Today's Education* 58 (November 1969): 49–51.
7. Graham and Heimerer, "Research on Teacher Effectiveness," p. 24.
8. Bill Meyer and Dan Zadra, "The Secret of the Slight Edge," *Young Athlete* (May–June 1976): 21.
9. "Trends: Teachers Suffer Stress Around the World," *Today's Education* 70 (November–December 1981): 6.
10. Katherine C. LaMancusa, *We Do Not Throw Rocks at the Teacher!* (Scranton, Penn.: International Textbook Co., 1966), p. 170.

Unit 2

1. Benjamin S. Bloom, ed., *Taxonomy of Educational Objectives, Handbook I: Cognitive Domain* (New York: David McKay Co., 1956).
2. David R. Krathwohl, Benjamin S. Bloom, and Bertram B. Masia, *Taxonomy of Educational Objectives, Handbook II: Affective Domain* (New York: David McKay Co., 1964).
3. Ann E. Jewett, L. Sue Jones, Sheryl M. Luneke, and Sarah M. Robinson, "Educational Change Through a Taxonomy for Writing Physical Education Objectives," *Quest* 15 (January 1971): 35–36.
4. Charles B. Corbin, *Becoming Physically Educated in the Elementary School,* 2d ed. (Philadelphia: Lea & Febiger, 1976), pp. 52–66.
5. Robert N. Singer and Walter Dick, *Teaching Physical Education: A Systems Approach* (Boston: Houghton Mifflin Company, 1974), 105–7.
6. Charles B. Corbin, "First Things First, But, Don't Stop There," *Journal of Physical Education, Recreation and Dance* 52 (June 1981): 12–13.

Chapter 6

1. David P. Ausubel, *The Psychology of Meaningful Verbal Learning: An Introduction to School Learning* (New York: Grune & Stratton, 1963), p. 16.
2. Ibid.
3. Bryce B. Hudgins, *Problem Solving in the Classroom* (New York: The Macmillan Company, 1966), p. 43.
4. Benjamin S. Bloom and Lois J. Broder, *Problem-Solving Processes of College Students: An Exploratory Investigation,* Supplementary Educational Monographs, no. 73 (Chicago: The University of Chicago Press, 1950), p. 25.
5. Robert M. Gagne and Leslie J. Briggs, *Principles of Instructional Design* (Chicago: Holt, Rinehart and Winston, Inc., 1974), pp. 8–11.
6. Robert M. Gagne, "Some New Views of Learning and Instruction," *Phi Delta Kappan* 51 (May 1970): 171–72.

7. Robert M. Gagne, *The Conditions of Learning,* 2d ed. (Chicago: Holt, Rinehart and Winston, Inc., 1974), p. 305.
8. Ausubel, *The Psychology of Meaningful Verbal Learning,* p. 16.
9. Dorothy R. Mohr, "Identifying the Body of Knowledge," *Journal of Health Physical Education Recreation* 42 (January 1971): 23.
10. Ibid., p. 24.
11. Ibid.
12. Katherine Ley, "Teaching Understandings in Physical Education," *Journal of Health Physical Education Recreation* 42 (January 1971): 21–22.

Chapter 7

1. Jewett, Ann E. and Marie R. Mullan, *Curriculum Design: Purposes and Processes in Physical Education Teaching-Learning* (Washington, D.C.: American Association of Health, Physical Education, and Recreation, 1977).
2. Henry, Franklin M. "Specificity Versus Generality in Learning Motor Skills," *Proceedings of the College Physical Education Association*, 61: 126–28, 1958.
3. Cratty, Bryant J. *Movement Behavior and Motor Learning,* 3d ed. (Philadelphia: Lea and Febiger, 1975), p. 387.
4. Ibid., p. 387 and 396–97.
5. Singer, Robert N. *Motor Learning and Human Performance: An Application to Motor Skills and Movement Behaviors,* 3d ed. (New York: Macmillan Publishing Co., Inc., 1980), p. 471.
6. Cratty, *Movement Behavior and Motor Learning,* p. 398.
7. Ibid., p. 389.
8. Nixon, John E. and Locke, Lawrence F. "Research on Teaching Physical Education," in *Second Handbook of Research on Teaching*, Travers, R. ed., 1973, p. 1217.
9. Cratty, *Movement Behavior and Motor Learning,* p. 364.
10. Singer, *Motor Learning and Human Performance,* p. 421.

11. Lawther, John D. *The Learning and Performance of Physical Skills*, 2d ed. (Englewood Cliffs, N.J.: Prentice-Hall, Inc., 1977), p. 144.
12. Ibid., p. 139.
13. Nixon and Locke, "Research on Teaching Physical Education."
14. Seagoe, M. V. "Qualitative Wholes: A Re-evaluation of the whole-part problem," *Journal of Educational Psychology*, 27, 1936, pp 537–45, in *Movement Behavior and Motor Learning*, 3d ed., Cratty, Bryant J. (Philadelphia: Lea & Febiger, 1973), p. 363.
15. Bilodeau, Edward A. and Ina McD. Bilodeau. "Motor-Skills Learning," *Annual Review of Psychology*, 12 (1961): 250, in *The Learning and Performance of Physical Skills,* John D. Lawther (Englewood Cliffs, N.J.: Prentice-Hall, Inc., 1977), p. 155.
16. Lawther, *The Learning and Performance of Physical Skills*, p. 55.
17. Jones, J. Richard. "Modify—To Simplify the Learning of Sports Skills," *Utah Association of Health Physical Education and Recreation Journal*, (Fall, 1977), pp. 4 and 10.

Chapter 8

1. David R. Krathwohl, Benjamin S. Bloom, and Bertram B. Masia, *Taxonomy of Educational Objectives, Handbook II: Affective Domain* (New York: David McKay Co., 1964).
2. G. W. Allport, "Values and Our Youth," *Teachers College Record* 63 (1961):211–19.
3. E. J. Shoben, Jr., "Potency in the Schools," Teachers College Record 63 (1962): 548–50.
4. S. B. Kahn and J. Weiss, "The Teaching of Affective Responses," in *Second Handbook of Research on Teaching*, R. M. Travers, ed. (Chicago: Rand McNally & Co., 1973), p. 789.
5. Klausmeier and Goodwin, in *The Affective Domain in Education,* Ringness, T. A. (Boston: Little, Brown & Company, 1975), p. 25.
6. Robert F. Mager, *Developing Attitude Toward Learning* (Palo Alto, Cal.: Fearon Publishers, 1965), pp. 50–57.
7. Arthur W. Combs, "The Human Side of Learning," *The National Elementary Principal* (January 1973): 38–42.
8. James Stephens, *The Crock of Gold* (New York: The Macmillan Co., 1942), p. 128.
9. Marion D. Hanks, "How to Listen," *The Improvement Era* 72 (March 1969): 16–19.
10. John Gustafson, "Teaching For Self-Esteem," *The Physical Educator* 35 (May 1978): 69.
11. Robert Rosenthal and Lenore Jacobson, *Pygmalion in the Classroom: Teacher Expectation and Pupils' Intellectual Development* (San Francisco: Holt, Rinehart and Winston, Inc., 1968).
12. Jere E. Brophy and Thomas L. Good, *Student-teacher Relationships: Causes and Consequences* (New York: Holt, Rinehart and Winston, Inc., 1974).
13. Dorothy Harris, *Involvement in Sport: A Somatopsychic Rationale for Physical Activity* (Philadelphia: Lea & Febiger, 1973).
14. Donald W. Felker, *Building Positive Self Concepts* (Minneapolis: Burgess Publishing Company, 1974).

Chapter 9

1. Harold Dunn, "Listen to Kids!" *Today's Education* 70 (November–December 1981): 37.
2. Abraham H. Maslow, "A Theory of Human Personality," *Psychological Review* 50 (1943): 370–96.
3. Larry Kehres, "Maslow's Hierarchy of Needs Applied to Physical Education and Athletics," *The Physical Educator* 30 (March 1973): 24–25.
4. Ibid., p. 25.
5. Robert M. Gagne, *The Conditions of Learning*, 2d ed. (New York: Holt, Rinehart and Winston, Inc. 1970).
6. Kehres, "Maslow's Hierarchy of Needs."
7. Edward L. Deci, et al., "Rewards, Motivation, and Self-Esteem, *The Educational Forum* 44 (May 1980): 429–33; Edward L. Deci, et al., "An Instrument to Assess Adults Orientations toward Control Versus Autonomy With Children: Reflections on Intrinsic Motivation and Perceived Competence," *Journal of Educational Psychology* 73 (October 1981): 642–50.

8. Bud Bertel, "Try What?" *Journal of Health, Physical Education, Recreation* 45 (May 1974): 24.

9. Lloyd Homme, et al., *How to Use Contingency Contracting in the Classroom* (Champaign, Ill.: Research Press, 1969), p. 18.

10. D. H. Ziatz, "How Do You Motivate Students to Learn?" *Journal of Physical Education and Recreation* 48 (March 1977): 26.

11. Howard E. Sundberg, "A Running Program That Works," *Alliance Update* (July–August 1981): 7.

12. David E. Corbin, "Prediction Races and Relays," *Journal of Physical Education and Recreation* 50 (June 1979): 58–59.

13. Eric L. Stein, "Run for Fun—A Program for All Ages," *Journal of Physical Education and Recreation* 49 (November–December 1978): 70.

14. H. Harrison Clarke, ed. "Computer Terminal in the Gym," *Physical Fitness News Letter,* Series 28 (November 1981).

15. Pat Sawley, Woods Cross High School, Woods Cross, Utah.

16. Michael Tenoschok, "Physical Education Appreciation," *Journal of Physical Education and Recreation* 50 (November–December 1979): 18.

17. Ron French, "The Use of Homework as a Supportive Technique in Physical Education," *The Physical Educator* 36 (May 1979): 84.

18. Lowell A. Klappholz, ed. "Half the PE Grade Is Based on Outside Activity," *Physical Education Newsletter,* (November 1980).

19. Doris A. Mathieson, "Interpreting Secondary School Physical Education—Take the Initiative," *Journal of Physical Education and Recreation* (January 1978): 51–52.

20. Dianne S. Ward and Bruce A. McClenaghan, "Special Programs for Special People: Ideas For Extending the Physical Education Program," *The Physical Educator* 37 (May 1980): 66.

21. Robert D. McLaughlin, "Chip-N-Block" For Parental Involvement," *Journal of Physical Education, Recreation, and Dance* 52 (June 1981): 22–23.

22. Marilyn E. Schuman, "Enrich the Curriculum and Your Own Style," *Today's Education* 70 (November–December 1981): 36.

23. Katherine C. LaMancusa, *We Do Not Throw Rocks at the Teacher!* (Scranton, Pa.: International Textbook Co., 1966), p. 80.

24. William L. Herman, "Have a Junk Day," *Journal of Physical Education and Recreation* 46 (October 1975): 35.

25. For more information on PEPI, contact the AAHPERD, 1900 Association Drive, Reston, Va. 22091.

26. Walter B. Clay, "First Class and Getting Better," *Journal of Physical Education, Recreation and Dance* 52 (June 1981): 19–21.

27. John M. Gray, "Enjoy Yourself and Be Flexible," *Today's Education* 70 (November–December 1981): 34–35.

Unit 3

1. Robert F. Mager, *Developing Attitude Toward Learning* (Palo Alto, Cal.: Fearon Publishers, 1968), p. vii.

Chapter 10

1. Hal A. Lawson and Judith H. Placek, *Physical Education in the Secondary Schools: Curricular Alternatives* (Boston: Allyn & Bacon, Inc., 1981), p. 80.

2. Richard W. Burns, *New Approaches to Behavioral Objectives* (Dubuque, Iowa: Wm. C. Brown Company Publishers, 1972), pp. 58–59.

3. Adapted from Blaine Nelson Lee and M. David Merrill, *Writing Complete Affective Objectives: A Short Course* (Belmont, Cal. Wadsworth Publishing Company, 1972).

4. Ibid., pp. 98–99.

5. Blaine R. Worthen and J. R. Sanders, *Educational Evaluation: Theory and Practice* (Worthington, Ohio: Charles A. Jones Publishing Company, 1973), p. 240.

6. Ibid., p. 241.

7. I. K. Davies, *Objectives in Curriculum Design* (New York: McGraw Hill, 1976), p. 66.

8. Ibid.

9. Worthen and Sanders, *Educational Evaluation,* p. 236.

10. Ibid., p. 243.

Chapter 11

1. Benjamin S. Bloom, J. Thomas Hastings, and George F. Madaus, *Handbook on Formative and Summative Evaluation of Student Learning* (St. Louis: McGraw-Hill, 1971).
2. Larry J. Sullivan, "Campus Comedy," *Reader's Digest* 117 (November 1980), p. 203.
3. Mike Bobo, "Skill Testing—A Positive Step toward Interpreting Secondary School Physical Education," *Journal of Physical Education and Recreation* 49 (January 1978): 45.
4. Adapted from Blaine Nelson Lee and M. David Merrill, *Writing Complete Affective Objectives: A Short Course* (Belmont, Cal.. Wadsworth Publishing Company, 1972).
5. B. E. Blanchard, "A Behavior Frequency Rating Scale for the Measurement of Character and Personality Traits in Physical Education Classroom Situations," *Research Quarterly* 7 (May 1936): 56–66.
6. Charles C. Cowell, "Validating an Index of Social Adjustment for High School Use," *Research Quarterly* (March 1958): 7–18.
7. June Breck, "A Sociometric Test of Status as Measured in Physical Education Classes" (Master's thesis, University of California, 1947).
8. Robert Fox, Margaret Barron Luszki, and Richard Schmuck, *Diagnosing Classroom Learning Environments* (Chicago: Science Research Associates, 1966), p. 73.
9. Lee and Merrill, *Writing Complete Affective Objectives,* p. 75.

Chapter 12

1. Paul Dressel, *Basic College Quarterly,* Michigan State University (Winter 1957): 6.
2. L. J. Weber and T. L. Paul, "Approaches to Grading in Physical Education," *The Physical Educator* 28 (May 1971): 59–62.
3. Carol Lee Stamm, "Evaluation of Coeducational Physical Activity Classes," *Journal of Physical Education and Recreation* 50 (January 1979): 68–69.
4. Ibid.

Chapter 13

1. Jack Canfield and Harold C. Wells, *100 Ways to Enhance Self-concept in the Classroom—A Handbook for Teachers and Parents* (Englewood Cliffs, N.J.: Prentice-Hall, Inc., 1976), p. 33.
2. Ibid., p. 32.
3. Ibid., p. 31.
4. Ibid., p. 53.
5. Ibid., pp. 50–52.
6. Ibid., p. 109.

Chapter 14

1. Bruce Joyce and Marsha Weil, *Models of Teaching,* 2d ed. (Englewood Cliffs, N.J.: Prentice-Hall, Inc., 1980), p. 478.
2. David E. Hunt, *Matching Models in Education: The Coordination of Teaching Methods with Student Characteristics* (Toronto, Ontario, The Ontario Institute for Studies in Education, 1971), pp. 9–10.
3. Robert C. Hawley, *Human Values in the Classroom: Teaching for Personal and Social Growth* (Amherst, Mass.: Education Research Associates, 1973).
4. Muska Mosston, *Teaching Physical Education,* 2d ed. (Columbus, Ohio: Charles E. Merrill Publishing Co., 1981).
5. Robert M. Gagne and Leslie J. Briggs, *Principles of Instructional Design* (Chicago: Holt, Rinehart and Winston, Inc., 1974), p. 64.
6. Lloyd Homme, et al., *How to Use Contingency Contracting in the Classroom* (Champaign, Ill.: Research Press, 1969), p. 45.
7. Merrill Harmin and Sidney B. Simon, "How to Help Students Learn to Think . . . About Themselves," *The High School Journal* (March 1972): 256–64.
8. Ibid.
9. Jack Canfield and Harold C. Wells, *100 Ways to Enhance Self-concept in the Classroom—A Handbook for Teachers and Parents* (Englewood Cliffs, N.J.: Prentice-Hall, Inc., 1976), p. 139.
10. Canfield and Wells, *100 Ways to Enhance Self-concept in the Classroom,* p. 187.

11. Harmin and Simon, "How to Help Students," p. 404 and Canfield and Wells, *100 Ways to Enhance Self-concept in the Classroom,* pp. 133–34. For information about current values realization materials and a schedule of nationwide training workshops, contact Sidney B. Simon, Old Mountain Rd., Hadley, Mass. 01035.
12. Canfield and Wells, *100 Ways to Enhance Self-concept in the Classroom,* p. 72.
13. Ibid., pp. 188–89.
14. Charles R. Hobbs, *The Power of Teaching with New Techniques* (Salt Lake City, Utah: Deseret Book Company, 1972), p. 117.
15. Kathryn Wright and Joy Walker, "Rainy Day Golf," *Journal of Health, Physical Education, Recreation,* 40 (November–December 1969): 83.
16. Hawley, *Human Values in the Classroom,* p. 16.
17. Ibid., pp. 60–61.

Chapter 15

1. Edgar Dale, *Audio-Visual Methods in Teaching,* Rev. ed. (New York: Dryden Press, 1954), p. 43.

Chapter 16

1. Robert F. Mager, *Developing Attitude Toward Learning* (Palo Alto, Cal.: Fearon Publishers, 1968).

Chapter 17

1. Rex Hardy, "Dressing Out in Physical Education: Probing the Problem," *The Physical Educator* 36 (December 1979): 191–92.
2. *Mitchell* v. *McCall,* 273 Ala 604, 143 S (2d) 629 (1962).
3. Hardy, "Dressing Out in Physical Education."
4. Katherine C. La Mancusa, *We Do Not Throw Rocks at the Teacher!* (Scranton, Pa.: International Textbook Co., 1966), p. 116.
5. Ibid., pp. 116–17.

Chapter 18

1. George H. Gallup, "The 13th Annual Gallup Poll of the Public's Attitudes Toward the Public Schools," *Phi Delta Kappan* 63 (September 1981): 33–47.
2. Thomas Gordon with Noel Burch, *T.E.T., Teacher Effectiveness Training* (New York: Peter H. Wyden, Publisher, 1974).
3. Wesley C. Becker, Siegfried Engelmann, and Don R. Thomas, *Teaching: A Course in Applied Psychology* (Palo Alto, Cal.: Science Research Associates, Inc., 1971), p. 157
4. Lloyd Homme, et al., *How to Use Contingency Contracting in the Classroom* (Champaign, Ill.: Research Press, 1969), p. 18.
5. Bruce Joyce and Marsha Weil, *Models of Teaching,* 2d ed. (Englewood Cliffs, N.J.: Prentice-Hall, Inc., 1980), p. 332.
6. Homme, et al., *How to Use Contingency Contracting,* p. 21.
7. Katherine C. La Mancusa, *We Do Not Throw Rocks at the Teacher!* (Scranton, Pa.: International Textbook Co., 1966), p. 146.
8. Homme, et al., *How to Use Contingency Contracting,* pp. 18–21.
9. Becker, et al., *Teaching,* p. 171.
10. John P. Glavin, *Behavioral Strategies for Classroom Management* (Columbus, Ohio: Charles E. Merrill Publishing Company, 1974), p. 52.
11. Homme, et al., *How to Use Contingency Contracting,* p. 9.
12. Becker, et al., *Teaching,* p. 97.
13. Murray Tillman, Donald Bersoff, and John Dolly, *Learning to Teach: A Decision-Making System* (Lexington, Mass.: D. C. Heath and Company, 1976), p. 361.
14. Becker, et al., *Teaching,* p. 158.
15. William Glasser, *Reality Therapy: A New Approach to Psychiatry* (New York: Harper & Row, Publishers, 1965).
16. Becker, et al., *Teaching,* p. 177.

Chapter 19

1. Daryl Siedentop, *Developing Teaching Skills in Physical Education* (Boston: Houghton Mifflin Co., 1976), pp. 271–75.
2. Max Rosenberg, "Test Your HRQ (Human Relations Quotient)," *Teacher* 90 (March 1973) or Marjorie C. Knutson, "Sensitivity to Minority Groups," *Journal of Physical Education and Recreation* 48 (May 1977): 24–25.
3. Dorothy B. Zakrajsek and Ronald R. Bos, "Student Evaluations of Teaching Performance," *Journal of Physical Education and Recreation* 49 (May 1978): 64–65.
4. Siedentop, *Developing Teaching Skills,* p. 30.
5. William G. Anderson, *Analysis of Teaching Physical Education* (St. Louis: The C. V. Mosby Co., 1980), p. 33.
6. Ibid., pp. 23–24.
7. Ibid., p. 32.
8. Siedentop, *Developing Teaching Skills,* pp. 99 and 265.
9. Edmund J. Amidon and Ned A. Flanders, *The Role of the Teacher in the Classroom* (Minneapolis: Association for Productive Teaching, 1971), p. 14.
10. Anderson, *Analysis of Teaching Physical Education,* p. 76.
11. B. L. Morgenegg, "Pedagogical Moves," In *What's Going on in Gym? Descriptive Studies of Physical Education Classes.* A special monograph of *Motor Skills: Theory into Practice,* 1978.
12. Anderson, *Analysis of Teaching Physical Education,* pp. 109–10.

Unit 5

1. Linda Bain, "Status of Curriculum Theory in Physical Education," *Journal of Physical Education and Recreation* 49 (March 1978): 25–26.
2. George H. Gallup, "The 13th Annual Gallup Poll of the Public's Attitudes Toward the Public Schools," *Phi Delta Kappan* 63 (September 1981): 33–47.
3. B. Frank Brown, *The Reform of Secondary Education.* (New York: McGraw-Hill Book Co., 1973), p. 8.

4. Robert C. Hawley, *Human Values in the Classroom: Teaching for Personal and Social Growth* (Amherst, Mass.: Education Research Associates, 1973), p. 70.
5. Denis Lawton, *Social Change, Educational Theory, and Curriculum Planning* (London: University of London Press LTD, 1973), p. 7.

Chapter 20

1. Robberta Mesenbrink, et al. "New Forms and Substances in Physical Education," in *Curriculum Report.* National Association of Secondary School Principals 4 (December 1974).
2. The NASPE Media Resource Center, College of Health and Physical Education, University of South Carolina, Columbia, South Carolina 29208.

Chapter 21

1. William Geiger and David Kizer, "Developing a Teaching Awareness," *The Physical Educator* 36, (March, 1979): 25–26.
2. Glen Hass, *Curriculum Planning: A New Approach,* 2d ed. (Boston: Allyn & Bacon, Inc., 1977), p. 233.
3. Ibid., p. 234.
4. Ibid., p. 234.
5. American Alliance for Health, Physical Education, Recreation and Dance, *"Basic Stuff"* Series (Reston, Va.: AAHPERD, 1981).

Chapter 22

1. Linda Bain, "Status of Curriculum Theory in Physical Education," *Journal of Physical Education and Recreation* 49 (March 1978): 25–26.
2. Rudolf von Laban, *Modern Educational Dance,* 2d ed., revised by Lisa Ullman (New York: Frederick A. Praeger, 1963).
3. Gerald S. Kenyon, "A Conceptual Model for Characterizing Physical Activity," *Research Quarterly* 39 (March 1968): 96–105.
4. Alvin Toffler, *Future Shock* (New York: Bantam Books, 1970), p. 420.

Chapter 23

1. Charles Bucher, "National Adult Physical Fitness Survey: Some Implications," *Journal of Health, Physical Education, Recreation* 45 (January 1974): 25.
2. Helen M. Heitmann, "Curricular Organizational Patterns for Physical Education." Paper presented to the NASPE Curriculum Academy Working Symposium, St. Louis, Missouri, November 4–6, 1978.

Chapter 24

1. Carl E. Willgoose, *The Curriculum in Physical Education,* 2d ed. (Englewood Cliffs, N.J: Prentice-Hall, Inc., 1974), pp. 137 and 140.

Chapter 25

1. "Classification of Students for Physical Education," *Journal of Health, Physical Education, Recreation* 38 (February 1967): 16–18.
2. American Association of Health, Physical Education, and Recreation, *Essentials of a Quality Elementary School Physical Education Program* (Washington, D.C.: AAHPER, 1970).
3. For a breakdown of requirements, see Howard Davis, *State Requirements in Physical Education for Teachers and Students* (Washington, D.C.: American Association of Health, Physical Education, and Recreation, 1973).
4. American Association of Health, Physical Education, and Recreation, *Essentials.*
5. The Society of State Directors of Health, Physical Education, and Recreation, *The School Program in Health, Physical Education, and Recreation: A Statement of Basic Beliefs* (Kensington, Maryland, 1976), p. 7.

6. Ibid.
7. President's Council on Youth Fitness, *Youth Fitness* (Washington, D.C.: U.S. Government Printing Office, July 1961), p. 11.
8. Linda L. Bain, "Socialization into the Role of Participant: Physical Education's Ultimate Goal," *Journal of Physical Education and Recreation* 51 (September 1980): 48–50.
9. American Association of Health, Physical Education, and Recreation. *Guidelines for Secondary School Physical Education* (Washington, D.C.: AAHPER, 1970).
10. Ibid.
11. American Association of Health, Physical Education, and Recreation, *Essentials.*
12. American Association of Health, Physical Education, and Recreation, *Essentials* and *Guidelines.*

Chapter 26

1. Rosalind Cassidy, *Curriculum Development in Physical Education* (New York: Harper & Row, Publishers, 1954).
2. Blaine R. Worthen and James R. Sanders, *Educational Evaluation: Theory and Practice* (Worthington, Ohio: Charles A. Jones Publishing Company, 1973).
3. American Alliance for Health, Physical Education, and Recreation, *Assessment Guide for Secondary School Physical Education Programs* (Washington, D.C.: AAHPER, 1977).

index